THE PROPHETS

Who They Were,
What They Are

NORMAN PODHORETZ

THE FREE PRESS

New York London Toronto Sydney Singapore

THE FREE PRESS
A Division of Simon & Schuster, Inc.
1230 Avenue of the Americas
New York, NY 10020

THE FREE PRESS and colophon are trademarks
of Simon & Schuster, Inc.

For information regarding special discounts for bulk purchases,
please contact Simon & Schuster Special Sales:
1-800-456-6798 or business@simonandschuster.com

Book design by Ellen R. Sasahara

Manufactured in the United States of America

10   9   8   7   6   5   4   3   2

Library of Congress Cataloging-in-Publication Data
Podhoretz, Norman.
The prophets: who they were, what they are/Norman Podhoretz.
p. cm.
Includes bibliographical references and index.
1. Bible, O.T. Prophets *(N'vi-im)*—Criticism, interpretation, etc.
2. Prophecy—Judaism. I. Title.
BS1286 .P63 2002
224'.06—dc21   2002024464
ISBN 0-7432-1927-9

Once more, for Midge

CONTENTS

INTRODUCTION:
THE BIBLICAL CONTEXT

ROUGHLY 2,750 YEARS AGO—around the time Homer was probably singing and/or writing the *Iliad* and the *Odyssey* in far-off
Greece—a man named Amos, who described himself in. the Bible as
" . . . an herdsman, and a gatherer of sycomore fruit . . ." left the village near
Jerusalem where he lived and traveled up to Samaria in the northern part of the
Land of Israel. Immediately he erupted like a volcano, denouncing its people in
the name of God for their sins and calling upon them to repent.

Thus did the first of the so-called classical prophets suddenly and mysteriously stride onto the historical scene, to be followed by, among many others, Isaiah, Jeremiah, Ezekiel, Hosea, and Micah. They were some of the greatest men
ever to walk the earth, and most of them, like Homer himself, were also, and not
so incidentally, among the greatest poets who ever lived. Then, three centuries
after Amos started this astonishing parade (and just when Socrates and Plato
were active in Athens), it ground to a halt as suddenly and mysteriously as it had
begun.

In the pages that follow I propose to tell the story of these blazing human
giants. Without quixotically attempting to dispel the entire mystery of the phenomenon they represented, I will try to shed a bit of light on it by examining
their roots in the history of ancient Israel as recounted so fascinatingly and with
such incomparable artistry in the Bible; by looking at how they reacted to the
conditions surrounding them at home, as well as to the bloody conflicts imping-
ing upon their people from abroad; and by speculating on how and why they
faded away when they did.

In telling this story, I will also try to correct certain stubborn misconceptions
about the classical prophets. A trivial example is the popular notion that these
turbulent and troublesome and tormented figures were saintly old characters
with long beards wandering about in loin cloths and issuing otherworldly moral
pronouncements in abstractly universal terms. Yet few of them were what nowadays passes for saintly; and far from dealing in abstractions floating above the

concrete details of daily life, all of them were always plunging down and dirty into the world around them.

For their story is, at bottom, the story of a war—among the most consequential in all of human history, and to my mind one of the most exciting. These men were the heroes of that war, but in waging it, the lethal instruments they wielded were not swords or lances. No, *their* weapons were words: words that in their own way could bring death as surely as swords and lances, but that could also do something beyond the power of swords and lances, which was to bring life and balm and healing, often to the wounds they themselves had made. I will be quoting many of those words, whose incandescent beauty and awful power ultimately vanquished an enemy as insidious and seductive as he was cruel and evil: the enemy they knew as idolatry. Yet I will conclude by arguing that this enemy keeps coming back under different names and in mutated forms that are not always easy to recognize as his. And I will ask, finally, whether the weapons that defeated him over two thousand years ago, and that are ready to hand in the Bible, may still be sharp enough to cut him down again today.

THE BIBLE: it is probably the most widely circulated book in the history of the world (or at least the Western world). Once upon a time it was so constantly and intensively read that it often blotted out all other books, provoking the great Victorian literary and social critic Matthew Arnold to protest in exasperation that "No man, who knows nothing else, knows even his Bible."* Well, that may have been so in 1869, and even into more recent times. But no longer. As I have discovered from innumerable conversations, most people nowadays have only the most general acquaintance with the Bible. Unless they happen to be students or regular devotional readers, they are usually familiar only with some of the more famous stories the Bible tells. Turning Matthew Arnold upside down, one could say that even people who know everything else, do not know their Bible.

Indeed, I have also learned from those innumerable conversations that many such people do not even know what the Bible contains. They vaguely remember that it is divided into two major sections, the Old Testament and the New Testament, and perhaps they recall that in some English translations there is also a section called the Apocrypha. But few are able to remember the names of more than a small number of the books in either of the two Testaments, and fewer still have more than the vaguest notion of what the Apocrypha is.

I have also run into Christians, both Protestant and Catholic, who are unaware, or have forgotten, that the original language of the Old Testament is

---

*Sources for all quotations, as well as other citations, can be found by looking up the appropriate page and the last three words of each reference in the Endnotes, starting on p. 365. For full tiles of abbreviated scriptural references in footnotes, see "A Key to Citations" on p. 363.

Hebrew* and that the New Testament was first written in Greek hundreds of years later. On the other hand, in my experience, virtually all Jews, no matter how secularized, know that the New Testament is not part of *their* Bible (or, to be more precise, the Bible of their forebears, for whom there was nothing old about the "Old Testament" except its age, and nothing in the "New Testament" that was true). Conversely, almost all Christians, even if they too are "lapsed," know that *both* Testaments are sacred to Christianity. Still, it can come as a surprise even to religious Christians that the Protestant and Catholic versions of the Bible are not precisely the same.

There has, then, been a general loss of intimate familiarity with the Bible throughout our culture. And yet, a Gallup survey taken in the year 2000 reported that more than eight out of ten Americans believed the Bible still spoke to us today and could even solve "most or all" of life's problems. At the same time, they admitted to finding the Bible as a whole "confusing" and often hard to understand.

This is not in the least surprising. In addition to containing many difficult passages, the Bible is not a book as that word is customarily used: it is, as the author of a popular work on it has correctly remarked, "a library" that took many centuries to compile and that features everything from "poetry, genealogy, prophecy, legal codes, parables, proverbs, theology, and history." From which it follows that "You can't read one portion the same as another," and most people who try to read it that way invariably run into trouble.

So far as strictly Orthodox Jews are concerned, God is the author of the Hebrew Bible, which He revealed to Moses at Mt. Sinai. Among fundamentalist Protestants, similarly, the Bible, from beginning to end, is the "inerrant" word of God. Gone are the days when vast numbers of American Protestants were in this camp. And yet, again according to Gallup, as late as about fifty years ago, two-thirds of the American people described themselves as fundamentalists, and even as of the year 2000, a full one-third of American adults still did.

But if strict fundamentalism suffered heavy losses during the past half-century, those who held on to the looser idea that everything in the Bible was in some undefined sense written under divine "inspiration and authority" remained steady at 80 percent. *Eighty* percent! This statistic is hard to reconcile with the results of my own highly informal and unscientific survey showing a dismal lack of knowledge of the Bible. But perhaps Gallup and I are both right—perhaps one can believe that the Bible is divinely inspired and still hardly bother to read it.

Probably the major cause of the drop in strict fundamentalism is the corrosive effect of the sciences—from cosmology to biology—on a literal understanding of the biblical text, beginning with "In the beginning": its very first words,

---

*Three of the later books—Ezra, Nehemiah, and Daniel—are, however, partly in Aramaic, a member of the same family of Semitic languages as Hebrew.

which introduce an account of the creation of the world.* But another major cause, coming from a very different direction, is the influence of the hordes of highly learned scholars (some of them pious Christians and Jews themselves) who, since the mid-nineteenth century, have steadily been undermining the assumptions of the strict fundamentalists. These scholars have asked, and labored mightily to answer, questions—especially about the Old Testament—that to some fundamentalists border on, if they do not actually cross over into, sheer blasphemy. Such as:

When was this or that book of the Bible originally written? Or was it first transmitted by word of mouth and then inscribed on parchment or stone tablets? If so, over how long a period did this process occur and how many authors were involved? When and by whom was the text as we now have it finally edited and established as "canonical" or authoritative? Is this text closer to the lost original than others that still exist, either in fragments on scraps of papyrus (like the Dead Sea Scrolls), or (like the Greek Septuagint) full translations into other languages from versions that have also been lost?

I would suppose that, unlike the strict fundamentalists, few members of Gallup's 80 percent would have any serious problems with the view that those who wrote and/or edited the books of the Bible were fallible human beings. Nor would they likely resist accepting that errors could easily have crept into the texts of these books through centuries of copying (as well as through translations containing errors of their own). Nor, finally, would they feel obliged to doubt that these errors—or some of them, anyway—can be corrected on the basis of philological, archaeological, and historical data deriving both from the Bible itself and from sources outside it.

It is on the basis of those assumptions about the part of the Bible that to Christians is the "Old Testament" and to Jews like myself simply the Bible, or the Hebrew Bible, that I have undertaken to tell the story of prophecy in ancient Israel. Though a Jew (with—as will become evident—rather idiosyncratic religious beliefs), I am addressing myself here as far as possible to everyone. "Everyone" embraces Jewish and Christian believers who may or may not be as soaked in the Bible as they (and particularly the Protestants among them) would have been in the not so distant past; non-believers to whom the Bible is one of the greatest treasures of world literature we possess and who take a keen interest in it as such; and even (I would hope) other non-believers who have hardly, if ever, encountered the Bible before.

•   •   •

*According to the same Gallup survey, done for the largest publisher of Bibles in the world, this account is for most people the hardest part of the Bible "to read and understand."

YET BECAUSE THE LEVEL of biblical literacy among us is no longer what it was in the past, it might be helpful if, before delving into the prophets themselves, I were to get some background information out of the way that might otherwise clog up the narrative and analysis to follow. Let me start, then, with a number of basic facts that are necessary for avoiding possible confusions and gratuitously distracting considerations up ahead.

For openers, since this is the story of prophecy in ancient Israel, I concern myself almost entirely with the Hebrew Bible, concentrating most heavily on one section of it, and rarely venturing into the New Testament except when I think it sheds light on a point I am working to clarify.

The (relatively) modern term in Hebrew for the Hebrew Bible is *TaNaKh,* an acronym composed of the titles of the three sections into which it is divided. The first, *Torah* (literally, "instruction" or "law"), is made up of the books of Genesis, Exodus, Leviticus, Numbers, and Deuteronomy; together these are called in English the First Five Books of Moses, or the Pentateuch (a Latinized Greek word that can be translated as "a volume of five books"). The second of the three sections is *N'vi-im* (or the Prophets—about whose contents more in a moment). The third is *K'tuvim* (Writings, or Hagiographa—another Latinized Greek word, this one meaning "sacred writings"), consisting of Psalms, Proverbs, Job, the Song of Songs, Ruth, Lamentations, Ecclesiastes, Esther, Daniel, Ezra, Nehemiah, First Chronicles, and Second Chronicles.

But a complication arises from the title of the second section, which is that *N'vi-im* has two subsections of its own: the Former Prophets and the Latter Prophets. In the Former Prophets are the Books of Joshua, Judges, First Samuel, Second Samuel, First Kings, and Second Kings. To complicate matters even further, these six books are not collections of prophecies. Rather, they constitute an account of the history of the people of Israel from the invasion and conquest of the Promised Land (then Canaan, later Palestine) in about 1250 B.C.E.* up to the expulsion of most of their descendants to Babylon nearly seven hundred years later. Prophets abound throughout this history, some of whom, like Samuel and Elijah, are among the most noteworthy. When they appear, however, it is as characters whose doings are recounted and a number of whose sayings are quoted; they are not the authors (or the putative authors) of the books themselves. The two volumes bearing the name of Samuel, for instance, do not claim to have been written by him (and, in fact, he dies before the second even begins).

---

*In line with the Jewish practice in dating ancient materials, which is also that of many non-Jewish scholars (among them devout Christians) who wish to avoid loading their historical accounts with theological implications, I will throughout this book be using the initials B.C.E., for "before the common era," rather than "B.C.," or "before Christ." The same principle applies to the substitution of "C.E." (common era) for "A.D." (the Latin abbreviation for *anno domini,* or "year of our Lord").

It is very different with the Latter Prophets, on whom I concentrate after surveying all the named prophets in the Pentateuch and the Former Prophets. With the exception of Jonah, the books of the Latter Prophets are all attributed in the introductory "superscriptions" to the men whose names are attached to them. Furthermore—and again with the exception of Jonah—these books are not stories *about* those men, but almost entirely collections of the prophecies they delivered (or supposedly delivered), interspersed here and there with narrative bridges.

Thus the Book of Isaiah begins: "The vision of Isaiah the son of Amoz, which he saw concerning Judah and Jerusalem in the days of Uzziah, Jotham, Ahaz, and Hezekiah, kings of Judah." From there, with no further ado, we are launched directly into the first of his prophetic utterances ("Hear, O heavens, and give ear, O earth: for the LORD hath spoken . . .").

This is why the Latter Prophets came to be dubbed the "writing" prophets, though most modern scholars (not all) agree that they themselves went around pronouncing "oracles" and preaching sermons that were transcribed by others. Nowadays, therefore, the standard term is the "canonical" prophets, or (in my own preferred designation) the "classical" prophets.

There are fifteen such books in the Hebrew Bible, and they in turn are divided into two sections, major and minor. The "major" prophets are Isaiah, Jeremiah, and Ezekiel, and the other twelve (Hosea, Joel, Amos, Obadiah, Jonah, Micah, Nahum, Habakkuk, Zephaniah, Haggai, Zechariah, and Malachi) are "minor." Theoretically, the word minor signifies not lesser moral or religious or literary stature but only lesser length. In practice, however, among the "minor" prophets only three (Amos, Hosea, and Micah) have over the centuries come to rank in importance, both intrinsic and in terms of influence, with their three "major" counterparts.

But we are not yet free of the complications in this picture. Modern scholars have demonstrated—if not without much debate among themselves as to crucial elements and details—that more than one hand is at work in every one of the fifteen Latter Prophets. To cite the least controversial case, the last twenty-six of the sixty-six chapters of the Book of Isaiah are without a doubt about events that took place about 150 years after those of the first thirty-nine. To strict fundamentalists, there is nothing strange about this: Isaiah, being a prophet, simply foresaw the future. But predicting the specifics of the future was something the classical prophets rarely did. In fact—as we shall see—whenever they tried doing it, they frequently turned out to be wrong.

And so, many years ago, the world was introduced to "Deutero" (or the Second) Isaiah, an anonymous prophet to whom chapters 40–66 were assigned. Still later, other scholars decided to take the last eleven chapters away from Deutero-Isaiah and give them to "Trito" (or the Third) Isaiah. Nor, as we shall also see, has it ended there.

Among the minor prophets, too—or so we are in addition assured by the scholars—there were a Deutero-Hosea and a Deutero-Zechariah. And besides these larger divisions, scattered passages in all fifteen of the classical prophets have been attributed to "schools" of their disciples, and others to later editors or "redactors" who may have added material of their own. For instance, in the relatively short Book of Amos alone (only nine chapters long), one twentieth-century scholar distinguishes seven different divisions, each one further divided into another seven parts deriving from what he posits to have been a long and complicated process of oral and written transmission. But the most extreme example—or what seems to me the *reductio ad absurdum* of this kind of textual analysis—is the Book of Obadiah, the shortest in the Hebrew Bible, consisting wholly of a single chapter of only twenty-one verses. Yet there are well-respected scholars who contend that these twenty-one verses represent either six or eight unrelated fragments that may have originated with as many different prophets.

Fifteen books, then, but at the very least seventeen or eighteen—or even possibly up to fifty or more—different authors and/or editors.

As TO THE FORMER PROPHETS, one theory is that these books were so classified because, to the rabbis of later generations, they showed how earlier prophecies had been fulfilled. In the Roman Catholic version of the "Old Testament," however, this entire corpus was not unreasonably placed among "The Historical Books."

The Book of Daniel came along after the section of the Hebrew Bible reserved for the Prophets had been closed, but it got into the still-open division of Writings. To Christians (first Catholics and then Protestants), however, Daniel belonged and was placed among the Prophets. So, too, with the Book of Lamentations. While Jewish tradition attributed it to one of the major prophets, Jeremiah, this book found a spot within the Writings section of the Hebrew Bible rather than being grouped with the Prophets. Still another Jewish composition connected with Jeremiah that became part of the Roman Catholic canon was the Book of Baruch. As the secretary and amanuensis of Jeremiah, Baruch figures prominently within the Hebrew Bible, but he has no book of his own there.

After their break with the Roman Catholic Church in the sixteenth century C.E., the Protestants developed a canon of their own. In their version, the "Old Testament" section tracked the Hebrew Bible more closely than the Roman Catholic canon did. But both Christian Bibles arranged certain of the books of the Old Testament in a different sequence from that of the *TaNaKh* (and from each other).

Another difference emerged in the treatment of a number of books or parts of books written by Jews roughly between the third century B.C.E. and the first century C.E. in Hebrew or Aramaic or Greek (or translated into Greek from

Hebrew or Aramaic manuscripts lost to us). There are—depending on how they
are divided and/or combined in different editions—either thirteen, fourteen, or
fifteen such books. Not deemed by the rabbinical Jewish authorities to be
divinely inspired, these books were not admitted into the Hebrew Bible. Among
them were Tobit, Judith, First Maccabees, Second Maccabees, The Wisdom of
Solomon (or The Book of Wisdom), and Ecclesiasticus (or The Wisdom of Ben
Sirach—and not to be confused with Ecclesiastes, which did get into the
Hebrew Bible as one of the Writings). Though all were denied entry into the
TaNaKh, they were (with some exceptions) eventually given full canonical status
by the Roman Catholic Church. Among Protestants, on the other hand, the status of these books was in constant dispute. In many Protestant editions of the
Bible, they were gathered into a section of their own, the one called the Apocrypha, and usually placed between the "Old" and the "New" Testaments; in others, they were omitted.*

The Hebrew Bible was fixed by the first century C.E., but variant readings
and versions remained in circulation. Hence it took nearly another thousand
years before a definitive text was established to the satisfaction of the rabbis who
devoted themselves to studying it and the scribes who had the awesome responsibility of copying it accurately over the centuries. This version, which then
acquired total authority among pious Jews, is the Masoretic text (MT), from a
Hebrew word, *m'sorah* ("tradition" or "handing down"). Today most biblical
scholars, whatever their religious affiliation may be, agree that the Masoretic text
is on the whole the most reliable one we have. Hence in consulting the Hebrew,
its readings are the ones to which I defer.

TO PARAPHRASE AMOS, I am neither a scholar nor the son of a scholar† but
rather an amateur. Yet I am using the word "amateur" in its radical meaning as
"lover"—much as an eminent literary critic of the mid-twentieth century, R. P.
Blackmur, did when he defined the art he practiced as "the formal discourse of
an amateur." It is, then, as a non-specialist, and a lover of the prophets, that I
approach them. This is precisely how non-specialists have always read the

---

*The word Apocrypha is Greek for "things that are hidden." According to the editors of the
Oxford Annotated Revised Standard Edition, "Some have suggested that the books were 'hidden' or withdrawn from common use because they were deemed to contain mysterious or eso-
teric lore, too profound to be communicated to any except the initiated. . . . Others have
suggested that the term was employed by those who held that such books deserved to be 'hidden' because they were spurious or heretical."

†"Son" is the literal translation of what Amos says ("I am neither a prophet nor the son of a
prophet"), but what "son of a prophet" actually means is something like "the member of a professional guild [or order] of prophets." I will comment further on these guilds later on.

prophetic literature, and it is what several relatively new scholarly methods of studying the Hebrew Bible in general have begun to do as well.

These newer methods have in varying degrees grown out of a rebellion against the enormously influential school of "Higher Criticism" of the Hebrew Bible that came before them. The designation Higher Criticism was invented to distinguish this approach from the "lower" criticism of the past, which consisted mainly of exegesis and interpretation of the text as given. But the Higher Criticism did not take the text as given. According to this school's "Newer Documentary Thesis," which was most closely associated with Julius Wellhausen, a German scholar of the late nineteenth century, there were four distinct sources or documents—J, E, D, and P—each deriving from a different period, that were stitched together by later editors to form the Pentateuch.* Analogous techniques were then applied by this school and its spin-offs—and with even greater disintegrative results to other books of the Hebrew Bible.

This entire line of analysis was at first resisted fiercely by believers. But in time it won over many of them who managed in one way or another to reconcile it with their own religiously based view of Scripture. By now, however, Wellhausen no longer bestrides the field of biblical criticism like a colossus. Even among his followers, "refinements" have been proposed and hotly debated in their turn, as has the issue of which passages belong to which of the four strands and the dating of each.

Furthermore, even allowing for a certain amount of overlapping, twelve—yes, twelve—other rival approaches to the interpretation of the Bible have entered the fray and are contending energetically and ambitiously with Wellhausen's school of Source (or Documentary) Criticism.†

---

*In German, "J" is pronounced like the English "Y," and because the Newer Documentary Thesis was most fully developed in Germany, the Yahwest strand, identified by its use for the name of God of four Hebrew letters transliterated as YHVH, came to be known as "J" rather than "Y." (For more about these letters, see p. 12.) "E" stands for Elohist (the author and/or editor who used *Elohim* rather than YHVH as the name of God); "D" for Deuteronomist (the presumed author of chapters 12–26 of the Book of Deuteronomy, about which much more later); and "P" for Priestly (the source of the Book of Leviticus and scattered passages in other books of the Pentateuch). Wellhausen was not the inventor of the Documentary Hypothesis (hence the "Newer"). In fact, its methods were born as early as the eighteenth century C.E. among students of ancient Greek texts working on Homer's epics and were then borrowed and applied to the Hebrew Bible. But the new approach did not really come into its own with the Hebrew Bible until the late nineteenth century, and it was Wellhausen who did more than anyone else to develop and establish it.

†Here is a list, as it appears in *To Each its Own Meaning: An Introduction to Biblical Criticisms and Their Application,* a collection edited by Steven L. McKenzie and Stephen R. Haynes: historical criticism; tradition-historical criticism; form criticism; redaction criticism; social-scientific criticism; canonical criticism; rhetorical criticism; structural criticism; narrative criticism; reader-response criticism; post-structuralist criticism; and feminist criticism.

What bothers many members of these newer schools is that, having broken the Bible apart, the Wellhausen approach never puts it back together, and leaves us—as one scholar has strikingly described it—with an unscrambled omelet. This is also the complaint of Brevard S. Childs, a leading exponent of the "canonical" school. Though he dislikes being classified as a canonical critic, Childs still insists (as do others who go by the name) that the final forms of each of the biblical books, as they have come down to us, are what really matter.

But there is an additional point to be made. It is connected with the widely held assumption that versions of a particular text that may be more ancient than those in the canon are more "authoritative" or genuine by virtue of their greater age. Canonical critics reject this assumption. In their opinion, it a hopeless task entirely to disentangle the "original" author from later "accretions." Furthermore, they say, the texts as we have them are, after all is said and done, the ones that have served to guide the thinking and practice of "communities of faith" throughout the centuries.

I am struck by a modern analogy, drawn from an area about as distant from the Bible as we can conceivably get: namely, policy proposals by government officials. There are "revisionist" American historians who, finding papers in the archives of the State Department containing proposals that were rejected, offer these as more revealing of the government's true intentions than the proposals that were actually acted upon. The analogy is not exact, but it does suggest that there is something perverse about treating a lost or discarded alternative as more genuine than the one that has survived as a living force.

Another form of complaint against the unscrambled omelet—framed largely in secular rather than religious terms—comes from the literary critics Robert Alter and Frank Kermode in a jointly edited anthology covering both the "Old" and "New" Testaments. The aim of Alter and Kermode is to stimulate "a revival of interest in the literary quality of these texts, in the virtues by which they continue to live as something other than archaeology" or sacred teaching. Not that Alter and Kermode ignore or sweep away discoveries or interpretations on which a considerable degree of consensus now exists, and that are the legacy of other schools of biblical criticism. "It would be absurd," they stipulate, "to prohibit the use of insights deriving from comparative religion, anthropology, philology, and so forth" in the course of subjecting the Bible to a primarily literary analysis.

From his standpoint as a scholar and a Protestant, Childs agrees, and so—speaking from yet another posture—do I. Where the story I am telling is concerned, this involves, first, acknowledging that two or more different hands are at work in some, or perhaps even all, the books of the classical prophets (though as it happens, I am not persuaded that there were two Hoseas). It also entails recognizing that in certain places the texts as we have them are "corrupt" as a result of mistakes of transmission and transcription. And it requires us, finally, to accept that a number of familiar phrases in English are mistranslations from the Hebrew based on either faulty understanding or tendentious theological interpretation.

Even though this is true of the King James Version of 1611, or KJV (sometimes also referred to as the Authorized Version, or AV), I have decided to use it almost every time I quote. After all, the King James Version *is* the Bible for most English readers. (An amusing example comes from G. B. Shaw's play *Pygmalion,* in which the linguist Henry Higgins, expressing his disgust with how the flower girl Eliza pronounces their native tongue when he first meets her, exclaims in exasperation, "English is the language of Shakespeare and the Bible.")

But the main reason for my decision is that of the various English translations I have consulted, the King James Version comes closest in syntax, cadence, locution, and spirit to the original Hebrew. Indeed, as has rightly been observed, it translates Hebrew idioms in such a way that they seem entirely native to English.

It has often been pointed out, and cannot be denied, that the King James Version tends to make books written in different styles sound alike; nor (in this, aping the look of the original Hebrew) does it distinguish between prose and poetry. Yet in my judgment Gerald Hammond is on the mark when, in his essay, "English Translations of the Bible," he summarizes the case for the King James translators as against all other versions in English:

> Through its transparency the reader of the Authorized Version not only sees the original but also learns how to read it. Patterns of repetition, the way one clause is linked to another, the effect of unexpected inversions of word order, the readiness of biblical writers to vary tone and register from the highly formal to the scatological, and the different kinds and uses of imagery, are all, like so much else . . . best open to them in the Authorized Version.

Still, where there are egregious errors, I attempt to correct them.*

A famous example is the voice crying from the wilderness, which has become a cliché in English. But in the Hebrew of the Book of Isaiah, no voice cries in the wilderness. The King James translators got the punctuation wrong here by failing to recognize that repeating the same idea in different words (parallelism), which is at the heart of biblical poetry, was being used by the prophet. What the verse actually says (in the much less elegant but more accurate translation of the New Jewish Publication Society) is: "A voice rings out:/'Clear in the

---

*For a description of the procedure I adopted, and the tools I used, in making these corrections, see "A Note on Translations," p. 15.

desert/A road for the LORD!/Level in the wilderness/A highway for our
God.'"

Which brings me to the difficult issue I have been struggling with ever since
I started working on this book: how to arrange the prose of the King James Version typographically when the passage in question is poetry, as the prophetic literature mostly is. After many long hours of making decisions and revisions that a
minute has reversed, I have come down on the side of letting the King James
Version be. Ancient Hebrew versification is another field of study that has
become vastly more technical than it used to be, with the result that translators
do not always agree about where lines set as though they were in prose should
be broken up to look like the poetry they in reality are. (Sometimes the experts
cannot even agree as to whether a particular passage is in prose or poetry.) For a
while I tried sticking to one or another contemporary model in which the lines
were broken up, and then applying it to the King James Version. But I repeatedly
became entangled in the problem of what to do whenever the translation I was
following constructed a sentence in a form that barely resembled the English of
the same sentence in the King James Version. In the end, throwing up my hands
in despair, I reached the conclusion that the cadenced prose of the King James
Version is itself so "poetic" that I might as well not tamper with it at all.

FROM MY PERSPECTIVE, the King James Version has yet another advantage
over the modern translations, which is that it eschews the so-called Tetragram-
maton "YHVH" (or its variants, "YHWH" and "Yahweh") in putting one of the
many biblical names of God into English. The Hebrew letters of which YHVH
is made up (*yod, hay, vav, hay*) used to be pronounced as "Jehovah," but pious Jews
have never pronounced it at all because there is a prohibition against doing so.
Anyhow, no one has ever known what the name is really supposed to sound like
since the days when there was a High Priest entrusted with the secret. Only
once a year, on Yom Kippur (the Day of Atonement), did he proclaim it before
the people. But the people were forbidden to speak it aloud themselves, and the
secret was lost after the Romans destroyed the Second Temple in 70 C.E. Whenever these letters appear, therefore, they are mouthed by Jews as *"Adonai,"* the
Hebrew for "our Lord," and this is the usage adopted by the King James Version,
but always in capital letters as "LORD."

I prefer LORD because YHVH in English willy-nilly makes God seem a
tribal deity (which is in fact what some scholars—wrongly, I believe—think He
was to the earliest of His Israelite devotees). Hence I allow it into this book only
when I am quoting someone else.

Another item of nomenclature that may seem strange to some readers is that
I usually avoid the terms "Hebrews" or "Jews." In the Bible itself, the people in

question are almost always "Israel" or "the children of Israel" or the "house of Israel"; once in a while they are "Jacob" or (as shorthand for the "Ten Lost Tribes" of the North) "Ephraim" or "Joseph"; but only very rarely are they "Hebrews." Not until the late fifth or early fourth century B.C.E.—at the very tail end of the prophetic period—did "Jews" begin entering into common currency as a synonym or substitute for "Israel."

Another term that is missing from this book is "Judaism." Obviously, Judaism as a religion is rooted in and grew out of the Hebrew Bible. But what we today recognize as Judaism was the creation of rabbis whose interpretations of every jot and tittle of the Bible were adumbrated first in the Land of Israel, beginning at some point in the second century B.C.E., and continuing in Babylon over the first five centuries or so of the common era. All this was then set down (mostly in Aramaic, not Hebrew) in the gigantic compendium known as the Talmud, from which the laws and practices of Judaism came to be drawn; these laws and practices were in still later centuries organized into codes that could more easily be consulted and followed, and were elaborated upon by further rabbinical interpretation. Therefore, to call the religion of the prophets "Judaism" smacks of anachronism.

In general, and before anything else, my intention is to figure out as best I can what the prophets were saying to their own contemporaries. And here again I agree with Childs when he remarks of the prophet Micah: "In spite of many good insights and interesting observations of detail, the growing confusion over conflicting theories of composition has increasingly buried the book in academic debris." I would extend the same observation to all the other prophets as well. Hence I make every effort in the pages ahead to dig the ones to whom I pay the most attention out of this debris.

At the same time, like Alter and Kermode, I lean heavily on the scholars for help in making sense of obscure and difficult passages. Moreover, because I chose to structure this book as the *story* of prophecy in ancient Israel, it became essential to determine the chronological sequence in which the prophets appeared. Unfortunately, this cannot be done simply by following the order of the prophetic books in the Masoretic Text itself: on that point, there is no disputing the evidence piled up by the scholars.

The trouble is that the scholars do not (putting it gently) always agree among themselves on the right chronology; in the estimating of dates, discrepancies can span centuries. Still, there is also a fair degree of consensus, and wherever it is to be found, I go along with it. No one, for example, disputes that Amos was the first of the classical prophets, even though his book is preceded by five others in the section of the Hebrew Bible devoted to those prophets.

On the other hand, no such consensus exists as to who was the last of the classical line. To go by the Hebrew Bible (and here the Catholic and Protestant

Bibles are in accord with the Hebrew and with each other), it was Malachi. Having been convinced, however, that there was a Second Zechariah and that he showed up about fifty years after Malachi, I end with him.

BUT WHY PILE yet another volume onto the thousands of books already written about the prophets? Being an amateur, I have nothing to contribute to the scholarly debates. Nor is it my aim to add to the inspirational literature on the prophets (not, at any rate, in the usual sense). What, then, am I up to?

I am not a very good Jew as measured by the very limited extent to which I observe the commandments of Judaism. Nor do I think that the world was created about six thousand years ago in only six days. Nor do I deny that elements of legend and the like crept into some or even many of the stories recorded in the Hebrew Bible. I do, however, believe that in general the Hebrew Bible is a reasonably reliable historical source for most of the period it covers.

A generation or so ago, archaeologists like William Fox Albright were telling us that their findings tended to confirm the Hebrew Bible's historicity. Now, inevitably, revisionists have noisily been asserting the opposite. But it is in the nature of things academic that these revisionists will themselves inevitably be revised by yet another generation of archaeologists. We will then be back again to giving the Bible the benefit of the doubt as to whether or not there was an exodus from Egypt, whether the Israelites were indigenous to the Land or Canaan or conquered it by force of arms, beginning with the city of Jericho around 1200 B.C.E., under the leadership of Joshua the son of Nun. (Not that the archaeologists or anyone else will ever be able to prove—or, in the eyes of believers, disprove—that those walls were toppled by the trumpets of the seven priests who accompanied Joshua.)

But what I believe or do not believe about its historicity is far less important than my conviction that the Hebrew Bible in general, and the prophets in particular, give awesome utterance to fundamental truths about the nature of human life. These are the truths I wish to explore in telling the story of prophecy in ancient Israel. And the reason I wish to do so is that, in my judgment, they have been obscured by commentators and clerics, as have the prophets themselves.

The most objectionable misuse of the prophets is the way selective quotation or outright misrepresentation has been employed to appropriate their backing for certain ideas that have to my mind done and are still doing great harm. I will accordingly make an effort to set the record straight by ferreting out what the prophets themselves seem in fact to have believed. Then, after pinning down as best I can what the prophets were saying to their own contemporaries, I want to explore the question of what they may still have to say to us today.

Yet, the worst thing of all that has been done to the prophets has not been to caricature or misrepresent but to ignore them. Even leaving the religious consequences aside, this is an immense intellectual and cultural tragedy. For so deeply rooted is Western civilization in the Hebrew Bible, and in the prophets who are among its greatest glories, that to forget them is to forget who we are and where we come from and where we ought to be going. To let them slip away is wantonly to scatter an inherited spiritual, intellectual, and literary fortune to the winds.

In writing this book, then, my deepest purpose, and my most fervent prayer, is that reading it will help others, as writing it has helped me, to recapture some idea of what we are losing when we turn our backs on the prophets. They spoke words of fire that could set the evils of their own time ablaze, and those words can do the same for the time we ourselves live in, if we can but cultivate the ability, and develop the willingness, to open our ears to them.

A NOTE ON TRANSLATIONS

AS I SAID ABOVE, all but a very few of the quotations from the Hebrew Bible in this book have been taken from the King James Version.* But as I also pointed out, the King James Version is not always accurate. Therefore I have continually checked it against my own reading of the Hebrew originals, as well as against six twentieth-century translations, which were based on knowledge about the Hebrew language that was unavailable in the seventeenth century.

One of these, the New Revised Standard Version (NRSV), was done by a committee of mostly Protestant scholars updating an earlier updated version of the King James Version, and another (the Jerusalem Bible, or JB) by a team of Roman Catholic experts. A third (Soncino) was produced by various

---

*Not all editions of the King James Version are identical in matters of punctuation (and there are also occasional differences in language). The one I have relied upon was edited by Robert Carroll and Stephen Prickett for the Oxford World Classics Series, and published by Oxford University Press in 1997 under the title *The Bible: Authorized King James Version With Apocrypha.*

Orthodox Jewish scholars, and a fourth (the New Jewish Publication Society—NJPS) by a group associated with the less traditionalist Conservative branch of American Judaism. I also consulted the even newer translations in the interdenominational Anchor Bible series (AB). Finally, in my chapter on the Pentateuch, I made use of the Schocken edition of *The First Five Books of Moses,* with translation and commentary by Everett Fox.

Whenever undeniable mistakes in KJV were corrected by these translations, or significant deviations from it occurred (as opposed to differences in phraseology that did not affect the essential meaning), I have so indicated in the footnotes.

Here is a list of the abbreviations by which these translations are cited in the footnotes:

KJV:	King James Version
NRSV:	New Revised Standard Version
Son:	Soncino
NJPS:	New Jewish Publication Society
JB:	Jerusalem Bible
AB:	Anchor Bible
Sch:	Schocken

One more point: in quoting Hebrew words, I have eschewed the standard scholarly systems of transliteration, which are very hard for the lay reader to vocalize. Instead, I have adopted a system of my own, designed to make it as easy as possible for anyone who does not know the language to get a reasonably clear notion of what the Hebrew sounds like.   •

PART ONE

Clouds of Ancestral Glory

CHAPTER ONE

IN THE BEGINNING

I N SPEAKING OF CLASSICAL PROPHECY as a mysterious phenomenon
at both ends of its three-hundred-year course, I also suggested that Amos
and those who followed in his footsteps neither materialized out of
nowhere nor eventually vanished into thin air. But we cannot appreciate the
force of that suggestion without first sketching the ancient Israelite matrix out of
which the classical prophets arose and back into which their words were eventually reabsorbed. When we arrive at the end of the story, I will take a stab at
explaining why no such words were heard again after they had been shattering
the air for three hundred years. But for now, there is the question of the original
emergence of the classical prophets.

In grappling with that question, one scholar, Shalom M. Paul, reaches all
the way forward to early nineteenth-century England for a line in William
Wordsworth's great poem, "Ode on Intimations of Immortality." Adapting this
line to Amos, Paul describes him as "trailing clouds of ancestral glory." The
allusion is to all those earlier prophets who did not leave books of their own
behind them but of whom we read in the Pentateuch and the Former
Prophets.

If the current scholarly consensus is right, the Pentateuch and the Former
Prophets did not exist in written form when Amos showed up in about 750
B.C.E. But it seems reasonable to some scholars—and to me as well—that the
history those books recount, and the stories they tell about the central figures in
that history, were in wide circulation long before being pulled together, written
down, and edited. It is not even impossible that some or much of this material
may already have been committed to writing by the middle of the eighth century B.C.E. But the main point is that the classical prophets of that century knew
from whence, from whom, and from what they had stemmed.

In later generations, the rabbis of the Talmud would speculate that not even all the prophets in the Pentateuch and the Former Prophets added together made up anywhere near the sum total of such spokesmen sent by God to reprove and instruct and comfort the children of Israel. According to one talmudic estimate, they amounted to "double the number of the children of Israel" who were led by Moses out of Egyptian slavery. But as a less fanciful talmudic count has it, only fifty-five prophets, including seven females, are mentioned in the Hebrew Bible, apart from the fifteen whose names are attached to books of their own. Still, whatever the number of predecessors he may have had, a very old tradition stood behind Amos of which he must have been aware.

How old? Well, we meet the word *navi* (the most common of the four Hebrew terms for prophet*) for the first time in Genesis, the very first book of the Hebrew Bible, when the pagan king Abimelech is told by God in a dream that the patriarch Abraham "is a prophet, and he shall pray for thee, and thou shalt live. . . ."

The context here is that on entering Abimelech's domain, Abraham has passed off his wife Sarah as his sister, having successfully pulled the same trick once before (when his name was Abram and hers Sarai) on Pharaoh in Egypt. In both cases, he does this because he fears, not without cause, that these monarchs will kill him in order to add so beautiful a woman to their own harems. God is thus warning Abimelech not to have sexual relations with Sarah, as Pharaoh— the text is silent on the matter—may have done (and which may be why he is then, like another Pharaoh in the future who will at first refuse to free his Hebrew slaves, hit " . . . with great plagues . . .").

In the next generation, poor Abimelech is put through the same paces by Abraham's son Isaac with *his* wife Rebekah. These three episodes, however, may constitute one of the numerous instances in the Hebrew Bible where different (and even conflicting) versions of the same story are told. Presumably the reason was that by the time such tales were written down, the editors or redactors did not dare to change or omit anything that had already become well-known, or sanctified, through oral transmission. (If so, this would lend additional credence to the supposition that Amos was conscious of the "clouds of ancestral glory" he himself was trailing.)

But where Abraham is concerned, the story—like many others we will pass along our way—also illustrates the Bible's amazing refusal to conceal the human weaknesses of even its most revered figures. (After Pharaoh takes Sarah into his "house," Abraham is rewarded with great riches, and shows no compunction

---

*The others are *ro-eh* (seer), which, we learn from the First Book of Samuel (9:9), was what in former times a *navi* was called; *khozeh* (visionary); and *ish ha-Elohim* (man of God).

about accepting them.) The prophets, I have said, were not saints as we under-stand the term, and that very much includes the first of them.

Some scholars, reasoning from the lack of evidence outside the Bible, and their own predispositions, hold that there never was such a person as Abraham, and that the name stands for a clan, perhaps legendary, into which later ideas and beliefs were retrojected. Other equally reputable scholars disagree, seeing noth-ing in the Bible itself, or in materials from other sources, that is necessarily inconsistent with the historicity of Abraham. If we cast our lot, as I do, with the theory that Abraham actually existed, we can reasonably guess that he was born in Mesopotamia around the year 2000 B.C.E., and that he grew up to become a wealthy semi-nomadic tent dweller. In that era, his family would, like everyone else in the world, have been idol worshipers. This is not mentioned in Genesis, but very likely only because it is taken for granted there.*

Then one day, with no warning or preparation, Abraham (still called Abram) hears the voice of God commanding him to " . . . Get thee out of thy country, and from thy kindred, and from thy father's house, unto a land that I will shew thee. . . ." This command is accompanied not by any promulgation of a new law, or of a new faith, but only by a promise: "And I will make of thee a great nation, and I will bless thee. . . . And I will bless them that bless thee, and curse him that curseth thee: and in thee shall all families of the earth be blessed."

God reiterates this promise again and again to Abraham, but such direct communication from Him, while a necessary condition for being designated in the Hebrew Bible as a prophet, is evidently not sufficient. Before Abraham there was his own remote ancestor Noah, to whom God also spoke and who " . . . found grace in the eyes of the LORD . . ." as " . . . a just man and perfect in his generations. . . ." Noah was accordingly spared from the universal destruction of the flood God had decided to bring upon the earth in order to wash away the wickedness that had spoiled His original creation, and thereby also to give it a new beginning. Yet Noah was never referred to as a prophet. More remarkably, neither will the title be given to Abraham's son Isaac or his grandson Jacob, even though they, along with him, will be reckoned among the three patriarchs of the special people that God has promised will develop out of their descendants.

Then there is the almost equally curious, and very significant, case of Joseph, one of Jacob's twelve sons. After being sold into slavery in Egypt by his brothers, who envy his status as the favorite of their father, Joseph gradually rises to great heights there by predicting the future through the interpretation of dreams and through practicing divination. Yet he is never deemed a prophet, either.

---

*Later, however, in the Book of Joshua (24:2), it is stated outright.

Here, then, is an early indication that, so far as the Hebrew Bible is concerned, prophecy does not mean the ability to foresee the future.* Just the opposite: though Joseph is not condemned or even criticized for it in Genesis, divination will be forbidden to the children of Israel in the third book of the Pentateuch, Leviticus.[†]

WHAT IS IT, THEN, that makes Abraham, and not any of the other patriarchs or their immediate descendants, a prophet? On the basis of the verse in which his being a prophet is associated with the ability to save Abimelech's life through prayer, the suggestion has been advanced by Shalom Paul and other authorities that the key element is this power to intercede with God for others. Other authorities, notably Francis L. Andersen and David Noel Freedman, writing in collaboration, disagree:

> A prophet may [intercede], because the situation makes such action possible, that is, he is in the presence of the divine king. That . . . , however, is not formally part of the status of prophet; it does not belong officially to the job description.

But in my view, the main factor in "the job description" is that Abraham alone plays the double role—involving a positive as well as a negative aspect—that all prophets will play throughout the history of Israel.

The positive side of this coin is the capacity to understand, and to make others understand, the revolutionary and previously unimaginable idea that there is only one God, not many gods; that He is invisible; that He alone created the heavens and the earth and all they contain or embrace; and that, for reasons He does not disclose, He has chosen to make the seed of Abraham (or the children of Israel, after the new name that will later be given to his grandson Jacob), the instrument through which His law and His commandments will be revealed first to them and then in due course to all other peoples as well.

With Abraham, we are still some seven hundred years away from the detailed contents of that revelation, which will take place through Moses on Mount

---

*True, the Bible is not completely consistent on this point, as witness Deuteronomy: "When a prophet speaketh in the name of the LORD, if the thing follow not, nor come to pass, that is the thing which the LORD hath not spoken, but the prophet hath spoken it presumptuously . . ." (18:22). I will be referring to this verse on a number of occasions later on.

†Consulting ghosts or " . . . familiar spirits . . ." will also be forbidden no fewer than three times in Leviticus (19:31, 20:6, and 20:27, in the last of which it will be declared punishable by death), as well as in Deuteronomy (18:10–11). The issue of wizardry and necromancy will arise again in the First Book of Samuel. But more of that, too, when we get to it.

Sinai. Meanwhile, however, Abraham " ... believe[s] in the LORD ..." and commits himself to " ... command his children and his household after him ... that they shall keep the way of the LORD, to do justice and judgment. ..."

No further definition is given of what justice means, or how Abraham can keep the way of God before its twists and turns have been disclosed. But as Andersen and Freedman comment about the oracles the classical prophets will deliver in the far future against the pagan nations:

> [These nations] are not to be blamed for failing to worship and serve Yahweh, whom they do not know as God. Hence they are not condemned [as Israel is] for apostasy, because never having known him they have not been guilty of abandoning him.

In spite of this, Andersen and Freedman go on, the crimes with which the pagan nations are charged "would be regarded as reprehensible behavior on anyone's part, anywhere, anytime. There seem to be underlying principles of justice and equity that are equally applicable to all."

In this illuminating perspective, what will be assumed by the classical prophets is "a kind of 'natural law,'" and I would suggest that some such assumption is also at work in connection with Abraham's commitment. Otherwise on what basis would Abraham argue and bargain with God, as he does (simultaneously appealing to "a kind of 'natural law'" and foreshadowing prophets of the classical era like Jeremiah) when He proposes to wipe the evil cities of Sodom and Gomorrah off the face of the earth: "Wilt thou also destroy the righteous with the wicked? ... Shall not the Judge of all the earth do right?"

We are entitled to conclude from all this—so it seems to me—that Abraham grasps the essence of the revolutionary idea of the one true and invisible God, which is why he ratifies his acceptance of it both for himself and his descendants through a "covenant" written by circumcision into the very organ of male generation.

In entering into this covenant with God, however, Abraham necessarily also takes upon himself the obverse or the negative aspect of the prophetic privilege and burden. He, the offspring of idolators, repudiates them so as to inaugurate a war against the religious ideas by which they and all other men have thus far always lived: that there are many gods; that images of wood, and silver, and gold can be fashioned of them; and that these images can then be worshiped and served. "Abominations"—as the Hebrew Bible never tires of characterizing them—are encouraged through this worship, and they must ultimately be extirpated, first among Abraham's own " ... children and his household after him ..." and the great people who will spring from his loins, and then among " ... all families of the earth. ..."

I should note that scholars exist who perceive no clear sign of the war against idolatry in the narratives about Abraham. Some even contend that Abraham brought the familial god with him when he left home, that this god was then identified with a local (Canaanite) deity, and that only after the time of Moses was it merged conceptually into the God of Israel. Yet surely the commission to set himself against the family god is inherent in God's command to Abraham that he go forth from the land of his birth and set out on a journey to a new place—or, as it might be phrased in a more modern idiom, a new world.

Then there is the story of the binding of Isaac, one of the greatest masterpieces of minimalist narrative art in the history of literature—an example *par excellence* of how much and how wide a range of emotion the Hebrew Bible can pack into just a few short verses, where what is omitted miraculously becomes as expressive as what is included. This story has frequently been interpreted as proof that the practice of child sacrifice associated with idolatry was not precluded at an early stage in the development of the Hebrew Bible's conception of God. But I would argue, paradoxical as the idea may seem at first sight, that the story should be understood as the first major shot ever fired in the war against idolatry.

Consider: when God commands him to sacrifice his beloved son Isaac as a " . . . burnt offering . . . ," Abraham, without a murmur of protest or a plea for mercy, immediately prepares to do so; only at the very last moment, when an angel stays his hand, is he prevented from consummating this dreadful act. Why does Abraham, who does not hesitate to argue with God over Sodom and Gomorrah, fail to argue with Him over his own beloved son?

One reason may be that child sacrifice is so common in the world around him that he sees nothing extraordinary about the command. As we have been taught by scholars like Jon D. Levenson, there is no need to assume that pagans who engaged in this practice loved their sons any less than Abraham loved Isaac. On the contrary: it is more likely that in appeasing or beseeching favor from the gods represented by their idols, they were sacrificing what was *most* precious to them.

But among the differences here is that what the idolators do voluntarily in pursuing a goal of benefit to them or theirs, Abraham is *ordered* by God to do, and for no such purpose or reward. Indeed, none is specified. The point is to put him through the most extreme of all imaginable tests of his readiness to obey. In passing this test, Abraham demonstrates an understanding that acceptance of the one true God who has been revealed to him first and foremost entails submission to His will. (One might say that, to the unresolved conundrum posed by Socrates in Athens many centuries later—"Is that which is holy loved by the gods because it is holy, or is it holy because it is loved by the gods?"—the Hebrew Bible has an unequivocal answer: it is holy because it is loved, or commanded, by God.)

But at the same time, Abraham has discovered that what God wills is radically at odds with what the many gods of all the pagan religions are believed to demand. Unlike the pagan gods, He will have nothing to do with child sacrifice, the most horrendous in the Hebrew Bible's eyes of all the many "abominations" closely associated with and flowing from idolatry.

Generation after generation of believers have been tormented by this story, asking why it was necessary for God to devise so cruel a test. My own theory is that only by undergoing the experience himself—in his own person, and on his own flesh—can Abraham come fully to realize that idolatrous practices are an ever-present danger even to God's chosen people, and that they can exert their insidious power even through the voice of God Himself.*

Having absorbed this hard lesson, Abraham becomes the first in what will be a long line of prophets charged with the burden of fighting against the idolatrous temptations to which his own descendants will constantly be subject—and that it will take them some fifteen hundred years to overcome.

AFTER ABRAHAM, there are no other prophets in Genesis. It is not until we meet Moses in Exodus, the second book of the Pentateuch, that the word *navi* turns up again. Yet when it does, it is attached not to Moses but to his brother Aaron, the more fluent and articulate of the two, and then to their sister Miriam. Moses himself, strangely, is not called a *navi* until Numbers, the fourth of the five books of the Pentateuch.

Title or no title, Moses is clearly *the* prophet (and I am assuming, as with Abraham, and again along with a reputable body of scholarly thought, that there actually was such a person—a Hebrew slave raised, according to a complicated series of events recounted in the Book of Exodus, as an Egyptian prince†). It is Moses who is appointed by God to lead the children of Israel out of slavery in Egypt somewhere around the year 1300 B.C.E. (when, in that same far-off land where Homer will sing of it, the Trojan war is raging). It is he to whom God also gives instructions in how to accomplish this feat. And it is he through whom God performs miracles in effecting the escape.

But most important of all, it is Moses who meets with God on Sinai and brings back the Ten Commandments. The first of these ratifies in concrete lan-

---

*This is a difficult concept and a theological stumbling block, but there are a number of other occasions in the Bible when God puts lies into the mouths of prophets who seem to be sent by Him. (See p. 99 for one such example, drawn from the story of King Ahab's death, 1 Kin 22). The purpose can be to test the people, but it can also serve to ensure that egregious sinners will stay on their path to a just punishment for which repentance can no longer avail.

†There have been those who, while accepting that Moses did indeed exist, posit that he was the illegitimate son of Pharaoh's daughter, passed off as an adopted slave baby who had been abandoned by his mother, and who, when grown up, was "adopted" by the Egyptian princess.

guage Abraham's more abstract conception of the war that has been declared against idolatry: "I am the LORD thy God. . . . Thou shalt have no other gods before me. Thou shalt not make unto thee any graven image. . . . Thou shalt not bow down thyself to them, nor serve them: for I the LORD thy God am a jealous God. . . ."

Simultaneously, it is given to Moses to move far beyond Abraham in specifying both the positive and negative obligations placed upon the children of Israel, and that the prophets will from now on always be driving home to their own people. The positive obligation to *obey* God (demonstrated by Abraham in the most unforgettable way through the binding of Isaac) Moses communicates by spelling out the ramifications—the fine print, as it were—of the Ten Commandments.

But these ramifications are not confined to the moral sphere alone: equally detailed and even more complicated regulations are also prescribed (largely though not exclusively in Leviticus, the third book of the Pentateuch) for sacrifice and other rituals that are no less obligatory and sacred than the moral laws. In some codifications of much later eras, the two sets of laws will be divided into those governing the relations between man and man, and those governing the relations between man and God. In the Pentateuch, however, no such neat division can be discerned. Only in another six centuries, when we get to the classical prophets, will the question of whether the two sets of laws are equally important become a—or perhaps *the*—central theme.

In the meantime, in Numbers, the book that follows Leviticus, we are presented, through a series of fascinating stories, with a clearer and clearer sense of what constitutes the negative mission imposed by the First Commandment and that goes along with the prophet's positive task of keeping an understanding of the laws alive. In prohibiting the children of Israel to bow down before other gods or to make graven images of them, the First Commandment amounts to a formal declaration of the war against idolatry that began only symbolically with Abraham.

The first group of these stories bears on the almost intolerable burden that the war against idolatry will impose on the prophets chosen by God to be, so to speak, its generals, starting with Moses himself. A mere two months or so after being freed from slavery and fleeing Egypt amid such spectacular miracles as the parting of the sea, the children of Israel begin hurling reproaches at Moses (" . . . Because there were no graves in Egypt, hast thou taken us away to die in the wilderness? . . .").

A few weeks later, and immediately after being provided with fresh water by divine intervention, they commence grumbling to Moses (and Aaron) again: " . . . Would to God we had died by the hand of the LORD in the land of Egypt, when we sat by the flesh pots, and when we did eat bread to the full; for ye have brought us forth into this wilderness, to kill this whole assembly with hunger."

God responds by raining down bread in the form of manna, which tastes like " . . . wafers made with honey." And still this " . . . stiffnecked people . . ." have the gall to disobey the prescribed system by which the manna is to be gathered.

Most astonishing of all is the episode of the "molten" (or golden) calf. To comprehend just how amazing this episode is, we have to remind ourselves that it immediately follows Moses' return from Mount Sinai with the Ten Commandments and the other laws he reads aloud to the people. Awed by " . . . the thunderings, and the lightnings, . . . and the mountain smoking . . . ," the people " . . . with one voice . . ." pledge their obedience (" . . . All the words which the LORD hath said, we will do"). On the next morning, having written it all down, Moses " . . . took the book of the covenant, . . ." and again read its contents to the people: " . . . and they said, All that the LORD hath said will we do, and be obedient."*

Moses then returns to Sinai to receive the two stone tablets " . . . written with the finger of God," but when he fails to get back soon enough to suit them, the people are hit by a veritable bout of amnesia. So far have they already forgotten what they have only just vowed to do, and not to do, that they now set about building an idol—the golden calf—to worship instead of God; and they force Aaron to acquiesce in this cardinal sin.

I think the story of the golden calf is there to underline how immensely hard it is for the people of Israel (as it would have been for any other people) to wrap their minds around the new religion—or even, having done so, to maintain a grip on the totally revolutionary idea that only one God exists; that He is invisible and can never even be pictured in a statue or a symbol; and that all the other gods worshiped by everyone else in the world are nothing but inanimate images of wood or stone or gold fashioned by men who then foolishly and vainly worship the work of their own hands.

Correlatively, the story shows us how easy it is to forget and slip back into the old ways—the ways, it bears repeating, of everyone else in the world, the Israelites themselves included until, as it were, only yesterday. These are people who have with their own eyes witnessed the wonders wrought by God, and who have directly experienced His awesome presence. Yet even *they* are unable to remain steadfast in their fidelity to Him, or their trust in Moses, who has given every conceivable sign of being His true servant and spokesman. Even *they* can, in the flicker of an eye, forget everything they have only just seen and heard and affirmed. Even *they* can blithely violate the principal and prime element of the oath they have only just made to obey Him.

---

*The literal translation is "We will do, and we will hear." The priority given in this declaration to doing over hearing has often been taken as the explanation of why Judaism later came to put so much more emphasis on obeying the commandments than on adhering to doctrine.

THIS IS WHAT MOSES—and all the prophets who will trail after him—are up against in the struggle to extirpate idolatry from within. Rooting it out, the story of the golden calf reveals, will take even more effort and more energy than might have been thought. So onerous will this struggle be that—as the classical prophets will never cease exclaiming in bewildered tones—not even the severest punishment ever seems to avail in bringing the people to their senses for more than a very short time, if at all.

We get the first example right here. Because of the sin of the golden calf, three thousand Israelites are slain by the sword, and others are visited by a plague. For the moment they build no more idols, but soon they resume their "murmurings" to Moses about the hardships they are being forced to endure in the wilderness. How much better, they complain, was the life they had led in Egypt, even as slaves. The cuisine there was especially good as compared with a diet exclusively composed of manna. And so

> . . . the mixt multitude that was among them fell a lusting: and the children of Israel also wept again, and said, Who shall give us flesh to eat? We remember the fish, which we did eat in Egypt freely; the cucumbers, and the melons, and the leeks, and the onions, and the garlick: But now our soul is dried away: there is nothing at all, besides this manna, before our eyes.

As will be the case with many prophets after him, Moses had resisted being singled out for this office in the first place: " . . . O my Lord, I am not eloquent, . . . but I am slow of speech, and of a slow tongue," and he had begged that someone else be sent in his place as God's agent. Now, having been laden with what feels like the last straw, Moses complains to God for having forced him " . . . to bear all this people alone, because it is too heavy for me."

God thereupon appoints seventy elders to share the burden with him: "And the LORD . . . took of the spirit that was upon him, and gave it unto the seventy elders: and it came to pass, that, when the spirit rested upon them, they prophesied. . . ." Joshua the son of Nun (Moses' main attendant, who will succeed him after his death and lead the people into the land God has promised to their ancestors and to them) is outraged by an apparent dereliction on the part of two of these newly exalted elders. But Moses (true to the description of him in the next chapter as the humblest of all men) replies, " . . . Enviest thou for my sake? would God that all the LORD's people were prophets. . . ."*

---

*The grammatical form of the main Hebrew term for prophet (*navi*) in this verse has been interpreted by some scholars to mean that the elders, rather than becoming prophets, only "acted like prophets." That is to say, they went into ecstatic frenzies or trances resembling those that were characteristic of the "mantic" prophets of the surrounding cultures of the Near East. Perhaps. Yet when Moses, in his reply to Joshua, declares that he wishes all the children of Israel were prophets, the term he chooses is the straightforward plural of *navi* (*n'vi-im*).

Joshua is jealous on Moses' account, but we are soon made witness to envy of Moses himself by his own brother and sister, Aaron and Miriam: "And they said, Hath the LORD indeed spoken only by Moses? hath he not also spoken by us? ..." At this God decides to leave no smidgen of doubt as to the special status of Moses among all the prophets, whether past, passing, or to come:

> And the LORD came down in the pillar of the cloud. . . . And he said, Hear now my words: If there be a prophet among you, I the LORD will make myself known unto him in a vision, and will speak unto him in a dream. My servant Moses is not so. . . . With him will I speak mouth to mouth, even apparently, and not in dark speeches; and the similitude of the LORD shall he behold. . . .*

Curiously, however (flashing back now to Exodus, where this mark of unique favor is first mentioned), no sooner does God speak " . . . unto Moses face to face, as a man speaketh unto his friend . . . ," than he is instructed that

> . . . Thou canst not see my face: for there shall no man see me, and live. And the LORD said, Behold, there is a place by me, and thou shalt stand upon a rock: And it shall come to pass, while my glory passeth by, that I will put thee in a cleft of the rock, and will cover thee with my hand while I pass by: And I will take away mine hand, and thou shalt see my back parts; but my face shall not be seen.

What is still more curious is that other characters in the Bible—before, during, and after the time of Moses—are permitted to survive the sight of God. Thus in previous generations, there was Jacob: " . . . I have seen God face to face, and my life is preserved." So, too, in Moses' own day:

> Then up went Moses, and Aaron, Nadab, and Abihu [Aaron's sons], and seventy of the elders of Israel: And they saw the God of Israel. . . . And upon the[se] nobles of the children of Israel he laid not his hand: also they saw God, and did eat and drink.†

---

*The words "even apparently" might more intelligibly be rendered as (in NRSV) "clearly" or (as in NJPS) "plainly." NRSV, NJPS, and other modern translations also give us "not in riddles" instead of KJV's "not in dark speeches." In any event, Miriam is punished for this presumption with an attack of leprosy, cured in only a week by Moses' plea to God. But Aaron—for reasons that have provided scholars with additional work to do in trying to unravel, and that remains puzzling to me—gets away scot free, just as he did when he acquiesced in the building of the golden calf.

†Interestingly, however, these same two of Aaron's sons are later punished when, as priests, they commit a ritual error by offering " . . . strange fire before the LORD, which he commanded

And in the future, there will even be a relatively obscure pre-classical prophet, Micaiah the son of Imlah, who survives seeing " . . . the LORD sitting on his throne, and all the host of heaven standing by him on his right hand and on his left." Then we will have the classical prophet (the First) Isaiah: "In the year that King Uzziah died I saw also the Lord sitting upon a throne. . . . Then said I, Woe is me! for I am undone; . . . for mine eyes have seen the King, the LORD of Hosts." But he is not undone.

Much exegetical ingenuity has been expended in efforts to explain away these contradictions, just as oceans of midnight oil have been burned by scholars in accounting for repetitions and/or different versions of the same events appearing side by side throughout the Pentateuch. I have no desire either to rehearse or participate in these efforts. Instead, I will take this occasion to reiterate my opinion that such puzzles add further plausibility to the theory—most forcefully promulgated among the scholars by Yehezkel Kaufmann—that whenever the biblical texts may have been set down in writing, the different oral traditions out of which they came had already acquired too much sanctity to be omitted or edited (which does not, of course, preclude simple human errors by copyists).

THE NEXT PROPHET we encounter in Numbers is Balaam. Not being an Israelite, and being moreover a practitioner of divination (which, as we have previously noted, is forbidden to the Israelites), Balaam cannot be considered one of the "clouds of ancestral glory" trailing behind Amos. But he deserves consideration here because when Balak, the king of Moab—one of the principalities Moses and his people encounter on their journey through the wilderness toward the promised land of Canaan—sends for him to curse the Israelites, God temporarily transforms this pagan seer into a Hebrew prophet.

It is a delicious tale, among whose marvels is the hilarious account of the ass on which Balaam is riding to meet Balak. (The ass, whose route is blocked by an

---

them not. And there went out fire from the LORD, and devoured them, and they died before the LORD" (Lev 10:1–2). No connection is made with the earlier ascent of Nadab and Abihu into the presence of God, and no clear explanation is offered as to what exactly they now did to merit being burned to death. But it is as though the consequence of seeing God face to face were finally realized after a long delay. I admit that this speculation is not, so far as I know, backed up by any authoritative student of Leviticus. Still, we do get this in Chapter 16, Verse 1 of that same book: "And the LORD spake unto Moses after the death of the two sons of Aaron, when they offered before the LORD, and died." Here, though, is one of those times when KJV is inaccurate. The literal sense of the Hebrew is "when they came near before God." These words are rendered by NRSV as "when they drew near before the Lord," while NJPS gives them as "when they drew too close to the presence of the LORD." Everett Fox in Sch (who strives for a "text in English dress but with a Hebraic voice") comes up with: "when they came-near before the presence of YHWH."

angel the animal can see but who at first remains invisible to Balaam, is given the power of speech to reproach his master for unjustly beating him when he swerves.) But despite this element of comedy, the story is in the main deadly serious, and it strikes me as a kind of portent of two elements we will repeatedly come upon in the realm of classical prophecy.

The first of these emerges from the complex narrative setting into which the story is deposited. Every time Balaam (spurred on by ever greater promises of reward from the king) tries to utter imprecations, God forces him to perform yet another of the tasks that will fall to the classical prophets—that of offering blessing and consolation to the same people they are otherwise always threatening and denouncing.

The lush blessings Balaam heaps upon the heads of the children of Israel, and the triumphant future over all their enemies that he paints, seem to follow naturally from a brief account of various Israelite military victories as they are making their way through the desert toward Canaan. Yet this string of successes has also been preceded by an insurrection against Moses that God punishes with extreme severity. (The earth opens up to swallow Korah, the leader of the rebellion, and his immediate entourage; 250 more of his followers are immolated; and another 14,700 die in a divinely ordained plague.) Then yet another rebellion breaks out near a place called Meribah that God orders Moses to quell by striking a rock with his rod to bring forth water for the people to drink. Moses, in the company of Aaron, does what he is told, but not before expressing a rather mild objection. It is for committing so apparently trivial a sin—and for this alone*—that he and his brother will never be permitted to enter the Promised Land.

By the time God informs them of this, we have already learned that all but two members of the generation who left Egypt with them will suffer the same fate. For when spies who had been sent on a reconnaissance mission (to " . . . search the land . . .") returned with " . . . an evil report . . . ," warning that the obstacles to conquest would be impossible to overcome, the people reverted to their inveterate "murmurings" against Moses and Aaron,

> . . . and the whole congregation said unto them, Would God that we had died in the land of Egypt! or would God we had died in this wilderness! And wherefore hath the Lord brought us unto this land, to fall by the sword, that our wives and our children should be a prey? were it not better for us to return into Egypt?

As he has often done before in analogous circumstances, Moses pleads with God not to destroy the entire people then and there (a plea that will also be made by many of the classical prophets). God once again grants his wish, but

---

*But see p. 34 for the different explanation given in Deuteronomy.

only in an overwhelming passage that picks up point by point and image by image the perverse prayer the people have just let loose from their lips:

> . . . As truly as I live, saith the LORD, as ye have spoken in my ears, so will I do to you: Your carcases shall fall in this wilderness, and all that were numbered of you, according to your whole number, from twenty years old and upward, which have murmured against me, Doubtless ye shall not come into the land, concerning which I sware to make you dwell therein. . . . But your little ones, which ye said should be a prey, them will I bring in, and they shall know the land which ye have despised. But as for you, your carcases, they shall fall in the wilderness.

Set against these frightful words, the blessings of Balaam seem puzzling. And all the more perplexing do they become when God forces him to declare that there is no " . . . iniquity in Jacob . . . [?!]." But it is precisely this near juxtaposition of the two passages—one of ferocious harshness and the other of effusively lyrical triumphalism—that resembles the alternation between oracles of condemnation and consolation that will be the dominant rhythm of classical prophecy from the time it emerges about six centuries later and throughout its three-hundred-year career.

The second foretaste of the classical prophets in Balaam's blessings is in the visions of the day when the potentates and princes of all the world will stream up to Jerusalem to pay tribute to and acknowledge the sovereignty of the one true God. To my ear, the third of Balaam's blessings points almost irresistibly in that very direction:

> How goodly are thy tents, O Jacob, And thy tabernacles, O Israel! As the valleys are they spread forth, as gardens by the river's side, as the trees of lign aloes which the LORD hath planted, and as cedar trees besides the waters. He shall pour the water out of his buckets, and his seed shall be in many waters, and his king shall be higher than Agag, and his kingdom shall be exalted. God brought him forth out of Egypt; he hath as it were the strength of a unicorn: He shall eat up the nations his enemies, and shall break their bones, and pierce them through with his arrows. He couched, he lay down as a lion, and as a great lion: who shall stir him up? Blessed is he that blesseth thee, and cursed is he that curseth thee.*

Though frustrated almost beyond endurance, King Balak does not punish the prophet for having thus betrayed him. But neither is Balaam rewarded by

---

*KJV's "He shall pour the water out of his buckets" is more accurately, if less beautifully, rendered by NJPS as: "Their boughs drip with moisture, Their roots have abundant water," while the "unicorn" at which KJV took a guess is actually "the horns of the wild ox."

God. When the people of Israel suddenly begin " . . . to commit whoredom with the daughters of Moab," who then induce (or seduce) these Israelites into bowing down before idols of the god Baal-peor, the Hebrew Bible subsequently blames "the counsel of Balaam" for having instigated this radical act of apostasy. Yet no mention is made of him in the original account of the seduction and its aftermath—a plague that disposes of another twenty-four thousand Israelites of the Exodus generation who, in yielding to the cardinal sin of idolatry after so many warnings against it, have once again shown themselves unworthy to enter the Promised Land. God then orders Moses to wage a war to the death against the Midianites, during which Balaam himself is put to the sword.

A strange and bloody conclusion to what had begun as a strange and delightful story.

AFTER BALAAM, there are no further references to prophets or prophecy (or diviners), whether Israelite or pagan, in the Book of Numbers. But in passing over to Deuteronomy, we enter a world that seems to belong more to the realm of classical prophecy than to any of the four books that have preceded this fifth and last volume of the Pentateuch.

By now it has been made abundantly clear that Moses is and will always remain the greatest of all prophets, a point that is to be stressed yet again toward the end of Deuteronomy just after he dies. But not until Deuteronomy does Moses assume a role similar to that of the classical prophets. Throughout Exodus, Leviticus, and Numbers, he often transmits the word of God to the people in his own voice. But as with the Former Prophets just up ahead in the order of the Hebrew Bible, there is a narrator in these three books who relates events as they occur, including many involving Moses himself. Another link between the Moses of these three books and the Former Prophets is that, like some of them, he performs miracles, which the classical Prophets almost never do.

Deuteronomy, however, leaps over the Former Prophets to tie in with the Latter. Here Moses takes over completely: so much so that, as the books of the classical prophets are called by their own names, so this one might well have been entitled "Moses."* Which is one of many reasons behind the scholarly consensus that Deuteronomy was either composed (or written down and/or edited) in the last decades of the seventh century B.C.E. It was then that a "Book of the Law" was discovered that is generally thought to have been some form or part of Deuteronomy. The possibility therefore exists that Deuteronomy could have

---

*The word Deuteronomy is a Latinized Greek word for "second law," which evidently derived from a misconstrual of the Hebrew name, *mishneh ha-torah ha-zot* ("copy of this Torah") by which it refers to itself (Deut 17:18). The Hebrew name by which it came to be and is still known is *D'varim* (Words).

been influenced by the classical prophets of the eighth century B.C.E. (Amos, Hosea, Micah, and the First Isaiah) rather than the other way around.

Yet to me, the alternative possibility sketched out by the historian and biblical scholar John Bright seems more convincing:

> Though no doubt reedited in the [preceding] generation . . . [Deuteronomy] was no new law, still less the "pious fraud" it has sometimes been called, but rather a homiletical collection of ancient laws that derived ultimately from the legal tradition of earliest Israel. . . . Its laws, therefore, could not have been for the most part very novel.

In the light of Bright's position, let me now look at Deuteronomy not as a product of the seventh century B.C.E. but as the concluding volume of the Pentateuch, which is where it was placed in the Bible that has come down to us in the Jewish, Catholic, and Protestant canons alike.

If we read it as such, one of the first things that strike us is the change in Moses. He, who was so " . . . slow of speech, and of a slow tongue" that God had to appoint Aaron to speak for him (to be, as it is put in Exodus, Moses' own "prophet"), has now become not only fluent but wonderfully eloquent. He has, in the critic Joel Rosenberg's formulation, found his voice. And this newfound power of eloquent articulation he now employs in the service of a lengthy farewell address to the children of Israel as they are poised " . . . on this side Jordan in the wilderness . . ." to invade the Promised Land to which he himself has been denied entry.

Forty years have gone by since the Exodus from Egypt, and along with the thinned-out ranks of the survivors of that flight, a new generation stands before Moses. It is for their benefit that Moses recapitulates the entire story and reiterates the laws that God has revealed through him (mainly those in the book of Exodus, but also others from Leviticus and Numbers). Toward the conclusion of this great speech, however, Moses emphasizes that it is addressed to future generations as well as to the people present at that moment: "Neither with you only do I make this covenant and this oath; But . . . also with him that is not here with us this day."

True, certain details both of the story and of the laws differ from the versions that came earlier. To choose only one of several examples, Moses now proclaims that " . . . the Lord was angry with me for your sakes, saying, Thou also shalt not go in thither [i.e., to the Promised Land]." He thereby attributes this punishment to the grumbling of the people after the return of the spies, whereas the explanation given in Numbers had to do with his apparent wavering over bringing forth water from the rock at Meribah.

So far as the laws go, there are also slight variations—most notably in the Ten Commandments when he repeats them here after having first recited them at

the foot of Mount Sinai. In Deuteronomy, the keeping of the Sabbath is tied to
the enslavement in and deliverance from Egypt, while in Exodus it is connected
to the fact that God rested on the seventh day after creating the world in six.

But these "reworkings" (to borrow Everett Fox's term), together with some
additional details, expansions, and extrapolations, do not amount to a real revi-
sion either of the story or of the laws emerging from it. The story is much the
same and the laws remain essentially what they were—with the important
exception of changes involving the abolition of scattered altars and the central-
ization of sacrifice in what will become Jerusalem.*

Through Moses, God instructs the people that living by these laws will bring
the blessings of prosperity and health and the admiration of the world. But if the
people deviate, they can expect to be cursed by eviction from their new home
and scattered throughout the realm of the pagans, whose idols they will end up
worshiping and whose most abominable practices (" . . . for even their sons and
their daughters they have burnt in the fire to their gods") the Israelites will emu-
late.

The prohibition against idolatry, and the war against it, are reaffirmed in
Deuteronomy even more strongly than before—with dire warnings of death to
all who yield or entice others to backslide into it. Not even brothers, sons,
daughters, wives, and friends are exempt if they are guilty of such enticement:

> Thou shalt not consent unto him, nor hearken unto him; neither shall
> thine eye pity him, neither shalt thou spare, neither shalt thou conceal
> him: But thou shalt surely kill him; thine hand shall be first upon him to
> put him to death. . . .

But what is still more interesting for our present purposes is that the same
fate is to be meted out to any

> . . . prophet or a dreamer of dreams [who] giveth thee a sign or a won-
> der, And the sign or the wonder come to pass, whereof he spake unto
> thee, saying, Let us go after other gods, . . . and let us serve them; Thou
> shalt not hearken unto the words of that prophet, or that dreamer of
> dreams: for the LORD your God proveth you, to know whether ye
> love the LORD your God with all your heart and all your soul. . . . And
> that prophet, or that dreamer of dreams, shall be put to death; because
> he hath spoken to turn you away from the LORD your God. . . . So
> shalt thou put the evil away from the midst of thee.

---

*About this, too, I will have more to say later.

What makes this passage so interesting is that, no matter his apparent bona fides, a putative prophet cannot be a true prophet if he preaches idolatry or infidelity to God. If he actually performs a wonder, and he may, he is able to do so only because God is using him to test the people's fidelity. But neither signs nor portents nor miracles can be taken as the mark of a true prophet if he tries to lead the people away from the love of God and the observance of His commandments.

IN NOTHING, HOWEVER, does Deuteronomy resemble the classical prophets so much as in its alternating passages of reproach and consolation. These are more extreme than the juxtaposition to which I pointed in Numbers of God's imprecations against the whining children of Israel and the blessings of Balaam that almost seem to cancel them out. The only comparably extreme precedent to the curses and blessings in Deuteronomy is at the end of Leviticus.

But for us today, the impact of this collection of curses and blessings in Leviticus is not so great as it is in Deuteronomy, perhaps because in Leviticus they cap a book dominated by material about priestly duties and animal sacrifice that is no longer relevant. By contrast, Deuteronomy, while in effect a summation of all that went before, concentrates for the most part on the nature of God's relation to this people that He has chosen. Consequently, these chapters acquire a power unsurpassed by the more or less parallel section of Leviticus.

In Deuteronomy, as in Leviticus, the curses curdle the blood more than the blessings comfort the soul. So it always seems to be, and not only in the Hebrew Bible. In Italy, in the fourteenth century C.E., for example, Dante will labor in vain to make the part about Paradise in *The Divine Comedy* as interesting as—let alone more appealing than—the one on Hell. And in England in the seventeenth century, John Milton's *Paradise Lost,* in spite of his best efforts, will turn out to be a much greater poem than its sequel, *Paradise Regained*—because, according to another major English poet, William Blake (writing more than a hundred years later), Milton was of "the Devil's party without knowing it." Be that as it may, evil does seem easier to portray than good. Even in the Hebrew Bible, *the* book of "God's party," the curses emit a spell that quite simply overwhelms the blessings.

So hard have these curses remained to swallow that on the days when the chapters containing them in Leviticus and Deuteronomy come around in the synagogue during the cycle of weekly readings from the Torah, they are chanted in an undertone. Everett Fox remarks that such curses were "fairly standard stuff in the context of [the] ancient Near Eastern treaties" between kings and their subjects that, we are informed by the school of Form Criticism, served in their basic structure as the model for the covenant between God and the children of Israel. Yet as in Percy Bysshe Shelley's poem of 1819 about Ozymandias, "king of kings," the makers of these treaties and the empires over which they ruled have long since crumbled to dust. The Hebrew Bible, however, lives on, and its words are fully capable of compelling belief and behavior, adoration and fear—and even, through their literary magnificence, of shaking the hidden depths of non-believers who expose themselves to its words.

The single most appalling of all the curses appears both in Leviticus and Deuteronomy. In Leviticus, it occupies only one short verse dealing with what will result from the famine that God threatens to bring if the people persist in refusing to repent and (in a refrain that is repeated over and over like a succession of blows to the head) "walk contrary unto me." Plagues, wild beasts, devastation of every kind are specified, but the nethermost reaches of horror are sounded by this: "And ye shall eat the flesh of your sons, and the flesh of your daughters shall ye eat."

In Deuteronomy it is a siege decreed by God that will bring this horror about, and the terseness of the lone verse in Leviticus is enlarged upon here with more unbearably graphic details:

> And thou shall eat the fruit of thine own body, the flesh of thy sons and of thy daughters, which the LORD thy God hath given thee, in the siege, and in the straitness, wherewith thine enemies shall distress thee: So that the man that is tender among you, and very delicate, his eye shall be evil toward his brother, and toward the wife of his bosom, and toward the remnant of his children which he shall leave: So that he will not give to any of them of the flesh of his children whom he shall eat: because he hath nothing left him in the siege, and in the straitness, wherewith thine enemies shall distress thee in all thy gates.

As if this were not bad enough:

> The tender and delicate woman among you, which would not adventure to set the sole of her foot upon the ground for delicateness and tenderness, her eye shall be evil toward the husband of her bosom, and toward her son, and toward her daughter, And toward her young one that cometh out from between her feet, and toward her children which she shall bear: for she shall eat them for want of all things secretly in the siege and straitness, wherewith thine enemy shall distress thee in thy gates.*

---

*In one detail, this passage is still more hideous than KJV makes it, since what it translates as "her young one that cometh out between her feet" actually means "the afterbirth that issues between her legs" (NJPS). Everett Fox (Scho) renders the phrase similarly as "her afterbirth that goes out from between her legs," and NRSV has "her afterbirth that comes out from between her feet."

In this vision of cannibalism, which goes to the outer limits of the imagination of disaster, the stress on the tenderness and the delicacy of the family is an added touch of genius in what stands as one of the most powerful expressions in all literature of the lowest reaches to which sinful human beings can fall.

Still, even if the curses are more compelling (and also more numerous) than the blessings, the blessings are also there, adumbrated both before and after the curses are set forth. Twice at the end of Deuteronomy, God assures the people through Moses that if they repent and follow His commandments, He will have compassion upon them, and gather them from all the nations through which they will have been scattered, and that He will take even greater joy in them than he did in their fathers. And in a passage to which we will have to return more than once before our story is done, he makes a key declaration:

> For this commandment which I command thee this day, it is not hidden from thee, neither is it far off. It is not in heaven, that thou shouldest say, Who shall go up for us to heaven, and bring it unto us, that we may hear it, and do it? Neither is it beyond the sea, that thou shouldest say, Who shall go over the sea for us, and bring it unto us, that we may hear it, and do it? But the word is very nigh unto thee, in thy mouth, and in thy heart, that thou mayest do it. . . . I call heaven and earth to record this day . . . that I have set before you life and death, blessing and cursing: therefore choose life, that both thou and thy seed may live.

This may not match the rhetorical or poetic intensity of the consolations offered by the classical prophets, especially the Second Isaiah. But as I hope to show before I am through, it has a better claim (particularly as bolstered by some of the surrounding verses) than anything anywhere else in the Hebrew Bible, including the classical prophets, to be regarded as the elusive "essence of Judaism" for which commentators have been searching from time immemorial.

This chapter, writes Everett Fox, "is usually taken to be a late addition"— that is, even later than the rest of the Book of Deuteronomy. But he also recognizes that it is "a fitting ending" to the speeches of Moses. So far as I am concerned, whenever it was written down, and by whomever, it alone establishes Moses as what the Pentateuch several times explicitly calls him: the preeminent prophet of Israel, rising above Abraham before him and the many who later (in the Bible as we have it, and not the one dissected and deconstructed by the scholars) will be pulled along in his mighty and turbulent wake.

CHAPTER TWO

WIELDING THE SWORD

R EACHING THE LAST SENTENCE of Deuteronomy, we come to
the end of the first section of the Hebrew Bible (the Pentateuch, or
the Five Books of Moses) and we then enter the division classified in
Jewish tradition as the Former Prophets (*N'vi-im Rishonim*). In the Hebrew
Bible, we recall, this section comprises six books: Joshua, Judges, First Samuel,
Second Samuel, First Kings, and Second Kings.*

---

*I should acknowledge that a number of objections of varying validity and/or plausibility can be
and have been made to this simple listing. To begin with, among Jews there was a time when the
two books of Samuel and the two books of Kings were regarded as one each. Among Christians,
as any reader of the King James Version of the Bible can see from the subtitles it uses, all four
books were (in the case of the 1 and 2 Samuel) "Otherwise Called, The First [Second] Book of
the Kings" and (in the case of 1 and 2 Kings) "Commonly Called the Third [Fourth] Book of
the Kings." Both the words "otherwise" and "commonly" referred to Roman Catholics who,
however, later adopted the Jewish and Protestant designations of 1 and 2 Samuel and 1 and 2
Kings, instead of merging them all into a single Book of the Kings. On the other hand, neither
Catholics nor Protestants agreed that these books belonged among the Prophets. In addition, in
both the Protestant and Catholic canons, Joshua and Judges were separated from Samuel and
Kings by the Book of Ruth, which in the Hebrew Bible was situated much further on, among
the Writings. So much for the differences among the Jewish and Christian canons with regard to
the Former Prophets (and there are a few others as well).

But then there are the modern critical-historical theories about these books. According to
one line of scholarly thought, all of them should be grouped with Deuteronomy, under whose
influence they were supposedly written and/or collated and/or edited by a person or persons to
whom they refer as the Deuteronomistic Historian (DtrH) in the sixth century B.C.E., but covering events that took place centuries earlier. Under this theory, the first division of the Bible
becomes a Tetrateuch rather than a Pentateuch, and it consists only of the first four books of
Genesis, Exodus, Leviticus, and Numbers. However, according to a competing though related
school of modern critical-historical thought, the first division of the Bible should really be considered a Hexateuch, consisting neither of five nor of four but of six books, with Joshua added
to the traditional First Five as their natural conclusion.

Since the debates over these theories still rage furiously, and will no doubt continue until the
End of Days, I feel free to go on accepting the divisions and the order established by the rabbis
who fixed the Jewish canon.

Given that these are all largely historical books, why were they placed among the Prophets? No doubt—as I hinted in the Introduction—one reason must have been that the actions and sayings of several important prophets such as Samuel, Elijah, and Elisha, who left no books of their own behind, are recorded in them. But I think that Brevard S. Childs makes a strong case for another explanation, to which I also alluded in the Introduction. As Childs would have it, the rabbis and scribes who by the first century C.E. had decided which of the many contenders in circulation merited inclusion in the Hebrew Bible, and also in what order they should be arranged, agreed that the purpose of these particular six books was "not to record history *per se*—whatever that might be—but to bear testimony to the working out of the prophetic word in the life of the nation."

Childs speaks as a Protestant, but a similar judgment is rendered by an Orthodox Jewish scholar, Dr. A. Cohen, who writes that these books

> do more than relate events in the early history of Israel; they also, and perhaps primarily, underline the doctrine that God and Israel are linked by a covenant, upon the faithful observance of which the national existence depended. They are written less from the standpoint of the historian than of the prophet.

But even apart from the general question of why these six books were defined as prophetic rather than historical, they present us with a problem involving the figure of Joshua himself. In Deuteronomy, shortly before the death of Moses, God assures him that He " . . . will raise them up a Prophet from among their brethren, like unto thee, and will put my words into his mouth; and he shall speak unto them all that I shall command him." Since we have already been told that Joshua will be the successor to Moses as the leader of the people, it seem obvious that he must also be the prophet to whom God is referring.

Furthermore, God had also said to Moses: " . . . Take thee Joshua the son of Nun, a man in whom is the spirit, and lay thine hand upon him"; then, after Moses' death, we are told that " . . . Joshua the son of Nun was full of the spirit of wisdom; for Moses had laid his hands upon him: and the children of Israel hearkened unto him. . . ." And here is how the Book of Joshua itself begins:

> Now after the death of Moses the servant of the LORD it came to pass, that the LORD spake unto Joshua the son of Nun, Moses' minister, saying, Moses my servant is dead; now therefore arise, go over this Jordan, thou, and all this people, unto the land which I do give to them, even to the children of Israel. Every place that the sole of your foot shall tread upon, that have I given unto you, as I said unto Moses. . . . There shall not any man be able to stand before thee all the days of thy life: as I was with Moses, so I will be with thee: I will not fail thee, nor forsake thee.

God then tells Joshua to "Be strong and of a good courage: for unto this people shalt thou divide for an inheritance the land, which I sware unto their fathers to give them."

Immediately thereafter, Joshua is once again exhorted to be strong and courageous, but this time it is not because he will have to gird himself for battle. What will require even more strength and courage of him, as is indicated by the addition to the first formulation of the word "very" ("Only be thou strong and very courageous . . .") is to

> . . . observe to do according to all the law, which Moses my servant commanded thee: turn not from it to the right hand or to the left. . . . This book of the law shall not depart from out of thy mouth; but thou shalt meditate therein day and night, that thou mayest observe to do according to all that is written therein. . . .

To this injunction, Joshua is so faithful that not once is he charged with a single sin, in this surpassing even Moses himself.

Underscoring what is hard to interpret from the plain text as anything short of an elevation of Joshua to the status of Moses (" . . . This day will I begin to magnify thee in the sight of all Israel, that they may know that, as I was with Moses, so I will be with thee"*), God performs a miracle parallel to the one that made the exodus from Egypt possible. The waters of the Sea of Reeds[†] were parted then, enabling the fleeing Israelite slaves to walk over it dry. Now (in about 1250 B.C.E.), something similar happens with the waters of the Jordan River that must be crossed before the land of Canaan on the other side of its banks can be conquered by a new generation of Israelites to whom God has promised it: these waters

> . . . which came down from above stood and rose up upon an heap. . . . And the priests that bare the ark of the covenant of the LORD stood firm on dry ground in the midst of Jordan, and all the Israelites passed over on dry ground. . . .

Joshua himself, in a speech to the people as they stand on the other bank of the river near Jericho, draws the parallel between the two miracles, and "On that day the LORD magnified Joshua in the sight of all Israel; and they feared him, as they feared Moses, all the days of his life."[‡]

---

*Both NRSV and NJPS have "exalt" rather than "magnify."

†This is the accurate rendering of *yam suf,* which KJV misunderstood as the "Red Sea," a misnomer we have been saddled with ever since.

God then commands Joshua to circumcise the new generation of males who for some reason had not been circumcised while in the desert, and, ever obedient, he does so. Following which, he becomes the beneficiary of yet another miracle: the toppling of the walls of Jericho at the sound of the people shouting and the rams' horns of the priests blasting away. The conquest of this city is only the first in a long string of extremely cruel and bloody battles. Joshua is the general and the strategist, but he always gives God the credit for victory—and indeed God repeatedly intervenes with exhortation and even tactical advice, as when He in effect directs the setting of an ambush against the city of Ai.

With Ai overrun and its inhabitants all brutally and mercilessly slaughtered, as were those of Jericho—all in accordance with God's command—Joshua takes time out to fulfill the injunction of Moses in Deuteronomy that an altar of plastered stones be built on this side of the Jordan and that all the words of the law be inscribed upon them. Joshua then proceeds to

> . . . read all the words of the law, the blessings and cursings, according to all that is written in the book of the law. There was not a word of all that Moses commanded, which Joshua read not before all the congregation of Israel. . . .

TERRIFIED BY THE REPORTS of what has been done by Joshua to Jericho and Ai, the people of Gibeon, who are next in line, surrender, becoming " . . . hewers of wood and drawers of water . . ." for the Israelites. Whereupon five Amorite "kings" (chieftains, really) join in an alliance to attack the now subdued Gibeonites, who appeal to their new Israelite masters for help. God then intervenes again, hurling hailstones down upon the Amorites, and He grants Joshua yet another miracle, the most spectacular of them all, to help him finish the job of defeating this coalition:

> Then spake Joshua to the LORD in the day when the LORD delivered up the Amorites before the children of Israel, and he said in the sight of Israel, Sun, stand thou still upon Gibeon; and thou, Moon, the valley of Ajalon. And the sun stood still, and the moon stayed, until the people had avenged themselves upon their enemies. . . .

Here, too, Joshua's status seems to surpass even that of Moses: this miracle of the sun standing still for an entire day is, we are told, unique. What is unique

---

‡(See page 41.) Again, NJPS and NRSV have "exalted" instead of KJV's "magnified." NJPS also gives us "revered" in place of "feared," and NRSV has "stood in awe of" rather than either "magnified" or "revered." Yet in a rare occurrence, KJV's "feared" is closer to the literal sense of the Hebrew than any of these modern alternatives.

about it, however, is not the miracle itself: it is that " . . . there was no day like that before it or after it, that the LORD hearkened unto the voice of a man. . . ." Even though this statement is an exaggeration, there being other instances recorded in the Hebrew Bible when " . . . the LORD hearkened unto the voice of a man . . . ," the very fact that the verse is there indicates how important Joshua is.

And so it goes, conquest after conquest, until Joshua has grown old. With death approaching, he convokes two assemblies of the twelve tribes making up the people of Israel.* In the first assembly, he assures the Israelites, who have already taken possession of portions of the land allotted to each of the tribes but not the whole of it, that in due course God will drive out the rest of the peoples still surrounding them. But there is a condition, and Joshua states it in almost exactly the same words as God directed at him before the crossing of the Jordan: "Be ye therefore very courageous to keep and to do all that is written in the book of the law of Moses, that ye turn not aside therefrom to the right hand or to the left."

To this positive injunction is appended the warning that defeat and expulsion will befall the Israelites if they mingle or marry with the idolators remaining in the land: " . . . neither make mention of the name of their gods, . . . neither serve them, nor bow yourselves unto them." If the Israelites do such things, " . . . for a certainty . . . these nations . . . shall be snares and traps unto you. . . ."

It is in this passage that the horrors of Joshua's military campaigns—normal enough by the standards of warfare prevailing in those days but nothing short of genocidal by ours—are set into the perspective that has guided them: the war against idolatry.

We have already seen† that idolatry is not yet prohibited among nations other than Israel. And from the classical prophetic literature, we will learn that only at the End of Days will all these nations finally smash their idols and bow down to the one true God who has revealed Himself to the Israelites and whose Law will go forth from Jerusalem. But so long as this vision‡ is unrealized, the main (if not always the exclusive) responsibility of the Israelites will remain what it has been since Abraham: to purge *themselves* of idolatry, to wipe it out from within.

Joshua, like Abraham and Moses, knows full well how revolutionary the new

---

*The twelve, each named after one of the sons of Jacob, are (listed in the order in which these sons were born to him): Reuben, Simeon, Levi, Judah, Zebulun, Issachar, Dan, Gad, Asher, Naphtali, Joseph, and Benjamin. Judah and Benjamin will settle in the south of what will become known as the Land of Israel, and ten others (minus Levi but with Joseph split into Manasseh and Ephraim, after his two sons) in the north..

†Chapter 1, p. 23.

‡The technical term for such a vision of the End of Days is "eschatology."

idea of God is, how lonely and isolated are the people who have accepted it, and how persistent is the temptation of the Israelites to slip back into the old habits and delusions and abominations of their own ancestors. Of all this, Joshua will soon remind them in the second of the two farewell addresses he delivers shortly before his death:

> And Joshua said unto all the people, Thus saith the LORD God of Israel, Your fathers dwelt on the other side of the flood in old time, even Terah, the father of Abraham, and the father of Nachor: and they served other gods.

From Joshua's exhortation to the people in this same speech to put away their " ... strange gods ... ," we realize that there are those among the Israelites who are worshiping idols even now. Which is why every precaution against further backsliding and seduction must be taken, ranging from the relatively mild prohibition against mixing and mingling with the surrounding setters of " ... snares and traps ..." (such as the women of Moab had been at Baal-peor*), and extending all the way to destroying them utterly by the sword.

This fundamental consideration imparts greater force to the description of the second assembly of the tribes of Israel that Joshua calls at Shechem to deliver what amounts to his last will and testament. There, like Moses before him on the plains of Moab, though very rapidly and in much briefer compass, he recapitulates the history of the Israelites from Abraham and the other patriarchs through Moses and the Exodus and up to the present moment. But it is all a prelude to his demand that they reaffirm the purpose for which this history has unfolded:

> Now therefore fear the LORD, and ... put away the gods which your fathers served on the other side of the flood, and in Egypt; and serve ye the LORD. And if it seem evil unto you to serve the LORD, choose you this day whom ye will serve; whether the gods which your fathers served ... or the gods of the Amorites, in whose land ye dwell: but as for me and my house, we will serve the LORD. And the people answered and said, God forbid that we should forsake the LORD, to serve other gods.†

---

*See Chapter 1, p. 33.

†For "if it seem evil," NRSV has "if you are unwilling," while NJPS give us "if you are loath." But the Hebrew word (*rah*) does indeed mean "evil," and thus KJV again comes closer to the literal meaning than the modern translations.

The reaffirmation by the children of Israel at Shechem of the covenant first made at Sinai is then sealed by Joshua by writing " . . . these words in the book of the law of God. . . ."

With the death of its hero, we arrive at the problem that the Book of Joshua presents as we try more fully to define the nature of prophecy in the Hebrew Bible. Despite the fact that God is in constant communication with Joshua and he with God, just as Abraham was; despite the fact that God's relation to him is put on a par with, and even higher in some ways than, His relation to Moses himself; despite the fact that he is an absolutely loyal transmitter of the Law and the covenant; despite the fact that God performs miracles on his behalf, just as He did for Moses (and will do for a select few of the Former Prophets in the books just ahead); despite the fact that (as the classical prophets will in later centuries) he exhorts the people in the name of God—despite all this, never is the title of prophet attached to Joshua.

The reason cannot be that he has so much blood on his hands. Moses, after all, smote the two kingdoms ruled by Sihon and Og on the other side of the Jordan (" . . . until there was none left him alive . . .") without losing the title of prophet, and some of the Former Prophets to come, including the greatest of them—Samuel, Elijah, and Elisha—will commit bloody deeds in the continuing war against idolatry. Nor can the reason be that Joshua's "job description" differs in various ways from that of the classical prophets, since the same thing can be said of all the Former Prophets.

One possible explanation is that, when the Book of Joshua was written down and/or first edited, "prophet" was not necessarily regarded as an honorific (Amos would even disclaim it in the middle of the eighth century B.C.E.). Therefore Joshua's stature would not be enhanced if he were called a prophet. But by the time the book was canonized, either this attitude toward prophecy had changed, or it had come to seem self-evident that Joshua was a prophet even though he was never named as such.

IF NONE OF THE WORDS for prophet (not *navi,* not *ro-eh,* not *ish-elohim*) appears in this, the first volume of the Former Prophets, the main one (*navi*) is found twice in the second volume, the Book of Judges. There it is accorded to a woman, Deborah, who is explicitly named " . . . a prophetess . . ."* and then to an anonymous figure who suddenly shows up with words of reproach in his mouth:

---

*What the Hebrew literally says of her is that she is "a woman, a prophetess," though "a woman" is omitted (as gratuitous, given the feminine form in the Hebrew, *n'viah?*) from KJV, RSV, and NJPS.

> ...Thus saith the LORD God of Israel, I brought you up from Egypt, and brought you forth out of the house of bondage; And I delivered you out of the hand of the Egyptians, and out of the hand of all that oppressed you, and drave them out from before you, and gave you their land; And I said unto you, I am the LORD your God; fear not the gods of the Amorites, in whose land ye dwell: but ye have not obeyed my voice.*

But is the presence of these two figures enough to have qualified Judges for inclusion in the prophetic section of the Hebrew Bible? I think not. Why then is the book sitting where it sits? Without dismissing the explanation Childs and Cohen apply to the Former Prophets as a whole, I would venture to supplement it by observing that where the Book of Judges in particular is concerned, the decisive element is that it goes on with the story of the war against idolatry. It is thus thematically and organically linked with the unfolding development of the prophetic mission in Israel.

From a narrative or historical point of view, Judges follows naturally from Joshua. Thus the book begins: "Now after the death of Joshua, it came to pass, that the children of Israel asked the LORD, saying, Who shall go up for us against the Canaanites first, to fight against them?"† The rest of this long first chapter consists of an account of mopping-up operations by the various tribes, which, however, still leave the conquest of the Promised Land incomplete.

But then there is an unexpected shifting of gears, as " . . . an angel of the LORD . . ." materializes out of nowhere to denounce the children of Israel for having failed to fulfill their part of the covenant with God:

> ... I made you to go up out of Egypt, and have brought you unto the land which I sware unto your fathers; and I said, I will never break my covenant with you. And ye shall make no league with the inhabitants of the land; ye shall throw down their altars: but ye have not obeyed my voice: why have ye done this? Wherefore I also said, I will not drive them out before you; but they shall be as thorns in your sides, and their gods shall be a snare unto you. And it came to pass, when the angel of

---

*Just as the Hebrew literally describes Deborah as "a woman, a prophetess," the literal meaning of the Hebrew here is "a man, a prophet"; and the "man" is omitted from KJV, RSV, and NJPS, as is the "woman" in connection with Deborah. In this instance, however, the reason may be to distinguish the anonymous prophet from the "angel of the LORD" who just as abruptly makes an appearance in the next verse.

†According to the Talmud, it was Aaron's grandson, Phinehas the High Priest, and not a prophet, through whom this question was asked.

the LORD spake these words unto all the children of Israel, that the people lifted up their voice, and wept.*

What immediately ensues, starting with the next verse, seems to be a flashback explaining why God has sent the angel to hurl these harsh words at the children of Israel. By this flashback we are apprised that after the death of Joshua (around 1200 B.C.E.), the Israelites continue serving God throughout " . . . all the days of the elders that outlived . . ." him. But with the passing of the elders, a new generation matures—presumably the one to whom the angel is speaking—and this generation not only violates the prohibition against mixing with the surrounding peoples but actually falls into the "snare" of their gods. They

> . . . did evil in the sight of the LORD, and served Baalim: And they forsook the LORD God of their fathers, which brought them out of the land of Egypt, and followed other gods, of the gods of the people that were round about them, and bowed themselves unto them, and provoked the LORD to anger.†

These verses form part of what is, in effect, an introductory summation of the rest of the book. In this overview, it is revealed that God has two other reasons besides the evil they have already done for not yet delivering the whole of the Promised Land into the hands of the Israelites. One is that He wishes to subject them to yet another test of their fidelity—to see whether they have the steadfastness and the stamina to keep (or rededicate themselves to) their part of the covenant. But failing that test by intermarrying with the remaining pagan peoples around them, by worshiping their gods, and by forgetting the LORD their God, the Israelites, just as God had warned through Joshua would happen, have become as weak militarily before their enemies as they are in the realm of faith. Hence the second reason is that God wants " . . . to teach . . . war . . ." to the next generations—those " . . . as had not known all the wars of Canaan." For there is much warring in store for them.

Very often, however, they will fight without success, since their apostasies will breed defeat, oppression, plundering, and vassalage at the hands of one local potentate after another. But on each occasion, after a period of suffering, God will take pity on the Israelites, and will send a "judge" to deliver them. These

---

*For "thorns in your sides," NJPS has "oppressors."

†The word "Baalim," which is carried over untranslated into KJV, is the Hebrew plural for *"Baal,"* a term that means "lord" or "master," and could refer to a specific pagan deity or could be used (as it probably is here) of idols in general.

judges have been succinctly characterized as a "series of charismatic leaders" who arise during the two hundred or so years (roughly the thirteenth to the eleventh centuries B.C.E.) between the death of Joshua and the advent of Saul, who—as we are shortly to discover in the First Book of Samuel—will become the first king of Israel. Except for Deborah, rather than acting in any legal capacity, the judges are military heroes upon whom " . . . the Spirit of the LORD . . ."* temporarily rests, and who lead single tribes or groups of tribes in campaigns to free Israel from periodic foreign oppression.

IF WE HAVE BEEN LEFT in any doubt by the Book of Joshua about how difficult it is to resist the temptations of idolatry and correlatively to remember what the belief in one God means and requires, Judges seems to have as its main purpose the piling up of a distressingly overwhelming body of evidence to support both points. Hard upon the death of every judge who is sent to rescue the Israelites, they once again begin to " . . . do evil in the sight of the LORD . . ." (a phrase that occurs in this book no fewer than eight times, always denoting the return to idolatry). More startling yet, three of the judges themselves fall into idolatrous traps.

The least culpable of the three is Gideon, who is summoned by an angel to " . . . save Israel from the hands of the Midianites . . . ," though his own father, Joash, is a worshiper of Baal. God therefore commands Gideon to tear down the altar Joash has built to Baal, as well as the sacred tree dedicated to the goddess Asherah next to it, and replace them with

> . . . an altar unto the LORD thy God. . . . Then Gideon . . . did as the LORD had said unto him: and so it was, because he feared his father's household, and the men of the city, that he could not do it by day, that he did it by night. And when the men of the city arose early in the morning, behold, the altar of Baal was cast down. . . . And they said to one another, Who hath done this thing? And when they enquired and asked, they said, Gideon the son of Joash hath done this thing. Then the men of the city said unto Joash, Bring out thy son, that he may die: because he hath cast down the altar of Baal. . . .

But paternal feeling wins out over piety toward Baal, and Joash refuses to turn his son over to the mob of idolatrous Israelites: "And Joash said unto all that stood against him, Will ye plead for Baal? Will ye save him? . . . if he be a god, let him plead for himself, because one hath cast down his altar."

---

*This term is used seven times in Judges.

Gideon having, as it were, established his credentials in action (and now given the nickname Jerubaal, or "contender against Baal"), is infused with "the Spirit of the LORD," enabling him to prevail in battles against the combined forces of " ... all the Midianites and the Amalekites and the children of the east. ... ." So successful is he that the Israelites ask him to become their king and establish a dynasty. But he refuses (" ... I will not rule over you, neither shall my son rule over you: the LORD shall rule over you"). Instead he asks that the golden earrings of the Midianites be awarded to him and, his request granted, he makes " ... an ephod thereof, and put it in his city, even in Ophrah: and all Israel went thither a whoring after it: which thing became a snare unto Gideon, and to his house."

The ephod here is clearly not the priestly garment to which the word sometimes refers in the Hebrew Bible, but a device for obtaining oracles. Because of its association with the High Priest's breastplate, it could not strictly be considered a pagan idol, and yet the one made by Gideon comes to be treated as such. Even Gideon, then, the "contender against Baal," and in other respects one of the most virtuous of the judges, becomes (inadvertently?) responsible for a resurgence of idolatry in his own lifetime. Then, after his death, it grows worse, as " ... the children of Israel turned again, and went a whoring after Baalim. ... ."

Next in line in Judges is Jephthah, who becomes guilty of the most serious of all the abominations connected with idolatry:

> And Jephthah vowed a vow unto the LORD, and said, If thou shalt without fail deliver the children of Ammon into mine hands, Then it shall be, that whatsoever cometh forth of the doors of my house to meet me, when I return in peace from the children of Ammon, shall surely be the LORD's, and I will offer it up for a burnt offering.

Having achieved his victory, Jephthah goes home,

> ... and, behold, his daughter came out to meet him with timbrels and with dances: and she was his only child. ... And it came to pass, when he saw her, that he rent his clothes, and said, Alas, my daughter! thou hast brought me very low ... : for I have opened my mouth unto the LORD, and I cannot go back.

Obediently acceding without argument, this nameless daughter asks only that, before being immolated, she be left " ... alone for two months, that I may go up and down upon the mountains, and bewail my virginity, I and my fellows." Jephthah grants her this request, and two months later he does " ... with her according to his vow which he had vowed: and she knew no man. And it was a custom in Israel, That the daughters of Israel went yearly to lament the daughter of Jephthah the Gileadite four days in a year."

This terrible tale is another vivid example of the unparalleled minimalist artistry of biblical narrative, through which a few short phrases perform the literary miracle of bringing characters and the full range of their emotions to life, and where what is omitted manages to become as eloquently expressive as what is included.

But in this case, I find one omission entirely incomprehensible: the absence of any reproach or punishment of Jephthah, a leader upon whom "the Spirit of the LORD" has rested, for committing the very sin against which—as we know from the binding of Isaac—the war against idolatry was originally declared.* Yet the presence of the story in this book may provide a clue to its underlying didactic purpose, which is further to deepen our sense of how hard it is for the Israelites—whether humble or high, whether leader or led—to purge themselves of idolatrous habits of mind and the abominations they generate.

ANOTHER FACET of this same truth is reflected in the story of Samson, whose hero's failures in the war against idolatry fall in seriousness between those of Gideon at the one extreme and Jephthah at the other. The Samson section is longer and more detailed than the chapter devoted to Jephthah, but it is no less minimalist in its parts. I would say that from a literary standpoint, its power to evoke character and feeling so richly with such economy is if anything even more wondrous.

Like at least two major characters in the Hebrew Bible both before (Isaac) and after (Samuel) him, Samson is born of a previously barren woman whose forthcoming conception is announced by yet another of the angels who fly in and out of the pages of Judges: "For, lo, thou shalt conceive, and bear a son; and no razor shall come on his head: for the child shall be a Nazarite unto God from the womb. . . ."† As a Nazirite, Samson (in accordance with what is prescribed in Numbers) will be forbidden to partake of grapes or the wine made from them, and will never be permitted to cut his hair. But the superhuman strength that

---

*Many centuries later, the rabbis of the Talmud will not let Jephthah off. First they will condemn him for ignorance of the law, through which he could have been absolved of his vow by paying ransom to the Temple treasury (though no Temple yet existed!). Then through their special homiletical methods, they will discover that Jephthah is later punished by contracting leprosy and losing his limbs one by one (though there is no word of any of this in the Bible). Historical scholars have naturally got into this difficult interpretative act as well, with one popular theory holding that the entire story is an etiological legend explaining the existence of the custom with which it concludes.

†The Hebrew word *nazir* (meaning "consecrated") is usually spelled Nazirite, and not as above in KJV. Usually, too, one became a Nazirite by vowing to consecrate oneself to the ritualistic service of God for a prescribed time as a kind of lay priest. But like Samuel, Samson is to be a Nazirite for life; unlike Samuel, however, he does not perform any ritualistic duties.

will go with this condition in Samson is not granted to any other Nazirite in the Hebrew Bible. God endows him with it so that he can begin freeing the Israelites from the Philistines, by whom they have long since been dominated as a punishment for doing " . . . evil again in the sight of the LORD. . . ."

The boy grows up, and (as with all the other judges) "the Spirit of the LORD" descends upon him. Yet Samson lusts after a Philistine woman, and though his parents ask, " . . . Is there never a woman among the daughters of thy brethren, or among all my people, that thou goest to take a wife of the uncircumcised Philistines? . . . ," he insists on marrying her. Defying his parents is bad enough, but Samson is simultaneously proposing to violate the commandment against intermarriage that God has earlier issued to the children of Israel. The narrator, however, justifies him: "But his father and his mother knew not that it [i.e., the proposed marriage] was of the LORD, that he sought an occasion against the Philistines. . . ."*

While the text does not say so openly, it is perhaps as a demonstration of God's support for this defiance of His own commandment that on the way to marrying the Philistine woman, the "Spirit of the LORD" enables Samson to tear a lion to pieces with his bare hands. Then, after he has married her, his wife not only betrays his confidence but is sexually unfaithful to him as well. Presumably having found the pretext he had sought, he retaliates by exacting a series of bloody revenges against her people (" . . . Now shall I be more blameless than the Philistines, though I do them a displeasure"). At this juncture, the men of the tribe of Judah, still fearful of the Philistines, capture Samson (who is a member of the tribe of Dan) and deliver him into the hands of their overlords. But he easily breaks loose from his bindings. With the "Spirit of the LORD" still upon him, " . . . he found a new jawbone of an ass, and put forth his hand, and took it, and slew a thousand men therewith."

If there was a divine purpose and a divine sanction behind Samson's marriage to the Philistine woman, no such justification is offered for the next two lustful liaisons he contracts. In Gaza he sleeps with a harlot, barely escaping capture by the Philistines who have been lying in wait for him outside her house. Then comes Delilah, with whom he actually falls in love. But it is an unreciprocated passion. When she is offered a bribe by " . . . the lords of the Philistines . . ." to discover and tell them the secret of his great strength " . . . and by what means we may prevail against him, that we may bind him to afflict him . . . ," she readily agrees. By turns coyly cajoling and nagging him " . . . so that his soul was vexed unto death," she finally finds out, and gets a man to shave off the seven

---

*Instead of KJV's "occasion," the modern translations have "pretext," and the traditional Jewish interpretation is that "he" in this verse is not God but Samson. This would make it a little less puzzling, but even so it remains hard to understand why the clear commission of a sin is justified here.

locks of his hair while he is asleep on her knee. Waking, " ... he wist not that the
LORD was departed from him. But the Philistines took him, and put out his
eyes, and bound him with fetters of brass; and he did grind in [the mills of] the
prison house."

Having blinded and turned him into a slave laborer, they entertain themselves by watching him stumble about. Meanwhile, however, Samson's hair is
growing back, and he prays to God to strengthen him "only this once, ... that I
may be at once avenged of the Philistines for my two eyes." The sequel indicates
that God has decided to grant his prayer:

> And Samson took hold of the two middle pillars upon which the house
> stood, and on which it was borne up, of the one with his right hand, and
> of the other with his left. And Samson said, Let me die with the
> Philistines. And he bowed himself with all his might; and the house fell
> upon the lords, and upon all the people that were therein. So the dead
> which he slew at his death were more than they which he slew in his life.

Unlike Jephthah, then, Samson in the end suffers retribution for his derelic-
tions in the war that he, as a judge with "the Spirit of the LORD upon him," is
supposed to be waging against idolatry. Even so, if the story—like so much of the
Book of Judges—illustrates the hold that idolatrous practices continue to exert,
Samson's tale is special in sharpening our understanding of how seductive (to use
a word that in this context seems especially appropriate) are the idolatrous cultures in whose midst the Israelites continue living.

DEBORAH, WHOSE STORY precedes those of Gideon, Jephthah, and Samson,
is very different from them and all the other dozen or so judges mentioned in
the book. Not only is she the only one to whom the title of prophet is attached;
she is also the only judge who actually does any judging ("And Deborah, a
prophetess, the wife of Lapidoth, she judged Israel at that time. And she dwelt
under the palm tree of Deborah ... : and the children of Israel came up to her
for judgment").

Yet there is no clear explanation of what makes her a prophet. True, she
speaks in the name of God, but so do other judges who are not regarded as
prophets. Furthermore, we never hear of God speaking to her, as He does to
some of the other judges. Even so, it is in the name of God that she summons the
warrior Barak and in effect orders him into combat against the forces of the
Canaanite King Jabin, under whose oppressive thumb the Israelites—as usual
because they have once more done evil in the sight of God—have been living.
These forces, led by the Canaanite king's commander Sisera, are so powerful that

Barak hesitates to take the field against them unless Deborah accompanies him (" . . . If thou wilt go with me, then I will go: but if thou wilt not go with me, then I will not go").

Why he insists on this condition we are not informed, but it seems even from the characteristically reticent text that he thinks the assurance she has given him that God will deliver Sisera into his hands requires her presence for fulfillment. Deborah agrees, but not before issuing an enchanting warning to Barak: " . . . I will surely go with thee: notwithstanding the journey that thou takest shall not be for thine honor; for the LORD shall sell Sisera into the hand of a woman. . . ." Barak, however, chooses the certainty of winning over the acquisition of glory. On the field of battle itself, he even delays his attack until Deborah gives him the word (" . . . Up; for this is the day in which the LORD hath delivered Sisera into thine hand. . . .").

Although Sisera's forces are in the event given into the hand of a woman, or a female-male team, Sisera himself is delivered into the hands of a woman alone. But the woman is not Deborah. Fleeing for his life, with Barak in hot pursuit, Sisera hides in the tent of Jael, under the false impression that, being a non-Israelite and a pagan, she is an ally. But

> . . . Jael . . . took a nail of the tent, and took an hammer in her hand, and went softly unto him, and smote the nail into his temples, and fastened it upon the ground: for he was fast asleep and weary. So he died. And, behold, as Barak pursued Sisera, Jael came out to meet him, and said unto him, Come, and I will shew thee the man whom thou seekest. And when he came into her tent, behold, Sisera lay dead, and the nail was in his temples.

And so Barak loses glory not once but twice to women. This does not, however, prevent him from joining with one of them, Deborah, in singing a song of triumph in which, furthermore, an entire passage is devoted to showering blessings on Jael for killing Sisera.

Still, notwithstanding the introductory words, "Then sang Deborah and Barak the son of Abinoam on that day . . . ," posterity has chosen to assign the authorship of the poem to Deborah alone, thereby doubly making good on her original warning to him about the glory he will lose in insisting on her participation in the battle.

For all its martial imagery and all its wallowing in bloody deeds, it is the marvelous passage toward the end of this poem picturing the anxiety of Sisera's mother as she waits for her son's return that has in all likelihood influenced posterity's verdict as to the authorship. For it is much easier to imagine that a woman—even a woman of martial valor—wrote it than a man:

> *Through the window peered Sisera's mother,*
> *Behind the lattice she whined:*
> *"Why is his chariot so long in coming?*
> *Why so late the clatter of his wheels?"*
> *The wisest of her ladies give answer;*
> *She, too, replies to herself:*
> *"They must be dividing the spoil they have found:*
> *A damsel or two for each man,*
> *Spoil of dyed cloths for Sisera,*
> *Spoil of embroidered cloths,*
> *A couple of embroidered cloths*
> *Round every neck as spoil."**

There is also another and yet more compelling reason for attributing this poem to Deborah. In celebrating the war against idolatry with a force and lucidity unmatched by anything said by any of her fellow judges, the Song of Deborah offers an implicit answer to the question of why she is the only one of them who is called a prophet(ess):

> *Deliverance ceased,*
> *Ceased in Israel. . . .*
> *When they chose new gods,*
> *Was there a fighter in the gates?*
> *No shield or spear was seen*
> *Among forty thousand in Israel!*

The poem goes on to sing the praises of the tribes of Israel who courageously fell in behind Deborah's own leadership (while condemning those tribes that did not participate in her struggle as a prophet against "new gods"):

> *Then was the remnant made victor over the mighty,*
> *The LORD's people won my victory over the warriors.*

And the Song concludes:

---

*Here, for a change, and in the other quotations from the Song of Deborah, I am deserting KJV and instead using NJPS. The King James translators understandably had trouble with the very obscure Hebrew that in a number of spots makes the Song of Deborah hard to unravel. But most of these linguistic difficulties have been overcome (if not entirely, then at least to a large extent) by modern philological scholarship, relying on the help of deciphered cognate Semitic languages and other tools unavailable in 1611.

So may all Your enemies perish, O LORD!
But may His friends be as the sun rising in might!

Finally, with respect to the prophetic tradition in Israel, there is yet one more point to be made. It is that the Song of Deborah links up in spirit and style to the triumphal Song of Moses in the Book of Exodus, and while thus forging a bond with the greatest of all the Hebrew prophets of the past, Deborah's poem simultaneously looks forward—again in style and spirit—to the great classical prophets of the future. For this alone, it earns a place among the clouds of ancestral glory that trail behind those prophets, and in so doing it also provides in itself another justification for classifying the book in which it appears as a prophetic work.

CHAPTER THREE

PLUNGING INTO POLITICS

U NLIKE THE BOOK OF JOSHUA, where there is no reference to any new prophet, or the Book of Judges, which has only two, the four volumes (First and Second Samuel and First and Second Kings) that follow them in the Hebrew Bible, completing the corpus of the Former Prophets, are awash in such figures. Among these are some of the most prominent of the entire line, and none more so than Samuel himself.*

As the First Book of Samuel opens, it is approximately a hundred years (1050 B.C.E.)† since the death of Deborah, and prophets have grown even scarcer than they were before. So few and far between have they become, we are told, that the word of God has hardly been making itself heard in the land.‡ Politically, Israel is still what it was in Judges—a loose confederation of tribes or clans, whose common ancestry and religion does not prevent them from engaging in bloody internecine conflicts on various occasions.

The land, yet to be fully conquered by the Israelites, is still dotted with pagan

---

*It is also in these books that such synonyms for *navi* as "man of God" (*ish-elohim*), "seer" (*ro-eh*), and "visionary" (*khozeh*) are also used more frequently than before. But *navi* remains the preferred term for "prophet." Interestingly, all these terms are at different points applied to Samuel.

†Here as elsewhere, the exact dates are difficult to pin down, partly because the chronologies supplied by the narrator of these books do not parse. But while modern historians disagree, it is not by that much.

‡KJV's rendition of the verse that conveys this information (" . . . And the word of the LORD was precious in those days; there was no open vision") is obscure. NRSV ("The word of the LORD was rare in those days; visions were not widespread") and NJPS ("In those days the word of the LORD was rare; prophecy was not widespread") both give a better sense of the Hebrew.

principalities, the most troublesome of which is that of the Philistines. Under
such circumstances, vicious battles also break out sporadically between one or
another of these principalities (or kingdoms, as, with a touch of grandiosity, they
are called) and one or another Israelite tribe.

To the limited extent that a leader exists in Israel, he is the High Priest Eli.
While presiding over the sanctuary in Shiloh, he is also a judge. But Eli does not
engage in military campaigns against the surrounding peoples as his predecessors
did in trying to ward off idolatrous snares and seductions from without. Nor,
going by the frequent references in this book to the possession of graven images
and other household gods by the Israelites, has significant progress been made in
the more important war against idolatry from within. Observance of the clause
in the first of the Ten Commandments prohibiting graven images is by now so
lax that many Israelites not only keep household gods but seem to think that
God Himself looks with favor upon such "syncretism."*

This much we have already gathered from the strange story in Judges about
an otherwise obscure resident of Mount Ephraim by the name of Micah (or
Micaihu), who builds himself a whole collection of household gods—" . . . a
graven image and a molten image . . ." and others to boot. When he then gets a
young Levite to become his private priest, he is actually confident " . . . that the
LORD will do me good. . . ."

But Micah is far from alone in this syncretistic illusion, since it must be on
the basis of the same theory that both his gods and his priest are soon stolen
from him by an armed contingent of the tribe of Dan. Nor—in a detail as
incomprehensible as the absence of any reproach to Jephthah in the same book
when he sacrifices his daughter because he believes that fulfilling a vow to the
God of Israel requires it of him—does the narrator throw out so much as a hint
in condemnation of this theory, or attempt to show that it is false. If anything, the
Danites are rewarded rather than punished. They go on to achieve a military victory over the city of Laish, which they rename Dan, and where " . . . they set
them up Micah's graven image, which he made, all the time that the house of
God was in Shiloh."

In this respect, the opening chapters of the First Book of Samuel leave us
with the impression that little has changed in the past hundred years. Astonishingly, it will emerge that even David, the future king of Israel, possesses a graven
image: David, who in the eyes of the Hebrew Bible, and of post-biblical Jewish
tradition as well, is seen (despite other sins he commits) as the most faithful to
God of all the many kings to come when, as will soon occur, a monarchy is

---

*This is another technical term we come upon often in the scholarly literature. In a religious
context, syncretism is the worship of different gods at the same time, or trying to reconcile
opposing systems of belief.

established in Israel. Nor, again incomprehensibly, is there any word of condemnation in the text against David for this lapse into idolatry.*

Both in the political and the religious realms, then, something is rotten among the children of Israel. But a change is in the offing.

OF A FAR-REACHING political transformation we have already received hints from the Book of Judges, which closes with a verse that repeats the same complaint made earlier in the same book: "In those days there was no king in Israel: every man did that which was right in his own eyes." Now, almost at the outset of the First Book of Samuel, we are put on notice through a story about the High Priest Eli that the religious situation is also about to change.

Eli has two sons who assist him in the sanctuary at Shiloh, and they are corrupt. When animal sacrifices are offered, these two wicked creatures confiscate, if necessary by threats of force, shares and portions that are supposed to be consecrated to God. Not only that, but " . . . they lay with the women that assembled at the door of the tabernacle of the congregation." Though the aged Eli chastises his sons when he hears of their " . . . evil dealings . . . ," he does nothing to stop them. God then dispatches an anonymous prophet to him with a ferocious denunciation of the wickedness of his sons and his own tepid response to their vile practices. Because of all this, God declares, speaking through the prophet, the High Priesthood will pass to another family: "And I will raise me up a faithful priest, that shall do according to that which is in mine heart and in my mind. . . ."

The priest to be raised up, as is clear from a number of other details in the prophet's speech, is not to be Samuel. And yet these words inevitably make us think of him. One reason is that the same message will shortly be delivered to Samuel himself, and directly by the voice of God, as a prelude to his own appointment as a prophet:

> And the LORD said to Samuel, Behold, I will do a thing in Israel, at which both the ears of every one that heareth it shall tingle. In that day I will perform against Eli all things which I have spoken concerning his house: when I begin, I will also make an end.

At the time of this revelation, Samuel is still a child, but he is already living in

---

*Whereas the rabbis of the Talmud will not let Jephthah off the hook, they will exonerate David by placing the blame on his then-wife for keeping the idols. Incidentally, the Hebrew word *teraphim* here is the same word used in Genesis for the household gods that Rachel steals from the house of her father Laban when she runs away with her husband Jacob.

the sanctuary at Shiloh and ministering " . . . unto the LORD before Eli. . . ." The reason he is there is that his previously barren mother, Hannah, vowed that if God were to open her womb and give her a son, she would dedicate the boy to His service forever:

> . . . O LORD of Hosts, if thou wilt indeed look on the affliction of thine handmaid, and remember me, and not forget thine handmaid, but wilt give unto thine handmaid a man child, then I will give him unto the LORD all the days of his life, and there shall no razor come upon his head.

Hannah's prayer is answered by the birth of Samuel, who becomes a Nazirite for life. But if, unlike Samson before him, he does not also acquire superhuman physical strength, he does, in becoming a prophet, acquire virtually superhuman spiritual power:

> And Samuel grew, and the LORD was with him, and did let none of his words fall to the ground. And all Israel . . . knew that Samuel was established to be a prophet of the LORD. And the LORD appeared again in Shiloh: for the LORD revealed himself to Samuel in Shiloh by the word of the LORD.*

Clearly, the end God has made in dealing with the High Priest Eli is indeed a new beginning. After having absented Himself for a long time and remaining silent, He is now returning to address the children of Israel, largely at first through Samuel and then through other prophets.

In fact, the verse in which we learn that prophecy was rare in those days serves as an explanatory introduction to the brilliantly vivid and utterly delicious story of Samuel's first encounter with God:

> . . . and Samuel was laid down to sleep; [and] the LORD called Samuel: and he answered, Here am I; And he ran unto Eli, and said, Here am I, for thou calledst me. And he said, I called not; lie down again. And he went and lay down. And the LORD called yet again, Samuel. And Samuel arose and went to Eli, and said, Here am I; for thou didst call me. And he answered, I called not, my son; lie down again. . . . And the

---

*KJV's "let none of his words fall to the ground" is a literal translation of the Hebrew, but NJPS's "He did not leave any of Samuel's predictions unfulfilled" is probably what the phrase intends to convey. As I have noted, the fulfillment of predictions is given in Deuteronomy (18:22) as one of the marks of the true prophet, but it bears repeating that the classical prophets will not predict the future except in the most general terms.

LORD called Samuel again the third time. And he arose and went to Eli, and said, Here am I; for thou didst call me. And Eli perceived that the LORD had called the child. Therefore Eli said unto Samuel, Go, lie down: and it shall be, if he call thee, that thou shalt say, Speak LORD; for thy servant heareth. So Samuel went and lay down in his place. And the LORD came, and stood, and called as at other times, Samuel, Samuel. Then Samuel answered, Speak; for thy servant heareth.

Besides becoming a prophet, Samuel, like his immediate predecessor among the Former Prophets, Deborah, also occupies a judicial office. But here, too, as with Samson, there is a change. Whereas Deborah sat under a palm tree to which people came for adjudication of their disputes, Samuel is a kind of circuit judge, moving from place to place.

IN THESE TWO CAPACITIES of prophet and judge, Samuel develops into the single most important leader of the Israelites since Joshua, and the only one whose authority is national in scope (rather than merely local or tribal, as with the judges preceding him). So important does he become that he even retains a position of great power and influence after the people acquire their first king, Saul, whom Samuel himself is instructed by God to seek out and anoint. Samuel obeys, but only reluctantly, since he has already resisted the clamor of the people for a king.

In part, this clamor is provoked (in a parallel to the story of the house of Eli) by the unworthiness of Samuel's own two sons. He has appointed them as judges but they " . . . walked not in his ways, but turned aside after lucre, and took bribes, and perverted judgment." Accordingly, the elders of the people come to him and say: " . . . Behold thou art old, and thy sons walk not in thy ways: now make us a king to judge us like all the nations."

Yet if (as subtly suggested by the text) Samuel's opposition to this demand contains an element of personal pique, God soon sets him straight:

And the LORD said unto Samuel . . . , they have not rejected thee, but they have rejected me, that I should not reign over them. According to all the works which they have done since the day that I brought them up out of Egypt even unto this day, wherewith they have forsaken me, and served other gods, so do they also unto thee.

Even so, perhaps still driven by personal resentment, Samuel feels constrained to warn the people of what will happen to them under the rule of an earthly king:

... He will take your sons, and appoint them for himself, for his chariots, and to be his horsemen; and some shall run before his chariots. And he will appoint him captains over thousands, and captains over fifties; and will set them to ear his ground, and to reap his harvest, and to make his instruments of war, and instruments of his chariots. And he will take your daughters to be confectionaries, and to be cooks, and to be bakers. And he will take your fields, and your vineyards, and your oliveyards, even the best of them, and give them to his servants. And he will take your menservants, and your maidservants, and your goodliest young men, and your asses, and put them to his work. He will take the tenth of your sheep: and ye shall be his servants. And ye shall cry out in that day because of your king which ye shall have chosen you; and the LORD will not hear you in that day.

Undeterred by this great speech,

... the people refused to obey the voice of Samuel; and they said, Nay; but we will have a king over us; That we also may be like all the nations; and that our king may judge us, and go out before us, and fight our battles. And Samuel heard all the words of the people, and he rehearsed them in the ears of the LORD. And the LORD said to Samuel, Hearken unto their voice, and make them a king. ...

Samuel's prophecy does not immediately come true in full, since the first two kings, Saul (about 1020–1004 B.C.E.) and David (roughly 1004–965 B.C.E.), will turn out to be relatively benign rulers. But then, commencing with the reign of David's son Solomon (about 965–928 B.C.E.) and the breakup after Solomon's death of the united monarchy into two—the Kingdom of Judah in the South, and the Kingdom of Israel in the North—the people (especially in the North) will have ample cause to remember Samuel's words.

In the meantime, Samuel searches out Saul and anoints him. Later, when Saul sins so greatly that God denies him a dynastic successor, it is Samuel again who is delegated to locate the man God has decided to make the next king—David the son of Jesse—and to anoint him as well, even before the death of Saul.

IN TRACKING THE STORY of prophecy in Israel, another significant development of which we must take account at this point is the rise of itinerant bands or schools or "sons" of prophets. We know from the scholars that this phenomenon was a familiar feature of the cultures of the ancient Near East, but we have thus far heard nothing about it in the Hebrew Bible. Now, though, Samuel himself seems to become the founder in Israel of such a school of prophets, and its leader and teacher, too.*

In the First Book of Samuel, none of these prophets is ever heard delivering oracles or practicing the forbidden arts of divination (as their counterparts did, often for pay, in the surrounding pagan cultures, and as some of their Israelite successors will do in the years ahead, incurring the wrath and contempt of the classical prophets). The only act we ever see them performing is to fall into ecstatic trances.† Not so the prophet Gad. While he flits rapidly in and out of the First Book of Samuel, giving a single verse's worth of advice to the as yet uncrowned David before departing the scene altogether, he returns in the next volume (and in the two Books of Chronicles‡) as the king's "seer."

But even though they rarely do much, the bands of prophets are on prominent display in this book. In fact, by the time we run into them in Ramah with Samuel at their head, they have already been present on several earlier occasions. The first mention of their existence comes just after Samuel has anointed Saul. Unable to believe that he has really been chosen as king, Saul asks Samuel: " . . . Am I not a Benjamite, of the smallest tribes of Israel? and my family the least of all the families of the tribe of Benjamin? . . ." As reassurance, Samuel gives him three signs, the last and most significant of which is that he will

> . . . meet a company of prophets . . . with a psaltery, and a tabret, and a pipe, and a harp, before them; and they shall prophesy: And the Spirit of the LORD will come upon thee, and thou shalt prophesy with them, and shalt be turned into another man.

This is exactly what happens, but

> . . . when all that knew him beforetime saw that, behold, he prophesied among the prophets, then the people said one to another, What is this that is come unto the son of Kish? Is Saul also among the prophets?

---

*I say "seems" because there is no definite statement to this effect in the text. But the inference can be drawn from the allusion (in KJV's rendering of 1Sa 19:20) to a " . . . company of the prophets prophesying, and Samuel standing as appointed over them. . . ." In NRSV's translation of the same verse, Samuel is "in charge of them," and NJPS has him "as their leader," though both of these modern translations acknowledge that the meaning of the Hebrew (*omed nitzav aleihem*) is uncertain. The place, situated in Ramah, is "Na'ioth," which some commentators take to mean "dwellings" or "house of instruction."

†The Hebrew verb (*nib'im*) in 1Sa 19:20, which KJV reasonably translates as "prophesying," becomes "in a frenzy" in NRSV and "speaking in ecstasy" in NJPS.

‡These two historical books, which are in the Writings section of the Hebrew Bible, overlap in many details with the Former Prophets and differ somewhat in others. They are, the scholars agree, more ideologically "Deuteronomistic" even than the Former Prophets.

This last question is asked yet again toward the end (or the middle?) of Saul's reign. He has by now become deeply depressed. He is also certain that a conspiracy is afoot against him led by the young former shepherd David, whom he has taken into his household as his armor-bearer. David also soothes Saul's melancholy with the harp that he is " . . . cunning in playing . . ."; he slays the Philistine Goliath with his slingshot; he becomes a highly successful military commander in Saul's army.

In spite of all this, but even more because of it, Saul begins to fear David and becomes convinced that he is out to usurp the throne. In a complicated maneuver " . . . to make David fall by the hands of the Philistines . . .," he offers his daughter Michal to the "comely" young man for a wife. Anticipating (or so the text intimates) that David will demur on the ground that he is unworthy to be the king's son-in-law, Saul lets it be known that the price for her is a hundred Philistine foreskins. Nothing daunted, David goes out and delivers twice that many, leaving Saul no choice but to honor the marriage bargain, but leaving him also " . . . David's enemy continually."

That Saul's attitude toward David exhibits all the symptoms of what today would be diagnosed as paranoia—but what the Hebrew Bible describes as " . . . the evil spirit from God [that] came upon Saul . . ."—does not mean that he has no rational ground for his suspicions. (As the twentieth-century American writer Delmore Schwartz once famously said during his own bout with this illness: "Even paranoids have real enemies.") He does not yet know that Samuel has secretly anointed David at God's command and that David will succeed him as king, but Samuel has already told him that he himself is not to be the founder of a royal dynasty.

Saul also suspects that his son Jonathan is willing to yield the succession to David, who has become his closest friend. This suspicion is borne out for us—if not for Saul—after David has gone into hiding in a forest for fear of being killed by the king:

> And Jonathan Saul's son arose, and went to David into the wood. . . .
> And he said unto him, Fear not: for the hand of my father Saul shall not
> find thee; and thou shalt be king over Israel, and I shall be next unto
> thee. . . . And they two made a covenant before the LORD. . . .

Unaware though he is of this meeting, Saul is only too aware that the people have been dancing and singing and shouting that " . . . Saul hath slain his thousands, And David his ten thousands." Saul's response upon first hearing this chant is also rational: " . . . They have ascribed unto David ten thousands, and to me they have ascribed but thousands: and what can he have more but the kingdom?"

Fearing David, then, " . . . because the LORD was with him, and was departed from Saul," the king makes repeated attempts on his protégé's life. To save himself, David again flees and is nowhere to be found, until Saul, receiving reports that he is with Samuel in Nai'oth, sends messengers to capture him. But the messengers, seeing the prophets prophesying (or writhing in ecstasy) with Samuel at their head, are touched by " . . . the Spirit of God . . . , and they also prophesied. And when it was told Saul, he sent other messengers, and they prophesied likewise. And Saul sent messengers again the third time, and they prophesied also."

Driven almost to the end of his tether, Saul now goes to Na'ioth himself. But there

> . . . the Spirit of God was upon him also, and he went on, and prophe-
> sied. . . . And he stripped off his clothes also, and prophesied before
> Samuel in like manner, and lay down naked all that day and all that
> night. Wherefore they say, Is Saul also among the prophets?

The first time we heard of the question "Is Saul also among the prophets?" being asked by the people, we were told that it had become " . . . a proverb. . . ." Yet if anything is clear from the unutterably poignant story of Saul, he is not among the prophets. This humble youth, whose only outstanding quality seems to be his great physical height but who rises to an even greater height of political power, achieves major military successes against the enemies of his people (mainly, at this period, the Philistines). But he now loses the favor of God precisely because he falters, as no true prophet could or would, in the war against idolatry.

This is not the only reason given for God's decision to deny dynastic succession to the house of Saul. There is another, which resembles in its bewildering triviality the incident over striking water from the rock at Meribah that kept Moses from ever entering the Promised Land. It consists of a sacrifice Saul offers before one of his battles with the Philistines instead of waiting for Samuel (who is late) to perform the rite. When Samuel finally arrives and discovers that Saul has performed the sacrificial rite on his own, the prophet turns on him with a vengeance:

> And Samuel said to Saul, Thou hast done foolishly: thou hast not kept
> the commandment of the LORD thy God, which he commanded
> thee: for now would the LORD have established they kingdom upon
> Israel forever. But now thy kingdom shall not continue. . . .

What makes this so hard to understand is that Saul's action is not, as Samuel contends, against the law. As an Orthodox Jewish commentator has observed:

Saul's sin cannot have been that he usurped the priestly prerogatives in offering the sacrifice. David and Solomon [would offer] sacrifices without censure, and it is clear that, in this period ... there was no prohibition of sacrifice by laymen at high places. There seems to be only one explanation: that his sin was that of impatience; he should have waited longer. The sin seems excusable and scarcely deserving of so heavy a punishment.

BUT IF THIS SIN SEEMS EXCUSABLE, the other one—to which much more attention and space are given while the issue of the sacrifice passes without further ado—involves an enormous moral shock. The shock, however, comes not from Saul's offense, but from the response to it by God speaking through Samuel.

In this account, Saul forfeits God's favor and will lose his own kingship and the dynasty it might have inaugurated because he falls short in carrying out the command to wipe out every last trace of the Amalekites. He has been told by God through Samuel: "Now go and smite Amalek, and utterly destroy all that they have, and spare them not; but slay both man and woman, infant and suckling, ox and sheep, camel and ass." Saul does go into battle and defeats the Amalekites, except that he does not kill their king, Agag, whom he has captured. He also allows his troops to take as spoil

> ... the best of the sheep, and of the oxen, and of the fatlings, and the lambs, and all that was good, and would not utterly destroy them. ...
> Then came the word of the LORD unto Samuel, saying, It repenteth me that I have set up Saul to be king: for he is turned back from following me, and hath not performed my commandments. ...

Unaware that he has sinned grievously, Saul greets Samuel after the battle with the words: " ... Blessed be thou of the LORD: I have performed the commandments of the LORD." In replying, Samuel provides us with one of those priceless touches that make this story (whatever else it may be) into a great work of literature: "And Samuel said, What meaneth then this bleating of the sheep in mine ears, and the lowing of the oxen which I hear?"

Immediately placed on the alert by this remark, Saul begins to justify himself: the people forced him to take the best cattle " ... to sacrifice unto the LORD thy God...." What, he implies, is wrong with that? Samuel's answer foreshadows an idea that will be expressed by some of the classical prophets in a totally different context but on which (as we shall see) it sheds an ironic light. What he says is this:

. . . Hath the LORD as great delight in burnt offerings and sacrifices, as in obeying the voice of the LORD? Behold, to obey is better than sacrifice, and to hearken than the fat of rams. For rebellion is as the sin of witchcraft, and stubbornness is as iniquity and idolatry. . . .*

As God now reminds Samuel, He has in the past vowed to wipe out the Amalekites because of the cruelty they showed toward the Israelites fleeing from slavery in the desert. So indeed He did:

And the LORD said unto Moses, Write this for a memorial in a book, and rehearse it in the ears of Joshua: for I will utterly put out the remembrance of Amalek from under heaven. And Moses. . . . said . . . the LORD hath sworn that the LORD will have war with Amalek from generation to generation.

And again, also from the lips of Moses: "Therefore. . . . thou shalt blot out the remembrance of Amalek from under heaven; thou shalt not forget it."

But it turns out that retribution for this past cruelty of the Amalekites toward Israel may be the least of it. The central point is that the Amalekites have become the quintessential embodiment of the idolatry against which Israel has been chosen by God to make war. In the Book of Joshua, other pagan peoples are targeted for total destruction as well (and in most of those cases, too, the seizing of booty is forbidden because the fight is not for the spoils of war but for the realization of God's promise and purposes). Even among these, however, the Amalekites have been singled out by the Hebrew Bible as special. They have come to represent not only the first but also the most intransigent enemy of Israel, and by extension of God Himself: the full-blown antithesis, as it were, of the new religion. Therefore no accommodation with them ever can or will be possible.

In significant contrast to his haste in offering a sacrifice before Samuel's arrival, Saul's sin in relation to Amalek consists of a less than wholehearted campaign against idolatry, caused by an inadequate understanding of the nature and significance of this campaign. After being excoriated by Samuel, however, he sees that he has done wrong and repents. But it is too late for forgiveness: God, Samuel tells him, is not a man and He does not change His mind. (Yet in the Hebrew Bible we often see God changing His mind—even right here, in regret-

---

*KJV's "stubbornness" can also be rendered as "defiance," which is preferred by NJPS. Others opt for "arrogance" or "presumption." But the sense remains more or less the same. In the Hebrew, the word KJV translates as the general term "idolatry" is again the more specific teraphim. But "idolatry" is certainly a fair enough rendering, and in my opinion it shows a keen understanding of what the passage is getting at.

ting that He had chosen Saul; but presumably because Saul's offense is so serious, going as it does to the heart of the matter, this time there can be no further change.)

At any rate, Samuel, who as a prophet grasps fully what is at stake, demands that Saul bring the Amalekite king, Agag, before him. The episode concludes with a gruesome passage that nevertheless compensates us with yet one more touch of literary genius:

> . . . And Agag came unto him delicately. And Agag said, Surely the bit-terness of death is past. And Samuel said, As thy sword hath made women childless, so shall thy mother be childless among women. And Samuel hewed Agag in pieces before the LORD in Gilgal.*

Subsequently it is disclosed that Agag was not the only Amalekite who was spared by Saul or who evaded him. He was lying either to Samuel or to himself in declaring that he had wiped the whole people out, since David (who by this juncture has taken the desperate measure of seeking refuge from Saul in the territory of the Philistines) keeps attacking the Amalekites with his small guerrilla army. Even then, they are powerful enough to retaliate by raiding David's stronghold while he is away, burning it down and kidnapping his wives.

Not being a prophet (in spite of the special place he will forever hold in the Israelite pantheon), David cannot consult God directly. But through the *ephod*† brought to him by the priest Abiathar, he is assured that if he pursues the Amalekites, he will find and vanquish them and recover all that they have stolen from him. Thus encouraged, David sets out, and winds up victorious. Even so, four hundred Amalekites escape, indicating how many more must have survived Saul's earlier victory.

Yet for no reason provided by the text, David is not reminded by God of His vow to wipe out Amalek from under heaven; God even looks silently and, for all we know, favorably, on David's looting of the Amalekites (though it has previ-

---

*NJPS has "with faltering steps" rather than "delicately"; it has "Ah bitter death is at hand," in place of "Surely the bitterness of death is past"; and it has "cut Agag down" instead of "hewed Agag in pieces." But JB goes KJV one better with "butchered." Though the Hebrew word, *va-y'shasef*, appears nowhere else in the Bible, these are all reasonable guesses based on the root *shsf*, meaning split or cleave.

†Sometimes this word signifies a simple linen garment worn by priests or their helpers (like the boy Samuel in 1Sa 2:18, or like David himself in 2Sa 6:14, when he dances in celebration of the arrival of the Ark of the Covenant to Jerusalem). But as I have already noted, it was also the item of apparel to which the High Priest's breastpiece was attached. Since this breastpiece could legally be employed for divinatory purposes (unlike the forbidden divinatory practices associated with idolatrous cults), *ephod* often becomes, as it does in this verse (and in the story about Gideon in the Book of Judges), a shorthand term for the sacred oracle.

ously been emphasized that they are in the category of peoples from whom no booty must be taken). Neither is David punished or even reproached for the same shortcoming for which Saul had been made to suffer so grievous a penalty.

But we are not yet done with Saul and David and the Amalekites. In a scene more reminiscent of the Romans of the future than the Israelites of that day (and also one that may well have inspired Shakespeare's description of the suicide of Antony in *Antony and Cleopatra,* which is uncannily close to it in detail), Saul, after being defeated in one of his battles with the Philistines and fearing that they will capture and make mock of him, asks his armor-bearer to run him through; when the armor-bearer refuses, Saul falls on his own sword. Shortly thereafter, a young man comes to David claiming to have administered the coup de grace to Saul, who, he says, was still alive after falling on his sword. Upon inquiry, the young man identifies himself as an Amalekite, and instead of being rewarded as David thinks he had expected to be, he is forthwith executed.

Thus, the somehow appropriate possibility is held out that Saul actually dies at the hands of an Amalekite. And there is also a possible clue to God's toleration of David's inadequacy in dealing with the Amalekites. For it is David who, as king, finally finishes them off, becoming the instrument through which God's vow to wipe them out from under heaven is at long last fulfilled.

AS WE WERE NOT DONE with the Amalekites after recounting the story of Saul's less than unconditional victory over them, neither have we heard the last of Samuel. We recall that he is already an old man when he anoints Saul (indeed, his advanced age—apart from the unworthiness of his sons to follow him—is one of the justifications the people give for asking him to get them a king). Yet we also recall that he retains his great influence even after being supplanted by Saul as the leader of the people, to the point where he is the one selected by God to anoint David. He also seems to retain his physical strength, considering that this self-described " ... old and grey-headed man ..." is still able to hack the captured king of Amalek into pieces with a sword.

Yet it is well before these events that Samuel delivers a farewell address to the people. Realizing that the establishment of the monarchy spells the end of his political position, Samuel chooses the moment just after Saul has become king to deliver this address, which is directly in the tradition of the ones given by Moses and then by Joshua as each is approaching his death.

There are two differences, however. First, unlike Moses and Joshua, Samuel introduces the speech with a defense of his own stewardship:

> ... I have walked before you from my childhood unto this day. Behold, here I am: witness against me before the LORD, and before his

anointed: whose ox have I taken? or whose ass have I taken? or whom have I defrauded? whom have I oppressed? or of whose hand have I received any bribe to blind mine eyes therewith? and I will restore it to you. And they said, Thou hast not defrauded us, nor oppressed us, neither has thou taken ought of any man's hand. And he said unto them, The LORD is witness against you, and his anointed is witness this day, that ye have not found ought in my hand. And they answered, He is witness.*

Coming so soon after the fierce warning he has given them of the oppressions they will suffer under a monarchy, this passionate outburst is difficult to read as anything other than Samuel's last fruitless protest against what they have forced him to do in giving them a king. It is also directed at Saul himself, who is in the audience, and who is being taught by the prophet how he is to behave as king.

The second part of Samuel's farewell address bears a greater resemblance to those of Moses and Joshua in presenting the people with a brief, if highly selective, run-through of their history—from the patriarch Jacob up to the period of the Judges. But Samuel places much more emphasis on the negative aspects of that history. His main theme is a rehearsal of the sins their forefathers committed, the consequent punishments they suffered, and the readiness of God to respond when they cried out to Him for deliverance. Now, Samuel proclaims to the assemblage of all Israel before him, you have sinned by demanding a king " . . . when the LORD your God was your king."

Then—and here is the second main difference between Samuel's farewell address and those of Moses or Joshua—he calls upon God for a miracle in the form of thunder and rain in a season when thunderstorms never break out in the Land of Israel, " . . . that ye may perceive and see that your wickedness is great, which ye have done in the sight of the LORD, in asking you a king." When God obliges, " . . . all the people greatly feared the LORD and Samuel. And all the people said unto Samuel, Pray for thy servants unto the LORD thy God, that we die not: for we have added unto all our sins this evil, to ask us a king."

This cry of repentance triggers a reversal of direction in Samuel's speech:

And Samuel said unto the people, Fear not: ye have done all this wickedness: yet turn not aside from following the LORD, but serve the LORD with all your heart; And turn ye not aside: for then should ye go after vain things, which cannot profit nor deliver; for they are vain. For

---

*KJV's "against you" is literally accurate, but NJPS's "to your admission" clarifies the meaning of the Hebrew idiom.

the LORD will not forsake his people for his great name's sake: because
it hath pleased the LORD to make you his people.*

The beauty of this passage of consolation is further enhanced by the personal
promise that seals it: "Moreover as for me, God forbid that I should sin against
the LORD in ceasing to pray for you: but I will teach you the good and the
right way."

Samuel's farewell address bears a family resemblance to the Song of Deborah
in reaching back to the past of prophecy while also anticipating its future.
Samuel remains a "Former Prophet"—a miracle worker and an ecstatic. Even
more telling, when we last see him, it is as a ghost whom Saul has persuaded a
witch—the witch of Endor—to conjure up, on the night before the battle in
which, the king rightly fears, the Philistines will defeat and kill him. In pressur-
ing the witch of Endor to practice her necromantic art, Saul is violating an
ancient Israelite prohibition, which he himself has reinstituted. But he is in desperate straits, because " ... God is departed from me, and answereth me no more,
neither by prophets, nor by dreams: therefore I have called thee, that thou mayest
make known unto me what I shall do."† This pathetic last-ditch plea is summar-
ily rebuffed by Samuel's ghost, and all the doomed king can elicit is an angry
confirmation of his worst fears.

While this kind of thing keeps Samuel anchored in the world of the Former
Prophets, his farewell address still looks both back and ahead. On the one hand,
there are strong reverberations of Moses in phrases like "serve the LORD with
all your heart," as well as in the substance of the speech. But on the other hand,
powerful intimations of the classical prophets of the future enter in the way fearsome denunciations are balanced with sweet consolation and the reaffirming of
God's eternal fidelity to the covenant He has cut with the children of Israel,
whom it has mysteriously pleased Him to make His people.

And so it is that Samuel, too, rises up, and even higher than Deborah does,
into the clouds of ancestral glory trailing behind the classical prophets to come.

---

*The "vain things" are, of course, idols.

†This is only one of many indications in the Hebrew Bible that the ancient Israelites believed in
the efficacy of magic. But because it was so closely tied to idolatry, its practice was banned.

CHAPTER FOUR

REBUKING THE KING

S AMUEL DIES IN THE ELEVENTH CENTURY B.C.E., probably during
its last decade or so (and well before the end of the first of the two
books bearing his name). From the moment of his death and until the
Second Book of Samuel begins, the only prophets of whom we hear are the
anonymous ones—presumably members of his "school"—who are sought out
in vain by Saul before he gets the witch of Endor to conjure up the ghost of
Samuel himself.

But shortly after entering the Second Book of Samuel, we are all at once
introduced to a new prophet, Nathan, of whom no mention has been made
before. As with Gad in the First Book of Samuel, we are in this initial glimpse of
Nathan told nothing about him. He is summoned by David, who has by now
been the king for more than seven years, and who asks him a question, to which
the prophet gives a brief answer. But unlike Gad, who immediately disappeared
after speaking a few words (though he will pop up again now and then during
David's forty-year reign), Nathan returns the next morning with a long message
from God that has been delivered to him during the night and that contradicts
his own quick reply to the king on the previous day.

We are now somewhere in the 990s B.C.E., and much has happened since the
death of Samuel in which up to this moment no part is ascribed by the Hebrew
Bible to any prophet. David, we remember, was secretly anointed once by
Samuel during the lifetime of Saul, and then upon Saul's death he was anointed
yet again, this time in public. Yet only the people living in the Southern territories apportioned to the tribes of Judah and (the much smaller) Benjamin have
accepted him as their king. In a portent of what will happen about 125 years
later, the Northern tribes, deciding in this instance that their loyalty is to the
house of Saul, choose one of his sons, Ishbosheth, as their ruler, and split off from
Judah.

71

A civil war ensues in which David ultimately prevails. Hence, in 1000 B.C.E. or thereabouts (when, according to the Second Book of Samuel, David is thirty years old), " . . . all the elders of Israel came to the king to Hebron; and king David made a league with them in Hebron before the LORD: and they anointed David king over Israel."

After this third anointing, and the establishment of a unified monarchy, David's next order of business is to conquer the well-fortified and geographically protected city of Jerusalem, then held by the Jebusites. Once he has taken this " . . . stronghold of Zion . . ." he renames it the " . . . city of David." He then moves his capital there from Hebron, where it has been for seven years. From now on, he will reign from Jerusalem for " . . . thirty and three years over all Israel and Judah."

There is disagreement over whether it is before (as in the text, though with certain contradictory indications) or after the conquest of Jerusalem that David triumphs in a war over the Philistines. It is also possible to surmise that a second mopping-up operation against the Philistines, and decisive victories over a host of other peoples, are recounted out of chronological order here. But whatever the exact sequence of events, David eliminates any threat from this formerly dominant power, of which he himself (while hiding from Saul) was a vassal.

After several misadventures and hesitations, David brings the Ark of God to Jerusalem. The Ark is the holiest of Israel's possessions, bearing within it the tablets on which Moses inscribed the Ten Commandments after he shattered the first set, written by God's own finger, in anger over the golden calf. (In some places in the Hebrew Bible, however, the Ark is said to contain the shattered tablets as well, and in other places God Himself is in some mysterious sense present within it.)

When not being carted around by the Israelites in their wanderings or carried into battle, the Ark has always been kept in a tabernacle. Now, after greeting its arrival in Jerusalem by leaping and whirling and dancing " . . . with all his might . . ." (much to the disgust of his wife Michal, the daughter of Saul, who considers such behavior unseemly for a king), David builds just such a tabernacle for it. It is at this juncture that he sends for Nathan:

> And it came to pass, when the king sat in his house, and the LORD had given him rest from all his enemies;* That the king said unto Nathan the prophet, See now, I dwell in an house of cedar, but the ark of God dwelleth within curtains.

---

*It is this phrase I had in mind in speaking above of certain contrary indications in the chronology, for if he had disposed of all his enemies, why would he have had to go so soon again into battle?

Realizing that David intends to build a more suitable dwelling for the Ark—a Temple to match or surpass his own new palace of cedar—" . . . Nathan said to the king, Go, do all that is in thine heart; for the LORD is with thee."

However, that same night, God lets Nathan know that he has spoken prematurely in assuring David that there is divine sanction for his desire to build a Temple. The prophet's orders now are to tell the king in the morning that God will build a "house" for *him,* but that one of David's sons, and not David himself, will build a "house" for God.*

NO REASON IS GIVEN in this passage for God's decision to withhold from David the privilege of building a Temple, but in later books, two separate but overlapping explanations are provided. The first comes from Solomon, the son (not yet born) who has been destined for the honor: " . . . David my father could not build an house unto the name of the LORD his God for the wars which were about him on every side . . ." The second, more elaborate, explanation is voiced by David himself when, shortly before his death, he instructs Solomon to build the Temple:

> And David said to Solomon, My son, as for me, it was in my mind to build an house unto the name of the LORD my God: But the word of the LORD came to me, saying, Thou hast shed blood abundantly, and hast made great wars: thou shalt not build an house unto my name, because thou hast shed much blood upon the earth in my sight.

There is no doubt that by the time of Nathan's initial appearance, David has shed a great deal of blood. For example, while taking refuge from Saul among the Philistines, he formed a guerrilla band that would regularly raid surrounding cities (some of which may have been Israelite) and wipe out every inhabitant, man and woman alike—not for any religious purpose such as was attached to the destruction of Amalek, but so that the word of his whereabouts would not get around. Yet the text records no rebuke offered for this by God or any prophet. Why then should it be held against him now? And why does God not bring the matter up through Nathan when he addresses David here? Conceivably it is because the main emphasis of the prophet's long speech moves in exactly the opposite direction from rebuke, culminating in a promise by God that He will never withdraw his favor from the Davidic dynasty, which " . . . shall be established for ever."

---

*The pun is more obvious in the Hebrew of 2Sa 7, where the word for house (*bayyit*) is repeatedly used to mean "dynasty" in the first instance and "Temple" in the second.

The historical influence of this speech cannot be exaggerated, and I will discuss it at some length below. But for now I want to move on to the next oracle pronounced by Nathan. Though not as historically weighty, it is much more famous, partly because it comes up in one of the most popular stories in the Hebrew Bible—the one about David and Bathsheba—and partly because it reaches so lofty a moral height.

One night, walking on the roof of his house, David spies " . . . a woman washing herself; and the woman was very beautiful to look upon." Though he knows that she is married to one of his soldiers, Uriah the Hittite, he arranges an adulterous liaison with her, from which she becomes pregnant. David then contrives to have Uriah killed in battle against the Ammonites so that he can make the widow his own wife.

Just after she gives birth to David's son, Nathan is sent by a "displeased" God with a parable for the king about a rich man with " . . . exceeding many flocks and herds," who steals a poor neighbor's pet lamb, the only one he possesses. Hearing this,

> . . . David's anger was greatly kindled against the man; and he said to Nathan, As the LORD liveth, the man that hath done this thing shall surely die: And he shall restore the lamb fourfold, because he did this thing, and because he had no pity.

To which Nathan replies:" . . . Thou art the man." And he immediately goes on:

> . . . Thus saith the LORD God of Israel, I anointed thee king over Israel, and I delivered thee out of the hand of Saul. . . . Wherefore hast thou despised the commandment of the LORD, to do evil in his sight? . . .

God then threatens David with all manner of punishments:

> . . . thou hast killed Uriah the Hittite with the sword, and hast taken his wife to be thy wife. . . . Now therefore the sword shall never depart from thine house. . . . Thus saith the LORD, Behold, I will raise up evil against thee out of thine own house, and I will take thy wives before thine eyes, and give them unto thy neighbor, and he shall lie with thy wives in the sight of this sun. For thou didst it secretly: but I will do this thing before all Israel, and before the sun.

A repentant David begs forgiveness through Nathan, who informs him that his life will be spared, but that the son Bathsheba has borne to him will die.

Despite David's prayers and fasting, the child does indeed die seven days later. In addition ("Now therefore the sword shall never depart from thine house"), two more of David's sons (Amnon and Absalom) will die violent deaths during his own lifetime.

Amnon will be the first to go, when Absalom has him killed for having raped their sister Tamar. Then Absalom himself will be slain for conspiring to seize his father's throne. In spite of the fact that he has been betrayed by this treacherous son, the first question David asks upon hearing that the rebellion has been squelched is this: " . . . Is the young man Absalom safe? . . ." The negative answer he gets elicits from David an unforgettable—and unforgotten—lament: "And the king was much moved, and went up to the chamber over the gate, and wept: and as he went, thus he said, O my son Absalom, my son, my son Absalom! would God I had died for thee, O Absalom, my son, my son!"

But since the curse has been cast upon David's "house," it will continue beyond his lifetime, when his newly crowned heir, Solomon, will execute his own older brother Adonijah, who is suspected of plotting to overthrow him.

As to the sexual retribution David is promised by Nathan in the form of seeing his wives sleep with another man in public, that prediction too will come true, not by the giving of those wives to his "neighbor," but in a more hurtful way. It will become part of the rebellion staged by his own beloved son Absalom (" . . . and Absalom went in unto his father's concubines in the sight of all Israel").

But all these horrors are still in the future when the first of them has materialized in the death of the child newly born of his sinful liaison with Bathsheba. Pulling himself together after a week of fasting and supplication to which God has paid no heed, David goes to comfort Bathsheba, " . . . and lay with her: and she bare a son, and he called his name Solomon: and the LORD loved him. And he sent by the hand of Nathan the prophet; and he called his name Jedediah, because of the LORD."*

NATHAN WILL REAPPEAR in another capacity at the beginning of the fifth volume of the Former Prophets, the First Book of Kings, but it is Gad to whom the next major mission of prophetic chastisement is assigned. This occurs in the last chapter of the Second Book of Samuel, which relates how God, angry with

---

*KJV's translation of the second verse, while literal, is a bit obscure. NJPS has "He sent a message through the prophet Nathan; and he was named Jedediah at the instance of the LORD," and both NRSV and JB give similar renditions. Solomon (*Shelomoh*) means "peaceful one" or "his peace," and Jedediah (*Yedidiah*), a name which is never again used of Solomon, means "beloved of God."

Israel (though we are not told why), puts it into the aged David's head to conduct a census—evidently a very great sin. When the census is concluded, David
recognizes that he has committed a terrible offense and prays for forgiveness. But

> . . . when David was up in the morning, the word of the LORD came
> unto the prophet Gad, David's seer, saying, Go and say unto David, Thus
> saith the LORD, I offer thee three things; choose thee one of them, that
> I may do it unto thee.

The three choices are seven years of famine, three months of flight from his
enemies, or three days of pestilence. David chooses the third, which results in the
death of seventy thousand of his people. Stricken and bewildered, "David spake
unto the LORD . . . and said, Lo, I have sinned, and I have done wickedly: but
these sheep, what have they done? let thine hand, I pray thee, be against me, and
against my father's house." Unbeknownst to David, however, even before this
prayer has been offered, " . . . when the angel stretched out his hand upon
Jerusalem to destroy it, the LORD repented him of the evil, and said to the angel
that destroyed the people, It is enough: stay now thine hand. . . ."

An Orthodox Jewish scholar, S. Goldman, has enumerated the various perplexities for the believer involved in this episode:

> If God was angry against Israel, He already had grounds for punishing
> them in the sin which had provoked Him to anger; why need He have
> instigated David to commit an act which brought punishment upon
> them? How can the statement that God "moved David" against
> Israel . . . be reconciled with the doctrine of free will? And if David was
> not a free agent, why should he have been punished? Why should sev-
> enty thousand of the people have died for David's sin? And wherein lay
> the sinfulness of the numbering of the people?

But it all becomes a little clearer if we look at the Second Book of Samuel
within its canonical context as a part of the Former Prophets. In this book there
is much less about the war against idolatry than there is in Joshua, Judges, and the
First Book of Samuel. Indeed, the only direct reference to that war is in the
account of how David, shortly after becoming king over all Israel, smites the
Philistines who have launched an attack against their former vassal. Retreating,
the Philistines " . . . left their images, and David and his men burned them."*

---

*Instead of "images," both NRSV and NJPS have "idols" and JB has "gods." But the modern
translations are more faithful to the Hebrew than KJV in describing what was done to these
images or idols or gods. The Hebrew says va-yisaem, which means, as all three modern translations rightly recognize, "carried them off [or away]." However, the parallel account in 1Chr
14:12, on which KJV seems to have relied, adds "and they were burned with fire."

On the other hand, David's *military* triumphs are a great contribution to the war against idolatry, securing as they do a solid base for the new religion carried by the children of Israel. But the Israelites, and especially their king, remain in need of further education as to the purpose of such triumphs. They need reminding that the goal is not to aggrandize their own power but to establish the rule of God—first within Israel itself, and then (though this will be fully revealed only by the classical prophets in a later age) among all other peoples.

In the meantime, we see in the Second Book of Samuel an extension and consolidation of the special tradition of prophetic instruction to the king that was inaugurated by Samuel himself. Both Nathan and Gad (the former implicitly and the latter explicitly) are directly attached to the royal court: they are the king's prophets. However, unlike their counterparts in the surrounding cultures, who mainly encourage their royal patrons, and who, on those rare occasions when they issue admonitions, do so very mildly, Gad and Nathan, like Samuel, dare to defy, contradict, and chastise the king.*

Nathan is especially interesting in this connection. When David first suggests that he wishes to build a house for the Ark, Nathan—acting like a typical court prophet of that period—almost automatically tells him to do what he wishes and glibly asserts that God is with him. But that very night, he learns better. And what he learns is that he knows nothing except what God wants him to know, and he also learns that when God sends him to deliver bad news to the king, that is what he must do (even, we may easily imagine, at the risk of being banished or executed). The same lesson is driven home even more forcefully in the story of David and Bathsheba, when Nathan, having opened David's sinful eyes with the divinely inspired parable of the rich man robbing from the poor, declares to the king's face: "Thou art the man."

Gad, too, becomes the instrument not of encouragement and flattery but of catastrophe when he is sent by God after the census to force David into choosing one of the three dire punishments that will be meted out to him and his people. Yet in this very aspect of a baffling story, we are confronted with another demonstration that the king of Israel—even the one with whose "house" God has made an eternal covenant—remains subject to divine rule.

What is remarkable is that the Hebrew Bible refuses to flinch from the fact that divine rule can seem capricious, arbitrary, and disproportionately harsh in meting out even well-deserved punishment (as with Sodom and Gomorrah), not to mention punishment that no evident sin has provoked (as here). And what is equally impressive is that when God acts in ways that seem wrong or that seem to contradict His own law and even His own nature as He Himself describes it,

---

*H. B. Huffmon, in *The Anchor Bible Dictionary* article on "Prophecy (ANE)," is very informative about the role of prophecy in the pagan cultures of the ancient Near East.

He is challenged in the Hebrew Bible with complete impunity. Abraham has already argued with Him over Sodom and Gomorrah; David has just issued his wrenching complaint over the death of innocent people for what he and not they have done; one of the major classical prophets, Jeremiah, will contend with Him over the question of why a God of justice permits the wicked to prosper; and the whole of the Book of Job will be devoted to the obverse question of why He makes the guiltless suffer.

The story of the census embodies one of the more disturbing demonstrations of this aspect of God's rule, and neither here nor in the other instances we will encounter does the Hebrew Bible explain it away or drown it in syrupy apologetics. But in trying to figure out why such a demonstration is put on at this moment, it helps to examine the Second Book of Samuel again a little more closely and to pay special attention to a few details that are not necessarily obvious on a first reading to the naked eye.

Among the critical scholars of that book, the consensus—and one in which I share—is that the census-plague chapter (24) is the last of three "appendices" to the main body of the book. It is preceded first by a hymn of praise and thanksgiving David sings to God who " . . . delivered me from my strong enemy, and from them that hated me. . . ." But in the midst of celebrating and expressing gratitude to God, David cannot refrain from praising himself as well:

> The LORD rewarded me according to my righteousness: according to the cleanness of my hands hath he recompensed me. For I have kept the ways of the LORD, and I have not wickedly departed from my God. For all his judgments were before me: and as for his statutes, I did not depart from them. I was also upright before him, and have kept myself from mine iniquity. Therefore the LORD hath recompensed me according to my righteousness; according to my cleanness in his eye sight.

Some pious commentators get around the blatant omission here of any allusion to Bathsheba or David's other sins by positing that the hymn is out of place, and properly belongs in the earlier section of the book where David's military victories are described. But I suspect that there was method behind the placement of this hymn by the editor of the book. For it reveals that David, in spite of his wonderfully lyrical sense of subordination to God, is at the same time convinced that he has won God's favor by deserving it through his virtues, and that he is not being truly honest when he proclaims a few verses after this little hymn to himself, " . . . thine eyes are upon the haughty, that thou mayest bring him down."

The impression of David's self-worship is underlined by the next appendix, which consists of an enumeration of his " . . . mighty men . . ." and his great military victories, with no mention at all of God's part in them. Again, despite his protestations of thanksgiving for these victories in the preceding hymn, David is actually taking all the credit for them himself.

So far as the sinfulness of the census itself is concerned, it is also worth remembering that Joab, his own commanding general, as well as "the captains of the host," opposed taking it:

> And Joab said unto the king, Now the LORD thy God add unto the people, how many soever they be, an hundredfold, and that the eyes of my lord the king may see it: but why doth my lord the king delight in this thing? Notwithstanding the king's word prevailed against Joab, and against the captains of the host. . . .

With all these considerations in mind, I would agree with Walter Brueggemann when he interprets the punishment for the census as a "Yahwistic foil to rapacious royal power." This interpretation, coming from a Protestant scholar, is rather different from what S. Goldman tells us about the Jewish perspective: "Jewish tradition held that the offense lay in the direct numbering of persons, or in the omission to pay the atonement money prescribed on the occasion of a census (Exod. 30:12)." But Goldman then comes very close to Brueggemann when he concludes "that the sin of the act lay in the vainglorious spirit which prompted it."

In other words, David is being hit with a brutal reminder of his proper place in the scheme of things. And he is further reminded that the people over whom he rules as earthly king cannot escape the consequences of his actions. Whether he wishes them to or not, and whether they deserve it or not, they will become the victims of his own misdeeds as king. For that he can escape neither responsibility nor the pangs of conscience.

Finally, there is Nathan, the more important by far of the two prophets in the Second Book of Samuel. Nathan never addresses himself, as the Latter Prophets almost always will, to the people at large, but only to the king. In this, like Deborah and Samuel, he is still rooted in the world of the Former Prophets. Yet Nathan also looks forward to the classical prophets more directly than several better remembered Former Prophets who will soon take the stage, particularly Elijah and Elisha. In contrast to Elijah and Elisha, Nathan is neither an ecstatic nor a miracle worker. His only role, like that of the classical prophets, is to speak the word that God speaks to him.

In common with the classical prophets, too, Nathan alternates curse (as in his furious rebuke to the king over Bathsheba and the murder of her husband) with blessing and consolation. The blessing is epitomized in Nathan's statements that while God will punish the sins of the children of Israel, never will they cease being His chosen people. In fact, he goes even further in the long oracle he delivers to David about the building of the Temple.

The oracle begins with an implicit reproach in denying this honor to the king, but it then offers compensation through a wholly new decision by God: the cutting of a covenant with David's royal line that is in effect a codicil to His covenant with the children of Israel:

> And when thy days be fulfilled, and thou shalt sleep with thy fathers, I
> will set up thy seed after thee, which shall proceed out of thy bowels,
> and I will establish his kingdom. He shall build an house for my name,
> and I will establish the throne of his kingdom for ever. I will be his
> father, and he shall be my son. If he commit iniquity, I will chasten him
> with the rod of men, and with the stripes of the children of men: But
> my mercy shall not depart away from him, as I took it from Saul, whom
> I put away before thee. And thine house and thy kingdom shall be
> established for ever before thee: thy throne shall be established for ever.

This oracle is so important that one wonders why it has never become as well known as some other less portentous prophecies recorded in the Hebrew Bible. My own supposition is that its fame has suffered from its inferiority as literature to those other prophecies. Yet though written in prose that borders on flatness, as compared with the magnificent poetry of the classical prophets, in its substance it can scarcely be surpassed in historical or theological significance by anything else in the Hebrew Bible.

Thus, in future centuries, when the Land of Israel will fall under foreign domination and when its people are driven into exile, the idea of a Messiah (the Anglicized version of *mashiakh,* or "anointed one" in Hebrew) descended from the house of David will grow out of the promise made by God through Nathan. The Messiah will be conceived as a liberator and an ingatherer, sent to make good on one part of Nathan's prophecy that will at many periods in Jewish history seem cruelly false in so many ways:

> Moreover I will appoint a place for my people Israel, and will plant
> them, that they may dwell in a place of their own, and move no more;
> neither shall the children of wickedness afflict them any more, as
> beforetime.

Then, nearly a thousand years after the death of David, a group of Jews will become convinced that the Messiah (*Christos* in Greek) has arrived in the person of Jesus of Nazareth and that he is literally the son of God. It is hard to resist the speculation that the words in Nathan's prophecy, "I will be his father, and he shall be my son," will serve as one of the influences shaping this belief.

Such, then, is the huge significance of Nathan's major oracle. Except for the immortal expostulation, "Thou art the man," Nathan is unequal in eloquence to Deborah or Samuel. But take him for all in all,* he deserves to be honored as yet another cloud of ancestral glory behind the classical prophets who will before too long begin arriving on the scene.

---

*Though according to 1Chr 29:29, we do not have all of him, or of Gad: "Now the acts of David the king, first and last, behold, they are written…in the book of Nathan the prophet, and in the book of Gad the seer." These books have been lost, and it is highly probable that "the book of Samuel the seer," which is also listed in this verse, is not the same as 1 and 2 Samuel, and has been lost as well.

CHAPTER FIVE

BEFORE AND AFTER ELIJAH

BEFORE LOSING SIGHT of Nathan altogether, we come upon him one more time, at the beginning of the First Book of Kings. There, however, he acts not as a prophet but rather as a member of a political faction at the royal court.

As David lies dying, with Amnon and Absalom gone, Adonijah (born to Haggith, one of David's concubines) is now the eldest surviving son, and he proclaims himself king. But Nathan and several other members of the court are opposed to Adonijah, on the ground that David has sworn to Bathsheba that he will make *her* son Solomon his successor to the throne. Nathan advises her to go and remind the king of this vow, and says that he himself will then back her up.

We know from the Second Book of Samuel that through Nathan (then acting in his capacity as prophet) God did send a message at Solomon's birth saying that He "loved" the baby. But there is no prior record of any vow by David to Bathsheba to install Solomon as king after him.* Even so, David confirms having made it:

> Then King David answered and said, Call me Bath-sheba. And she came into the king's presence, and stood before the king. And the king sware and said. . . . Even as I sware unto thee by the LORD God of

---

*Not even in the two Books of Chronicles, which as usual both resemble and differ in some details from the historical narratives in the Former Prophets. In the First Book of Chronicles, however, David makes a statement to an assemblage of Israel's leaders—not to Bathsheba—that has no counterpart in the Second Book of Samuel or the First Book of Kings: "And of all my sons (for the LORD hath given me many sons,) he hath chosen Solomon my son to sit upon the throne of the kingdom of the LORD over Israel" (1Chr 28:5).

Israel, saying, Assuredly Solomon thy son shall reign after me, and he shall sit upon my throne in my stead; even so will I certainly do this day.

Nathan, after obeying David's order that he participate in the anointing of Solomon, then disappears from this book.*

Soon thereafter (in the 960s B.C.E.), David dies at the age of seventy, having ruled for a total of forty-plus years. Then, for nearly the whole of Solomon's reign (which seems to have lasted into the 920s B.C.E.) no mention is made of any other prophet. When God speaks, he speaks directly to Solomon without the intercession of a prophet. The first time is in a dream in Gibeon. This is a hill or a "high place" on which an altar consecrated to God exists and where sacrifices to Him are customarily offered. Solomon has gone there for that purpose because of its prestige as the highest of the "high places" in the vicinity:†

> . . . and God said, Ask what I shall give thee. And Solomon said. . . . I am but a little child: I know not how to go out or come in. And thy servant is in the midst of thy people which thou hast chosen, a great people, that cannot be numbered nor counted for multitude. Give therefore thy servant an understanding heart to judge thy people, that I may discern between good and bad. . . .‡

This request pleases God so much that He not only grants it but much more:

> And God said unto him, Because thou hast asked this thing, and hast not asked for thyself long life; neither hast asked riches for thyself, nor hast asked the life of thine enemies. . . . Behold, I have done according to thy words: lo, I have given thee a wise and understanding heart; so that there was none like thee before thee, neither after thee shall any arise like unto thee. And I have also given thee that which thou has not asked, both riches and honor: so that there shall not be any among the kings like unto thee all thy days. And if thou wilt walk in my ways, to

---

*A Nathan, who may be the same person, is later listed as the father of one of Solomon's top officials, but the Nathan who is the father of yet another official seems to be someone else, since he is called "Nathan the priest" (1Kin 4:5), rather than Nathan the prophet.

†In later centuries, offering sacrifices in such "high places" will be forbidden, partly because the only legitimate venue for sacrifice will become the Temple Solomon himself will build, and partly because they are also associated with idolatrous rites. Certain trees and groves or gardens, which were also the venue of idolatrous rites, will be forbidden as well. Of course (see p. 92 on Ahab), it is already a great sin to set up such places when they have been dedicated to "strange gods."

‡NJPS and JB are closer to the Hebrew than KJV or NRSV in rendering *na-ar kattan* as "a young lad" or "a young man" rather than "a little child."

keep my statutes and my commandments . . . then I will lengthen thy days.

Approximately four years later, God again speaks to Solomon (as the son of David whom God chose even before he was born to build the Temple when his father was forbidden to do so). On this occasion He confirms the covenant first made through Nathan with David about both the Davidic line and the children of Israel:

And the word of the LORD came unto Solomon, saying, Concerning this house which thou art in building, if thou wilt walk in my statutes, and execute my judgments, and keep all my commandments to walk in them; then will I perform my word with thee, which I spake unto David thy father: And I will dwell among the children of Israel, and will not forsake my people Israel.

After another seven years, Solomon has just finished building the Temple (God's "house"), and installed the Ark within its innermost sanctuary, only to ask: "But will God indeed dwell on the earth? behold, the heaven and heaven of heavens cannot contain thee; how much less this house that I have builded?" Nevertheless, with the promise that "I will dwell among the children of Israel" still fresh in his memory, he begs God to infuse the Temple with His presence. To this end, he offers a long dedicatory prayer beseeching God never to forsake His chosen people, the children of Israel; to listen to their supplications from within the Temple or the prayers raised up outside but toward it; and to forgive their sins " . . . (for there is no man that sinneth not) . . ." when they repent.

Up to this moment, the blessings God said He would shower upon the newly crowned Solomon have fully been realized, as they will continue to be for a long time to come. The wise and understanding heart the newly crowned king asked for has been granted and is put to the test when two prostitutes come to him, each claiming that she is the mother of the surviving one of two babies born to them at the same time:

And the king said, Bring me a sword. And they brought a sword before the king. And the king said, Divide the living child in two, and give half to the one, and half to the other. Then spake the woman whose the living child was unto the king, for her bowels yearned upon her son, and she said, O my lord, give her the living child, and in no wise slay it. But the other said, Let it be neither mine nor thine, but divide it. Then the king answered and said, Give her the living child, and in no wise slay it: she is the mother thereof.

This story spreads far and wide within Israel, " . . . and they feared the king: for they saw that the wisdom of God was in him, to do judgment." But Solomon's reputation reaches far beyond Israel itself:

And God gave Solomon wisdom and understanding exceeding much. . . . And Solomon's wisdom excelled the wisdom of all the children of the east country . . . and his fame was in all nations about. . . . And there came of all people to hear the wisdom of Solomon, from all kings of the earth, which had heard of his wisdom.

But it is a queen, the Queen of Sheba, rather than a king, of whom we are specifically told in this connection:

And when the queen of Sheba heard of the fame of Solomon . . . she came to him with hard questions. . . . And Solomon told her all her questions. . . . And she said to the king, It was a true report that I heard in mine own land of thy acts and of thy wisdom. . . . Happy are thy men, happy are these thy servants, which stand continually before thee, and that hear thy wisdom. Blessed be the LORD thy God, which delighted in thee, to set thee on the throne of Israel: because the Lord loved Israel for ever, therefore made he thee king, to do judgment and justice.

The Queen of Sheba, however, is not only overwhelmed by Solomon's wisdom. She is also left breathless by the degree of his prosperity, to which she herself gratuitously contributes with a great quantity of expensive gifts before returning to her own country. So do all the other potentates who follow in her trail " . . . to hear his wisdom. . . ."

On top of all this is the wealth Solomon acquires " . . . of the merchantmen, and of the traffick of the spice merchants, and of all the kings of Arabia, and of the governors of the country."

The description of Solomon's possessions here borders on the lascivious:

And king Solomon made two hundred targets of beaten gold: six hundred shekels of gold went to one target. And he made three hundred shields of beaten gold. . . . Moreover the king made a great throne of ivory, and overlaid it with the best gold. . . . And all king Solomon's drinking vessels were of gold . . . none were of silver: it was nothing accounted of in the days of Solomon. For the king had at sea a navy . . . : once in three years came the navy . . . , bringing gold, and silver, ivory, and apes, and peacocks. . . . And Solomon gathered together chariots and horsemen: and he had a thousand and four hundred chariots, and twelve thousand horsemen. . . .

The awed tone of this description does not (I think it fair to say) reflect the narrator's weakness for such things. What he is trying to convey, rather, is the fulfillment of God's promise to give this king much more than the wisdom he requested as a youth just ascending the throne. The wealth and honor he did not then covet (not even half of which, exclaims the Queen of Sheba, did she imagine from the reports she received) have also been bestowed on Solomon.

Everything, then, is going wonderfully well in Israel under David's first successor. But in one of those abrupt switchings of gears typical of the Hebrew Bible, both the tone and the substance now change direction. For we are about to discover that Solomon is not upholding his part of the bargain with God: he is not, that is, observing His statutes and His commandments.

IN THE EARLY DAYS of his reign, Solomon marries a daughter of the Pharaoh of Egypt without being rebuked by God, despite the fact that such a marriage would seem to contravene God's earlier prohibition against taking pagan women for wives. Now, however, we read that

> . . . king Solomon loved many strange women, together with the daughter of Pharaoh, women of the Moabites, Ammonites, Edomites, Zidonians, and Hittites; Of the nations concerning which the LORD said unto the children of Israel, Ye shall not go in to them, neither shall they come in unto you: for surely they will turn away your heart after their gods: Solomon clave unto these in love.*

In the First Book of Kings where we hear of Solomon's marriage—his first—to the Egyptian princess, there is a suggestion that it is a political alliance. Here, by contrast, we are told that he loved these foreign women.† Since he eventually accumulates seven hundred wives and three hundred concubines, we are left to wonder about the breadth of his affections.‡

In any case, God's warning that such intermarriages must lead to a lapse into

---

*Rabbinical tradition, unimpressed by the distinction between the two kinds of marriage, will explain the text's silence about the one to Pharaoh's daughter by exegetically determining that she had converted to the religion of Israel and turned her back on her native gods.

†"Foreign" is a better translation than KJV's "strange."

‡The English poet John Dryden, in "Absalom and Achitophel," a deliciously irreverent satire written in 1681, attributes the same quality to Solomon's father David: "In pious times, e'r Priest-craft did begin,/Before Polygamy was made a Sin;/When Man on many multiplied his kind,/E'r one to one was cursedly confin'd,/When Nature prompted and no Law deni'd/Promiscuous use of Concubine and Bride;/Then Israel's monarch, after Heaven's own heart,/His vigorous warmth did, variously, impart/To Wives and Slaves: And, wide as his Command,/Scatter'd his Maker's image through the Land."

idolatry is now borne out by Solomon to an extraordinarily surprising degree. And it becomes all the more surprising when we consider that he has thus far been the paragon of wisdom, and a follower in the religious footsteps of his father, David, who, for all his other sins, never lapsed into idolatry while sitting on the throne. Yet Solomon, betraying the most essential part of his duty as king of Israel, now

> . . . went after Ashtoreth, the goddess of the Zidonians, and after Milcom the abomination of the Ammonites. . . . Then did Solomon build an high place for Chemosh, the abomination of Moab, . . . and for Molech, the abomination of the children of Ammon. And likewise did he for all his strange wives, which burnt incense and sacrificed unto their gods.

His anger kindled against this evil, God speaks for the last time to Solomon:

> Wherefore the LORD said unto Solomon, Forasmuch as this is done of thee, and thou hast not kept my covenant and my statutes, which I have commanded thee, I will surely rend the kingdom from thee, and will give it to thy servant.

However, for the sake of David, God will not do this in Solomon's lifetime, but in his son's. Furthermore, while tearing most of the kingdom away from that son (still unidentified, as he himself was when the kingdom had been promised to him), He will allow Solomon's successor to keep Judah, again for David's sake but also because it is where Jerusalem, " . . . which I have chosen," is located.

Much the same message is soon delivered to the "servant" to whom God has just told Solomon the rest of the kingdom will pass. But to this "servant" the message is not communicated directly; it comes through a prophet, Ahijah of Shiloh. Like Nathan and Gad, who previously turned up without any introduction or prior mention, this prophet is entirely new to us. And what he comes to announce is almost as historically important as Nathan's oracle about the eternity of the Davidic dynasty—which to some extent Ahijah reverses. The shock value of Ahijah's words, however, is diminished by virtue of the fact that they are a more or less verbatim repetition of what we have already heard God saying to Solomon. The only additional detail is the name of the "servant" to whom Ahijah speaks: it is Jeroboam the son of Nebat, whose identity God had for some reason chosen not to reveal to Solomon.

Using the prophetic formula, " . . . thus saith the LORD, the God of Israel . . . ," Ahijah informs Jeroboam that he has been chosen by God to rule over all of Israel except for the small Southern territory of Judah (with the even smaller portion of Benjamin thrown in) after Solomon's death. God also makes the same promise to the future ruler of the Northern Kingdom that he made to David: if

Jeroboam remains faithful to God's commandments, God will ensure that *his* house is established as a lasting dynasty over the other ten of the twelve tribes of Israel. Nevertheless, the covenant with David remains in force. God will allow the Davidic line to continue, albeit in a severely reduced condition: though He has resolved to " ... afflict the seed of David ... ," it will not be " ... for ever."

AHIJAH NOW FADES AWAY, and then, with the death of Solomon, his son Rehoboam accedes to the throne. The split prophesied by Ahijah occurs almost immediately when the new king brutally turns down a plea by the Northerners to lighten the load of taxes and forced labor that Solomon had placed upon them: " ... My father made your yoke heavy," Rehoboam snarls at them, "and I will add to your yoke: my father also chastised you with whips, but I will chastise you with scorpions." Infuriated by this response to their plea, the Northerners " ... rebelled against the house of David unto this day," and in 922 B.C.E. (or thereabouts) they make Jeroboam (who, ironically, had been Solomon's overseer of forced labor at one time) the first ruler of their new Kingdom of Israel.

Rehoboam, driven south down to Jerusalem to rule over the much smaller Kingdom of Judah, gathers his forces for an assault on Jeroboam. But another " ... man of God ... " of whom we have never heard before nor will again in the Former Prophets (though he does appear in the Second Book of Chronicles) is dispatched by God to prevent the impending civil war:

> ... the word of God came unto Shemaiah the man of God, saying, Speak unto Rehoboam, the son of Solomon, king of Judah and Benjamin, ... and to the remnant of the people, saying, Thus saith the LORD, Ye shall not go up, nor fight against your brethren the children of Israel: return every man to his house; for this thing is from me. They hearkened therefore to the word of the LORD, and returned to depart, according to the word of the LORD.

But if on this occasion Rehoboam obeys, the truce is soon broken, "And there was war between Rehoboam and Jeroboam all their days." Furthermore, Jeroboam, far from following God's commandments, presides from the outset of his reign in the North over lapses into idolatry that are even worse than Solomon's. Forgetting that it was on account of such sins that a kingdom was given to him, Jeroboam fashions two golden calves. In part his motive is political. If the people should travel to the Temple in Jerusalem to sacrifice, he fears, they might return to Rehoboam. So, in an act of apostasy that could scarcely be more outrageous or extreme, he declares to them of the golden calves: " ... It is too much for you to go up to Jerusalem: behold thy gods, O Israel, which brought thee up out of the land of Egypt."

At this, another anonymous " . . . man of God . . ." is sent from Judah to the altar Jeroboam has built at Bethel. This man of God prophesies the destruction by Josiah, a yet-to-be-born future king of Judah, of the new idolatrous cult, and he even gives a miraculous sign to persuade Jeroboam that he is a true prophet. But the king pays him no heed: "After this thing Jeroboam returned not from his evil way. . . ."

Living in what today we would recognize as a state of denial, Jeroboam is entirely oblivious of the punishment he will inevitably incur, though it is already setting in with the illness of one of his sons. So blind is he that he sends his wife to consult Ahijah of Shiloh, the very same prophet who first brought him the news that he would reign over the new Kingdom of Israel while simultaneously putting him on notice that if he failed to keep God's commandments, his dynasty would be wiped out.

Ahijah, now old and blind, is alerted by God to the queen's impending arrival, and he greets her " . . . with heavy tidings":

> Go, tell Jeroboam, Thus saith the LORD God of Israel, Forasmuch as I . . . made thee prince over my people Israel, And rent the kingdom away from the house of David, and gave it thee: and yet thou has not been as my servant David, who kept my commandments. . . . But hast done evil above all that were before thee: for thou hast gone and made thee other gods, and molten images, to provoke me to anger, and hast cast me behind thy back: Therefore, behold, I will bring evil upon the house of Jeroboam, and will cut off from Jeroboam him that pisseth against the wall, . . . and will take away the remnant of the house of Jeroboam, as a man taketh away dung, till it be all gone. Him that dieth of Jeroboam in the city shall the dogs eat; and him that dieth in the field shall the fowls of air eat: for the LORD hath spoken it. Arise thou therefore, get thee to thine own house: and when thy feet enter into the city, the child shall die.*

Scalding imagery like this, descended from the curses in Leviticus and Deuteronomy, will resound in the air again, and even more loudly, in the prophecies of doom by the First Isaiah and other classical successors to Ahijah. But through this oracle, Ahijah becomes for the time being the major exponent of the prophetic tradition's war against idolatry from within.

---

*"Him that pisseth against the wall" is the literal translation of a Hebrew idiom or metaphor for "male," which is how prissier translators than the Jacobeans of KJV have usually rendered it. The phrase "him that dieth," which will be used of other wicked kings besides Jeroboam, means not at the hand of whichever monarch is being condemned, but members of his entire house.

This alone would be enough to stake a claim for his importance. But Ahijah—who in prophesying the establishment of the Northern Kingdom under Jeroboam partially reversed Nathan—is now also commanded to pronounce another oracle reversing himself. This new oracle reaches beyond the prediction that Jeroboam's dynasty will be cut off; it extends to the entire Northern Kingdom and all its people:

> For the LORD shall smite Israel, as a reed is shaken in the water, and he shall root up Israel out of this good land, which he gave to their fathers, and shall scatter them beyond the river. . . . And he shall give Israel up because of the sins of Jeroboam, who did sin, and made Israel to sin.*

Important as are the oracles of Ahijah, he is so overshadowed by Elijah, who follows him some forty or fifty years later (perhaps in 875 B.C.E.), that the older prophet's name has been almost entirely forgotten.

A similar fate has befallen Jehu the son of Hanani, the one other prophet of whom we read not long before the advent of Elijah. Jehu is sent to Baasha, the third ruler of the Northern Kingdom of Israel and the instrument through which Ahijah's prophecy of doom against Jeroboam's dynasty comes to be fulfilled. Baasha first assassinates Jeroboam's son and successor Nadab, who followed in the sinful footsteps of his father. Then, having usurped the throne of the Northern Kingdom, Baasha wipes out every member of the former royal family.

Yet because he himself is now also treading the evil path taken by both Jeroboam and Nadab, God curses him through Jehu as He cursed Jeroboam through Ahijah, and in almost exactly the same horrific terms:

> Forasmuch as I . . . made thee prince over my people Israel; and thou hast walked in the way of Jeroboam, and hast made my people Israel to sin. . . . Behold, I will take away the posterity of Baasha, and the posterity of his house; and will make thy house like the house of Jeroboam the son of Nebat. Him that dieth of Baasha in the city shall the dogs eat; and him that dieth of his in the fields shall the fowls of the air eat.

MEANWHILE, things have improved in the Southern Kingdom of Judah—though only after a period during which the religious situation was scarcely better than in the North. Under Solomon's son Rehoboam, ruling after the split,

---

*"Israel" here is of course the Northern Kingdom. But in other places, the name is applied to the entire people, including those in Judah. To avoid confusion, therefore, I am using the term "Northern Kingdom," reserving "Israel" or "the children of Israel" or the "house of Israel" for the whole people, wherever they might be living.

. . . Judah did evil in the sight of the LORD, and they provoked him to jealousy with their sins which they had committed, above all that their fathers had done. For they also built them high places, and images, and groves, on every high hill and under every green tree. And there were also sodomites in the land: and they did according to all the abominations of the nations which the LORD cast out before the children of Israel.*

Rehoboam's successor, Abijam, who persists in these evil ways, reigns only three years in Jerusalem, but (still, we are told, for the sake of David) no prophet comes to announce the destruction of his line. Instead, and without prophetic prodding, the next king of Judah, Asa, pursues a program of radical religious reform during his long forty-year reign (roughly 913–873 B.C.E.). Even while the Northern kings with whom he overlaps are sunk in the abominations of idolatry, Asa resumes the battle against it, doing " . . . that which was right in the eyes of the LORD, as did David his father." Among other things,

> . . . he took away the sodomites out of the land, and removed all the idols that his fathers had made. And also Maachah his mother, even her he removed from being queen, because she had made an idol in a grove; and Asa destroyed her idol, and burnt it by the brook Kidron.†

During this same period, however, conditions are growing worse and worse in the Northern Kingdom. The house of Baasha suffers the doom pronounced upon it by God through the prophet Jehu, when the king's son Elah, " . . . drinking himself drunk . . . ," is assassinated by one of his own military commanders, Zimri. Once he has seized the throne, Zimri (in a mere seven days!) does unto the house of Baasha what Baasha did unto the house of Rehoboam: " . . . he left him not one that pisseth against a wall, neither of his kinsfolks, nor of his friends."

A civil war then breaks out within the Northern Kingdom. In the course of this war, Zimri dies in a fire he himself has set in the royal palace while under siege by the forces of a rival military commander, Omri. This provokes yet another civil war that ends with the victory and coronation of Omri. In the six

---

*KJV's "sodomites" are "male temple prostitutes" in NRSV, and "sacred prostitutes" in JB. These renditions are more precise than KJV, which misses the connotation of "consecrated" in the Hebrew word *k'deshim,* the masculine form of the term elsewhere used of female temple prostitutes.

†"Asa's heart" is said in the rendition of KJV to have been "perfect with the LORD all his days," but in Hebrew the phrase is *l'vav Asa hayya shalem.* This means not that his heart was "perfect" but that it was "full." "Wholehearted" (NJPS) and "the heart of Asa was wholly . . ." (JB) are better translations.

years of his reign, Omri does " . . . worse than all that were before him." But in the cardinal sin of idolatry, he will soon be bested by his son Ahab, who ascends the throne in 869 B.C.E.:

> And it came to pass, as if it had been a light thing for him to walk in the sins of Jeroboam the son of Nebat, that he [Ahab] took to wife Jezebel, the daughter of Ethbaal king of the Zidonians, and went and served Baal and worshiped him. And he reared up an altar for Baal in the house of Baal, which he had built in Samaria. And Ahab made a grove; and Ahab did more to provoke the LORD God of Israel to anger than all the kings of Israel that were before him.*

Thus, the Northern Kingdom, which from the very day it came into being surrendered to the lure of idolatry instead of resisting it, has now sunk in this respect to the lowest level in its approximately fifty years of existence. But there is a backlash, as many prophets begin springing up in opposition to the idolatrous abominations that have spread throughout the North. When the queen, Jezebel, institutes a purge of these enemies of her gods, a certain Obadiah, who, though Ahab's steward, " . . . feared the LORD greatly, . . . took an hundred prophets, and hid them by fifty in a cave, and fed them with bread and water."

THE STAGE IS NOW SET for the advent of Elijah. Like Nathan and Gad before him, he materializes with no preliminary introduction and without (at first) even being called a prophet: "And Elijah the Tishbite . . . said unto Ahab, As the LORD God of Israel liveth, before whom I stand, there shall not be dew nor rain these years, but according to my word." Only after predicting this drought to the king (where and how he has acquired access to Ahab we are never informed) is his status as a prophet confirmed for us, when " . . . the word of the LORD came unto him, saying, Get thee hence, and turn thee eastward, and hide thyself . . ."—presumably from the vindictive wrath of Ahab.

Elijah, we now discover, is the greatest wonder worker among the prophets of Israel since Moses himself. In quick succession, we see him as the beneficiary of one miracle (being fed by ravens during a famine) and the performer of a series of others. The first of these occurs in the home of a widow to whom God has sent him during the drought accompanying the famine. When Elijah asks the widow for " . . . a morsel of bread . . . ," and she replies that all she has is

---

*The Zidonians, according to NJPS's rendition, were the Phoenicians. "As if it were a light thing" is faithful to the Hebrew *nakel*, but the sense is captured more clearly by NJPS with "Not content to follow" and JB's "The least that he did was to follow." KJV's "grove," from the Hebrew *asherah*, becomes "sacred pole" or "post" in the modern translations.

... an handful of meal in a barrel, and a little oil in a cruse: and, behold, I am gathering two sticks, that I may go in and dress it for me and my son, that we may eat it, and die. And Elijah said unto her, Fear not; go and do as thou hast said: but make me thereof a little cake first, and bring it unto me, and after make for thee and for thy son. For thus saith the LORD God of Israel, The barrel of meal shall not waste, neither shall the cruse of oil fail, until the day that the LORD sendeth rain upon the earth. And she went and did according to the saying of Elijah: and she, and he, and her house, did eat many days. And the barrel of meal wasted not, neither did the cruse of oil fail, according to the word of the LORD, which he spake by Elijah.

But the culmination of Elijah's powers as a miracle worker is reached when the widow's son falls so ill

... that there was no breath left in him. And she said unto Elijah, ... O thou man of God? art thou come unto me ... to slay my son? And he said unto her, Give me thy son. And he took him out of her bosom, and carried him up into a loft, where he abode, and laid him upon his own bed. And he cried unto the LORD, and said, O LORD my God, has thou also brought evil upon the widow with whom I sojourn, by slaying her son? And he stretched himself upon the child three times, and cried unto the LORD, and said, O LORD my God, I pray thee, let this child's soul come into him again. And the LORD heard the voice of Elijah; and the soul of the child came into him again, and he revived. And Elijah took the child ... and delivered him unto his mother: and Elijah said, See, thy son liveth. And the woman said to Elijah, Now by this I know that thou art a man of God, and that the word of the LORD in thy mouth is truth.

Impressive as are some of the other miracles Elijah goes on to perform (such as splitting the waters of the Jordan with his mantle), none can be ranked with the bringing back to life of a dead child. Combined with the provision of food to a starving family, this supremely wondrous act shows Elijah as a life-giving force, and it serves as a kind of balancing prelude to the Elijah we see in the very next chapter as a ruthlessly bloody warrior for God and against idolatry.

Three years have now passed, and with drought and famine still raging, God commands Elijah to present himself to Ahab, after which " ... I will send rain upon the earth." Obeying, Elijah with some difficulty manages to meet the king, who greets him by asking:" ... Art thou he that troubleth Israel?"*To which Eli-

---

*Here is a rare instance when, even on literary grounds, I prefer the modern translations to KJV. NRSV:"Is it you, you troubler of Israel?" JB:"So there you are, you scourge of Israel." NJPS:"Is that you, you troubler of Israel?"

jah responds: " . . . I have not troubled Israel; but thou, and thy father's house, in that ye have forsaken the commandments of the LORD, and thou hast followed Baalim."*

Elijah then issues a challenge. Let the 450 prophets of Baal† contend against him alone in a test on Mount Carmel before the people of Israel. Ahab agrees, and when the people are assembled, Elijah demands of them: " . . . How long halt ye between two opinions? if the LORD be God, follow him: but if Baal, then follow him. And the people answered him not a word." Silently, but eventually signaling their approval, they wait as the test is set up. Both he and the prophets of Baal will each prepare a bullock for sacrifice; the Baalists will then call upon their god to send down fire upon it, and Elijah will call upon God of Israel to do the same—" . . . and the God that answereth by fire, let him be God. . . ."

The prophets of Baal go first, but neither their repeated cries nor their leapings on the altar elicit an answer from Baal. No fire comes even when they " . . . cut themselves after their manner with knives and lancets, till the blood gushed out upon them." All the while, Elijah taunts and mocks them: " . . . Cry aloud: for he is a god; either he is talking, or he is pursuing, or he is in a journey, or peradventure he sleepeth, and must be awaked."‡

Baal's prophets having failed, it is now Elijah's turn. With the help of the people, he repairs and sanctifies the altar and has trenches dug around it filled with water, which is also poured on the altar itself, on the bullock, and the wood beneath it. This accomplished,

> . . . Elijah the prophet came near, and said, LORD God of Abraham, Isaac, and of Israel,§ let it be known this day that thou art God in Israel, and that I am thy servant, and that I have done all these things at thy word. Hear me, O LORD, hear me, that this people may know that thou art the LORD God, and that thou hast turned their heart back again. Then the fire of the LORD fell, and consumed the burnt sacrifice, and the wood, and the stones, and the dust, and licked up the water that was in the trench. And when all the people saw it, they fell on their faces: and they said, The LORD, he is the God; the LORD, he is the God.

---

*Instead of translating, KJV again carries the Hebrew plural of *Baal* over into English.

†He also throws in four hundred more who serve the Asheroth, or sacred posts, but they seem to be forgotten as the story unfolds.

‡Instead of "pursuing," Son has "gone aside," a euphemism for answering a call of nature.

§The other name by which the patriarch Jacob was called, and after which, obviously, the people who came to descend from him were usually designated.

Hearing this, " . . . Elijah said unto them, Take the prophets of Baal; let not one of them escape. And they took them: and Elijah brought them down to the brook Kishon, and slew them there."*

In slaughtering the prophets of Baal, Elijah goes Samuel (who only butchered a single person, the king of Amalek) 450 times better. But Samuel was contending solely with the enemy from without. By contrast, the enemy being fought by Elijah through this ruthless deed has (with the formidable royal patronage of Jezebel) moved from the outside into the very heart of Israel, contaminating and corrupting the people from one end of the Northern Kingdom to the other.

Under these circumstances, Elijah is not only carrying on a reprisal against Jezebel's campaign to wipe out all the Israelite prophets. He is backing up the spiritual war against idolatry that is his primary prophetic responsibility with what amounts to military action against it. Doing what in the circumstances is required, he is, as it were, conducting a kind of guerrilla operation against the spiritual enemy that has been occupying the whole of the North of Israel.

But just as this bloody episode is preceded by a picture of Elijah as the bringer and saver of life, so it is concluded in the same way when, in accordance with the promise God made in directing him to seek out Ahab, the rains finally pour down to end the drought and the famine.

IN PLAYING OUT this dual role, Elijah seems to enter into a more intimate relationship with God than any prophet before him except Moses. And indeed, images and events are sprinkled in the text that irresistibly conjure up the memory of Moses. The most vivid of these enter into the story immediately after Elijah's triumph over the prophets of Baal.

When Elijah slaughters those prophets, Ahab does nothing to punish him. Possibly the king, like the rest of the people who have witnessed the contest, experiences a temporary revival of belief in the God of Israel, which is then confirmed when the skies darken in accordance with Elijah's prediction of rain. At Elijah's urging, Ahab takes to his chariot before the rain comes and speeds off to Jezebel in Jezreel, while the prophet, with " . . . the hand of the LORD . . ." upon him, runs on foot ahead of him in what looks (to us) like a manic dance.

Elijah is described as a hairy man, and the picture drawn of him by the always dazzling minimalist art of the narrator evokes qualities of ebullience, high energy, and even raucousness, all of which come out in his taunting of the

---

* "Slew" is weak for the Hebrew *va-yishkhatem*. Both NJPS and JB have "slaughtered," which is more precise.

prophets of Baal, and in his general manner of speech. But the sense of triumph that overcomes him after his great victory soon gives way to a deep depression. It is triggered when Jezebel, hearing from Ahab what Elijah has done, sends a messenger swearing that she will kill him by the next day.

Forced by this threat to flee for his life, he seeks refuge beyond her domain, in the Southern Kingdom of Judah. There, he goes " . . . a day's journey into the wilderness, and came and sat under a juniper tree: and he requested for himself that he might die; and said, It is enough; now, O Lord, take away my life. . . ." Falling asleep under the tree, he is awakened by the touch of an angel, who instructs him to " . . . Arise and eat. And he looked, and behold, there was a cake baken on the coals, and a cruse of water at his head. And he did eat and drink, and laid him down again."* But the angel wakes him up once more, and once more tells him to eat because otherwise he will lack the strength to make the journey ahead.

It is in this journey that Elijah recapitulates in microcosm the experience of Moses some five centuries earlier. Moses went without food for forty days and forty nights on Mount Sinai, and so does Elijah on his way to Sinai (here called Mount Horeb, as it was when Moses first encountered God there).† Like Moses, too, who was sent into " . . . a clift of the rock . . ." to shield him from the glory of God that was about to pass by, Elijah goes into a cave in advance of a similar manifestation, or (in the technical term) "theophany." The only difference is that before entering the cave Elijah is not cautioned by God, as Moses was, about what will soon happen. However, as he sits there in the depths of his distress,

> . . . behold, the word of the LORD came to him, and he said unto him, What doest thou here, Elijah? And he said, I have been very jealous for the LORD God of hosts: for the children of Israel have forsaken thy covenant, thrown down thine altars, and slain thy prophets with the sword; and I, even I only, am left; and they seek my life, to take it away.

In claiming to be the only one of God's prophets left, Elijah is exaggerating. Some commentators have proposed that all the others are still in hiding after having survived Jezebel's purge. Yet we soon encounter three anonymous prophets, one of whom is identified as a member of a prophetic guild (" . . . a certain man of the sons of the prophets . . ."). Then there will be a fourth, Micaiah the son of Imlah, whose prophetic standing is such that, as I have remarked in another context, he even " . . . saw the LORD sitting on his throne, and all the

---

*The word KJV translates as "coals" actually means "hot stones," and the juniper is a broom bush or tree.

†The same identification of Horeb with Sinai is found in many other passages in the Bible.

host of heaven standing by him on his right hand and on his left." And none of this is to take account of the four hundred prophets—prophets speaking not in the name of Baal but in the name of the God of Israel—who are also consulted by King Ahab along with Micaiah.

Be that as it may, God's response—providing us with another link to Moses—is to command that Elijah

> . . . Go forth, and stand upon the mount before the LORD. And, behold, the LORD passed by, and a great and strong wind rent the mountains, and brake in pieces the rocks before the LORD; but the LORD was not in the wind: and after the wind an earthquake; but the LORD was not in the earthquake; And after the earthquake a fire; but the LORD was not in the fire: and after the fire a still small voice.*

And there is yet one more reminiscence of Moses in this "theophany": being granted a direct contact with the presence of God, Elijah does what Moses himself did upon his first direct experience of the divine in a burning bush. Like Moses, who " . . . hid his face; for he was afraid to look upon God," Elijah, presumably out of the same fear, wraps " . . . his face in his mantle. . . ."

Yet so deeply is Elijah sunk in despair that not even this experience lifts him out of it. When he leaves the cave and God asks him again, " . . . What doest thou here, Elijah?," the prophet repeats what he has said before, and in exactly the same words. But now, as though to persuade him that his work will not have been in vain, God commands him to go back and anoint Hazael as the new king of Aram (Syria) and Jehu as the new ruler of the Northern Kingdom of Israel. He is also to appoint his own successor (Elisha), who will, we gather, combine the same two roles as Elijah has done of prophet and soldier in the war against idolatry:

> And it shall come to pass, that him that escapeth the sword of Hazael shall Jehu slay: and him that escapeth from the sword of Jehu shall Elisha slay. Yet I have left me seven thousand in Israel, all the knees which have not bowed unto Baal, and every mouth which hath not kissed him.†

---

*The literal meaning of *kol d'mamah dakkah* is "a voice [or sound] of thin silence." I for one like KJV's "a still small voice" better than NRSV's "a sound of sheer silence" or NJPS's "a soft murmuring sound," let alone JB's "the sound of a gentle breeze."

†The editor of the Soncino edition points out, however, that no such slaughter by Elisha is ever recorded in the Bible. Nor is there any mention of anointing in connection with a prophet anywhere else in the Bible. The best guess is that the word is used here to mean "appoint," which Elijah will soon do not by pouring oil on Elisha's head, but in throwing his mantle over him.

So far as the appointment of Elisha is concerned, no sooner commanded than accomplished. Elijah comes upon him plowing a field, and casts " . . . his mantle upon him. . . . Then he arose, and went after Elijah, and ministered unto him."*

BUT ELIJAH'S WISH FOR DEATH, for which the appointment of Elisha would seem to be a preparation, is not yet granted. Before he can depart this world, he still has a number of unfulfilled tasks to perform. Primary among them is to deal with Ahab and Jezebel who, we are reminded, are the acme of evil:

> . . . there was none like unto Ahab, which did sell himself to work wickedness in the sight of the LORD, whom Jezebel his wife stirred up. And he did very abominably in following idols, according to all things as did the Amorites, whom the LORD cast out before the children of Israel.

These two great sinners hand Elijah a perfect opportunity when the king's offer to buy the neighboring vineyard of a man named Naboth is turned down, and Jezebel hatches a plot to get the recalcitrant owner stoned to death on a false charge. When the news of Naboth's death reaches her, she tells Ahab that he can now seize the vineyard, which he then does. But

> . . . the word of the LORD came to Elijah the Tishbite, saying, Arise, go down to meet Ahab king of Israel . . . : behold, he is in the vineyard of Naboth, whither he is gone down to possess it. And thou shalt speak unto him, saying, Thus saith the LORD, Hast thou killed, and also taken possession? And thou shalt speak unto him saying, Thus saith the LORD, In the place where dogs licked the blood of Naboth shall dogs lick thy blood, even thine.

Ahab, one imagines from his reply, has come to feel that for him there is no escaping this "troubler of Israel": "And Ahab said to Elijah, Hast thou found me, O mine enemy? And he answered, I have found thee: because thou hast sold thyself to work evil in the sight of the LORD." Elijah then pronounces much the same curse upon Ahab that has been directed at the other idolatrous kings who reigned over Israel before him:

---

*The literal meaning of the Hebrew that KJV translates as "ministered unto him" is "served him" (*va-y'shartehu*), no doubt as an assistant or even apprentice.

Behold, I will bring evil upon thee, and will take away thy posterity, and will cut off from Ahab him that pisseth against the wall.... And will make thine house like the house of Jeroboam the son of Nebat, and like the house of Baasha the son of Ahijah, for the provocation wherewith thou hast provoked me to anger, and made Israel to sin.... Him that dieth of Ahab in the city the dogs shall eat; and him that dieth in the field shall the fowls of the air eat.

So frightened is Ahab that when he

... heard those words, that he rent his clothes, and put sackcloth upon his flesh, and fasted, and lay in sackcloth, and went softly. And the word of the LORD came to Elijah the Tishbite, saying, Seest thou how Ahab humbled himself before me? because he humbleth himself before me, I will not bring the evil in his days: but in his son's days will I bring evil upon his house.

For Jezebel, a separate curse is reserved: "And of Jezebel also spake the LORD, saying, The dogs shall eat Jezebel by the wall of Jezreel."

But if full recompense for Ahab's sins is deferred until the next generation as a result of his bout of repentance, it is too late for Ahab himself to escape altogether. Misled by the four hundred prophets he consults—because God (in one of those theological stumbling blocks I mentioned in Chapter One*) puts lying words into their mouths—Ahab goes into battle against Syria, and meets his death. But Elijah, though still alive, is nowhere in sight when this happens or when the dogs do indeed lick up Ahab's blood; and by the time Jezebel is put to death some years later, Elijah will be gone.

He himself, however, does execute the evil fate God has in store for Ahab's son Ahaziah, who also " ... walked in the way of his father, and in the way of his mother. . . ." As Elijah executes this judgment, we get one more picture of this prophet both as a miracle-worker and as a bloody avenger. First he lets it be known that Ahaziah, who is bedridden after accidentally falling through a trellis, will shortly die because he has dispatched messengers to Baal-zebub the god of Ekron (a nearby Philistine city) to find out whether he will recover. Enraged by what Elijah has predicted, the king sends fifty men to bring the prophet down from a hill on top of which he has been sitting. From the bottom of the hill, the captain of this contingent

---

*See footnote, p. 25.

... spake unto him, Thou man of God, the king hath said, Come down. And Elijah answered and said to the captain of fifty, If I be a man of God, then let fire come down from heaven, and consume thee and thy fifty. And there came down fire from heaven, and consumed him and his fifty.

The same drama of immolation is replayed when another fifty are sent. But when the third contingent reaches the hill, the captain begs Elijah for mercy, and an angel orders Elijah to spare them and go to Ahaziah. Once in the royal palace, the prophet informs the king to his face that he will never leave his bed because he has " ... sent messengers to enquire of Baal-zebub the god of Ekron ..." as if there were " ... no God in Israel to enquire of his word. ... So he died according to the word of the LORD which Elijah had spoken. ..."

From the death of Ahab's son Ahaziah, we move—in a leap from ignominy to glory—to the death of Elijah himself. The day comes when Elijah knows that he is to be taken up " ... into heaven by a whirlwind ..." and as he makes his way by degrees from Gilgal to the Jordan, Elisha, despite his master's repeated requests, refuses to leave his side, needing to assure himself that Elijah's spirit will be infused into him. "And it came to pass, as they still went on, and talked, that, behold, there appeared a chariot of fire, and horses of fire ...; and Elijah went up by a whirlwind into heaven."

Elisha is permitted to see this. He also then takes " ... the mantle of Elijah that fell from him ..." and performs the same miracle with it that Elijah himself has just done in parting the waters of the Jordan. In this way is it confirmed that he has truly been chosen as his master's prophetic heir.

AS SUCH—and assuming against certain schools of scholarly thought that Elisha too is a historical rather than a legendary figure, even if some of the stories about him are obviously legendary—in the roughly fifty years of his prophetic career (about 850–800 B.C.E.), he attends to some business that Elijah never got around to finishing.

Weeping because of the destruction that he foresees will be wreaked on his people by Hazael, he still maneuvers to make him king of Syria, as Elijah had been commanded by God to do. Then, in another mopping-up operation, he sends one of his disciples to anoint Jehu as king of Israel. The new king loses no time in carrying out the still unfulfilled curse against Jezebel, who has outlived her husband by some fifteen years. It is an unforgettable scene of enormous imaginative force. Sensing that she is about to be killed by Jehu, the queen—for she *is* a queen and " ... a king's daughter"—neither flees nor cowers but paints her face and sets her hair before her executioners arrive. When they do, " ... they threw her down: and some of her blood was sprinkled on the wall, and on the horses. ..." Jehu himself then treads her under foot with his chariot,

And when he was come in, he did eat and drink, and said, Go, see now this cursed woman, and bury her: for she is a king's daughter. And they went to bury her: but they found no more of her than the skull, and the feet, and the palms of her hands. Wherefore they came again, and told him. And he said, This is the word of the LORD, which he spake by his servant Elijah the Tishbite, saying, In the portion of Jezreel* shall dogs eat the flesh of Jezebel: and the carcase of Jezebel shall be as dung upon the face of the field in the portion of Jezreel; so that they shall not say, This is Jezebel.

Jehu also fully and bloodily carries out the curse of extinction that God had hurled through Elijah at the house of her husband Ahab, murdering every last member of it.

Elisha is not involved, as Elijah would surely have been, when Jehu follows up on this massacre by destroying the Baalim (though not " ... the golden calves that were in Beth-el, and that were in Dan"). And when Elisha counsels magnanimity to a defeated foe, he demonstrates that he is not the prophet-cum-warrior that Elijah was, and that he himself might have been expected to become on the basis of the role staked out for him by God in deciding upon his appointment. Rather, as someone has aptly characterized him, he is much more the prophet as statesman or diplomat than the prophet as warrior.

There are other contrasts between Elisha and Elijah as well. For one thing, Elisha is an ecstatic, using music to put himself into prophetic trances ("But now bring me a minstrel. And it came to pass, that when the minstrel played, that the hand of the LORD came upon him"). Also, as against the relatively solitary Elijah, Elisha is surrounded by " ... sons of the prophets. ..." These bands of disciples, or prophetic guilds, have grown so numerous that they complain to Elisha about how cramped their living space is, and they get his permission to build larger quarters (during which he works a rather trivial miracle in causing an iron axe that has fallen into the water to rise so that it can be retrieved).

But the other miracles Elisha goes on to work are much more consequential. In performing them, he, like Elijah, shows both a life-giving and a destructive side—though it is not always possible, as it is with Elijah, to detect any connection between the destructiveness and the war against idolatry. Thus, on the one hand, right after donning the mantle of Elijah, he heals the befouled water of Jericho which has been causing death and miscarriages; later he will decontaminate a store of food. Here we have the life-giving aspect of Elisha's miracle-working powers. Yet when he is mocked by a group of little children (" ... Go up, thou bald head; go up, thou bald head"), he curses them in return " ... in the

---

*That is, the place that had been Naboth's vineyard.

name of the LORD." At this, two she-bears emerge from the woods and tear forty-two of the children to pieces.

The life-giving aspect returns, however, in Elisha's next miracle. This also involves water, which he provides to a tripartite alliance of the kings of Israel, Judah, and Edom in a war against the Moabites. But then the destructive side expresses itself again, when he orders the alliance to " ... smite every fenced city, and every choice city, and ... fell every good tree, and stop all wells of water, and mar every good piece of land with stones." Yet this is one occasion when Elisha's destructive side is definitely connected with the war against idolatry. For he is directing the divine wrath against an enemy who will, upon recognizing that he has been defeated, take " ... his eldest son that should have reigned in his stead," and offer him "for a burnt offering upon the wall. . . ."

All the rest of Elisha's miracles are also life-giving. He cures a Syrian captain of leprosy and makes a convert out of him to the God of Israel (" ... thy servant will henceforth offer neither burnt offering nor sacrifice unto any other gods, but unto the LORD"). He saves himself from a marauding Syrian army when at his plea God surrounds him with " ... horses and chariots of fire. . . ." He rescues a woman's children from being sold into slavery. He arranges for the provision of food where it is either lacking or insufficient, and he even ends a famine in Israel so severe that women are boiling their own children and cannibalizing them.

But, as with Elijah, Elisha's miraculous powers are consummated in the greatest feat of all: the revival of the dead. Also as with Elijah, this great miracle is performed upon the child of a woman who has fed him and in whose house he has been a guest:

> And when Elisha was come into the house, behold, the child was dead and laid upon his bed. He went in therefore, and shut the door upon them twain, and prayed unto the LORD. And he went up, and lay upon the child, and put his mouth upon his mouth, and his eyes upon his eyes, and his hands upon his hands; ... and stretched himself upon him: and the child sneezed seven times, and the child opened his eyes.

Even after he himself dies, this power of resurrection does not depart from him:

> And Elisha died, and they buried him. And the bands of the Moabites invaded the land at the coming in of the year. And it came to pass, as they were burying a man, that ... they cast the man into the sepulchre of Elisha: and when the man was let down, and touched the bones of Elisha, he revived and stood up on his feet.

.   .   .

THERE ARE THOSE who think that Elisha is on a par with his master, but to me he seems much less impressive, a blurrier carbon copy (and certainly less of a "hard-liner," so to speak, in the war against idolatry). Jewish tradition and folklore agree. Elijah will come to be featured as one of the greatest heroes of the past with an even more important role to play in the future as the herald of the Messiah.*

No doubt, this exaltation of Elijah owes much to the fact that he is singled out to be transported to heaven in a flaming chariot. Furthermore, in the conclusion of the Book of Malachi, at the tail end of the era of classical prophecy, God will promise: "Behold, I will send you Elijah the prophet before the coming of the great and dreadful day of the LORD." But Elijah's great importance may have even more to do with the parallels to Moses that are drawn in the story of his encounter with God at Mount Sinai. Nor can I resist the conviction that a literary component is once again at work. There is the especially vivid portrait of Elijah drawn through the stories about him, which are as miraculous in their art as the miracles they describe—so much so that it becomes virtually impossible to put one's finger on their literary secret, on how the narrator does it. Then there is the "theophany" at Mount Sinai, surely one of the greatest passages in the entire Hebrew Bible, combining an unparalleled evocation of human poignancy and despair with a sense of the divine whose profundity is also impossible to analyze.

Interestingly, this particular sense of the divine stands in the sharpest possible contrast to what—from a literary if not a theological point of view—is probably its other most awesome manifestation in the Hebrew Bible. I am referring to the voice from the whirlwind toward the end of the Book of Job (a very different whirlwind from the one that sweeps Elijah's fiery chariot into heaven†), in which God is all thunder, roaring out an endless stream of images to stress His creative power and to show that the human mind is too limited to understand it. With Elijah, God's presence manifests itself not in violent wind, or earthquake, or fire, but in that "still small voice" that one must strain oneself to hear. It would seem that the power of God over all things and all creatures can reveal itself, when He chooses, in the most intimate whisper and not only in ear-shattering and fearsome disturbances of nature.

Except, perhaps, for the enchanting detail of the seven sneezes of the child whom Elisha restores to life, there is nothing in what scholars call the Elisha "cycle" that reaches the literary heights scaled by the chapters about Elijah. But

---

*Every year at the seder, the festive meal that Jews celebrate at Passover in memory of the deliverance of their ancestors from slavery in Egypt, a special cup of wine is set aside for Elijah, and at a certain point the door is opened to let him in as the assemblage sings a melodious prayer asking that he come to them soon accompanied by the Messiah.

†Though the same Hebrew word, *s'arah,* is used in both places.

the disciple is as great a miracle worker as, or even greater than, the master. I stress this element of their powers because—to repeat a point I have harped on before—miracle working will disappear almost entirely from the classical prophets. What they will do is *speak,* and when they act, it will take the form of symbolic representations in their own bodies and in their own lives that will be calculated to dramatize their words.

However, this difference will not extend in any significant degree to the *content* of the oracles or sermons that the classical prophets will deliver. Most commentators allege that there is a sharp break between the pre-classical and the classical prophets. But as I will be arguing in the following pages, I see no such break where substance is concerned. What I see is the classical prophets carrying on the same war against idolatry fought by their pre-classical forebears, going all the way back to Abraham. The difference is that they fight it by other means.

BUT WE ARE NOT YET quite ready to meet this new line of prophets, since the last of the six volumes constituting the Former Prophets does not end with the death of Elisha (some time around 800 B.C.E.). Being in its own right—and not merely because it compiles tales of individual prophets—a prophetic work, the Second Book of Kings goes on to give a fundamentally religious history both of the North and the South for approximately another two hundred years.

This takes us through momentous events. The Northern kings, without exception, pursue their evil ways, and finally God's patience comes to an end. In 722 B.C.E., He " . . . rejected all the seed of Israel, and afflicted them, and delivered them into the hands of spoilers, until he had cast them out of his sight . . . as he had said by all his servants the prophets. . . ." The instrument of this ultimate punishment is the Assyrian empire, which conquers the Northern Kingdom, disperses the Israelites (who will become the "Ten Lost Tribes" of legend), and colonizes the area with its own people.

In the Southern Kingdom of Judah, however, a few good kings alternate with the bad ones. But so bad are the bad ones that the good are unable to make up for them. For example, Ahaz, who rules in the late eighth century B.C.E., " . . . made his son to pass through the fire, according to the abominations of the heathen. . . ." Later (in the early to the mid-seventh century B.C.E.) comes his grandson Manasseh who also " . . . made his son pass through the fire . . ." among other major, if lesser, idolatrous abominations. The consequence is that

> . . . the LORD spake by his servants the prophets, saying, Because Manasseh king of Judah hath done these abominations, and hath done wickedly above all that the Amorites did, which were before him, and hath made Judah also to sin with his idols: Therefore thus saith the

LORD God of Israel, Behold, I am bringing such evil upon Jerusalem and Judah, that whoseoever heareth of it, both his ears shall tingle. . . . And I will forsake the remnant of mine inheritance, and deliver them into the hand of their enemies; and they shall become a prey and a spoil to all their enemies.

Now, Manasseh's father Hezekiah was a good king in the eyes of God, and his grandson Josiah becomes an even better one. It is in fact during Josiah's reign in the last decades of the seventh century B.C.E. that a " . . . book of the law . . ."* is discovered while the Temple built by Solomon (now more than two hundred years old) is being repaired. Reading it causes King Josiah to institute a sweeping reformation to undo all the evil done by his grandfather. But not even this can avert the doom of the Southern Kingdom of Judah as pronounced once again by the prophetess Hulda. All it can do, she declares in the name of God, is spare Josiah himself from seeing " . . . all the evil which I will bring upon this place. . . ."

The narrator heaps unprecedented praises upon Josiah while denying to his virtues the power to save Judah:

And like unto him there was no king before him, that turned to the LORD with all his heart, and with all his soul, and with all his might, according to all the law of Moses; neither after him arose there any like him. Notwithstanding the LORD turned not away from the fierceness of his great wrath, wherewith his anger was kindled against Judah, because of all the provocations that Manasseh had provoked him withal. And the LORD said, I will remove Judah also out of my sight, as I have removed Israel, and will cast off this city Jerusalem which I have chosen, and the house of which I said, My name shall be there.

The working out of this threat is sketched by the Second Book of Kings through a succession of rulers down to the Babylonian conquest of Judah, the looting and the destruction of Solomon's Temple in 586 B.C.E., and the ensuing deportation to Babylon of most residents of Jerusalem.

But there is one extremely strange feature about it all. The Second Book of Kings covers a period in which at least eight of the classical prophets—Amos, Hosea, Micah, the First Isaiah, Zephaniah, Nahum, Habakkuk, and Jeremiah— walk the Land of Israel, both in the North and the South, and when Ezekiel and the Second Isaiah are active among their fellow exiles in Babylon. Yet of them

---

*As already noted, this was some portion or form of what would become the Book of Deuteronomy.

all, only Isaiah the son of Amoz (the First Isaiah) is mentioned by name. Most uncharacteristically for a classical prophet, moreover, he performs a miracle.*

These two facts have led some, myself included, to suspect that the Isaiah in Kings is actually some other prophet to whom the name later gets attached. But even if the story is about the real First Isaiah, the absence from the Second Book of Kings of all the other classical prophets who live during the period it traverses remains puzzling.

Perhaps the reason is that the prophets of interest to the narrator of the Second Book of Kings are mainly men of action, who have more direct access to the rulers than most of the classical prophets ever do. If the Isaiah who appears here is really Isaiah the son of Amoz, his own connection with the royal circles of his day may be why he is noticed at all.

IN THE HEBREW BIBLE, the Book of Isaiah is placed right after the Second Book of Kings and stands at the head of the Latter Prophets. Historically, however, Isaiah the son of Amoz actually was the third (or perhaps even the fourth) of the classical prophets. Because I am trying here to tell a more or less continuous story, I am about to break the pattern I have so far followed. That is, I will from now on disregard the biblical in favor of the historical order insofar as the current state of scholarly knowledge makes this possible.

Which carries me back once again to the middle of the eighth century B.C.E., and to Amos, the first of the classical prophets to burst out of the clouds of ancestral glory whose course I have been following up to this point in an effort to show that he and the other classical prophets do not come out of nowhere. Yet that they do not come out of nowhere tells us nothing about *why* they come when they do.

In some measure, the explanation lies in a new wave of expansionist imperial energy that is beginning to gather force among the great rival powers of the area—Assyria, Egypt, Babylonia, Persia—in the eighth century B.C.E. and that will over the next three hundred years bring with it the calamities described in the Second Book of Kings. Above all else, it is because the earliest of the classical prophets sense the approach of such calamities, and because the later ones struggle out of the same sense to teach the people how to ward off others of a like nature, that they are driven to speak.

Yet politically shrewd though the classical prophets can sometimes—if by no means always—be, it is not through political analysis that they see what they see.

---

*The chapters in the Second Book of Kings in which Isaiah makes an appearance (19–20) reappear with some variations in Chapters 36–39 of the Book of Isaiah itself, where they are placed between the end of the First Isaiah's prophecies and the beginning of the Second's.

To them, it is always the relation of the people to God that constitutes the decisive factor in the national fate. Being unfaithful to God by apostasy (putting other gods *before* Him) or syncretism (putting other gods *beside* Him) will doom them to subjugation and exile from which the only hope of escape and restoration is to repent of these terrible sins and to turn back and walk in His ways. It will be the mission of the classical prophets to preach this doctrine, while simultaneously explaining what the religion of Israel means and demands. And as in performing the first part of this mission they will almost always meet with resistance in the immediate present, so in performing the second part will their words just as often meet with misunderstanding in the far distant future, up to and including our own day.

PART TWO

Eruption

CHAPTER SIX

AMOS: THE LION ROARS

I T IS EASY TO SEE WHY Amos has been taken as the beginning of a turning point in the development of religious thought in Israel and eventually
in the entire history of the Western world. The path-breaking change supposedly inaugurated in the eighth century B.C.E. by this first of the classical
prophets is most often said to be from a primitive emphasis on ritual (especially
animal sacrifice, but also the observance of festivals, or even the singing and playing of hymns of praise to God) to a higher and nobler stress on morality; from a
narrowly tribalistic mentality to an all-embracing universalist outlook (or, in the
more standard parlance, from "particularism" to "universalism"). It has even been
argued that the religion of Israel only becomes truly monotheistic with Amos
and the other prophets of the eighth century B.C.E.—Hosea, Micah, and the
First Isaiah.

In all probability, the influence of Darwin's theory of evolution had more
than a little to do with this interpretation: having spread far beyond the confines
of biology into almost every area of thought, evolutionism eventually invaded
(perhaps in some cases subliminally) even the study of the Hebrew Bible.*

The evolutionary approach came, so to speak, as a Godsend to a disparate
collection of interested parties. One of these was Christian believers—scholars as
well as educated laymen—who accepted the Hebrew Bible (or the "Old Testa-

---

*The evolutionary approach, however, could and did accommodate a twist given to it by Julius
Wellhausen, whom we met in the Introduction as the leading exponent of the "Newer Documentary Thesis" with its J, E, D, and P scheme. According to Wellhausen, beginning in the late
sixth century B.C.E., the great progress that had already been made in the previous two hundred
years toward a higher development was interrupted and reversed when the priests took over
from the prophets. The result was, he wrote, a concomitant loss of the prophetic emphasis on
ethical concerns and a resurgence of ritualism, legalism, and exclusivism. I will discuss this
notion more fully, and take issue with it, in Chapter 14..

ment") as Scripture but who regarded it as a long prelude to the New Testament. For them, the evolutionary approach provided "scientific" warrant to the ancient "Christological" reading of the classical prophets as heralds of the purification, the elevation, and the true understanding of all things that the arrival of Jesus would bring in the fullness of time.

Another interested party was composed of people who had been brought up as good Protestants and then unhappily lost their faith under the assaults of modern science. But having been raised in a religion that encouraged the constant study of Scripture, they remained on intimate terms with the Hebrew Bible. This was not true either of lapsed Roman Catholics or of formerly Orthodox Jews who had undergone a similar process of secularization. For fear that the layman might misinterpret the Bible if left to his own devices, Orthodox Jews rarely read it on its own without the mediation of rabbinic commentaries, while Roman Catholics were discouraged from reading it at all.

To many lapsed Protestants, by contrast, the "Old Testament" was still of great value, and the books of the classical prophets were among the most appealing, since they appeared to be more closely in congruence with "enlightened" modern ideas about spirituality and morality than most of what preceded them in the canonical biblical order, from the Pentateuch through Kings. These lapsed Protestants, too, were thus attracted to an approach that could salvage some of their favorite books from the general wreckage.

There was also a great advantage in the evolutionary approach to certain Jews who mainly lived in Germany (the headquarters, as it were, of the new Higher Criticism of the Hebrew Bible). These were people who sought to modernize their religion by purging it of embarrassingly "archaic" and "obsolete" elements, and who were driven by this impulse to create the movement known as Reform Judaism. Still being Jews, they could not share in the view that the prophets (or some of them) were halfway on the road to Christianity, or even Christians *avant la lettre*. But the Reformers could, and did, place a much greater emphasis on the prophets than had been the case among Jews before. Some even declared that the ever elusive "essence of Judaism" was to be sought in the classical prophets—by which they generally meant certain carefully selected sayings culled from them and then ripped out of context. (It must, however, be admitted that the rabbis of the Talmud, for whom most of the early Jewish Reformers had little use, had not been above doing this kind of thing themselves when it suited their fancy.)

So great was the impact on all sides of the new evolutionary reading of the classical prophets that it still maintains a grip on the minds even of people who know little else, if anything, about the Bible. Yet in revisiting their books, I have discovered that the truth about the classical prophets is more complex, and also more interesting, than what is by now the stereotypical view of them. Indeed, not even Amos—who perhaps fits the conventional modern paradigm more closely than any of his successors—can be placed into it without ignoring his roots in a past that he is frequently admired for repudiating, and without blinding ourselves to key elements of his prophecies.

In arguing that there was no radical break between the pre-classical prophets and the line that begins with Amos in the eighth century B.C.E., I am not saying that nothing whatever changed. Nor am I denying that—even beyond the working of miracles—differences existed between the pre-classical and the classical prophets. It is impossible, for example, to imagine Amos slaughtering 450 prophets of Baal, as Elijah did, or, like Elisha, encouraging the horrendous massacre Jehu carried out against the house of Ahab. These bloody deeds belonged entirely to the era of pre-classical prophecy, when the war against idolatry, supported by royal power and patronage, called for the sword as much and as often as, from now on, it would depend on the teaching of the Law and the warnings of punishment for violating it.

Yet, as I have announced I hope to show, the classical prophets were far more continuous with their predecessors than we have been led to believe. Furthermore, the idea that the classical prophets represented a break, a new development, or a "higher stage" in the "evolution" of the law revealed to Moses at Sinai—or, for that matter, the conception of God that in my opinion actually did originate with Abraham—cannot withstand an open-minded reading of their books within the matrix of the Hebrew Bible as a whole.

WHEN, SOMEWHERE BETWEEN 760 and 750 B.C.E., Amos leaves his hometown of Tekoah in the Southern Kingdom of Judah and travels to the Northern Kingdom of Israel to pronounce its doom in the name of God, it has been between fifty and a hundred years since prophets of the stature of Elijah and Elisha have been active up there.

However, bands of prophets like those Elisha headed have continued roving from place to place in the long stretch of time since his death. These "sons of prophets" are still around on the fateful day when Amos hears God commanding him to leave his flocks and his sycamores in Judah so that he can go and warn the people of the Northern Kingdom that, for all the prosperity and power they are at the moment enjoying, disaster is heading their way.

From the fact that Elisha himself was the head of just such a band or bands (as Samuel had been before him), we may infer that in the eyes of the Hebrew Bible (or anyway the Books of Samuel and Kings), they are "true" prophets, loyal to the God of Israel. But from a story in the Book of Amos, written in the third person (and therefore by someone other than Amos himself), it appears that the prophetic guilds—as well as their anonymous masters—have by now degenerated into charlatans, soothing their clients with whatever syrupy words they want to hear, and accepting money for such services. (Even Elisha himself seems to have prophesied for pay on occasion.) Possibly, too, they are engaging in the forbidden practices of divination and magic.

All of which is probably why, in an angry confrontation with Amaziah, the priest who presides at the shrine of Beth-el, Amos indignantly distances himself from these professional prophetic guilds:

> . . . Amaziah said unto Amos, O thou seer, go, flee thee away into the land of Judah, and there eat bread, and prophesy there: But prophesy not again any more at Beth-el: for it is the king's chapel, and it is the king's court. Then answered Amos, and said to Amaziah, I was no prophet, neither was I a prophet's son; but I was an herdsman, and a gatherer of sycomore fruit: And the LORD took me as I followed the flock, and the LORD said unto me, Go, prophesy unto my people Israel.*

Yet when Amos denies that he is a prophet or the "son of a prophet," he is obviously not denying that he experiences himself as a prophet in the sense of being compelled to speak the words God commands him to speak. Nor is he denigrating prophecy in general. Just the opposite. God says through him in recounting the blessings He has showered upon the Israelites that He " . . . raised up of your sons for prophets. . . ." Moreover, He accounts it as one of the great sins of the same Israelites that they " . . . commanded the prophets, saying, Prophesy not." But Amos's attitude becomes clearest of all when he declares that "Surely the LORD God will do nothing, but he revealeth his secret unto his servants the prophets." *Nothing* is kept from the prophets by God: it is an extraordinarily bold claim.

But why has God sent Amos from his home in the Kingdom of Judah to what is after all a foreign country? True, the two kingdoms are inhabited by people of the same stock and ancestry, and they are all formally devotees of the same religion. But since the secession of the North after the death of Solomon more than one hundred and fifty years earlier, there have been many periods with no love lost between the two kingdoms. Often they have even entered into rival or mutually hostile alliances leading to war.

When Amos is dispatched on his prophetic mission, however, relations

---

*KJV translates *ve-ekhal sham lekhem* literally, and hence fails to give an accurate sense of the meaning of this idiom. Instead of telling Amos to "eat bread" in Judah, Amaziah, as NRSV, NJPS, and JB all recognize, is telling him to go there and "earn his bread"—that is, his living. There are two insinuations in this attack on Amos. One is that he belongs in Judah, not in Israel (JB: "get back to the land of Judah"), and the other is that he prophesies for money. To which Amos answers that he is no professional, but that he has undertaken this mission at God's command. (Incidentally, to my ear, the present tense used by some translations—such as NRSV's "I am no prophet . . . etc." and NJPS's "I am not a prophet, . . . etc."—rings truer to the Hebrew *lo navi anokhi v'lo ben navi anokhi* than the past tense in KJV and JB.)

between the North (then ruled by Uzziah) and the South (where Jeroboam II is on the throne) happen to be unusually good. This harmony makes it possible, or easier, for Amos to intervene in the internal affairs of the North (though even under such circumstances, the priest Amaziah does not hesitate to challenge him a seditious outside agitator). Still, why Israel and not Judah?

I have found no satisfactory answer to this question in the scholarly literature. The explanation most frequently given by historians is that under Jeroboam II, the Northern Kingdom, taking advantage of the temporary quiescence of the then great imperial powers in the region (Assyria and Egypt), has been able to reconquer land that was lost before, and even to expand its domain over territories it did not previously rule. One result is that major trade routes now pass through areas held by the Northern Kingdom, and this naturally generates greatly increased economic prosperity. But far from having, as we would say today, a trickle-down effect, the new wealth of the kingdom is heavily concentrated in a few hands—or, again as we might say today, the gap between rich and poor has grown even wider than before. Nor are the rich content with the great abundance they already enjoy. They therefore contrive to fatten themselves even further by squeezing everything they can out of the poor, mostly by illegal means that they manage to employ by bribing the judicial authorities.

Yet during this same period, the Southern Kingdom of Judah is also expanding its territory and also growing more prosperous than ever before. Are the rich in the South behaving any more virtuously toward the poor than their coreligionists in the North? If so, there is no indication of it in the Book of Amos.

In fact, although Amos concentrates most of his fire on the Northerners, he reserves a fair amount of ammunition for Judah as well. On occasion, Judah is also included even when God is explicitly addressing the people of the Northern Kingdom: "Also I brought you up from the land of Egypt, and led you forty years through the wilderness. . . ." Or, and even more emphatically: "Hear this word that the LORD hath spoken against you, O children of Israel, against the whole family which I brought up from the land of Egypt, saying, You only have I known of all the families of the earth. . . ." Of course, it is not only the ten Northern tribes that God brought out of Egypt, and "the whole family" undoubtedly embraces Judah along with Israel.

All this means that Amos would have had sins aplenty to denounce in his own country without having to travel up North.* Why Israel and not Judah,

---

*The references in Amos to the sins of Judah are regarded by many scholars as a late addition by the hand of a disciple or an editor. So, too, is the idyllic vision of a restored Davidic kingdom in the last chapter of the book, to which we will come in due course. Many would also relegate to a later date the other two verses I just quoted in which Judah is implicitly included. But there are also scholars like Francis L. Andersen and David Noel Freedman who (in their edition of Amos) strongly believe that Amos consistently had Judah in his sights, even if they do not necessarily ascribe all the disputed verses to him.

then? Simply because, Amos himself tells the priest Amaziah—and us—God sent him there, and he had no choice but to go.

Francis L. Andersen and David Noel Freedman wisely caution that "Whatever we may privately believe about prophets and prophecy, especially in the Bible," we must recognize that "these were sincere men and women who believed that God was in touch with them and had spoken to them or otherwise communicated with them, and that it was their duty to report what they had seen or heard." We can, if we wish, translate this into rationalistic or secular language. We can say that in the inner ear of genius through which he imagines he hears the voice of God, Amos can already detect, amid the din of luxurious living, the distant rumblings of the Assyrian chariots that will in only a few decades overrun the place and send its people into permanent exile. That Assyria in particular will be—as the First Isaiah will later call it—the instrument of God's wrath* in this instance (and subsequently in others), Amos does not know; if this knowledge had been vouchsafed to him by God, or by his own political acumen, he would have communicated it. But what he does know is that the people of the North have lost their moral and religious bearings, and that unless they find their way back to God, and soon, they will be truly lost. It is not yet too late for them to be shaken out of their confused and degraded religious condition into a new awareness of what serving the God of Israel involves, and what it does *not* involve. But time is running out.

BY FAR THE GREATEST of the shocks Amos administers is a series of harsh attacks on the sacrifices offered at shrines like Beth-el, Gilgal, and Dan. These attacks have been read by traditionalist Jewish commentators as being directed not against sacrifice itself but on the performance of them anywhere other than Jerusalem. Does not Amos proclaim in the name of God "That in the day that I shall visit the transgressions of Israel upon him, I will also visit the altars of Beth-el. . . ."†? And does he not then sarcastically add, "Come to Beth-el, and transgress; at Gilgal multiply transgressions. . . ."?

The problem with this traditionalist interpretation, though, is that approximately another hundred years will pass before the book generally taken to be Deuteronomy is discovered and before the offering of sacrifices to the God of Israel will, in accordance with its command, be prohibited anywhere except in Solomon's Temple in Jerusalem.

Yet even if it is still permissible to worship God at Beth-el, Gilgal, and Dan, it is also true that pagan practices and the idols that go with them have come to

---

*Isaiah's exact phrase (10:5) is " . . . the rod of mine anger. . . ."

†KJV's "visit" means "punish" (as in the modern translations).

be syncretistically mixed in there with the lawful worship of the God of Israel. As we have seen, the first king of Israel after the secession in 922 B.C.E., who was also named Jeroboam, even set up golden calves at Beth-el. By this act, he desecrated the most ancient of Israel's holy sites—the one near which Abraham built an altar, and where God spoke, in a dream, to Jacob, who then erected a monument there and an altar nearby as well.

Even so, when Amos witheringly invites the people to come sin at Beth-el and Gilgal, the things they do there, as he goes on to describe them, are not unlawful or sinful in themselves. When he derides the people, he almost seems to be mocking them for being over-zealous in their observance:

> . . . [you] bring your sacrifices every morning, and your tithes after three years: And offer a sacrifice of thanksgiving with leaven, and proclaim and publish the free offerings: for this liketh you, O ye children of Israel, saith the LORD.*

And if there is no blinking the fact that Amos is attacking lawful sacrifices to the God of Israel, even (or especially) when they go beyond the minimum requirement, neither can one avoid recognizing how savage these attacks are:

> I hate, I despise your feast days, and I will not smell in your solemn assemblies. Though ye offer me burnt offerings and your meat offerings, I will not accept them; neither will I regard the peace offerings of your fat beasts.†

God even contemptuously spurns the hymns they sing to Him and the music accompanying them: "Take thou away from me the noise of thy songs; for I will not hear the melody of thy viols." This refrain is sounded again as part of a longer condemnation of the rich who " . . . are at ease in Zion . . ." and who " . . . chant to the sound of the viol, and invent themselves instruments of musick like David."

What God demands, Amos proclaims, is this: "Seek good, and not evil, that ye may live: and so the LORD, the God of hosts, shall be with you. . . . Hate the evil and love the good, and establish judgment in the gate. . . ." And what God demands is this: "But let judgment run down as waters, and righteousness as a

---

*The Hebrew is "days" (*yamim*) and not, as KJV mistakenly has it, "years," while KJV's "this liketh you" is more clearly translated by NRSV as "for so you love to do," and by NJPS as "For you love that sort of thing."

†"Smell" (of the burnt offerings) is literally accurate, but NJPS renders it as "I will not be appeased," which strikes me as conveying the true sense better than any of the other modern alternatives such as NRSV's "take no delight" or JB's "take no pleasure."

mighty stream."* And what this variously phrased demand entails is that the rich cease " . . . treading . . . upon the poor, and [taking] from him burdens of wheat. . . ."† These are the sins for which sacrifices and hymns and tithes can make no atonement:

> Thus saith the LORD; For three transgressions of Israel, and for four, I will not turn away the punishment thereof; because they sold the righteous for silver, and the poor for a pair of shoes; That pant after the dust on the head of the poor, and turn aside the way of the meek. . . .

And again, using some of the same overpowering imagery:

> Hear this, O ye that swallow up the needy, even to make the poor of the land to fail, Saying, When will the new moon be gone, that we may sell corn? and the sabbath, that we may set forth wheat, making the ephah small, and the shekel great, and falsifying the balances by deceit? That we may buy the poor for silver, and the needy for a pair of shoes; yea, and sell the refuse of the wheat? The LORD hath sworn by the excellency of Jacob, Surely I will never forget any of their works.‡

Much—and, by some, everything—has been made of this contemptuous denigration by Amos of sacrifice (or, if one prefers technical language, the "cult") and his correlatively passionate concern over the oppression of the poor by the rich (or, in our own contemporary terminology, issues of social justice and the distribution of wealth and income). But is he breaking sharply with the past in this? How new—let alone revolutionary—is he being?

THE FIRST STEP in dealing with that question is to ask whether there are any precedents in the Hebrew Bible for such an interpretation of God's laws and statutes. To that question, the answer is an unequivocal yes. Furthermore, Amos himself relies on these precedents in condemning the sins not only of the North but also of the South:

---

*"Justice" (as in the modern translations) rather than "judgment" would be better here and in the quotation preceding it, and both "everflowing" (NRSV) and "unfailing" (NJPS and JB) stream are closer to, if not more literal than, KJV's "mighty stream" for *nakhal eitan.*

†"Burdens" means levies or taxes.

‡Son's gloss here is that "By making the measure [ephah] small and the coin [shekel] heavier in weight, they were guilty of gross fraud." And like other modern translations, Son corrects KJV's "excellency of Jacob" and translates it as "pride of Jacob."

Thus saith the LORD; For three transgressions of Judah, and for four, I will not turn away the punishment thereof; because they have despised the law of the LORD, and have not kept his commandments, and their lies caused them to err, after the which their fathers have walked.

Now, it is important to understand that the term in this passage for "the law" is *torah*. S. M. Lehrman remarks: "The Higher Critics . . . define *torah* here as the verbal directions of the priests." That is, even the Higher Critics—to whom Amos is a key figure in the opposition they normally draw between prophet (good) and priest (bad)—read him as ratifying "the verbal directions of the priests." We can therefore be sure that Amos is castigating the Judahites for violating the very laws to which he is allegedly opposed. We can also be confident, having noticed earlier the way the moral teachings of that *torah* are indiscriminately mixed in the Pentateuch itself with the ritual obligations it imposes, that to Amos there is no contradiction between the two.

Right after prophesying the doom of the Southern Kingdom of Judah for these sins, Amos gets around to his main subject—the sins for which the Northern Kingdom of Israel is facing total destruction and exile. Having cited a few items from the list he compiles, I want now to quote this glorious passage more fully:

Thus saith the LORD; For three transgressions of Israel, and for four, I will not turn away the punishment thereof; because they sold the righteous for silver, and the poor for a pair of shoes; That pant after the dust of the earth on the head of the poor, and turn aside the way of the meek: and a man and his father will go in unto the same maid, to profane my holy name; And they lay themselves down upon clothes laid to pledge by every altar, and they drink the wine of the condemned in the house of their god. Yet destroyed I the Amorite before them. . . . Also I brought you up from the land of Egypt, and led you forty years through the wilderness. . . . And I raised up of your sons for prophets, and of your young men for Nazarites. Is it not even thus, O ye children of Israel? saith the LORD. But ye gave the Nazarites wine to drink; and commanded the prophets, saying, Prophesy not.

What is for our present purposes most interesting about this passage is that, like the Pentateuch, it lists ritual and moral violations together, along with outright idolatrous practices as well. Moreover, by bringing up the Exodus from Egypt and the forty years in the desert and the conquest of the Promised Land, Amos defines everything he is condemning as prohibited since ancient times. For example, the actions he excoriates in the verses about selling the poor for silver or a pair of sandals, and about going to sleep in "pledged" (i.e., pawned) clothes are explicitly forbidden in the Book of Exodus:

If thou at all take thy neighbor's raiment to pledge, thou shalt deliver it
unto him by that the sun goeth down: For that is his covering only, it is
his raiment for his skin: wherein shall he sleep? and it shall come to pass,
when he crieth unto me, that I will hear; for I am gracious.

In the same chapter of Exodus, a theme is also struck that is very close to the
moral element so important to Amos:

Ye shall not afflict any widow, or fatherless child. If thou afflict them in
any wise, I will surely hear their cry; And my wrath shall wax hot, and I
will kill you with the sword; and your wives shall be widows, and your
children fatherless.

This precept is harped upon so often—one might even say obsessively—in
the Book of Deuteronomy that Everett Fox labels the stranger, the widow, and
the orphan as the "three classic powerless groups in Israel."*

Another of Amos's great concerns is the perversion of justice through
bribery: "For I know your manifold transgressions and your mighty sins: they
afflict the just, they take a bribe, and they turn aside the poor in the gate from
their right." In Deuteronomy a special point is similarly made about judging
both justly and impartially, and the taking of bribes by judges is very harshly
condemned.† And this is not even to mention the injunction "Thou shalt not
bear false witness against thy neighbor" which is one of the Ten Commandments
that first appears in Exodus and is then repeated with slight variations in phraseology in Deuteronomy.

Even stipulating that Deuteronomy had not yet been discovered (or perhaps
even written) in the time of Amos, and even granting, as we must, that the cen-
tralization of sacrifice commanded by it was an innovation, it is nearly impossible to believe that many of the book's other doctrines—and especially the moral
ones—had not been in the air for a very long time.

I would press much the same point about many of the "Deuteronomistic"
ideas contained in the Former Prophets. Admittedly, it was not until the late
sixth or early fifth centuries B.C.E. that these six books were put into the shape
in which they have come down to us. Yet this still gives us no solid ground for
doubting that there was a prophet named Samuel in the eleventh century B.C.E.,
another named Elijah in the ninth century B.C.E., and so on, and that the stories

---

*"The stranger" is always included with the widow and the orphan in Deuteronomy, and usu-
ally also in Exodus, as in 22:21.

†It is interesting that Deuteronomy (1:17) expressly forbids judges from showing partiality not
just to the rich but to the poor as well: each case is to be decided on its own merits.

about them were based on traditions handed down from generation to generation before being committed to writing. In addition, we have to keep bearing in mind that such traditions were steadily becoming more and more sanctified. This means that special care would have been taken not to tamper with them.

For my money, all these considerations make the entire body of "Deutronomistic" literature—including the Book of Deuteronomy itself—fair game in the hunt for precedents on which Amos and the other classical prophets could draw. Like John Bright, Andersen and Freedman provide scholarly authority for such a position in their edition of Hosea, a slightly younger contemporary of Amos: "The affinities of Hosea with Deuteronomy are well-known. . . . Questions of literary dependence are vexing and perhaps beyond solution, and it is safer to speak of a common tradition from which both draw."

Or again: "Hosea's discourses . . . are threaded with Deuteronomic ideas in a way that shows they already were authoritative in Israel." And Andersen and Freedman—bolstering their case with a reference to the work of another scholar, Walter Brueggemann—continue: "Whether already written in an early form, or still largely oral, Deuteronomic material served as background for much of Hosea's thought." Much the same, I would add, can be said for Amos.

Yet Deuteronomy aside, moral considerations are not exactly absent from the other four books of the Pentateuch which were not yet "official and established scriptures," but to which Andersen and Freedman apply the same argument:

> [W]e can say that material that eventually found its way into the Pentateuch, or at least material closely resembling it, already existed in the time of the monarchy, some of it coming down from the age of Moses himself. This traditional moral code provides a prevailing backdrop to prophetic judgment speeches.

A great deal was painted on that backdrop, from the saving of Noah from the flood because he was "just," through Abraham's argument with God over Sodom and Gomorrah (cities to which Amos himself refers, proving that he had the story in mind), to the Ten Commandments, of which more than half (depending upon how one counts) are concerned with the moral relations between man and man rather than the ritual obligations of man to God.

So much, then, for the idea that the emphasis on morality and justice in Amos constitutes a break with the past, or is revolutionary in spirit. But what about the obverse or corollary idea that Amos is repudiating the ritual or priestly component of the religion of Israel?

In search of an answer to *that* question, we can do no better than look again at his compendium, of the people's transgressions. There we notice that one of them has to do with Nazirites. As we have learned in discussing Samson and Samuel, Nazirites were people (they could be women as well as men) who had taken a vow to dedicate themselves wholly to God for a certain period of time. This not only gave these laymen the temporary status of priests, but imposed even more stringent restrictions upon them. For example, only when the High Priest entered the Holy of Holies—the inner sanctum—of the shrine was he enjoined from wine, whereas the Nazirite was throughout the entire period of his vow forbidden " . . . wine and strong drink, and shall drink no vinegar of wine, or vinegar of strong drink, neither shall he drink any liquor of grapes. . . ." That Amos should single out as a major sin of the people that they have corrupted Nazirites by inducing them to get drunk surely demonstrates that he continues to set great store by the priestly or "cultic" traditions on the basis of which such a thing is forbidden.

But there are also two other fascinating precedents in the Bible for Amos's attitude toward the relation of ritual observance to ethical behavior. The first is in the speech the prophet Samuel makes to King Saul from which I quoted before in a different connection in Chapter 3: " . . . Hath the LORD as great delight in burnt offerings and sacrifices, as in obeying the voice of the LORD? Behold, to obey is better than sacrifice, and to hearken than the fat of rams." To be sure, what Samuel is saying—that obedience to God is more important than sacrifice—contains nothing about morality. Yet it does indicate that the prophetic tradition behind Amos is already infused with the idea that sacrifice is not a sufficient means of atoning for or escaping punishment from sin, and certainly not a substitute for observing God's commandments in other areas, or an excuse for ignoring them.

The second precedent to which I want to call attention brings us from Samuel to the other most important pre-classical prophet, Elijah. According to one interpretation of the detail Amos twice uses of "a pair of shoes" or sandals (na'alayim), "the rich accept bribery from the neighbors of the poor man's field to force the latter to surrender his title deeds and thus 'close in' (na'al) all the fields together."* This may be too ingenious by half. But it reminds us that when Elijah prophesies the bloody end of the royal house of Ahab, it is *not* as punishment for the idolatry this wicked king has permitted under the influence of his Baal-worshiping wife Jezebel. It is, rather, because they have stolen the vineyard of their neighbor Naboth after she has arranged for his judicial murder.

What this tells us is that not even the surrender to idolatry—against which Elijah has been conducting a war whose zealotry could hardly be exceeded—is more heinous in his eyes, which (since he is a prophet) are the eyes of God, than the *moral* crime Ahab and Jezebel have committed against Naboth. It is, incidentally, a compound crime, in that—as Ahab must or should have known—it would have been a sin for Naboth to accept the king's original and seemingly

---

*So Son's paraphrase of the great medieval Jewish exegete Rashi.

reasonable offer to exchange the vineyard either for a better one or for money ("And Naboth said unto Ahab, the LORD forbid it me, that I should give the inheritance of my fathers unto thee").

In short, Amos is not—as many have imagined—the revolutionary harbinger of a new and higher stage of religion in which morality takes precedence over ritual.

NOR CAN AMOS without distortion or selective quotation be represented as the first biblical figure who grasps the inner meaning of monotheism, freeing it from the shackles of "tribalism" or "particularism" and carrying it to its logical conclusion in a "universalistic" conception of God not as the God of Israel but as the God of all peoples.

Some who have represented Amos in this manner contend that, before the classical prophets came along, the people of Israel did not actually believe in, or at least understand, the monotheism for whose discovery they have been given credit. I am not thinking here of those scholars who have devoted themselves to robbing the Hebrew Bible of this credit by searching for earlier evidence of monotheism in every piece of pottery or every bit of parchment archaeologists have dug up from the cultures of the ancient Near East. Nor am I focusing on the veritable glee with which in certain quarters it was declared, after the discovery in 1901 of the Code of Hammurabi (who ruled over Babylonia in the eighteenth century B.C.E., or about five hundred years before Moses), that it exposed even the Ten Commandments as an unoriginal contribution. So far as that order of issues goes, Yehezkel Kaufmann, the great historian of the religion of Israel, has persuasively shown that the ancient Israelites were not primitive nomads but members of a high civilization of their own surrounded by other high civilizations from which they borrowed bits and pieces that they then forged into something entirely new.

What I do have in mind is the related but distinct argument that the correct term for describing the religion of the ancient Israelites is not monotheism but "monolatry." Monolatry is defined as an intermediate phase between paganism, with its many gods, and monotheism with its one God. Under the aegis of monolatry, a single God is worshiped, but the existence of other gods is acknowledged.

But were the children of Israel who lived before the advent of the classical prophets monolatrous in some such sense rather than monotheistic? Not according to Kaufmann, who, on this matter, too, makes a strong case for the very early emergence of monotheism in Israel, not only among the elites but also among the people at large. As it would be going too far afield to reproduce his argument, I will do no more than state my emphatic agreement with it. But in any event, the main issue as it bears on Amos, and the classical prophets who follow

him, can be condensed into the contention of the monolatry party that the God
we encounter in the Hebrew Bible before they come along is exclusively the
God of Israel. Which is to say that He is a tribal deity named YHVH.

I passed hastily in the Introduction over this jaw-breaker, where I explained
that it is the English transliteration of the Hebrew letters *yod, hay, vav, hay*. Now
that the older transliteration, "Jehovah," has all but disappeared, "Yahweh" has
become the most fashionable substitute. I also proposed in the Introduction to
avoid both YHVH or Yahweh in referring to God (except when quoting others)—and precisely because it makes Him sound too much like a tribal deity.

In the present context, I would expand on the same point by adding that the
name YHVH or Yahweh seems to me almost inescapably to carry with it an
implication of monolatry. I hasten to admit that there are plenty of scholars who
do not regard early Israel as monolatrous but still go with YHVH or Yahweh in
their translations and commentaries. In part (I would guess) the reason is that the
name has an appropriately primordial ring to it. But the more important reason
may be that they feel obliged to differentiate between the strands of the Hebrew
Bible that the "Newer Documentary Thesis" identifies with the redactor who
called God *Elohim* and the one who called Him *YHVH*.*

Without denying the general validity of the Documentary Thesis, however, I
would still insist that in the Hebrew Bible, the God of Israel is never envisaged as
a tribal god among other gods. Andersen and Freedman:

> The tradition that Yahweh was the Creator and Lord of Heaven and
> earth (i.e., of everything) was not a new insight of Amos himself or a
> new development of his time; it was an ancient and essential ingredient
> of the faith of Moses, and certainly from that time on.

But I would trace this tradition back to an even earlier time. From the first
verse of Genesis to the last verse of the Second Book of Chronicles—that is,
throughout the whole of the Hebrew Bible—God is the one true God, the creator of heaven and earth and the ruler of all the creatures inhabiting them. That,
out of an inscrutable love, He chooses the people of Israel to be His own and to
make an everlasting covenant with them, does not imply that they possess any
special merit or greatness. On the contrary, it throws upon their shoulders the
burden (against which they are always rebelling) of being " . . . a kingdom of
priests, and an holy nation . . ." charged with the special responsibility of upholding the laws of God—moral, ritual, civil—in all their manifold specificities.

---

*It is usually "Yahweh" rather than "Yahveh" for the same reason the Documentary Thesis uses
"J" rather than "Y"—because "w" in German, the language in which this thesis was first developed and adumbrated, is pronounced as "v."

Nor does His covenant with Israel entail God's indifference to the moral behavior of other peoples. What the rabbis of the Talmud in later centuries will isolate as the seven laws of Noah (prohibitions against murder, robbery, adultery, etc.) are applied, albeit in non-codified form, to all the peoples who live before Abraham and his progeny. No less than the children of Israel, they too are made " . . . in the image of God. . . ." Hence, as Israel is punished by God when it sins against His laws, so are the other peoples punished for violating the (far fewer) laws incumbent upon them.

The distinction is that whereas God has taken it upon Himself never totally to abandon Israel no matter how severely He may make them suffer, He has entered into no such covenant with the idolaters. Meanwhile, these idolaters practice their abominations and remain a snare and a delusion to Israel itself. But—as several of the classical prophets make entirely explicit in their visions of the End of Days—the time will come when they will learn better, and all will worship the God of Israel as the only true God.

RETURNING NOW TO AMOS in the light of this ancient picture into whose frame he steps in the middle of the eighth century B.C.E., we can perceive how harmoniously it fits him and he it. It becomes clear, first of all, that—again contrary to much received opinion—nothing radically new can be inferred from the order in which he places the denunciatory prophecies that he pronounces in the first chapter. There is, however, an element of surprise in the construction of this chapter.

After the "superscription" written by an editor who introduces "The words of Amos, who was among the herdsmen of Tekoa, which he saw concerning Israel in the days of Uzziah king of Judah, and in the days of Jeroboam the son of Joash king of Israel . . . ," the prophet's "words" are what we naturally anticipate hearing. And our expectation is heightened by the first of them that we do hear: " . . . The LORD will roar from Zion, and utter his voice from Jerusalem; and the habitations of the shepherds shall mourn, and the top of Carmel shall wither."

But—and here is the surprise—before he even gets around to Judah (symbolized by Zion and Jerusalem) and Israel (epitomized in Mount Carmel), Amos dwells first on a number of neighboring pagan peoples. They have been or still are enemies of his own people, and yet he mainly castigates them *not* for what they have done to the children of Israel but for their dealings with one another. These include atrocities like the excessive cruelty in war (" . . . because they have threshed Gilead with threshing instruments of iron"); treachery (" . . . because he did pursue his brother with the sword, and did cast off all pity, and his anger did tear perpetually, and he kept his wrath for ever"); inhuman brutality (" . . . because they have ripped up the women with child of

Gilead . . ."); and the like. For doing such things, their cities will be burned
down and their palace will be devoured.

A modern Christian student of the prophets (R. F. Horton), commenting on
one of these sections, writes:

> It is very characteristic of Amos that the punishment falls on Moab, not
> for his endless inroads and devastations of Israel, but for a deed of impi-
> ety . . . against a king of Edom, Israel's foe. Nothing could better show
> the ethical and theological impartiality of the prophetic word in Amos.

But what the prophet is implying when he starts with the non-Israelites before
turning to his own people is that, bad as the surrounding nations are, the children of Israel—both North and South—are worse *precisely* because they were
chosen by Him to obey His law and His commandments and have failed to
do so.

> Hear this word that the LORD hath spoken against you, O children of
> Israel, against the whole family which I brought up from the land of
> Egypt, saying, You only have I known of all the families of the earth:
> therefore I will punish you for all your iniquities.

Yet is this not contradicted when God later asks: "Are ye not as children of
the Ethiopians unto me, O children of Israel? . . . ," and when he then adds that
just as He " . . . brought up Israel out of the land of Egypt . . . ," so He did " . . .
the Philistines from Caphtor, and the Syrians from Kir"?

For many commentators, both Jewish and Christian, these statements
amount—as the Roman Catholic Jerusalem Bible puts it in the heading of its
translation of them—to this: "No special privileges for Israel." The New Jewish
Publication Society translation shows that it too accepts the same interpretation:
"To Me, O Israelites, you are/Just like the Ethiopians/—declares the
LORD./True, I brought Israel up/ From the land of Egypt,/ But also the
Philistines from Caphtor/And the Arameans from Kir."

But another interpretation is possible. Quoting the exegete A. B. Ehrlich—
who reads the clause as "Do you not behave toward me as do the children of the
Ethiopians?"—the Soncino edition continues:

> The point of the comparison is to be found in the question [posed by
> the prophet Jeremiah], "Can the Ethiopian change his skin, or the leop-
> ard his spots?," from which it is seen that the "Ethiopian" was used by
> the prophets to indicate an unchangeable type. Amos asserts that the
> people of Israel are fixed in their evil ways and will not reform.

This interpretation is more consonant with the point of view of the Hebrew Bible that I believe Amos neither departs from nor transcends, and it is also more in line with the Book of Amos itself.

As for the second clause drawing a parallel among the Israelites, Philistines, and Syrians, the implication here cannot conceivably be to equate the three in the eyes of God. This would fly in the face of every other word in the Hebrew Bible, besides cavalierly nullifying the covenant that God has made with Israel. Yet He has already reaffirmed that covenant through Amos once before in speaking of " . . . the remnant of Joseph" that will survive the impending devastation, and He will do so again in the very next verse after the clause about bringing up the Philistines and the Syrians: "Behold, the eyes of the LORD God are upon the sinful kingdom, and I will destroy it from off the face of the earth; *saving that I will not utterly destroy the house of Jacob, saith the LORD.*"* Even so— even though a remnant of "the house of Jacob" will always remain—what the reference to the Philistines and the Syrians does is instruct Israel that the covenant is not one-sided, and that it cannot be relied upon to release the human party from keeping the divine laws and commandments.

THE PEOPLE OF the Northern Kingdom—but also of Judah—having complacently shown by their behavior that they need such instruction, Amos lets them have it with all the stops pulled out. God, who brought them up out of Egypt, has already stricken them with one of the plagues that forced Pharaoh to free them then ("I have sent among you the pestilence after the manner of Egypt . . ."). Thus, having afflicted the Egyptians with plagues on Israel's behalf, God is now giving the sinful children of Israel themselves a taste of the same medicine.

Yet not even this has caused them to mend their evil ways. Nor have they been chastened by the other disasters—such as famine, drought, and defeat in war—that have befallen them in the past. They are "at ease in Zion" now that life has become luxurious for them thanks to the prosperity brought by Jeroboam's military and economic successes, and then swollen by their own unscrupulous squeezing of the poor. In this condition, they are in no doubt that they will be protected by God so long as they pay the proper ritual obeisances to Him; and this is why they are beyond saving:

> The virgin of Israel is fallen; she shall rise no more; she is forsaken upon her land; there is none to raise her up. . . . Therefore the LORD, the God of hosts, the LORD, saith thus; Wailing shall be in all streets; and they

*The italics are of course mine.

shall say in all the highways, Alas! alas! and they shall call the husbandman to mourning, and such as are skilful of lamentation to wailing. And
in all vineyards shall be wailing: for I will pass through thee, saith the
LORD.

Again, He will do *to* the children of Israel what he did *for* them in Egypt when
they were slaves there, and when He Himself " . . . pass[ed] through to smite the
Egyptians. . . ."

And there is yet another daring reversal in Amos. Previously, the "Day of the
LORD" has popularly been imagined as a time of joy when God will finally dis-
patch His people's enemies, but Amos dramatically turns the tables in his invoca-
tion of this concept:

Woe unto you that desire the day of the LORD! to what end is it for
you? the day of the LORD is darkness, and not light. As if a man did
flee from a lion, and a bear met him; or went into the house, and
leaned his hand upon the wall, and a serpent bit him. Shall not the day
of the LORD be darkness and not light? even very dark, and no
brightness in it?

Descriptions pile up of the fate that is in store for the Northern Kingdom,
and first of all the greatest of its sinners—the wives of the rich, those " . . . kine
of Bashan . . ." who egg their husbands on in oppressing the poor so that they can
get even more than they already have, and who will themselves therefore be led
away like cows to the slaughter.

There is nothing in these descriptions as grisly as the images in Leviticus and
Deuteronomy of starving parents eating their own children, of mothers devouring the afterbirth streaming down their legs, and of people gnawing on their
own flesh. But there is one verse that approaches them in horror:

Thus saith the LORD; As the shepherd taketh out of the mouth of the
lion two legs, or a piece of an ear; so shall the children of Israel be taken
out that dwell in Samaria in the corner of a bed, and in Damascus in a
couch.*

Yet even leaving this verse aside, Amos's visions of doom are frightening
enough. There will be no escaping that doom. Neither swiftness of foot nor the

---

*There is a textual problem here that other translators and exegetes have plausibly solved by
interpreting "Damascus" as standing for luxurious fabrics and furniture that the rich have
imported from Syria.

courage of the soldier nor ingenuity of concealment will avail. No matter where the Israelites try to flee, God will seek them out and cut them down:

> Though they dig into hell, thence shall mine hand take them; though they climb up to heaven, thence will I bring them down: And though they hide themselves in the top of Carmel, I will search and take them out thence; and though they be hid from my sight in the bottom of the sea, thence will I command the serpent, and he shall bite them: And though they go into captivity before their enemies, thence will I command the sword, and it shall slay them. . . .*

But in a sense, the worst—and probably the most original—of the punishments decreed by God through Amos is spiritual rather than physical:

> Behold, the days come, saith the LORD God, that I will send a famine in the land, not a famine of bread, nor a thirst for water, but of hearing the words of the LORD; And they shall wander from sea to sea, and from the north even to the east, they shall run to and fro to seek the word of the LORD, and shall not find it.

All these visions of physical and spiritual human calamity are encompassed and multiplied by images of natural destruction—earthquake, flood, fire, famine, even the blotting out of the noontime sun—that in themselves evoke the inescapability of the fate awaiting the Israelites. Expressed in language that is dense, compact, and vivid, the visions cascade down upon us with the relentless force of a malignant cataract. And yet they are not permitted to have the last word. In a startlingly sudden shift that is effected without any transition at all, the book ends with a gorgeous oracle of hope for the future.

Never mind that critical scholars generally agree that this passage, as well as the two earlier statements that a remnant of the children of Israel will always survive any general national devastation, are later additions, tacked on after the Assyrian conquest of the North and the deportation of the "Ten Lost Tribes." Reading the book as it has come down to us, we are left with the promise that in the future everything that has been destroyed will be rebuilt and that the exiled people of the North will return for good to an idyllically abundant and peaceful land.

---

*It is misleading to translate the Hebrew word *sheol* as "hell," since there is nothing comparable in the Hebrew Bible to what that concept signifies. NRSV, NJPS, and JB all wisely refrain from even trying to find an English equivalent and simply use the word *sheol* itself. Son has "netherworld," while correctly pointing out that "Sheol was to the Hebrews the abode of the dead. Believed to be located in the depths of the earth, it is a simile for inaccessibility."

These sumptuously lyrical verses—which fall upon our ears with something of the same effect made by the last movement of Beethoven's Sixth Symphony, entitled by the composer "glad and grateful feelings after the storm"—may or may not have issued from the mouth and the mind and the imagination of Amos. But if not, whoever composed them was in my opinion a literary artist worthy of Amos himself:

> In that day will I raise up the tabernacle of David that is fallen, . . . and I will raise up his ruins, and I will build it as in the days of old. . . . Behold, the days come, saith the LORD, that the plowman shall overtake the reaper, and the treader of grapes him that soweth seed; and the mountains shall drop sweet wine, and all the hills shall melt. And I will bring again the captivity of my people of Israel, that they shall build the waste cities, and inhabit them; and they shall plant vineyards, and drink the wine thereof; they shall also make gardens, and eat the fruit of them. And I will plant them upon their land, and they shall no more be pulled up out of their land which I have given them, saith the LORD thy God.*

UNFORTUNATELY, there is no scene in this book (such as there is in Isaiah, Jeremiah, and Ezekiel) telling us in detail how Amos becomes a prophet. But from the little he reveals we can infer that, like Moses before and Jeremiah after him, he is reluctant to become the spokesman of God: "The lion hath roared, who will not fear? the LORD God hath spoken, who can but prophesy?" The image of the lion unavoidably suggests a degree of coercion. And when Amos denies to the priest Amaziah that he is either a prophet or the son of a prophet, he may well be asserting not only that he is not a professional and that he makes his living by other means; he may also be saying that God has forced him into this way of life: "And the LORD took me as I followed the flock, and the LORD said unto me, Go, prophesy unto my people Israel."

In carrying out this command, Amos, as the first prophet whose oracles were collected together into a book bearing his name, set so high a literary standard that we might have doubted it could ever be reached again if we did not know that it would be matched over and over—and sometimes surpassed—by other prophets even then waiting in the wings. I believe it would be a great mistake to ignore this factor or relegate it entirely to the realm of aesthetics rather than religion, since one answer to the intriguing question posed by Andersen and Freedman, "Why is there a book of Amos but not a book of Elijah?," must be literary. Because Amos was a

---

*"Melt" (which is the literal meaning of the Hebrew *titmogagnah*) is rendered as "flow with it [i.e., wine]" by NRSV and JB. But NJPS has "wave [with grain]."

greater orator than any of the Former Prophets who preceded him, he collected an audience of listeners on whom he made so huge an impact that they could not bear the thought of losing his words and hence wrote them down on some sort of scroll and/or memorized them for subsequent transcription.

Or was it that Amos did this himself—that he was not only an orator but a *writer*? No one can say for certain. But there are scholars who entertain the hypothesis that the sections of the book deemed "authentic" or "original" may well have come from Amos's own hand. Part of their case is built on the general rejection of the old assumption that Amos was a simple peasant. Under that assumption, it was further snobbishly supposed that no ordinary "rustic" could have been as knowledgeable about the affairs of the world and as culturally sophisticated as the author of this book had to have been. (This is rather like the argument that Shakespeare—who, as Ben Jonson, his reverential but much better educated contemporary, marveled, had "small Latin, and less Greek"—could never have written the plays attributed to him.) But with modern scholarship having come around to what the rabbis of the Talmud always held about Amos, almost everyone nowadays thinks, as those rabbis did, that he was no peasant but rather a wealthy farmer or rancher. The current consensus—also tinged with snobbery—is that, as a rich man, his mind and sensibility were no less cultivated than his property, and that he could easily have done his own writing.

If so—if, that is, Amos really was a "writing" prophet—that would represent a genuine break with the biblical past, as opposed to the two much more wide-spread notions that he was a revolutionary who rejected ritual entirely in favor of morality and that he was also the first true monotheist in the history of ancient Israel, or at least the exponent of a purer form of it than existed before.

Besides the evidence I myself have mustered on these latter points, a number of scholars have argued that no man of Amos's time could possibly have imagined religious worship and devotion that did not include the offering of sacrifice. It is even less conceivable that a believer in the God of Israel could call for abolishing the observance of other ritual commandments, such as the Sabbath and the festivals. No more than Amos is a Christian *avant la lettre* is he an early member of the Society for Ethical Culture or (as his attacks on the oppression of the poor by the rich have led some to imagine) the founding father of socialism.

Indeed, it is only because Amos takes the sanctity of the rituals for granted that he can permit himself to sound as though God has sent him to call for their abolition. Being familiar with "the material that eventually found its way into the Pentateuch," Amos knows that no neat division—or rather no division at all—can be drawn in the religion of Israel between the moral and ritual spheres. To repeat: the commandments governing each are set down in the Books of Exodus and Leviticus with so little distinction of importance or priority made among them that often they are all mixed up together (as they are in his own catalogue of the sins of the Northern Kingdom).

Thus, it does not occur to Amos that the contemptuous attack he is launching on the religious devotions of the people will fall on their ears as anything other than a violent reminder of what they have forgotten and desperately need to remember: that the moral dimension of their faith is inseparable from the ritual.

But what about the rhetorical question: "Have ye offered unto me sacrifices and offerings in the wilderness forty years, O house of Israel?" This strongly seems to suggest that sacrifices are unnecessary and that, in the earliest phase of Israel's relations with God, there was no such intermediary approach to Him. Yet I wonder how much more there is in such a suggestion than the device of conjuring up a mythical Golden Age of the past with which to beat up on the present.

Moreover, as Yehezkel Kaufmann correctly asserts, "in order to take this verse at face value," one must assume that Amos is ignorant of the numerous references in the Book of Exodus to sacrifice—an assumption contradicted by internal evidence. Kaufmann's interpretation is that "Amos wishes to contrast the present multitude of offerings that the people daily 'give' to God and by which they set great store, with the age of the Wandering. . . . Yet that age, when they were unable to make daily offerings to him," because, living exclusively on mannah, they had nothing to give, "was the time of favor and grace! Amos does not fundamentally depart from tradition even here."

Nor would he be departing from tradition if Andersen and Freedman are right in their reading of what he is saying about sacrifice—that "the temples are so corrupt that it is better to stay away entirely and have nothing to do with sacrifice at all than to join worship of that kind"—the kind that is run and supported by religious and political officials who "swear by false gods," who are "apostates and idolators in irreconcilable conflict with their true God."

I DO NOT WISH to be understood as asserting that, apart from having perhaps been a writer as well as an orator, Amos brings nothing new at all into the religion of Israel. But if not in an abolitionist position on the cult and the concomitant elevation of monotheism to a new level, where do we find the truly novel element in Amos?

In the opinion of Kaufmann, it lies in the fact that no one before Amos has ever tied the fate of the *entire nation* to its "everyday moral sins." This is true, though Kaufmann is a bit (in one of his own favorite words) "hyperbolic" when he writes that "what underscores the novelty of this evaluation is Amos's almost complete silence regarding idolatry, the chief offense which the early literature held crucial for the destiny of the people."

The qualifier "almost" gives the game away, since Amos does in fact tie the "everyday moral sins" of the rich Israelites directly to idolatry and to an idolatrous frame of mind. We can even refute Kaufmann's argument that Amos does not share the earlier idea that only idolatry (as opposed to moral sin) threatens "national doom and exile" by glancing again at how the prophet himself expands upon his allusion to the absence of sacrifice in the desert:

> But ye have borne the tabernacle of your Moloch and Chiun your images, the star of your god, which ye made to yourselves. *Therefore* will I cause you to go into captivity beyond Damascus, saith the LORD, whose name is The God of hosts.*

It would seem that Kaufmann is once more being "hyperbolic" when he dismisses these verses—which are explicit, emphatic, and forceful—as "almost incidental." What becomes unmistakable through them is that concentrating most of his attention on the issue of morality is not for Amos tantamount to a resignation from the war against idolatry. He is, rather, adumbrating one of the major purposes for which God has chosen the prophets to wage this war.

While there can be no question that Amos stresses the oppression of the poor by the rich over any of their other sins, there can also be no question that he traces their behavior to idolatry. They use *legitimate* ritual as a loophole and a cover, but it is their obeisance to alien gods that is the ultimate cause of their wicked ways.

This theme runs like an undercurrent throughout the whole book, surfacing here and there with varying degrees of clarity. The most obvious instance, perhaps, is the verse in which God says that " . . . a man and his father will go in unto the same maid, to profane my holy name"—an allusion, as everyone agrees, to the pagan practice of sacred prostitution. And as further evidence that Amos makes no firm distinction between social injustice and ritual sin, it is worth recalling that these words about the resort to sacred prostitution comprise the second half of a verse that begins with a condemnation of the rich who " . . . pant after the dust on the earth at the head of the poor, and turn aside the head of the meek. . . ." Similarly with the next verse: "And they lay themselves down upon clothes laid to pledge by every altar, and they drink the wine of the condemned in the house of their god." Here Amos takes a practice prohibited, as I have previously observed, in the Book of Exodus and puts it together with ritual sexual intercourse in a pagan shrine.

But the link Amos forges between idolatry and the life led by the rich of the North often emerges more subtly. Take those "That lie upon beds of ivory, and stretch themselves upon their couches . . ."—an image that can be (and has often been) understood as a picture of the erotic licentiousness fostered by idolatry. I would further propose that the same thematic undercurrent breaks through the surface when, after contemptuously characterizing the married women in the mountains of Samaria as "kine [cows] of Bashan" who egg their husbands on to

---

*The italics are mine.

bring them more and more wine, Amos proceeds to lament the fall of "The virgin of Israel." Given the proximity of the two images, we are irresistibly drawn into foreseeing the fallen virgins being transformed into just such a herd of matrons, or even sacred prostitutes, whose drunken revels are a prelude to the venery encouraged by obeisance to Baal.

In banging away at the same point, Amos's near contemporary Hosea will, in his characteristic fashion, be more open and more explicit. He will rave against " . . . the children of Israel who look to other gods, and love flagons of wine"; he will juxtapose " . . . whoredom and wine and new wine . . ." with the consultation of idols; and at one moment, going all the way, he will declare: "Ephraim* is joined to idols. . . . When their drinking is ended, they indulge in sexual orgies."†

Amos makes the same association of wine with lechery and idolatry in his more veiled attack on the "kine of Bashan." But there is nothing veiled or subtle at all when he draws a parallel between the Northern Kingdom and Sodom and Gomorrah, which were of course destroyed by God for their pagan sexual abominations.

ONE EMINENT SCHOLAR, Joseph Blenkinsopp, calls Amos a "dissident intellectual." But I would opt for the coinage of the historian Robert M. Seltzer, to whom Amos is a "conservative radical." The two sides—the conservatism and the radicalism—are captured by a nuanced and complex analysis in which Kaufmann brilliantly improves on some of his hyperbolic formulations:

> [T]he opinion that Amos unconditionally rejected the cult, especially the cult of sacrifice . . . is quite out of the question. . . . [But] the new stress on morality has as its concomitant a new attitude toward the cult. . . . The absolute and autonomous value that paganism placed on the cult . . . vanished. God is in no way dependent on the cult of men; on the contrary, the cult is a manifestation of his grace to man. Its purpose is to serve as a symbol and expression of the "knowledge of God," a memorial to his covenant. Hence its value is conditional, not absolute.

---

*Ephraim is usually a synonym for the Northern Kingdom of Israel (as is Joseph in Amos). But since Hosea sometimes seems to distinguish between the two, evidently restricting the former to the hill country of the North, scholars have speculated that at some point during the late eighth century B.C.E., but before the fall of the entire kingdom, it was partly conquered and divided into two.

†This is NRSV's translation of a verse that completely baffled KJV. JB is equally forthright: "Ephraim is wedded to idols,/They sprawl in the company of drunkards;/ whoring is all they care about." NJPS is a little prissier: "They drink to excess—/Their liquor turns against them,/They 'love' beyond measure."

And Kaufmann continues:

> Morality, on the other hand, is an absolute value, for it is divine in essence. . . . Moral goodness makes man share, as it were, in the divine nature . . . ; both cult and morality are God's command and part of his covenant, and both are expressions of the "knowledge of God." But while cult is sacred only as a symbol, morality is essentially godlike, being a reflection of the qualities of God.

I think the only thing wrong with this characterization is that it still goes a bit too far in insisting upon a greater—and more invidious—distinction between morality and ritual than is warranted by the ideas of Amos and the classical prophetic tradition he inaugurates.

Reverting now to Kaufmann's general point of view toward the religion of ancient Israel, and applying it more consistently to Amos than he himself sometimes does, I also think that, far from transforming "monolatry" into monotheism or elevating a primitive monotheism to a higher stage of development, this first of the classical prophets is indeed trailing clouds of ancestral glory. By this I mean that he is carrying forward the work of the Former Prophets and their even older predecessors by fighting a more insidious form of the idolatry that always seems to creep into and undermine the revolutionary new faith of the children of Israel. His prophetic predecessors did it with the sword or through miracles; Amos does it with words.

Which is yet another reason that the greatness of Amos as a literary artist—like that of the classical prophets who will follow in his wake over the next three hundred years—cannot be relegated entirely to the realm of aesthetics. Their literary power must be reckoned as in itself a major factor, first in the establishment, and then in the maintenance, of their enormous religious influence over the minds and souls of so many people in so many places and over so long a period of time.*

---

*Perhaps the most audacious statement of the importance of the literary power of the classical prophets is the description in the 1790s C. E. by the great Romantic English poet William Blake in "The Marriage of Heaven and Hell" of a "memorable fancy" that came to him of having dinner with Isaiah and Ezekiel: "Then Ezekiel said: 'The philosophy of the east taught the first principles of human perception: some nations held one principle for the origin & some for another: we of Israel that the Poetic Genius (as you now call it) was the first principle, and all the others merely derivative . . . that all Gods would at last be proved to originate in ours & to be the tributaries of the Poetic Genius . . . and we so loved our God, that we cursed in his name all the deities of surrounding nations . . . : from these opinions the vulgar came to think that all nations would at last be subject to the jews [sic]. This,' said he, ' . . . is come to pass; for all nations believe the jews' code and worship the jews' god. . . .' I heard this with some wonder, & must confess my own conviction."

CHAPTER SEVEN

HOSEA AND THE WHORE

HERE IS NO RECORD of what ultimately became of Amos. It may be that he was simply expelled from the Northern Kingdom, returned home to his flocks and his sycamores, and—with his mission completed—spent the rest of his life in Judah without again being compelled by God to prophesy.

But it is just as easy, or easier, to picture his being arrested and then executed in the North for predicting (mistakenly) that King Jeroboam II would fall by the sword. This prediction, reported to the king by the priest Amaziah not as a prophetic oracle but as a piece of seditious advocacy, might well have led to Amos's execution. Certainly, he would have been lucky to get off with nothing more severe than expulsion after his savage riposte to Amaziah's order that he leave Israel and go back to Judah and do his prophesying there. Here is how he responded to Amaziah:

> Now therefore hear the word of the LORD: Thou sayest, Prophesy not against Israel. . . . Therefore thus saith the LORD; Thy wife shall be an harlot in the city, and thy sons and thy daughters shall fall by the sword, and thy land shall be divided by line; and thou shalt die in a polluted land: and Israel shall surely go into captivity forth of his land.

But just when or shortly after Amos was forced by one means or another into silence, a new prophet arrived to take his place. As it was given to Amos to resume the war against idolatry after the long hiatus that set in with the death of Elisha, the task of heating up the war was now handed to the second of the classical prophets. He was an Israelite, and hence a local rather than an intruder from Judah, and he seems to have been active in the 740s B.C.E. His name was Hosea the son of Beeri.

Or was it? Not according to an influential school of thought among students of the Book of Hosea. Even though its first verse (the "superscription") sets him historically in the mid-to-late eighth century B.C.E., this group of scholars argues that Hosea the son of Beeri actually lived about a hundred years earlier, probably during the reign of Ahab and Jezebel, and that only the first three of the fourteen chapters of the book bearing his name are by and about him. The remaining eleven chapters (4–14)—minus a few later editorial interpolations and plus a host of emendations of a supposedly corrupt text—are, these scholars maintain, made up of the oracles of some other prophet whose name has never been uncovered. To his proponents, this other prophet is "Deutero-Hosea" or "Hosea B," and it is his oracles they place in the eighth century B.C.E. along with, but a little later than, those of Amos.

Yet unlike the positing of a Deutero- or Second Isaiah and a Deutero-Zechariah, with which by now almost no one disagrees (though, as we shall see, not everyone accepts the further wrinkle that there is a Third, or "Trito"-Isaiah, or even many more Isaiahs than that), this splitting of Hosea into two has failed to command universal assent. The latest trend even seems to be moving in the other direction, toward the view that the bifurcation of the Book of Hosea rests on insufficient evidence and ultimately unconvincing arguments.

This is another of those disputes that will not be settled until the End of Days, if then, involving as they all do highly technical linguistic and historical questions. Indeed, it is less of a strain to imagine a realization of the eschatological vision of the lion lying down with the lamb that we will encounter in the Book of Isaiah than to picture the contentious specialists in the field of critical biblical scholarship ever surrendering their hard-won theoretical lucubrations. I will therefore skip over the debate, and merely report that, from my own repeated readings of this very difficult text,* and from having reviewed the cases made by the two sides, I wind up casting my lot with the one-Hosea party.

More than anything else, what has pushed me into this position is a strong disagreement with the main *non*-technical factor in the two-Hoseas thesis (a factor I will identify in a minute, and that I suspect is the true driving force behind much of the incredibly erudite and often convoluted fiddling by translators and commentators with an already convoluted text).

It must be stipulated that such translators and commentators have a more complex understanding of the classical prophets than the various groups we have encountered who think that, beginning with Amos, a sharp break with the past

---

*"The text of Hosea," write Francis L. Andersen and David Noel Freedman in their edition of it, "competes with Job for the distinction of containing more unintelligible passages than any other book of the Hebrew Bible" (*The Anchor Bible Hosea*, p. 66). Andersen and Freedman are two of the leading proponents of the one-Hosea theory. Yehezkel Kaufmann and H. L. Ginsberg are among the most eminent of their opponents.

occurs, ushering the religion of Israel into a new and higher phase of its development. Specialists in modern critical biblical studies know very well—how as experts in the history of ancient Israel could they not?—that there is a much greater degree of continuity between the classical prophets and the religion they inherit than the interested parties I discussed earlier have stubbornly gone on insisting. They also recognize that the fury of these prophets—in which William Blake heard "the voice of honest indignation" raised to the level of genius—is squarely aimed at the religious and political conditions prevailing in their own times rather than at the traditional faith of the children of Israel (or "Yahwism," as most scholars persist in calling it).

Nevertheless—and here we arrive at the non-technical factor I mentioned a minute ago—not even these specialists are immune to the conventional conception that locates the distinguishing mark of the classical prophets in their alleged belief that morality is more important than ritual. Where Hosea is concerned, this idea is buttressed by the book's famous verse: "For I desired mercy, and not sacrifice; and the knowledge of God more than burnt offerings."* Yet in reading such specialists, one can sometimes sense the intellectual struggles they undergo in tortuously trying to salvage as large a dose of this tenacious conception as they can from their own better knowledge.

In the preceding chapter, I examined an example of those struggles in the passing flashes of inconsistency and incoherence that mar an otherwise illuminating and logically stringent analysis of Amos by Yehezkel Kaufmann. And the same is true of Kaufmann's reading of Hosea. Even this great opponent of the evolutionist scheme of Israelite religion, this great champion of the view that true monotheism was there, among both the elites and the people at large, at least from the time of Moses, concludes that the first three chapters of Hosea must be "a product of pre-classical prophecy." Why? Because

> The chastisements of chapters 1–3 follow early motifs . . . , idolatry alone is the cause of doom. The prophecy of restoration follows the pattern of the ancient promises of peace and prosperity. *There is no universal ideal.* A new idea appears in the concept of eschatological repentance. . . . The faithless nation will realize its error and return to God; then God will renew his relations with the people. But the idea is expressed most naively; the motive seems to be longing for material blessing, *and the repentance is cultic only.* [italics added]

---

*All the modern translations put this verse in the present tense, not the past. But in place of KJV's "mercy" (for the Hebrew *khesed*) we get "steadfast love" from NRSV, "love" from JB, and "goodness" from NJPS. Also NJPS substitutes "obedience to God" for "knowledge of God" (though the Hebrew does in fact say "knowledge"—*da'at*).

So, too, H. L. Ginsberg, who bases more of his brief for the existence of two Hoseas on philological and historical details than Kaufmann does, but who hacks his way through these thickets to the same conclusion on the same grounds:

> His [the first Hosea's] message is, in effect, pre-classical. There is nothing here of the great innovation of the eighth-century prophets: the primacy of the ethical law and the doctrine that ethical sins no less than ritual and cultic ones may bring about the very destruction of the nation. Hosea son of Beeri has only one theme: Israel has broken faith with YHWH and embraced idolatry: consequently YHWH denounces his covenant with Israel; but YHWH will reduce Israel to destitution, and it will come to its senses; then YHWH will restore Israel to grace.

To Ginsberg, thus, the "primacy of the ethical law" is the key signature of the eighth-century prophets. But then—in another example of the struggle I am pointing to—his profound scholarship gets the better of him, and he cannot in all honesty help adding that the destruction of the nation can be caused by "ethical sins *no less* than ritual or cultic ones" (my italics). He thereby takes away with one clause what he gives with the other—the primacy of ethical over ritual sins—and leaves them hanging there as *equally* serious in the eyes of the eighth-century prophets.

Which is exactly how they are regarded, in the last eleven chapters of the book as well as in the first three. The point of view of those latter chapters exhibits no radical contrast with the earlier—and most especially when it comes to idolatry. Why then divide the book into two?

AS TO THE FIRST THREE CHAPTERS, in them we are told about Hosea's marriage to a whore named Gomer, whom God commands him to take for his wife. Is this shocking and extraordinary story fact, or parable, or just a mere vision that never was acted out? Each of these three interpretations has had its advocates, but I myself read the story as fact transmuted into parable. That is, Hosea really does marry Gomer, and his marriage then becomes an allegory.

If that is correct, it would not in the least be unusual. Other prophets we will be meeting later on will also perform certain acts both in their public and private lives intended to dramatize the messages they are delivering from God. Yet however bizarre these may appear—and even though they will sometimes earn the prophets who perform them a reputation as madmen—they all grow pale when set beside what God orders Hosea to do in the first chapter of this book:

The beginning of the word of the LORD by Hosea. And the LORD said to Hosea, Go, take unto thee a wife of whoredoms and children of whoredoms: for the land hath committed great whoredom, departing from the LORD. So he went and took Gomer the daughter of Diblaim. . . .*

In quick succession, Gomer presents Hosea with a boy, then a girl, and then another boy. Each of these babies, in accordance with God's instructions, is given a name that signifies an aspect of the fate lying in store for the Northern Kingdom—a fate that will turn out to be more complex than we are originally led to suppose.

Of the firstborn, " . . . the LORD said unto him, Call his name Jezreel. . . ." Jezreel (which literally means "God sows") was, we know, the place where Naboth's vineyard was located and where his murderess, Jezebel, was in turn murdered by Jehu (as Elijah had prophesied she would be). The assassin, having gone on to massacre everyone in sight associated with the Omride dynasty of her late husband Ahab, then seized the throne for himself. Now his great-great-grandson, Jeroboam II—the very king whose death by the sword Amos incorrectly predicted and for whom Hosea has no love either—still rules in the North.

The name of the first child born to Hosea by Gomer summons all this history up and, as God informs the prophet, points to the future doom of the dynasty founded by Jehu:

 . . . for yet a little while, and I will avenge the blood of Jezreel upon the house of Jehu, and will cause to cease the kingdom of the house of Israel. And it shall come to pass at that day, that I will break the bow of Israel in the valley of Jezreel.†

The second child is named Lo-rukhamah, again on God's orders, " . . . for I will no more have mercy upon the house of Israel; but I will utterly take them

---

*Here we go with the aforementioned difficulties in the text. On this verse and a half alone, there is a vast literature. To single out the main problem, it is with the Hebrew term *eshet z'nunim,* which KJV, choosing the literal path (also followed by NJPS), translates as "a wife of whoredoms," while JB simply has "whore," and Son "a wife of harlotry." All these seem acceptable, though AB's "promiscuity" is in my opinion more questionable.

†Another much-debated question onto which I do not intend to pile answers of my own is how we can explain why God has decided to "avenge the blood of Jezreel upon the house of Jehu" when He told Jehu that He approved of what he had done to the house of Ahab (2Kin 10:30). To be sure, the report of divine approval was followed by this verse: "But Jehu took no heed to walk in the law of the LORD God of Israel with all his heart: for he departed not from the sins of Jeroboam [the First], which made Israel to sin" (2Kin 10:31). On the other hand, it is not this but the massacre of Ahab and his entire family that God promises to avenge here.

away."* Finally, upon the birth of the third and last child, "Then said God, Call his name Lo-ammi: for ye are not my people, and I will not be your God."†

The details of Hosea's personal life, then, are so intertwined with the relations between God and the Northern Kingdom that there is simply no disentangling them. The prophet's marriage to Gomer is in part an enactment of, and in part a commentary on, the history of God's espousal of the people of Israel, so that the narrative keeps switching from one to the other, almost as though there were no distinction between them.

One of the endless controversies that this story has triggered is whether Gomer is already a whore when Hosea marries her, or whether she becomes one afterward. If, as I read the text, she already is a whore, this would imply that Amos's "virgin of Israel" had already "fallen" by the time God originally chose her. The idea seems not so far-fetched when we remind ourselves that Abraham himself, the founding father of the children of Israel, stemmed from a family of idol-worshipers before being introduced to the one true God.

But whenever she became one, Israel—and here the prophet is evidently talking about the Northern Kingdom and not the whole people—is undoubtedly a whore *now.* This is confirmed by God's explanation to Hosea of why he is to seek out and marry a whore himself—" . . . for the land hath committed great whoredom, departing from the LORD." In response to this adulterous behavior, God is preparing to be merciless. Not only will He cast her out; He will also arrange for her to be utterly destroyed: "I . . . will cause to cease the kingdom of the house of Israel."

NOW, HOWEVER, comes the first of the violently abrupt switches from repudiation to reconciliation that occur throughout Hosea. With nary a syllable of transition from His escalating threats of rejection, culminating in the declaration "I will not be your God," we are presented with this:

> Yet the number of the children of Israel shall be as the sand of the sea, which cannot be measured nor numbered; and it shall come to pass, that in the place where it was said unto them, Ye are not my people, there it shall be said unto them, Ye are the sons of the living God. Then shall the children of Judah and the children of Israel be gathered together, and appoint themselves one head, and they shall come up out of the land; for great shall be the day of Jezreel.

---

*Lo rukhamah has been variously translated as "Not-accepted" (NJPS), "Unloved" (JB), "Not pitied" (NRSV), and "the unpitied one" (Son).

†Lo-ammi means "Not my people."

Here everything is wonderfully reversed. In Jezreel—the very place selected by God for the defeat and destruction of Israel as envisaged in the living symbol of the name given to Hosea's first son—great things will happen instead. Far from being decimated, the whole house of Israel will grow too numerous to count,* and all will gather in Jezreel itself where the two monarchies will be reunited under one king (subsequently to be identified as a descendant of David rather than one of the many, mostly faithless, royal lines that have been coming and going in the Northern Kingdom). Hence mercy and love will descend upon the "Unpitied," and those who were "Not My People" will be transformed into " . . . the sons of the living God."

But no sooner has this blazing sun broken through the storm clouds than the sky darkens again, and the wrath of God with the Northern Kingdom, expressed through the direst of threats against Gomer, comes thundering back in full force. But again it is difficult to distinguish between, as it were, the public and the private—between the voice of God addressing the people of the North and the voice of Hosea, or that of God Himself, talking about Gomer who, now that her children are grown, has relapsed into (or never given up?) being a whore.

For instance, the firstborn son Jezreel is ordered (whether directly by God, or by Hosea, or by God speaking through Hosea, it is impossible to tell) to get his siblings to

> Plead with your mother, plead; for she is not my wife, neither am I her husband: let her therefore put away the whoredoms out of her sight, and her adulteries from between her breasts; Lest I strip her naked, and set her as the day that she was born. . . . And I will not have mercy upon her children; for they be the children of whoredoms. For their mother hath played the harlot: she that conceived them hath done shamefully: for she said, I will go after my lovers, that give me my bread and my water, my wool and my flax, mine oil and my drink.

In these verses there is little doubt that Gomer is the object, but as the details of her "whoredoms" come pouring out, she turns into a symbol of the Northern Kingdom:

> I will also cause all her mirth to cease, her feast days, her new moons, and her sabbaths, and all her solemn feasts. And I will destroy her vines

---

*Are we supposed to see in this vision a reaffirmation of the promise to Abraham: " . . . Look now toward heaven, and tell the stars, if thou be able to number them: and he [God] said unto him, so shall thy seed be" (Gen 15:5)? Such a reading would be consistent with Hosea's habit of dropping allusions to earlier biblical traditions or stories without spelling them out.

and her fig trees, whereof she hath said, These are my rewards that my
lovers have given me: and I will make them a forest, and the beasts of
the field shall eat them.

This said, it is back again to Gomer, but she now becomes *both* herself and
Israel: "And I will visit upon her the days of Baalim, wherein she burned incense
to them, and she decked herself with her earrings and her jewels, and she went
after her lovers, and forgat me, saith the LORD."

In such passages, the worship of idols is identified—and with no ifs or buts
or subtle Amos-like suggestions—as the source of sexual abandon, from accepting pay in the manner of an ordinary prostitute to a married woman committing
adultery. Gomer's infidelity to Hosea is a personal figuration of the nation's infidelity to God in whoring after strange gods by making graven images of Baal
out of their silver and gold. Hence the retribution—still shuttling back and forth
from the private to the public—will be the same, though naturally on a different
scale in each of the two interrelated realms.

Gomer herself is now forcibly prevented by her husband from pursuing her
lovers, and she then decides that she has no choice but to stay with him, and that
it is the better part of prudence for her to become faithful. Yet he will still punish her with various forms of material deprivation as well as humiliation ("And
now I will discover her lewdness in the sight of her lovers, and none shall deliver
her out of mine hand"*). The people of the North, who, like Gomer, do not realize that the prosperity they are currently enjoying under Rehoboam II is the gift
of God, not of Baal, will, again like Gomer, suffer the punishment of being
stripped naked and rendered destitute.

NOW WE ARE taken by surprise by another switch for which we are also
unprepared. Furthermore, following immediately upon the dire threats I have
just been citing, this second switch violates normal logic even more than the first
by beginning with the word *lakhen,* or "Therefore."

Instead of heralding another string of curses, this "therefore . . . ," we are star-
tled to discover, is the first word of a passage in which God takes back everything
He has just said. He will restore the vineyards to Israel that He has only a minute
ago consigned to the beasts of the field, and she (the whole house of Israel now,
or still just the Northern Kingdom?) will respond " . . . as in the days of her
youth, and as in the day when she came up out of the land of Egypt." He will
make her forget the Baalim, and then He will marry her again, this time forever

---

*The modern translations (except for AB) tend to have "shame" rather than KJV's "lewdness."

" . . . in righteousness, and in judgment, and in lovingkindness, and in mercies"
and—with the source of her former harlotry expunged through the removal of
the idolatrous cult—even in "faithfulness" to God, whom she now knows as her
true husband.

And there is more. In an idyllic picture that anticipates the eschatological
visions of the glorious End of Days that will greet us in the Books of Micah and
Isaiah, God portrays a world of peace and of harmony between beasts and men.
In that world, the heavens and the earth will "hear" each other, so that " . . . the
corn, and the wine, and the oil . . ." God has only just before threatened to take
away from Gomer-Israel (because she has given the credit for them to Baal) will
under this new "covenant" become abundantly available to her.

The same idyll also ends with a series of plays on the names of Hosea's children (those same "children of whoredom" upon whom God and/or Hosea have
only moments earlier declared they will have no mercy). Drawing on the literal
meanings of Jezreel as "God will sow," of Lo-rukhama as "no pity," and of Lo-
ammi as "not my people," God declares: "And I will sow her unto me in the
earth; and I will have mercy upon her that had not obtained mercy; and I will say
to them which were not my people, Thou art my people; and they shall say, Thou
art my God."

In the next chapter, there is a return to normal logic. Having portrayed in
glowing eschatological colors His own future reconciliation with an Israel that is
still whoring after other gods, God now commands Hosea to anticipate Him by
taking his wife back, even though she is at this very moment engaged in yet
another adulterous affair. He obeys, but in doing so, he sets conditions, to which
we must assume Gomer agrees: "And I said unto her, Thou shalt abide for me
many days; thou shalt not play the harlot, and thou shalt not be for another man:
so will I also be for thee."*

These particular conditions are one more symbolic or allegorical reflection
of God's relations to the children of Israel, who

> . . . shall abide many days without a king, and without a prince, and
> without a sacrifice, and without an image, and without an ephod, and
> without teraphim: Afterward shall the children of Israel return, and seek

---

*My summary represents a controversial position. Because it seems to me the more plausible of
the competing interpretations, I assume that it is Gomer with whom Hosea arranges a provi-
sional reconciliation rather than yet another whore he seeks out to marry at God's command.
An additional controversy also surrounds the promise Hosea makes to her in return ("so will I
also be to thee"): Is he pledging fidelity, or is he saying that for the time being she will not even
have him to sleep with? I opt for the latter because it fits better with these two verses about the
children of Israel. So does NRSV: "you shall not have intercourse with a man, nor I with you."
NJPS, too, has "even I [shall not cohabit] with you."

the LORD their God, and David their king; and shall fear the LORD and his goodness in the latter days.*

With this, we arrive at the end of what Kaufmann, Ginsberg, and others believe to be the entire book of Hosea the son of Beeri and which they place in the ninth rather than the eighth century B.C.E. I have already indicated that I agree with Andersen and Freedman, who think that all fourteen chapters belong to Hosea the son of Beeri and that he alone is the second of the classical (eighth-century B.C.E.) prophets. But before going briefly into that issue and plunging ahead with the rest of the book, let me say something about the literary character of the first three chapters that also has bearing on the eleven to come.

FOR MOST PROFESSIONAL STUDENTS of the Book of Hosea, it is a very strange text. From the few abrupt reversals I have already examined, so much seems to be out of order, and there is the added difficulty of figuring out in many verses along the way who is speaking to whom and about what. This difficulty is exacerbated by pronouns that do not match their antecedents, by the singular where the plural is grammatically required and vice-versa, and by puzzling changes from the first person to the second or the third.

Vexation with these peculiarities has given rise to the conclusion that the text has been corrupted by errors in the course of its transmission through the generations, and the temptation is to emend, emend, emend in the hope of making sense out of what can occasionally appear to be beyond the understanding of a rational mind. Few scholars can resist falling into this temptation, and though Hosea is not the only text that has invited them to exhibit their vast stores of learning and ingenuity, it may well be one of the juiciest targets in the Hebrew Bible. As a result, words and phrases are changed—in some cases into their opposites—and passages are transposed to where this or that scholar thinks they really belong.

Yet there also exist staunch defenders of striving to understand the book as it has come down to us instead of trying to reconstruct some supposedly more accurate version. Among the most formidable of these are Andersen and Freedman, who conclude that the stylistic and grammatical difficulties I have mentioned are too closely woven into the fabric of the text to be written off as the errors of copyists.

---

*NJPS differs from KJV in many details here and is no doubt more accurate: "For the Israelites shall go a long time without king and without officials, without sacrifice and without cult pillars, and without ephod and teraphim. After, the Israelites will turn back and seek the LORD their God and David their king—and they will thrill over the LORD and over His bounty in the days to come."

In endorsing this attitude, I would observe that to anyone at home in the modernist poetry of our own time, Hosea is not so peculiar as it seems to the many colleagues of Andersen and Freedman who differ in their approach. Considered strictly as literature, this book, *mutatis mutandis* (or *l'havdil,* to substitute for the Latin a similar Hebrew term that is more appropriate in this context, since it designates an impending shift from the sacred to the secular), might even be usefully compared to T. S. Eliot's poem of the early 1920s, "The Waste Land." That poem is also hard to follow because of the way voices that are not readily identifiable float in and out at apparent random, and also because the logical sequence of the narrative that the reader senses moving under the surface is frequently jumbled. All this is done deliberately by Eliot, in order to achieve certain effects. And I think that Hosea—even allowing for a corrupted verse here and a copyist's error there—is far more aware of what he is doing than the scholars have generally perceived in their yearning for neatness and their rage for emendation.

Just taking the first three chapters alone as an illustration, I would maintain that the confusion of voices there reinforces the words of God that the prophet believes he has been sent to speak. By making the extraordinary details of his own marriage into a living paradigm of God's "marriage" to Israel, Hosea provides a very powerful running commentary on the significance of the divine scheme.

In his edition of the Book of Ezekiel, Moshe Greenberg speaks of "the modern critical allergy to variety in prophetic moods," and contrasts this with the ancient redactor of Ezekiel, "perhaps the prophet himself," who "saw no impropriety or grotesqueness in depicting a variety of moods not only within one of the periods of the prophet's career but within a single oracle." This same "allergy" often breaks out in the treatment of the two sudden reversals in the first three chapters of Hosea. So disturbed are many scholars (and even some translators) by these reversals that they have taken it upon themselves to join the two together and transpose them to the end of Chapter 3.

Such a rearrangement may make the whole smoother and easier to grasp, but it also weakens its force. The structure of the text as we have it, unemended, conveys its own message, which is that God is at once jealous and loving, and that either of these attributes can manifest itself at will and without warning. My own experience as a reader of these three chapters is that the second shift from jealousy to lovingkindess, which is the longer and more lyrical and visionary of the two, conveys this lesson with greater power and beauty on its own than it does when put together with the first.

The two-Hoseas party either ignores or is unimpressed with the fact that such stylistic idiosyncrasies are as marked in the last eleven chapters of the book as they are in the first three. Of course, since this can be explained away by positing a single editor, it need not testify to a single prophet. But the proponents of a Hosea-B or Deutero-Hosea point to two other factors as well. One is that all traces of Gomer or any other wife disappear after Chapter 3. The other is that Hosea the son of Beeri's focus on idolatry as against morality places him in the ethos and the era of pre-classical prophecy. "The primacy of the ethical law" over the ritual or cultic—to cite H. L. Ginsberg's succinct formulation again—only becomes a feature of the book, they say, in Chapters 4 through 11.

YET IF THERE REALLY ARE two Hoseas, what this would show is precisely that the break between pre-classical and classical prophecy is not so sharp as has commonly been supposed, and emphatically not where idolatry is concerned. For while Gomer may fade from sight after Chapter 3 of the book, her ghost, as it were, lingers on, in that the nexus between whoredom and idolatry that she embodies remains a, or even *the,* major theme of the last eleven chapters of the book.

At least a dozen times in those chapters, Hosea pounds on this theme. Whoredom or playing the harlot or committing adultery can denote the infidelity of the people of the North to God, her "husband," in worshiping pagan gods. Or it can allude to sexual intercourse with temple prostitutes (of both sexes). Or it can encompass all these elements (just as Gomer's harlotry is simultaneously an act of infidelity to her human husband and idolatrous apostasy against God).

Needless to say, thunders the prophet in the last eleven chapters (sometimes speaking in his own voice, sometimes quoting God, sometimes doing both at once), none of this searching for benefits from pagan rites will do any good. Misled by priests who are themselves utterly corrupted, and are betraying the trust that has been lodged in them to teach the Law, "My people ask counsel at their stocks, and their staff declareth unto them: for the spirit of whoredoms hath caused them to err, and they have gone a whoring from under their God."*

But the Northern Kingdom as a whole is also guilty and will also be punished (" ... like people, like priest ...") for having departed from " ... the knowledge of God. . . ." Bereft of this knowledge, the people are now fools who have forgotten that God is the only true source of the blessings they have enjoyed and still seek. Here we get yet another transmutation into straightforward terms of

---

*The "stocks" and the "staff" are generally interpreted and/or translated as idolatrous fertility— or even, in modern parlance, phallic—symbols. For example, NJPS has "stick" and "rod" and glosses them as "phallus, meaning 'its lust.'" It then translates the next verse as "A lecherous impulse has made them go wrong." JB and Son see the stick as a sacred pole dedicated to Asherah, the fertility goddess and consort of Baal, and the rod as a diviner's magical wand. Still, whatever the most precise rendering may be, the meaning is clear enough.

the Gomer parable: she too gives credit to her lovers (gods) for the clothes and food she actually receives from her husband (God).

Gomer has three children.* But they have only been given to her in order to send a message from God through their names. No comparable bounty will come to the people of the North through bowing and blowing kisses to idols and fornicating in pagan shrines (and also—so it is hinted—copulating beside altars not even dedicated to Baal but to God Himself): " . . . they shall commit whoredom, and shall not increase: because they have left off to take heed to the LORD."† If, perchance, children do get born out of such simultaneously adulterous/idolatrous copulation, they will be " . . . strange: . . . now shall a month devour them. . . ."‡ And even if they survive beyond the first month, they will not live long: "As for Ephraim, their glory shall fly away like a bird, from the birth, and from the womb, and from the conception. Though they bring up their children, yet will I bereave them. . . ." Into this fearsome statement of God's intentions, Hosea's own voice breaks with a commensurately vengeful prayer: "Give them, O LORD: what wilt thou give? Give them a miscarrying womb and dry breasts." To which God in effect replies Amen: "Ephraim is smitten, their root is dried up, they shall bear no fruit," and He reiterates that even if " . . . they bring forth, yet will I slay even the beloved fruit of their womb."

As with children, so with crops. Previously Gomer was threatened with the loss of her " . . . vines and her fig trees, whereof she hath said, These are my rewards that my lovers have given me: and I will make them a forest, and the beasts of the field shall eat them." Now the people of the North are told directly rather than allegorically or symbolically that the same action will have the same consequence: "Rejoice not, O Israel, for joy, as other people: for thou hast gone a whoring from thy God, thou hast loved a reward upon every cornfloor." But this payment for harlotry will not suffice: "The floor and the winepress shall not feed them, and the new wine shall fail in her. They shall not dwell in the LORD's land; but Ephraim shall return to Egypt, and they shall eat unclean things in Assyria."§

---

*According to some traditional commentators, only the first is Hosea's, but it takes an exegetical stretch to reach this conclusion.

†Of the five modern translations I have checked, four agree with KJV, while choosing words of their own to express the same meaning. But NJPS has: "They shall swill, but not be satisfied,/Because they have forsaken the LORD/To practice/lechery." I would go with the majority here.

‡Instead of "strange" (which seems an accurate rendition of the Hebrew *zarim*), NRSV has "illegitimate" and JB, agreeing, has "bastards." But this time NJPS confirms KJV, as do Son and AB. As for "month," it is faithful to the Hebrew, but the precise meaning of the whole verse is very obscure, and it has therefore lent itself to many different interpretations. On the other hand, as so often with obscurity of detail in Hosea, the general sense is not that hard to grasp.

§To Hosea, as to Amos (7:17), the food of heathen nations is unclean.

Bad as this deprivation is ("For they have sown the wind, and they shall reap the whirlwind: it hath no stalk: the bud shall yield no meal: if so be it yield, the strangers shall swallow it up"), the Northern Kingdom's punishment for idolatry will not be confined to famine and drought and invasion by foreign armies who will confiscate their property. In a prophecy that seems to echo Amos (5:17), we learn that the punishment will be executed not only through the devastations wreaked in war by (unwitting) agents of God like Egypt and Assyria, but by God Himself.

In this, as in the prophecy of failed crops, we get one more adumbration (by the supposed Deutero-Hosea) of the parable of Hosea's marriage to Gomer. Thus, the repudiation signified by the child named "Not my people" reappears in more abstract guise:

> . . . O Ephraim, thou committest whoredom, and Israel is defiled. They will not frame their doings to turn unto their God: for the spirit of whoredoms is in the midst of them, and they have not known the LORD . . . : therefore shall Israel and Ephraim fall in their iniquity; Judah* also shall fall with them. They shall go with their flocks and with their herds to seek the LORD; but they shall not find him; he hath drawn himself from them.†

He hath drawn himself from them, and He will depart from their midst and " . . . will go and return to my place . . ."—a place they will be unable to reach. There are even scattered threats (again echoing Amos, though going beyond him) of the most radical rejection imaginable—a reversal of the Exodus, as when God proclaims: " . . . they shall return to Egypt" and " . . . Ephraim shall return to Egypt. . . ." And why not? They are no longer His people, and He no longer loves (or pities) them. This is what He has said through the name of one of the children born to Gomer and Hosea (Lo-ammi) before reversing Himself. But now He takes back what He took back before: " . . . for the wickedness of their doings, I will drive them out of mine house, I will love them no more. . . ."‡

All this—especially the verse about seeking the LORD and failing to find Him—is again reminiscent of Amos, when he heartbreakingly conjures up a

---

*Almost everyone emends all references to Judah in Hosea and turns them into "Israel." The idea is that later editors inserted these references after the destruction of the Northern Kingdom to make them relevant to the South. It is a plausible theory, but (along with Andersen and Freedman) I myself vote for the original, even though as prophecy it took much longer to work out in Judah than it did for the North.

†NJPS has "He has cast them off" in place of "he hath drawn himself from them," but the other modern translations are essentially in accord with KJV, and so am I.

‡NJPS is again the odd man out, with "accept" rather than "love."

vision of "the fair virgins and young men" wandering about in search of the word of God, and experiencing their failure to hear it as a worse famine and a worse drought than the physical ones they are suffering. But here too, Hosea goes beyond Amos: in executing the punishment Himself, God will " . . . be unto Ephraim as a moth, and to the house of Judah as a rottenness."* He, He Himself, will gnaw at their innards from within.

And He will also attack them from without: "For I will be unto Ephraim as a lion, and as a young lion to the house of Judah: I, even I, will tear and go away; I will take away, and none shall rescue him." Reaching back to this image in a later chapter, He intensifies it:

> Therefore I will be unto them as a lion: as a leopard by the way will I observe them: I will meet them as a bear that is bereaved of her whelps, and will rend the caul† of their heart, and there will I devour them like a lion: the wild beast shall tear them.

FOR ALL THIS FEROCITY, which is expressed over and over, God keeps switching in no particular order to mercy and forgiveness, and then back again—arbitrarily, as it seems—to the most extreme condemnation. This is the same pattern that was established in the Gomer-Hosea parable, and it has the effect of conveying the same sense. Whereas the jealous God of the Ten Commandments, speaking in much the same words through Hosea (" . . . I am the LORD thy God from the land of Egypt, and thou shalt know no god but me . . ."), is, so to speak, predictable in punishing Israel's faithlessness to Him, the merciful and forgiving God is more complicated and ultimately inscrutable. He can be counted upon to manifest this attribute when sinners repent, but He can also turn them away if He deems their change of heart to be only temporary and evanescent.

For example, as though having actually heard His declaration that He will abandon the children of Israel " . . . till they acknowledge their offense, and seek my face: in their affliction they will seek me early," they say:

> Come, and let us return unto the LORD: for he hath torn, and he will heal us; he hath smitten, and he will bind us up. After two days will he revive us: in the third day he will raise us up, and we shall live in his sight. Then shall we know, if we follow on to know the LORD: his

---

*This time, most of the modern translations improve upon KJV, with words like "canker" and "larvae" instead of "moth."
†"Caul" is an archaic term that means "covering" (NRSV) or "casing" (NJPS).

going forth is prepared as the morning; and he shall come unto us as the rain . . . unto the earth.

To which God immediately replies: "O Ephraim, what shall I do unto thee? O Judah, what shall I do unto thee? for your goodness is as a morning cloud, and as the early dew it goeth away."

God, then, can refuse to accept repentance that is unlikely to last. On the other hand, He can also decide to be merciful even when the sinful people have done nothing to deserve His forgiveness. In one of the most tender passages in the book, the Northern Kingdom becomes not God's spouse but His son whom He taught to walk as a child and whom He guided " . . . with bands of love . . . ," but who then turned away from Him and "sacrificed unto Baalim, and burned incense to graven images." At this thought, God's anger flares up and explodes into a string of curses. Then comes yet one more startling turnabout:

How shall I give thee up, Ephraim? how shall I deliver thee, Israel? How shall I make thee as Admah? how shall I set thee as Zeboim? mine heart is turned within me, my repentings are kindled together. I will not execute the fierceness of mine anger, I will not return to destroy Ephraim: for I am God, and not man; the Holy One in the midst of thee. . . .

There are two things about this passage that have been highlighted as extraordinary. One is that it shows us God arguing with Himself. In the Bible, humans—from Abraham to Moses, and from Amos to Jeremiah to Job—often argue with God, but nowhere else is God represented as engaging in a tumultuous internal debate.

The second feature that has been found extraordinary here is that God changes His mind. Which is why some translators and commentators eliminate the negative in the Hebrew as an error, and then read the passage as saying not that God has changed His mind, but that, on the contrary, He *will* return to destroy Israel and *will* visit upon it the fate of Admah and Zeboim, the two cities that perished along with Sodom and Gomorrah.

It is true that this interpretation makes better theological sense than its opposite, especially when we summon up the memory of passages we ourselves have already come across that supply evidence for it. In the Pentateuch, Balaam tells Balak that "God is not a man . . . that he should repent: hath he said, and shall he not do it? or hath he spoken, and shall he not make it good?" In the Former Prophets, Samuel declares in similar words that " . . . the Strength of Israel . . . is not a man, that he should repent."

Yet God has only the day before told Samuel himself that "It repenteth me that I have set up Saul to be king. . . ." And there is also this, just before God is about to drown the world in the great flood in the Book of Genesis:

And God saw that the wickedness of man was great in the earth, and that every imagination of the thoughts of his heart was only evil continually. And it repented the LORD that he had made man on the earth, and it grieved him at his heart. And the LORD said, I will destroy man whom I have created from the face of the earth; both man, and beast, and the creeping thing, and the fowls of the air; for it repenteth me that I have made them.

But then God changes His mind again by saving Noah and all the animals to make a new beginning. And one can also cite another passage (a very familiar one to Jews because in later centuries a truncated version of it came to be—and still is—recited in the synagogue whenever the scrolls of the Torah are removed from the Ark on festivals that fall on weekdays):

> . . . The LORD, The LORD God, merciful and gracious, long-suffering and abundant in goodness and truth, Keeping mercy for thousands, forgiving iniquity and transgression and sin, and that will by no means clear the guilty. . . .

Andersen and Freedman, who usually do their best to avoid emendations, make an exception in this case. Here they support eliminating the negative in "I will not execute" and "I will not return." They also refer to God's description of Himself in the passage from the Book of Exodus I have just cited. But they argue that

> even that supreme revelation cannot eliminate the ambivalence, for it makes the contrary assertion that "he will by no means clear the guilty." . . . Yahweh is long-suffering and slow to anger. Theoretically his wrath could be held in check indefinitely. . . . His responses are not automatic. . . . At best, [the verse in Hosea], if negative, declares a reluctance, not a permanent decision.

They then flesh out this argument with an analysis of Hosea's own theology:

> [I]n Hosea's theology the divine compassion is expressed, not by deflecting or annulling just anger, but by restoration after the requirements of justice have been satisfied by inflicting the penalties for covenant violations.

Persuasive though this is on its face, it seems less so when confronted with the contrary instances in which God changes His mind, like those I have cited. Be that as it may, I for one would be very loath to lose the supreme beauty of

God's reluctance in the unemended text. And as for the Andersen-Freedman analysis of Hosea's "theology," it perhaps strains for more philosophical consistency than so unsystematic and even incoherent a book can sustain.

In Hosea, God, who (in the Gomer section, but also elsewhere) can rage like a husband engaged in a lover's quarrel with his wife, here sounds like a parent who at one moment would like to kill a troublesome son and at the next cannot bear the thought of any harm coming to the child he has adored since infancy. The God of the Hebrew Bible is indeed God and not man that (in spite of the noted exceptions) He should repent. And yet, considering that in Hosea He is in general conceived in what from a strictly theological point of view are dangerously anthropomorphic terms, the assignment to Him of human-like emotions strikes a less discordant note than it would in a different literary setting.

Nor does the immediate rekindling of His rage at the persistence of Ephraim's idolatrous ways, and the promise of additional punishment that accompanies this explosive return of anger, seem out of keeping with the idea of a father torn by conflicting emotions toward his son. With this son, nothing works: not love, not guidance, not chastisement, not threats, and not even the prospect of being forgiven. He is hopelessly stuck on his wicked path, and the more his father tries—with every means he can think of—to draw him back, the more frustration mounts at his failure, igniting another explosion of rage.

The final nail in the coffin of the Hebrew negative, according to Andersen and Freedman, is that "The historical events evince wrath against Israel, not mercy for it": God, that is, never does repent of His determination to destroy Ephraim. Yes, but the Book of Hosea ends before the fall of the Northern Kingdom, and it closes on a vision of mercy. The word of God, having been wielded as a sword throughout most of the book, now brings not disease and death but restored health and new life. Earlier, such a healing and life-giving word unaccountably breaks in when God—in the guise of a lion, a leopard, and a she-bear who has lost her cubs and is about to pounce and tear the Northern Kingdom to pieces—interrupts Himself with the cry:

> O Israel, thou hast destroyed thyself; but in me is thine help. I will be thy king. . . . I will ransom them from the power of the grave; I will redeem them from death: O death, I will be thy plagues; O grave, I will be thy destruction. . . .*

---

*Unfortunately for the case I am constructing with the help of these verses, they too are taken by the modern translations (except, for a change, NJPS) to mean the opposite of what they seem to say both in the Hebrew and KJV. Nonetheless, I will stick to the view that this is not a smoothly logical bridge between the passages above and below it, but rather one of the many abrupt reversals that come without warning throughout Hosea.

Yet just as unexpectedly as it has occurred, the interruption is concluded when, without a pause, the word of life is immediately trumped by the word of death:

> Though he be fruitful among his brethren, an east wind shall come, the wind of the LORD shall come up from the wilderness, and his spring shall become dry, and his fountain shall be dried up. . . . Samaria shall become desolate; for she hath rebelled against her God: they shall fall by the sword: their infants shall be dashed in pieces, and their women with child shall be ripped up.

AS WITH THE VISIONS of destruction in Amos, however, this prophecy of the conquest of the Northern Kingdom by Assyria (the "east wind"?) is not given the last word in the Book of Hosea, which ends before the events just painted in such horrific detail. The concluding chapter holds out a last hope by painting an obverse picture—this one of the Northern Kingdom's repentance and God's forgiveness—that is as gorgeous as the vision of the conquest is frightful.

It begins: "O Israel, return unto the LORD thy God, for thou hast fallen by thine iniquity. Take with you words, and turn to the LORD: say unto him, Take away all iniquity, and receive us graciously. . . ." In this state of mind and spirit, the people of the North now understand that alliances with foreign powers (Egypt, but especially Assyria!) cannot avert the destruction that these very powers are prepared to wreak upon it as unwitting instruments of God's punishment for deserting Him:* "Asshur [Assyria] shall not save us; we will not ride upon horses:† neither will we say any more to the work of our hand, Ye are our gods: for in thee the fatherless findeth mercy."

This is all that God wishes to hear, and so He answers: "I will heal their backsliding, I will love them freely: for mine anger is turned away from him." Sending even sweeter music into His ears, "Ephraim shall say, What have I to do any more with idols? I have heard him, and observed him. . . ."‡ At this, God revisits images—dew, leafy trees, corn, vines—that have cropped up earlier in contexts denoting Israel's faithlessness and the punishments this faithlessness will bring.

---

*In the First Isaiah, as I remarked earlier, the idea that Assyria is an unwitting instrument of God's wrath will be open and explicit. Here there is only a hint of it.

†The horses are generally taken as alluding to an alliance with Egypt.

‡This is yet another passage that some interpret very differently as God rather than Ephraim speaking, and in interrogatives. The Hebrew is obscure, but KJV's rendering is supported (as usual in less archaic and less elegant English) by most of the modern ones I have consulted, and I think it more consonant with the spirit of the entire chapter.

Now, however, God restores to them the life-giving properties they should by nature possess, and waxes lyrical:

I will be as the dew unto Israel: he shall grow as the lily, and cast forth his roots as Lebanon. His branches shall spread, and his beauty shall be as the olive tree, and his smell as Lebanon. They that dwell under his shadow shall return; they shall revive as the corn, and grow as the vine: the scent thereof shall be as the wine of Lebanon.

Alas, Israel never takes the path that will lead to such a destination, and therefore—as the later prophets will see it—forfeits its only chance of the divine mercy that alone can bring survival. Whether there is one Hosea or two, the prophecies that all the scholars date to the 740s B.C.E. will have to wait almost another twenty years (until 722 B.C.E.) to be fulfilled by the fall of the Northern Kingdom at the hands of the Assyrian empire and the scattering of its populace to the winds.

In the meantime, Hosea is dismissed as a fool and a madman (" . . . the prophet is a fool, the spiritual man is mad . . ."). Yet the very fact that his oracles are preserved and eventually set down in writing indicates that not everyone shares the opinion that he is crazy. When he is vindicated by the disappearance of the Northern Kingdom, his prophecies—together with those of Amos—will be considered equally applicable to the Southern Kingdom of Judah.

The Southern Kingdom will outlast the North by about 130 years before its turn comes to be conquered—not by Assyria but by Babylon, which will by then have overthrown Assyria. But in the eyes of the prophets, Judah's fall will be attributable to the same sin of idolatry for which the Northern Kingdom was punished.

In the eyes of the classical prophets, too, these bloody developments will be seen as political manifestations, or epiphenomena, of the deeper war in which the whole house of Israel is involved—the spiritual war against idolatry that God has chosen this people to wage. It is a war that cannot be won in the world as a whole until it is won within the children of Israel themselves through the "knowledge of God" that Hosea says has been lost to them and abandoned by their corrupt priests. Because of this, the word of God spoken through the prophets must be not only a sword but also a *torah:* a positive means of teaching the people why and in what ways idolatry is a lie in itself and the cause of evil in those who submit to it, and why and in what ways fidelity to the one true God is good in itself and the cause of good in those who love and stand in awe of Him.

The particular evil Amos strives to expose as a microcosmic consequence of the surrender to idolatry is social injustice; to Hosea, it is sexual lewdness in men and whorishness in woman. The message of both prophets is that to live as their people are living is to be sterile and diseased, rotting from within, and therefore all the more defenseless against the horrors of conquest from without.

Conversely, resisting the seductive temptations of such a life—seductive because, although poisoned at the root, they are so alluring on the surface— opens the way to blessings that are fruitful and nourishing and bountiful, and that will breed inner satisfactions denied to the worshipers of strange gods who are actually serving nothing but their own base and foul desires.

CHAPTER EIGHT

MICAH: *PAX ISRAELITICA*

J UST AS NO ONE has any idea of what ultimately became of Amos, so
there is no indication on which to base even a speculation about what, if
anything other than death, befell Hosea when he ceased prophesying. Was
Gomer still around, and did he live happily ever after with her as a symbolic
statement of the reconciliation between God and Israel in the last chapter of the
book? This is more or less how the rabbis of the Talmud would see it in one of
those charming fables (*midrashim*) they liked to spin about events in the Bible:

> When God spoke to the prophet about the sins of Israel, expecting him
> to excuse or defend his people, Hosea countered by telling God to
> choose another people. It was then that Hosea was commanded to take
> Gomer to wife. When, after a time, God asked him to follow the exam-
> ple of Moses, who parted from his wife as soon as he was called to
> prophecy, Hosea replied that he could not send his wife away since she
> had borne him children, whereupon God said to him: "If thou, whose
> wife is a harlot and whose children are the children of harlotry and thou
> knowest not whether they are thine or not, canst not separate from her,
> how then can I separate Myself from Israel, from My children, the chil-
> dren of My elected ones, Abraham, Isaac and Jacob?" As soon as he real-
> ized his sin, Hosea entreated God to pardon him, whereupon he was
> told: "Instead of asking mercy for thyself, ask mercy for Israel against
> whom I have decreed three decrees because of you." Thereupon Hosea
> prayed as he was bidden and the impending threefold doom was averted.

Less fanciful is the theory that Hosea survived until the brutal Assyrian conquest of the Northern Kingdom in 722 B.C.E., suffered deportation, and became
a member of the Ten Lost Tribes. But we simply have no idea.

This much, however, we do know: shortly after Amos disappeared from the North, and probably a little before Hosea did, down in the South two other prophets became active. While mainly concerned with Judah, they also had something to say about Israel (which was still in existence during the earlier phase of their prophetic careers). The name of one was Micah (for whom no patronymic but only a hometown—the small rural village of Moresheth—is supplied) and the name of the other was Isaiah the son of Amoz of Jerusalem.

These two were themselves such close contemporaries—both prophesying more or less between 740 and 700 B.C.E.—that no consensus has been forged on which one came first. Of the authorities whose work I have consulted, a majority give chronological priority to Isaiah, but only hesitantly. Others are even less sure. Hence there is no definitive guidance from the experts about whether our story of the four prophets of the eighth century B.C.E. should continue with Isaiah and then conclude with Micah, or the other way around. Left free to make a choice, I have decided to take up Micah first. Because (as everyone agrees) Isaiah is the greatest of the four, it seems fitting that he should be placed in a position where his words can most clearly be seen as the grand climax of this first phase of classical prophecy.

LIKE MUCH OF the classical prophetic literature, the Book of Micah is not only difficult in itself but bedeviled by textual corruption. The Andersen-Freedman team, in the edition of Micah they added to the ones they did of Amos and Hosea, ranked the latter with the Book of Job in the number of unintelligible passages it contains. Now they put Micah into the running for the same dubious distinction. Wrestling with one particularly recalcitrant verse, they make a comment that might well be extended to the book as a whole:

> The general content . . . is clear. When it comes to specific details, the passage is as obscure as any in the Hebrew Bible, perhaps the most obscure. . . . The text is incoherent to the point of unintelligibility. Yet all the individual words are familiar and their meanings are plain. It is on the level of composition that the arrangements are meaningless; or, rather, the meaning eludes us.

Yet there is one verse in Micah whose meaning eludes no one. It has become so celebrated that rare is the person unfamiliar with it—and this includes people who know nothing else about Micah or any other book in the Hebrew Bible, and may not even have the faintest notion of where the saying comes from. It is, of course, this: "He hath shewed thee, O man, what is good; and what doth the LORD require of thee, but to do justly, and to love mercy, and to walk humbly with thy God."*

Why has Micah's injunction acquired such enormous fame and popularity? At first glance, the answer seems so obvious as to make the question sound silly. If we look at it in its historical context, the injunction expresses the essence of the turning point that the classical prophets of the eighth century B.C.E. are assumed by almost everyone to represent: the elevation—to say it yet again, as I unavoidably must do—of morality over ritual and sacrifice.

And the answer seems equally obvious—though somewhat more complicated—if we look at Micah's statement from a modern perspective. When the German philosopher Friedrich Nietzsche proclaimed in 1882 that God was "dead," he was saying out loud what many in their heart of hearts felt had finally been wrought by the astounding progress of modern science. But at the same time, they could not bring themselves to face the prospect of a world in which, as the great Russian novelist of the same period, Feodor Dostoevsky, warned (prophetically sensing the rise of totalitarianism in the next century, as surely as Amos and Hosea experienced intimations of the rise of Assyria in their own day), "everything" would become possible. Nor could even many who agreed with Nietzsche accompany him to his more optimistic conclusion that, liberated from the shackles of religion, mankind could now move to a stage "beyond good and evil."

Like those ex-believers for whom the evolutionist approach of the Higher Criticism provided a middle ground on which to take temporary refuge from a wholesale repudiation of the Bible, the people of a more philosophical bent who joined their ranks were unable or unwilling to let go of the influence of their religious upbringing. (Writers like George Eliot and Matthew Arnold in England and Ernest Renan in France, along with the Jewish founders of the Society for Ethical Culture in America, immediately spring to mind, but there were scores of others.) They, too, went on a mission to rescue whatever could be salvaged from the traditional biblical faith. And so there arose a host of efforts to extract and preserve the moral core that to the "modern mind" remained valid even if no God existed to command and enforce it.

No wonder, then, that in culling through the Bible they should have pounced

---

*KJV's translation is the most frequently quoted, but not necessarily the most accurate. NRSV has "do justice" instead of "do justly," and "kindness" instead of "mercy." NJPS has "Only to do justice/And to love goodness,/And to walk modestly with your God." JB, in slightly different wording, follows KJV, except that it gives us "to love tenderly" rather than "love mercy." The only truly significant difference among these readings has to do with the Hebrew word *v'hatzhayah.* On this Son has a note (pp. 181–82) that explains NJPS's rendering: "One is reluctant to question a phrase which has sunk so deeply into the religious consciousness of mankind; yet it is doubtful whether *humbly* is an adequate translation of the Hebrew. In the Bible the root *tsana* is found only here and in Prov. 11:2 (elsewhere *anav* is used to express humility). The lexicon turns to Rabbinic Hebrew for elucidation of its meaning, and there the word signifies 'modesty, decency, chastity, personal purity.' It follows that a more accurate rendering of Micah's phrase is 'to walk modestly [in the sense of "in decency, chastity, and purity"] with thy God.'"

upon Micah's summation of "what is good." No wonder that one leading English biblical scholar of the nineteenth century, G. A. Smith, should have called it "the greatest saying of the Old Testament," and another, Robertson Smith, should have given it the place of honor in an influential lecture he delivered on "The Prophets of Israel." And no wonder that in the twentieth century the formidable Canadian literary critic Northrop Frye should have praised it "as one of the great moral breakthroughs in history."

Andersen and Freedman put their finger on the main point: "The 'good life,' as defined here [by Micah], is not 'religious' at all, not if religion is thought of in terms of institutions (temple, synagogue, church) and ceremonies." No better definition could be framed of what vast numbers of people raised as pious Christians and Jews—now turned skeptics and basically secularized but still very far from being cut off from their biblical moorings—were searching for.

But it would be misleading to suggest that Micah's saying appealed in the nineteenth century, or continued appealing in the years ahead, only to people mining the Hebrew Bible for a "humanist" conception of the "good life," stripped of everything but the most generalized moral precepts and addressed not exclusively to the people of Israel but to "man" in general. Even in the Talmud, Micah's saying is characterized as a summation of all 613 commandments that the rabbis extrapolated from the Bible. (At first sight, this is baffling, since Micah seems to omit the ritual commandments affecting the relations "between man and God" to which equal standing is generally accorded by the rabbis of the Talmud. But on reflection one realizes that the rabbis correctly understood Micah's idea of walking with God to involve obeying *all* His commandments.)

Yet if it appears almost self-evident at first glance why Micah's statement should have attained such widespread importance, interesting questions begin to arise when we consider it more carefully, both in connection with the prophetic literature of the eighth century B.C.E. as a whole, and within the narrower confines of the Book of Micah itself. To those questions, the answers are anything but self-evident.

Thus, before Micah, both Amos and Hosea made similar statements. Amos: "Seek good, and not evil, that ye may live: and so the LORD, the God of hosts, shall be with you. . . . Hate the evil, and love the good, and establish judgment in the gate. . . ." And Hosea:

> Hear the word of the LORD, ye children of Israel: for the LORD hath
> a controversy with the inhabitants of the land, because there is no truth,
> nor mercy, nor knowledge of God in the land. By swearing, and lying,
> and killing, and stealing, and committing adultery, they break out, and
> blood toucheth blood.

Indeed, Micah himself would seem to be referring to these very statements by Amos and Hosea when he prefaces his own with "He hath shewed thee, O man, what is good. . . ." As most of the modern translations recognize, the Hebrew says "told," not "showed" you, which strengthens the suspicion that Micah was alluding specifically to the prophecies of his older contemporaries.

Considering the similarity among the three oracles, why has Micah's been singled out for special glory? A possible reason is the very simple one that its greater pithiness makes it more memorable. Less simple is another possibility: that tendentious interpretations of Micah have created the impression that he provides an even more unambiguous warrant than Amos and Hosea are thought to do for dismissing any need for the "cult." Even Yehezkel Kaufmann contributes to this impression: "The doctrine of the primacy of morality is asserted with particular force in Micah, first because of the absence . . . of an attack on idolatry." And, Kaufmann continues, what gives the famous verse its force "is the unparalleled idea," going beyond Amos, "that these are God's *sole* demand of man."

Yet after revisiting Micah with a fresh eye, I am convinced that this impression is as false to Micah's prophetic message as it is to the Book of Amos. As with Amos—and Hosea—what emerges from a reading that takes the whole of Micah into consideration, and not just the passages that are most palatable to modern moral tastes, has much, or even everything, to do with idolatry.

Therefore, as against the standard view, I will try to demonstrate that, in common with his two somewhat older contemporaries who have recently been preaching in the North, Micah, taking his stand in Judah, is engaged with all his might in the war against idolatry, especially (though not so exclusively as Amos and Hosea) from within. Like Amos and Hosea, too (more forthrightly than the former, but not quite so clearly as the latter), he establishes two relationships: a negative one between the particular evils he denounces and idolatry; and a positive one between the good and fidelity to God (which, again contrary to the stereotyped interpretation of this book, embraces *both* ritual and morality).

IT DOES NOT REQUIRE fancy exegetical or homiletical maneuvers to show that Micah was as much a general in the war against idolatry as Amos and Hosea. Nor is it necessary to go searching in the heavens above or beyond the sea to uncover the necessary evidence. Proof stares us in the face in the very passage from which the famous saying is always conveniently ripped.

That passage describes a contention between God and Israel, which is at first presented in the form of a legal dispute, with the whole of nature serving as a kind of jury:

Hear ye now what the LORD saith; Arise, contend thou before the mountains, and let the hills hear thy voice. Hear ye, O mountains, the LORD's controversy, and ye strong foundations of the earth: for the LORD hath a controversy with his people, and he will plead with Israel.*

God then indicts the children of Israel for ingratitude. They have forgotten everything He has done for them since bringing them out of slavery in Egypt, and are acting instead as though He were a tiresome burden: "O my people, what have I done unto thee? and wherein have I wearied thee?" He then invites them to "testify against me."†

But it would make no sense for God to bring a case against Israel if the offense were only ingratitude. What the lawsuit implies is a breach of contract: the children of Israel have broken the covenant they have made with God. As He reminds them in detail, *He* has honored His part of the bargain, but they have violated theirs. One might expect that He would then spell out the ways in which they have done so, and that they would then eagerly accept His invitation to defend themselves or even accuse *Him* of violating the covenant.

But no: neither of these things happens. No bill of particulars is recited by God, and the people do not defend themselves. In effect they simply enter a plea of *nolo contendere* and, having thus admitted their guilt, ask what they can do to be forgiven. Or rather—carrying through with the lawsuit imagery as it applies to that period—they ask what they can do to recompense the injured or defrauded party. "Wherewith shall I come before the LORD, and bow myself before the high God? . . ."

The switch here from the plural to the singular is one of the details in Micah that has bred much scholarly debate (just as with many passages in Hosea, where both the syntax and the grammar of the Hebrew are at least as peculiar). But the meaning remains the same whether the "I" is a spokesman for the entire people; or the prophet himself asking rhetorical questions; or (as I think) the literary artist in Micah further personalizing a dispute that has already been made intimate by God's use of the term "My people" and the tenderly imploring tone He adopts when an accusatory or angry note might have seemed more suitable.

---

*NJPS renders these two verses differently (though the basic idea is the same): "Hear what the LORD is saying:/Come, present [My] case before the mountains,/And let the hills hear you pleading./Hear, you mountains, the case of the LORD—/You firm foundations of the earth!/For the LORD has a case against His people,/He has a suit against Israel." JB's language is not identical with NJPS's, but it too reflects the idea of a "case" (or *riv*, as "Form Criticism" calls it) being argued in court.

†NJPS translates this verse a little more freely: "What wrong have I done you?/What hardship have I caused you?" But NJPS goes along with KJV's "testify," which JB more literally renders "Answer me."

Responding, then, in one voice, the people agree to pay damages. Yet—again confounding normal expectations—they do not negotiate for a plea bargain that would get them off with as little as possible. Instead, they themselves keep upping the value of the settlement they are prepared to reach. " . . . Shall I come before him [God] with burnt offerings, with calves of a year old?" And if this precious gift is not enough, "Will the LORD be pleased with thousands of rams . . . ?" And if even this extravagant price is too low, how about " . . . ten thousands of rivers of oil . . ."? Will that suffice?

Perhaps because of God's silence in response to these deals, they think not, since without pausing for an answer, and still speaking in a single voice, they escalate to the ultimate sacrifice, the greatest one of all: " . . . shall I give my first-born for my transgression, the fruit of my body for the sin of my soul?"

It is *this*—not the lawful sacrifices proposed before—that provokes God into uttering the famous injunction. Having pronounced it, but without (for the moment) specifically expressing His disgust at the abominable proposal the people have made, God launches a string of denunciations enumerating the sins of which the people are guilty and the punishments that will be meted out to them.

The sins with which He begins have already been denounced by Micah in two earlier chapters of the book, and they are similar to those emphasized by Amos. The first time around, Micah excoriates the rich for expropriating the property of small landholders, for bribing the judges (presumably in order to give their thievery legal cover), and in general for committing crimes against the poor:

> Woe unto them that devise iniquity, and work evil upon their beds! when the morning is light, they practice it, because it is in the power of their hand. And they covet fields, and take them by violence; and houses, and take them away: so they oppress a man and his house, even a man and his heritage.

And this is not all:

> . . . ye pull off the robe with the garment from them that pass by securely as men averse from war. The women of my people have ye cast out from their pleasant houses; from their children have ye taken away my glory for ever.*

---

*In Hebrew, these verses are a very tough nut to crack, as the wide divergences among the modern translations demonstrates. But as always with Micah (and Hosea), the general sense is clear, even if the details are virtually impossible to pin down with real precision.

But there is even worse, when Micah, turning to the rulers, employs grue-some imagery, complete with one of the more repulsive suggestions of cannibal-ism in the Hebrew Bible, to evoke the injustices these leaders both commit and tolerate:

> And I said, Hear, I pray you, O heads of Jacob, and ye princes of the house of Israel; Is it not for you to know judgment? Who hate the good, and love the evil; who pluck off their skin from off them, and their flesh off their bones; Who also eat the flesh of my people, and flay their skin from off them; and they break their bones, and chop them in pieces, as for the pot, and as flesh within the cauldron.

It is to such sins as these (from Chapter 3) that God returns (in Chapter 6) when he rejects the people's amazing offer to atone for them by sacrificing their own firstborn. But in this second round, He passes over the social realm quickly, and speaks in relatively milder terms mainly of how the rich cheat the poor:

> Are there yet the treasures of wickedness in the house of the wicked, and the scant measure that is abominable? Shall I count them pure with the wicked balances, and with the bag of deceitful weights? For the rich men thereof are full of violence, and the inhabitants thereof have spo-ken lies, and their tongue is deceitful in their mouth.

BUT WHERE, it may reasonably be asked, is the connection with idolatry in all this? Where is there even an open expression of astonishment at the fantastic idea broached by the people to God Himself that they might atone for their sins against their covenant with Him through the grossest possible violation of that very covenant—that is, by resorting to the worst of all the abominations associ-ated with the idolatry the covenant itself requires them to renounce?

According to Andersen and Freedman, when Micah speaks of the introduc-tion of the "sins of the house of [the Kingdom of] Israel" into Jerusalem, he is pointing to his own contemporary, King Ahaz of Judah, who (as we have learned from the Second Book of Kings) is not only an idolator but practices human sacrifice: "But he [Ahaz] walked in the way of the kings of Israel, yea, and made his son pass through the fire, according to the abominations of the heathen, whom the LORD cast out from before the children of Israel."

But Micah provides us with an even more powerful piece of evidence than this that he is fusing social sin with idolatry. It comes in a verse containing the bill of indictment that God finally issues after He has spurned the offer of human sacrifice by telling the people what they should have known already about jus-tice and mercy—having, as He says, been told before. In this highly significant verse, it is a Northern dynasty that is brought in as an epitome of everything wicked that is being imitated by the Southern Kingdom: "For the statutes of Omri are kept, and all the works of the house of Ahab, and ye walk in their counsels...."

Because this verse is preceded by a list of social injustices, a number of commentators (both Jewish and Christian) have interpreted it as referring not to the royal patronage of Baal worship during the reigns of Omri and his son Ahab, husband of Jezebel, but rather to "oppression and injustice" or "to the luxury of the upper classes, and social injustice."

Yet these commentators miss a crucial element, which is that the house of Ahab embodied a perfect synthesis of idolatry and social oppression. It was during this king's reign that, we recall, Elijah treated the two classes of sin as equally serious, first by slaughtering 450 prophets of Baal after his contest with them on Mount Carmel, and then by cursing Ahab and Jezebel with a bloody end for the murder of Naboth and the theft of his vineyard.

The underlying premise of Elijah's twin actions, I would contend again, was that the theft and the murder flowed from the idolatry, or, conversely, that they were the fruits of faithlessness to the commandments of the God of Israel. In harking back to "the house of Ahab," which necessarily includes Jezebel, even though she is not named here, Micah the literary artist returns to the bloody crossroads where sins against God meet and marry crimes against man, and the two classes of violation become indistinguishable from each other.

So intent are many people on reading Micah solely as a tract against social injustice, and seeing him as building on the non-religious or "humanist" foundation they imagine has already been laid by Amos, that they almost literally blind themselves to the even more outspoken and unambiguous denunciations of idolatry scattered through this book. Yet the very first chapter begins with several such denunciations (in at least one of which—involving the image of harlotry—we have a resonant echo of Hosea):

> ...What is the transgression of Jacob? is it not Samaria? and what are the high places of Judah? are they not Jerusalem? Therefore ... all the graven images thereof shall be beaten to pieces, and all the hires thereof shall be burned with the fire, and all the idols thereof will I lay desolate: for she gathered it of the hire of an harlot, and they shall return to the hire of an harlot.

Later, in a vision of the future purification of the " ... cities of thy land, ..." there is more. But it is embedded in and surrounded with complexities that have to be unraveled before we can grasp that Micah is saying something very different from what appears on the surface, and from what a host of commentators have taken it to be.

•   •   •

To BEGIN WITH, in the superscription we are informed that "The words of
the LORD that came to Micah the Morasthite . . ." concern *both* Samaria (the
then capital of the Northern Kingdom, which has not yet fallen) and Jerusalem
(the capital of Judah), and while he concentrates on his native Judah, he so often
embraces the North in his prophecies that we can safely take the "cities" in the
purification vision as the two capitals and therefore standing for the entire Land
of Israel.

The purification that Micah foresees begins with an apparent act of demilita-
rization: "And it shall come to pass in that day, saith the LORD, that I will cut off
thy horses out of the midst of thee, and I will destroy thy chariots." But if we read
this verse as a "pacifist" statement, we are puzzled by how completely it contradicts the visions immediately preceding it. There, far from employing the language
of what we might today regard as an advocate of disarmament, Micah envisages a
fiercely warlike Israel achieving victories over its more powerful enemies:

> Now also many nations are gathered against thee, that say, Let her be
> defiled, and let our eye look upon Zion. But they know not the
> thoughts of the LORD, neither understand they his counsel: for he shall
> gather them as the sheaves into the floor. Arise and thresh, O daughter
> of Zion: for I will make thine horn iron, and I will make thy hoofs
> brass: and thou shalt beat in pieces many people; and I will consecrate
> their gain unto the LORD, and their substance unto the LORD of the
> whole earth.

Despite this assurance of ultimate victory, Micah prophesies a prior succession of battles in which Israel will be defeated by unnamed foreign forces. But
then a remnant of Judah, apparently swollen by returning exiles, will rally under
a new king of the house of David, and under him they will (also apparently)
reconquer all that has been lost:

> And he shall stand and feed in the strength of the LORD, in the majesty
> of the name of the LORD his God; and they shall abide: for now he
> shall be great unto the ends of the earth. And this man shall be the
> peace, when the Assyrian shall come into our land: and when he shall
> tread in our palaces, then shall we . . . waste the land of Assyria with the
> sword, and the land of Nimrod in the entrances thereof: thus shall he
> deliver us from the Assyrian, when he cometh into our land, and when
> he treadeth within our borders. And the remnant of Jacob shall be in the
> midst of many people as a dew from the LORD, as the showers upon
> the grass, that tarrieth not for man, nor waiteth for the sons of men. And

the remnant of Jacob shall be among the Gentiles in the midst of many people as a lion among the beasts of the forest, as a young lion among the flocks of sheep: who, if he go through, both treadeth down, and teareth in pieces, and none can deliver. Thine hand shall be lifted upon thine adversaries, and all thine enemies shall be cut off.*

Traditionalist commentators interpret all this as a messianic or eschatological vision for the distant future (when the scion of David will be born) and—somehow managing to overlook the nationalistic and warlike triumphalism of this passage—they concentrate all their attention on the verse about dew and rain as metaphors for the teachings of God. This reading is a great aid to resolving the apparent contradiction that arises in the next verse, when God declares that He will rid Israel of its military equipment (chariots and horses): for, as is axiomatic to the traditionalists, in the messianic age there will be no further need for reliance on weaponry.

But in an interpretation of this verse that is more plausible, since it looks forward to the attack on idolatry that follows, and to which it works as an introduction, Andersen and Freedman propose that the horses and chariots may have been connected with elements of an idolatrous practice. In support of this interpretation, they cite the fact (reported in the Second Book of Kings) that King Josiah, in later conducting his purge of anything smacking of idolatry, "took away the horses that the kings of Judah had given to the sun, at the entrance to the house of Yahweh, . . . and he burned the chariots of the sun with fire."

But even without this illuminating bit of information, one has no trouble refuting the notion that Micah (supposedly like Amos before him) is on the whole indifferent to the war against idolatry. After all, Micah continues in the name of God to promise in the most unambiguous terms that an end will be made in Jerusalem (and Samaria?) to all manner of idols, to the sacred groves in which they are worshiped, and to the forbidden arts of divination. For the "extraordinary tenacity" of divination among the people of Israel, Andersen and Freedman write, "seems to have been an integral part of persistent paganizing trends, with the making of idols . . . as its most overt expression." Thus Micah:

And I will cut off witchcrafts out of thine hand; and thou shalt have no more soothsayers: Thy graven images also will I cut off, and thy standing

---

*The modern translations differ from KJV in many details, the most significant of which (shades of the debates in the State of Israel today!) are the substitution of "safety" and "security" for "peace" and "fortresses" for "palaces." The justification for rendering *shalom* as "safety" or "security" rather than as "peace" is that Micah applies it to what will happen in the event of an Assyrian invasion, which he certainly does not envisage as a state of peace. Several of the modern translations also use the conditional "should" instead of "will" in the verses about an Assyrian invasion.

images out of the midst of thee; and thou shalt no more worship the work
of thine hands. And I will pluck up thy groves out of the midst of thee....

BUT THERE IS ANOTHER messianic or eschatological vision in Micah, which
creates problems both for the widely accepted "universalist" picture of this
prophet and for the more "particularist" (and less pacifist) idea of him that I have
been trying to demonstrate is truer to the book as we have it. The same vision
creates even thornier problems for the scholars, because it duplicates almost
word for word one of the most frequently quoted passages in the Book of Isaiah.
Here is how it appears in Micah:

> But in the last days it shall come to pass, that the mountain of the house
> of the LORD shall be established in the top of the mountains, and it
> shall be exalted above the hills; and people shall flow into it. And many
> nations shall come, and say, Come, and let us go up to the mountain of
> the LORD, and to the house of the God of Jacob; and he will teach us
> of his ways, and we will walk in his paths: for the law shall go forth of
> Zion, and the word of the LORD from Jerusalem. And he shall judge
> among many people, and rebuke strong nations afar off; and they shall
> beat their swords into plowshares, and their spears into pruninghooks:
> nation shall not lift up a sword against nation, neither shall they learn
> war any more. But they shall sit every man under his vine and under his
> fig tree; and none shall make them afraid: for the mouth of the LORD
> of hosts hath spoken it. For all people will walk every one in the name
> of his god, and we will walk in the name of the LORD our God for
> ever and ever.*

Except for what comes after, there are only thirteen minor differences
between this passage and the one in the second chapter of the Book of Isaiah. In
the useful list constructed by Andersen and Freedman, seven possible explanations have been put forward:

1. Isaiah and Micah each composed an identical prophecy independently.
2. An earlier prophecy was taken over and used by each prophet independently.
3. Micah composed it; Isaiah borrowed it.

---

*Several modern translations have "instruction" instead of "law" and "arbitrate" rather than
"rebuke" the distant nations. They also either translate or gloss "word" as "oracle" (though the
Hebrew *d'var* plainly means "word of").

4. Isaiah composed it; Micah borrowed it.
5. An oracle originally part of the Micah tradition but not necessarily original with the prophet was put into his book and later introduced into the book of Isaiah in one of its many revisions.
6. An oracle originally part of the Isaiah tradition but not necessarily original with that prophet was put into his book and later borrowed into the book of Micah.
7. An independent oracle, not originally associated with either prophet, and written later than either book, perhaps much later on, found its way independently into both books.

While recognizing that this "mystery" is not yet solved, and may never be, and while also acknowledging that theirs is very much a minority view among their fellow scholars, Andersen and Freedman incline toward Micah as the author and the First Isaiah as the borrower.

Yet most other scholars, along with the rest of the world, attribute the passage to the First Isaiah (and I suspect that, except for readers steeped in the Bible, hardly anyone is even aware that these hallowed words occur anywhere but in the Book of Isaiah). And there is indeed a good reason for regarding the passage as having originated with the First Isaiah and inserted into the Book of Micah by Micah himself or someone else. When, shortly, we come to the First Isaiah, I will have a bit to say about why it fits very well with him. For now, however, let me indicate why I think it does *not* fit smoothly into Micah.

For this purpose, a good way to begin is by quoting the veritably rhapsodic characterization of the passage by Andersen and Freedman:

> This apocalypse is perhaps the most famous of all the visions to come
> from the imagination of the prophets of Israel, or revealed by the God
> of Israel. . . . It is global in scope, tranquil in mood, an impossible dream
> for all humankind, as hard to believe now as it must have been then . . .
> it is remarkable that it comes from an age of wars and tumults, of cru-
> elty and chaos. It comes from a time of imperialist devastation, demoli-
> tion, and domination of smaller nations by powers advanced in the
> technology of war, ruthless in conquest and control.

Now let me set this eloquent description beside Kaufmann, turning to him this time in agreement rather than dissent. Kaufmann generally accedes to the standard conception of Micah as a pacifist and a universalist that I am at pains to complicate or even throw out. But he also contradicts himself (or comes close to doing so) in explaining why he believes the duplicated passage in question is more likely to have issued from the mouth (or pen, as he would maintain) of the First Isaiah than from Micah.

As a prelude to his discussion of the duplicated passage, Kaufmann looks back at the purification vision I analyzed above:

Micah's prophecies of salvation are inspired by the popular idea of the "day of YHVH."* They are purely national, and are pervaded by the theme of national revenge. . . . The Davidic monarchy will return to its former glory, and the enemies of Israel will be crushed and despoiled by the new king, who is described as a ravaging bull or a lion. . . . In this setting the Isaianic vision of the temple mount is particularly out of place . . . it is a foreign body in Micah.

It is on just such a note of national vindication as Kaufmann describes that the Book of Micah will end. But not before, like all the other classical prophets, Micah repeatedly warns of impending catastrophes whose details rival or sometimes even surpass their counterparts in the Hebrew Bible in frightfulness and horror. To the people of his own time, the most frightful of these must be his prophecy of the destruction of Jerusalem. No one before him has ever dreamed that God will permit harm to come to His own city—the city where His own "house" is located. The First Isaiah, for example, will specifically assure King Hezekiah of this in 701 B.C.E., when the Assyrian king Sennacherib swallows much of Judah and is laying siege to Jerusalem. But Micah has the incredible daring to proclaim that "Therefore shall Zion for your sake be plowed as a field, and Jerusalem shall become heaps, and the mountains of the house as the high places of the forest."†

In measuring how deep an impression Micah's audacity makes, we have to jump ahead more than a century to another prophet, Jeremiah. His opponents will advocate that Jeremiah be put to death for prophesying that Jerusalem could suffer the same fate as the by then long defunct capital of the Northern Kingdom and that Solomon's Temple could be destroyed just as the Northern sanctuary of Shiloh had been. But Jeremiah's defenders will save his life by citing the precedent of Micah:

Then rose up certain of the elders of the land, and spake to all the assembly of the people, saying, Micah the Morasthite prophesied in the days of Hezekiah king of Judah, saying, Thus saith the LORD of hosts;

---

*Just as a reminder: this is the conception that Amos reverses in representing it not as a day of salvation or national vindication but as one of dreadful judgment and retribution against Israel. However, see p. 175.

†Where KJV incorrectly has "the mountains of the house" for *har ha-bayyit,* NJPS accurately translates it as "the Temple Mount," and JB as "the mountain of the Temple." NJPS is also closer to the Hebrew than KJV with "a shrine in the woods" instead of "the high places of the forest."

Zion shall be plowed like a field, and Jerusalem shall become heaps, and
the mountain of the house as the high places of a forest. Did Hezekiah
king of Judah and all Judah put him at all to death? did he not fear the
LORD, and besought the LORD, and the LORD repented him of the
evil which he had pronounced against them? . . .

Omitted from the quotation in the Book of Jeremiah are the words "for your
sake" which appear in Micah as a preliminary to "Zion shall be plowed as a
field." But for whose sake? Whom is Micah talking about? The answer to that
question hurls us smack up against one more fascinating aspect of the Book of
Micah, and another of its major themes.

I HAVE THUS FAR looked at three of the groups Micah has in mind and
whom he has (metaphorically?*) accused of being cannibals: the thieving rich,
the oppressive rulers, and the corrupt judges, who among them conspire to
defraud people possessing less land and less power than they themselves own. But
there is a fourth group on whom Micah vents his fury at even greater length: the
prophets who are his rivals and opponents.

Even though Micah sometimes flings the insult "diviners" at them, these are
not prophets of Baal such as Elijah challenged, or devotees of some other pagan
god or gods; they are prophets who claim to speak, no less than Micah does, in
the name of the God of Israel. His stormy confrontations with them begin when
they (or possibly the rulers he has been denouncing) demand, as Amaziah the
priest did of Amos, that he stop prophesying:

Prophesy ye not, say they to them that prophesy: they shall not prophesy to them, that they shall not take shame. O thou that art named the
house of Jacob, is the spirit of the LORD straitened? are these his
doings? . . .

The King James translators are understandably flummoxed by this passage,
which is one of those in Micah that Andersen and Freedman pick out as among
the most obscure in the entire Hebrew Bible.† The general thrust would seem to
be that Micah is being excoriated himself not only for the charges he has been
making against the leading citizens of Judah, but also for blasphemously imply-

---

*I raise the question because some commentators believe that Micah is talking about *actual*
human sacrifice, which in accordance with the procedures followed in animal sacrifice, might
have ended with the eating of portions of the victim's body. Naturally other commentators violently disagree.

ing that God is no longer with His people. Micah, however, throwing in a few
more charges and threats of punishment (no doubt to show that he is not intimidated), then shoots back contemptuously with: "If someone were to go about
uttering empty falsehoods, saying, 'I will preach to you of wine and strong
drink,' such a one would be the preacher for this people!"*

But Micah is only just warming up. Before going on to develop his attack on
these lying and drink-pushing prophets, he again demonstrates that he is not
intimidated by escalating his excoriation of the leaders (through those compar-
isons cited above between them and wild beasts ripping up their prey, or perhaps
even as cannibals devouring the humans they have first sacrificed and then
chopped " . . . in pieces, as for the pot, and as flesh within the cauldron . . .").

Having done that, Micah turns his full and virulent attention on the
prophets in particular. In rather homey images (Micah is, after all, a country
boy), he sneers that they will tell anyone who pays them that all is and will continue to be well, while vilifying those from whom they can extort no such assurances: "Thus saith the LORD concerning the prophets that make my people err,
that bite with their teeth, and cry, Peace; and he that putteth not into their
mouths, they even prepare war against him."† The punishment for this will perfectly fit the crime:

> Therefore night shall be unto you, that ye shall not have a vision; and it
> shall be dark unto you, that ye shall not divine; and the sun shall go
> down over the prophets, and the day shall be dark over them. Then shall
> the seers be ashamed, and the diviners confounded: yea, they shall all
> cover their lips; for there is no answer of God.

That takes care of them. And he himself? "But truly I am full of power by the
spirit of the LORD, and of judgment, and of might, to declare unto Jacob his
transgression, and to Israel his sin."

---

†(See page 171.) The modern translations offer guesses that are at least comprehensible. NRSV:
"'Do not preach'—thus they preach—/'one should not preach of such things;/disgrace will not
overtake us.'/Should this be said, O house of Jacob?/Is the LORD's patience exhausted?/Are these
his doings?" NJPS: "'Stop preaching,' they preach./'That's no way to preach;/Shame shall not overtake [us]./Is the House of Jacob condemned?/Is the LORD's patience short?/Is such His practice?'" JB: "'Do not rave,' they rave/'do not rave like this./No shame is going to overtake us./Can
the House of Jacob be accursed?/Has Yahweh lost patience?/Is that his way of going to work?'"

*Instead of remaining with KJV, which could not decode this verse, I am using NRSV here,
whose rendering in my judgment finds the meaning and expresses it more elegantly than the
other modern versions.

†NRSV has "when they have something to eat" in place of KJV's more literal "bite with their
teeth," and JB has a similar formulation. NJPS is best here, I think, with "when they have something to chew."

Micah's absolutely self-assured assertion of his own prophetic legitimacy is not backed up in the book by any indications (like those we are given in Hosea and in Amos, and the much more extensive scenes we will get in Isaiah, Jeremiah, and Ezekiel) of his being called by God. We have only his word for it. But that word is fortified by the authority with which he speaks it—an authority that to his audience must sound more compelling than any exhibited by the rival prophets with whom he exchanges charges of fraud. What else can account for the survival of his preachings when theirs all disappear?

It cannot be proved that the power of Micah's oracles and sermons and visions is the crucial element behind their preservation. But we can be certain that he does not become part of the prophetic canon by virtue of the accuracy of his predictions, since one of those is that the Assyrians will be defeated in battle if they invade the country. The opposite, of course, will all too soon happen in the North, and the Babylonians will later invade the South, and conquer it.

Still, even if his political judgment is off (in the short run, anyway), Micah does get the main point right when—wielding the word with the force of a lethal sword—he dismisses the principal idea that his rivals are preaching:

Hear this, I pray you, ye heads of the house of Jacob, and the princes of the house of Israel, that abhor judgment, and pervert all equity. They build up Zion with blood, and Jerusalem with iniquity. The heads thereof judge for reward, and the priests thereof teach for hire, and the prophets thereof divine for money: yet will they lean upon the LORD and say, Is not the LORD among us? none evil can come upon us.

What Micah—in the true tradition of classical prophecy—is telling the whole lot of them is that God's covenant with Israel is not, as they foolishly and complacently assume, unconditional, and that evil can indeed come upon them if they fail to fulfill their obligations under it. And that is when he audaciously carries this fundamental truth all the way by including Jerusalem itself in the coming calamities. (This prophecy, unlike the one about Assyria, does eventually come to pass.)

AND YET—in the true rhythm of classical prophecy, with its leaps from condemnation to consolation without a trace of any logical moral pattern (not even necessarily from repentance to forgiveness)—the immediate sequel to the vision of Jerusalem destroyed is the Isaianic vision of Jerusalem restored and more glorious than ever it was before.

The same rhythm is picked up again, when, following Micah's vision of the national restoration that will come about with the advent of a new king of the house of David—a kingdom that will be as dominant among the nations in the political realm as the Temple will be in the spiritual—the prophet unleashes another string of curses. In their malignity, these curses are a negative counter-point—both physical and spiritual—to the balm of the blessings and the hopes he has soothingly uttered. In their physical aspect, they are redolent of Hosea:

> Thou shalt eat, but not be satisfied; and thy casting down shall be in the midst of thee; and thou shalt take hold, but shalt not deliver; and that which thou deliverest will I give up to the sword. Thou shalt sow, but thou shalt not reap; thou shalt tread the olives, but thou shalt not anoint thee with oil; and sweet wine, but shalt not drink wine.*

But the curses that describe the *spiritual* accompaniment of these physical sufferings are closer to Amos than to Hosea. Amos, remember (8:11–13), envisions the young men and the virgins of Israel who, faint with thirst for the word of God, wander about in search of it, and never find it. Micah now paints a different scene, but in its stress on the spiritual element of the punishment to come, it has a kind of affinity with the poignant prophecy of Amos. It is a searing picture of radical disorder, an overturning of the conditions that normally govern the closest and most intimate relations of human life:

> Trust ye not in a friend, put ye not confidence in a guide: keep the doors of thy mouth from her that lieth in thy bosom. For the son dishonoreth the father, the daughter riseth up against her mother, the daughter in law against her mother in law; a man's enemies are the men of his own house.

Nor does this exhaust his catalogue of horrors. Yet as with all the classical prophets, evil tidings are not accorded the last word, which is always given (whether by the prophet himself, or by his disciples or redactors) to consolation and hope:

> Therefore I will look unto the LORD; I will wait for the God of my salvation: my God will hear me. Rejoice not against me, O mine enemy: when I fall, I shall arise; when I sit in darkness, the LORD shall be a light unto me. I will bear the indignation of the LORD, because I have sinned against him, until he plead my cause and execute judgment

---

*KJV's "thy casting down, etc.," is rightly understood by the modern translations as "a gnawing hunger within you" (NRSV) or, better, "a gnawing at your vitals" (NJPS). What KJV renders as "take hold" probably means "conceive." The idea, as in Hosea 9:11–16, is that if they conceive, they will not give birth, and if they give birth, their children will be slain in war.

for me: he will bring me forth to the light, and I shall behold his righteousness.

It is a hymn (or a psalm) of great sublimity, and in this instance the moral
logic of sin, punishment, repentance, and forgiveness is definitely present. And
the same note, infused with the same beautiful mixture of humility and exaltation, is struck in another psalm-like hymn a little further on:

Who is a God like unto thee, that pardoneth iniquity, and passeth by the
transgression of the remnant of his heritage? he retaineth not his anger
for ever, because he delighteth in mercy. He will turn again, he will have
compassion upon us; he will subdue our iniquities; and thou wilt cast all
their sins into the depths of the seas.

But what the standard view of Micah omits is that for him the public consequences of God's mercy and forgiveness will be to vindicate His people and take
revenge upon the enemy who has been rejoicing at their fall. There is no mention here of "the Day of the LORD," but the popular conception of it that Amos
turns upside down—warning that it will be a day of doom and not of triumph—is turned back by Micah to its original state:

Then she that is mine enemy shall see it, and shame shall cover her
which said unto me, Where is the LORD thy God? mine eyes shall
behold her: now shall she be trodden down as the mire of the streets. . . .
According to the days of thy coming out of the land of Egypt will I
shew unto him marvelous things. The nations shall see and be confounded at all their might: they shall lay their hand upon their mouth,
their ears shall be deaf. They shall lick the dust like a serpent, they shall
move out of their holes like worms of the earth: they shall be afraid of
the LORD our God, and shall fear because of thee.*

So the question inevitably arises: which is the true Micah? Is he the nationalist (or "particularist") of the concluding chapter, or the "universalist" who in
the name of God addresses "man," and not the children of Israel alone, in the
most famous statement he ever pronounces? And what, correlatively, are we to
make of the relation between the eschatological vision with which he leaves the
stage and the "Isaianic" one that appears earlier in his book?

One of the reasons Kaufmann believes that Micah is the borrower of the
prophecy of the Temple Mount from the First Isaiah is that he thinks the real

---

*"At all their might" is better translated as "for all their might."

Micah is the nationalist of the last chapter, and that as such he is unable to rise to the spiritual heights attained by Isaiah. I take a rather dimmer view of those heights than Kaufmann does, and I will have something to say about why in the concluding section of this book. But here I want to enter a speculation of my own into the never-ending dispute over how the Temple Mount prophecy found its way into the Book of Micah.

REVIEWING THAT DISPUTE, I have been persuaded by Kaufmann and the many other scholars who assign the prophecy to the First Isaiah. Yet as against Kaufmann, my (possibly wild) guess is that whoever borrowed and stuck it into the Book of Micah—and it pleases me to think that it was Micah himself—did so precisely because the passage presented a perfect opportunity to assert the compatibility of Isaiah's eschatological vision with his own.

The point is that for Micah no contradiction exists between Isaiah's idea that all peoples will some day embrace the faith of Israel, and his own prophetic conviction that a resurgent Israel—unified as in the days before the splintering of the monarchy, and led once again by a scion of King David—will subdue all the mighty nations of the world (epitomized by Assyria) through the force of arms. Far from being in conflict, these two visions are dependent on each other.

Which is to say that the precondition of the First Isaiah's "universalist" prophecy coming to pass is the fulfillment of Micah's "particularist" one. This is why Micah can describe the Davidic future as "peace" even as he is dwelling almost lovingly on the fierce and cruel blows the future king will deliver to all the Assyrias of the world. For it is only after the winning of these wars—only after God has executed " . . . vengeance in anger and fury upon the heathen . . ."—that "the remnant of Jacob shall be in the midst of many people as a dew from the LORD, as the showers upon the grass. . . ." Only then, nourished by the purified faith raining upon them from the influence of the religion of Israel, will all peoples come to God " . . . from Assyria, and from the fortified cities, and from the fortress even to the river, and from sea to sea, and from mountain to mountain."*

With this verse, Micah, in terms that sound very much like his own, stretches an eschatological hand out to the First Isaiah whom he has earlier been quoting.

The universal peace of the First Isaiah's vision, in short, emerges from its placement in Micah as a kind of *pax Israelitica* that has been established by God through the armed conquests of His own people. It is a peace, moreover, that rests on the utter destruction of idolatry. Some, most notably Kaufmann, have

*What KJV reads as "fortified cities" is correctly understood by the modern translators as "the cities of Egypt."

said that Micah is relatively indifferent to the issue of idolatry. Yet I hope I have
shown that he, like Amos, never doubts that the moral crimes and sins he spends
much of his time denouncing are inextricably intertwined with idolatry. To the
war against idolatry Micah, like all the classical prophets, brings the mighty
weapon of words, leaving the sword to be wielded, when necessary and when
possible, by other servants of God.

His job, and the job of the other prophets of the eighth century B.C.E., is to
go on uncovering the evils whose extirpation is the aim of the war against idolatry. But simultaneously, and conversely, what Hosea calls "the knowledge of
God"—which its priestly custodians are failing to hold dear and pass on—must
be kept alive and fresh by the prophet in order to remind the people of the great
good that the abolition of idolatry will liberate in all its glorious fullness.

CHAPTER NINE

THE FIRST ISAIAH AND THE
BLOOD OF BULLOCKS

UCH AS I WOULD LIKE to go on to Isaiah without further ado, I
am forced to begin by elaborating on a problem I have already
touched on several times, though only in passing. It is a very old
problem, but it has lately been growing thornier and thornier—as thorny, one
might say, as the briers and thistles that are used repeatedly in the Book of Isaiah
itself as an image of the aridity of despoliation.

For a long time—ever since the Middle Ages—it was suspected on the basis
of internal historical evidence that there were two different prophets in the
Book of Isaiah whose oracles had been stitched together under the name of the
first, Isaiah the son of Amoz. Among Jews, beginning with the great rabbinical
exegete of the twelfth century C.E., Abraham Ibn Ezra, fully traditionalist commentators have existed who were willing to entertain this possibility. As Jon D.
Levenson explains, the more daring Jewish exegetes of the Middle Ages "did not
really care" who had a hand in writing the books of the Bible. For "if the real
author is God, it is of no account which human vessel He inspired with any
given verse." A modern traditionalist expression of the same medieval attitude
comes from Rabbi J. H. Hertz:

> This question can be considered dispassionately. It touches no dogma,
> or any religious principle in Judaism; and, moreover, does not materially
> affect the understanding of the prophecies, or of the human conditions
> of the Jewish people that they have in view.

There are, however, strict Orthodox Jews who have never ceased insisting on
a single Isaiah, and they are joined by fundamentalist Protestants who believe in

the "inerrancy of Scripture." As for Roman Catholics, a Biblical Commission in 1908 cautioned exegetes of that faith against the splitting up of Isaiah, but today, according to the editors of the Jerusalem Bible, "a growing number of Catholic interpreters" now accept the modern critical view.

Accepting "the modern critical view" once simply involved surrendering to the large measure of agreement that had been reached by the end of the nineteenth century C.E. that only the first thirty-nine of the sixty-six chapters—and possibly not even all of those—were either by or about Isaiah the son of Amoz. Hence he became the First Isaiah, or Isaiah of Jerusalem, after the city in which he lived. But apart from being his home, Jerusalem was of enormous importance to his message throughout the four decades, running from about 740–700 B.C.E., of his prophetic career.

A correlative consensus also coalesced around chapters 40–66. It held that about two hundred years following the advent of the First Isaiah, an anonymous prophet arose in Babylon, to which—along with many thousands of his fellow Judahites—he had been deported after the sacking of Jerusalem and the depopulation by Nebuchadnezzar of the Southern Kingdom in 586 B.C.E. To this prophet the remainder of the Book of Isaiah (that is, Chapters 40–66) was long ascribed. He therefore was given the name of "Deutero-Isaiah" or the Second Isaiah or (more rarely) Isaiah of the Exile.

So far, so good. But then (in 1875) along came a German scholar (Bernard Duhm) who concluded that Deutero-Isaiah could not have been the author of the last eleven chapters (55–66) because, among other reasons, the prophecies contained in these chapters seemed to have emerged from Jerusalem rather than from Babylon. Thus was born "Trito," or the Third, Isaiah. Unlike the Second Isaiah, however, the putative Third ran for a while into scholarly skeptics who saw no good ground to posit his existence at all. But such skeptics were eventually outnumbered by converts to Duhm's theory—at least for a while.

For as time wore on, backers of the Third Isaiah, taking exactly the opposite tack from the skeptics, started wondering why they should stop with him when under the scholarly microscope they could discern not just one but many Isaiahs even in Chapters 40–66. These chapters they then classified as an "anthology" of oracles by a bevy of prophets of the "school of Isaiah." In response to this new approach, C. C. Torrey, a prominent proponent of the single-author theory of the Second Isaiah, complained in the 1920s that "the paring process, begun with a penknife, is continued with a hatchet, until the book has been chopped into hopeless chunks" (which did not prevent Torrey himself from chopping Chapters 37–38 out of the First Isaiah and giving them to the Second).

EXACTLY THE SAME COMPLAINT lodged by Torrey about the Second Isaiah might with equal justice be made about what the critical hatchet has done to the

First Isaiah. For a start, an entirely separate book entitled "The Little Apocalypse" or "The Isaian Apocalypse," consisting of Chapters 24–27, was carved out of the First Isaiah and thrown from the eighth century B.C.E. into the sixth, when—in line with one hypothesis—it was written by or under the influence of none other than the Second Isaiah; another theory pushed "the Isaian Apocalypse" up to as late as the second century B.C.E.

But even "The Isaian Apocalypse" itself was put on the block, where the hatchet went on chopping. There were short or isolated passages within these four chapters that some dated earlier and some dated later, while assigning each to separate members of the "school of prophecy" supposedly founded by the First Isaiah, and to which the ever growing tribe of "pseudo-Isaiahs" presumably also belonged.

Nor has even this extra bit of hacking exhausted the wielders of the exegetical hatchet on Chapters 1–39. In the 1970s H. L. Ginsberg (in a scholarly tradition that went back to J. G. Einhorn in nineteenth-century Germany) discriminated among passages that were "definitely or probably Isaian," those that were "definitely neither by nor about Isaiah," and "tantalizing in-betweens." Other critics denied to the First Isaiah not only "The Isaian Apocalypse" but also Chapters 34–35.

By now we have an even more extreme position, which is that the first thirty-nine chapters of the book are themselves a compilation or anthology of five separate collections (usually demarcated as 1–12, 13–23, 24–27, 28–35, and 36–39).* All these, we are told, were written and/or compiled at different times (anywhere from the sixth to the second centuries B.C.E.). They were then lumped together with the anthology or anthologies of Chapters 40–55 and 56–66 (many of which, we were also told, actually predated much, or most, of the first thirty-nine), and all were eventually "redacted" as the oracles of Isaiah the son of Amoz.

This move away from the old division of Isaiah first into two and then into three and toward God alone—and I mean God alone—knows how many more prophets, is what Joseph Blenkinsopp, in his edition of Chapters 1–39 (published in the year 2000), styles a "paradigm shift." Given this shift, he remarks,

> It is . . . not surprising that interest in the person and personality of an historical Isaiah has receded, for some commentators to the vanishing point. Few critical scholars today would feel justified in emulating Samuel Rolles Driver by writing on "Isaiah, His Life and Times," and

---

*The idea of the First Isaiah as an anthology, however, is not an invention of contemporary biblical criticism. It too originated with Eichhorn, and was further developed in 1821 by W. Gesenius, yet another of the German scholars who dominated the field in the nineteenth century. But Swedish, British, and American scholars gradually got in on the act as well.

many would be uncomfortable with George Buchanan Gray's contention that it is the task of the commentator to disengage the work of the prophet from the accretions which it has received.

We have, then, reached the point where not even Ginsberg's "definitely Isaian" passages are so confidently ascribed to the First Isaiah, and even Ginsberg's "tantalizing in-betweens" have been consigned to the dustbin of scholarly history. In the early 1980s, about ten years after Ginsberg wrote his article, a contemporary German exegete, O. Kaiser, concluded that only a few verses in Chapters 1 and 28–31 could with any certainty be traced back to the First Isaiah. With this, poor Isaiah the son of Amoz of Jerusalem all but vanishes, and what is left of him reminds me of the verse in Amos about the shepherd who " . . . taketh out of the mouth of the lion two legs, or a piece of an ear. . . ."

But Blenkinsopp, while in general yielding to this "paradigm shift," comes to the rescue (if not exactly with all colors flying) by refusing "to disallow a significant eighth-century B.C.E. Isaian substratum, . . . however overlaid it may be by the literary deposit of subsequent rereadings before and after the disasters of the early sixth century B.C.E." In the age of the "new paradigm," this is no small mercy, and I for one am grateful for it.

NOT THAT I AM PREPARED to dismiss all the immensely learned efforts to clear up the multitude of obscurities and structural confusions—as well as the historical anomalies—that are bound to strike any careful or well-informed reader of Isaiah. Martin Luther, in working on his great translation of the Bible into German, grew annoyed when he came to the classical prophets, all of whose books are bedeviled to one degree or another with the same problems of obscurity and confusion as Isaiah's. But as one scholar speculates, Luther probably had Isaiah especially "in mind when he spoke of the prophets' 'queer way of talking, like people who, instead of proceeding in an orderly manner, ramble off from one thing to the next, so that you cannot make head or tail of them or see what they are getting at.'"

Luther no doubt depended on the grace of God to solve these problems for him so that he could render the texts into intelligible German. But I must confess that, for me, resorting to the modern interpretative tools forged from the disciplines of philology, archaeology, and history has all too often served to compound rather than to clarify the difficulties of the text.

Nor am I alone in this. I learn from Blenkinsopp himself that Matthew Arnold, who in 1883 put out an edition of *Isaiah of Jerusalem in the Authorised English Version with an Introduction, Corrections, and Notes,* lamented that "the apparatus to Isaiah is so immense that the student who has to handle it is in danger of not living long enough to come ever to enjoy the performance of Isaiah himself." But if this was a problem in 1883, it has grown into a much greater one with the exponential increase in philological, archaeological, and historical knowledge in the past century or more.

It would be presumptuous of any amateur like myself simply to ignore the critical scholarship on Isaiah (and the other prophets). And it would also be ungrateful to deny what has become by now abundantly evident: that I have often been helped by the modern exegetes (as was Matthew Arnold himself in making his "corrections") to get a better grip on verses of which, like Luther, I could not at first "make head or tail."

Furthermore, there is no blinking the fact that passages throughout this book almost certainly belong to different periods than those below or above them. Conceivably some were altered at a later date by the First Isaiah himself. Or (to borrow a term from Blenkinsopp) they could have been "recycled" by others after the First Isaiah was already gone, in order to make them seem more applicable to the particular conditions prevailing in those later periods.

But even if we were to assume that the First Isaiah was the source of all the oracles (and the subject of the third-person stories) in Chapters 1–39, it would still be difficult, if not impossible, for anyone acquainted with the history of the last four decades of the eighth century B.C.E. not to notice that the prophecies collected in those chapters are often in scattered chronological order, sometimes wildly so. That modern exegetes are perhaps a touch too ingenious, and a little too free with their emendations or rearrangements of the text, does not alter the fact that they are grappling with real problems.

All that having been stipulated, it must be added that there is, in the words of Blenkinsopp, "a degree of consistency of language, subject matter, and theme throughout Isaiah 1–39 that allows us to speak of an Isaian tradition carried forward by means of a cumulative process of reinterpretation and reapplication." Which is to say that the Book of Isaiah "did not reach its present shape as a result of a haphazard accumulation" of editorial additions, but rather through "a developing textual and interpretative religious tradition."

Sharing this perspective, I will now go ahead and use the name the First Isaiah in talking about the first thirty-nine chapters of the book. Not only that, but I will attempt to view them as though they emanated from this one prophet who lived in Jerusalem in the eighth century B.C.E. where he spent the last four decades of that century describing the "vision"* that he had no doubt had come to him from God and that God had commanded him to express in words.

Furthermore, when I arrive down the road in our story to the sixth century B.C.E., I intend to commit an even greater sin against the new paradigm, and

---

*This is the very first word—*khazon* in Hebrew—in the book, and the term by which Isaiah's prophecies are introduced.

even against the old tripartite one that it has just about succeeded in replacing. For I will read Chapters 40–66 in much the same way I now plan to deal with 1–39: as comprising the spiritual and intellectual essence of a single prophet, the Second Isaiah, who had strong thematic and other links to the tradition of the First.

I will also take my stand with another minority view. This one holds that the Second Isaiah left Babylon for Jerusalem in the late sixth century B.C.E., when the Persian king Cyrus, who had by then conquered the Babylonians, permitted the exiles from Judah to return home. I will then treat Chapters 56–66 as having been spoken or written by the Second Isaiah himself after his arrival in Jerusalem—and not by a Third Isaiah, or another twenty, or fifty, or a hundred.

BUT BACK NOW to the last four decades of the eighth century B.C.E. and to the "performance" of the First Isaiah. In the simpler days of yore when we had only one Isaiah, he was generally considered the greatest of all the classical prophets, and even when we had two, the First held onto this reputation, though the Second was deemed great enough in his own right to be worthy of inclusion in the same book. Thus A. Cohen, an Orthodox Jewish commentator writing in 1949: "By general consent, the Book of Isaiah is regarded as the supreme example of the prophetic literature of the Hebrew Bible. In loftiness of thought, beauty of diction, and rhetorical force the Book occupies a place of its own."

Especially coming from a pious Jew, what this assessment reveals is that one of the major factors at work in establishing the immense prestige of the Book of Isaiah was—and is—its literary stature. Whether emanating from a single person or several, the first thirty-nine chapters of the Book of Isaiah unquestionably are a treasure house of some of the greatest poetry ever written in any language.* And even against the stiff competition these chapters get from Amos, Hosea, and Micah, they carry the day. Amos, Hosea, and Micah are all great poets themselves, and their books contain passages that are on a literary par with the First Isaiah. But he is more consistent in the overwhelming power that is generated by an imagination expressing itself through compressed verses that somehow keep escaping the bounds of their incredible brevity and exploding into spectacular flashes of light that blind the eyes with their brilliance and sear the mind and the soul with their heat.

At the same time, the First Isaiah exhibits a special skill and delight in wordplay, in assonance, in metaphor and symbol, in unexpected turns of phrase, in bold alterations of meter, and in shifts of tone from the reverential to the sarcas-

---

*For the reasons set forth in the Introduction, however, I will continue quoting from the cadenced prose of the King James Version.

tic. Not surprisingly, many of his phrases have infiltrated common discourse (" . . . let us eat and drink; for to morrow we shall die"; " . . . LORD, how long? . . ."; " . . . Watchman, what of the night?"; " . . . and a little child shall lead them"; and on and on and on).

Would aesthetic considerations have kept the Book of Isaiah, and the prophetic literature of which it is a part, alive all by themselves? There is no way of knowing. Still, without going so far as William Blake did, critics like Robert Alter and Hillel Halkin, who study the Bible as literature, suspect that such considerations exerted an influence (perhaps unconscious) over the decisions by the rabbis who would shape the biblical canon in the centuries ahead, and who had to determine which of the many candidates for inclusion were divinely inspired and which were not.

This suspicion is heightened by the debates among those rabbis over The Song of Songs, an erotic poem with no overt religious content that won a place in the Hebrew Bible through being interpreted as an allegory written by King Solomon of God's love for Israel (for which Christians later substituted Christ's love for the Church). Toward the end of the first century C.E., Akiva, the leading rabbi of his generation, suppressed the doubts that had been voiced by his colleagues about the sanctity of the book by exclaiming: "For all the world is not worthy as the day on which the Song of Songs was given to Israel, for all the Writings are holy, but the Song of Songs is the Holy of Holies." The overstatement is a giveaway: Akiva adored this book so much that he would go to practically any hyperbolic lengths to make sure that it was preserved.

For all that, I doubt that it was primarily for its poetry that the Book of Isaiah achieved its reputation as the "supreme" volume in the whole of prophetic literature. The main factor, I would say, was that this book lent itself even better than those of the other prophets of the eighth century B.C.E. to the purposes of that same amalgam of groups we have already run across twice before—Higher Critics, nineteenth-century religious reformers (both Jewish and Christian), and ex-believers (also both Jewish and Christian) who credited the classical prophets with the invention or the purification of monotheism, or were unwilling or unable to throw out the Bible with the bathwater of faith. True, and as we have seen, the aims of this group could be and were served both by Amos and Micah (though not by Hosea to anything like the same degree). But Isaiah, a longer and richer book, was even more useful.

There was also another group—one we have only previously brushed against in the course of this story—that made more of the Book of Isaiah than that of any other prophet. This group was much older than the nineteenth-century amalgam, having come into the world as a byproduct of the birth of Christianity. The earliest Christians, all of whom were of course Jews, took to combing the "Old Testament" for prefigurings and promises of the future Messiah, and for "prooftexts" that this Messiah would be Jesus. For the mills of a

"Christological" reading of the Hebrew Bible, no other prophetic book provided more or juicier grist than Isaiah.

The net result of the activities of all these groups, to put it bluntly, was that the Book of Isaiah earned its special reputation on false premises. To be sure, the false premises are not its own. They are, rather, the ones imposed on it first by Christians who misinterpreted key passages by reading meanings into those passages that were not there, and then by "enlightened" readers who picked and chose what pleased their sensibilities and ignored what seemed offensive to them.

WORKING HISTORICALLY BACKWARD, I will begin with the nineteenth-century groups and revisit the issue of the relation between ritual and morality. In discussing Amos, I raised the question of why God sent him from Judah to the Northern Kingdom to denounce the economic injustices that the prosperity of that period had evidently brought about. After all, I remarked there, the Southern Kingdom was also enjoying prosperity at the same time, so that sinners must have been around for Amos to fulminate against without having to leave home to find them. In that sense, when the priest Amaziah angrily told Amos to go back where he came from and do his prophesying there, he may have had a point.

Not, however, in the estimate of the great American archaeologist W. F. Albright. Writing in the 1940s, Albright said of Judah's prosperity that it

> was not canalized for the exclusive benefit of the aristocracy and the
> wealthy merchants, as was apparently true of the Northern Kingdom in
> the eighth century. . . . All private houses so far excavated reflect a sur-
> prisingly narrow range of variation in the social scale. . . . In other
> words, there was no period in Judah during which was such concentra-
> tion of wealth in the hands of individuals as to destroy the social order.

Yet in the first chapter of the Book of Isaiah, the prophet is much like Amos in his focus on the economic crimes committed in Jerusalem under cover of judicial corruption:*

---

*I am fully aware that many scholars divide Chapter 1 into several different parts, some dating either from the early 730s or 701 B.C.E., when Jerusalem's condition was anything but prosperous. Indeed, the passage I am about to quote is often placed in 740 B.C.E., when Jerusalem *was* prosperous and when the First Isaiah set out on his prophetic mission. But to say it one last time, I am proceeding as though there really was an Isaiah the son of Amoz who was active between 740 and 701 B.C.E., and that sense can still be made of much of the book we have before us if we read it as it goes along.

... put away the evil of your doings from before mine eyes; cease to do evil; Learn to do well; seek judgment, relieve the oppressed, judge the fatherless, plead for the widow. ... Thy princes are rebellious, and companions of thieves: every one loveth gifts, and followeth after rewards: they judge not the fatherless, neither doth the cause of the widow come unto them.*

In this same chapter, there is also a trace of Hosea's main preoccupation when the First Isaiah bursts out: "How is the faithful city become an harlot! ..." But then he reverts to the spirit of Amos's overriding concern with the mistreatment of the poor:

The LORD standeth up to plead, and standeth to judge the people. The LORD will enter into judgment with the ancients of his people, and the princes thereof: for ye have eaten up the vineyard; the spoil of the poor is in your houses. What mean ye that ye beat my people to pieces, and grind the faces of the poor? saith the LORD God of hosts.†

Like Amos, too, who places additional blame on the women of the North (the "kine of Bashan"), the First Isaiah lets loose with an assault on the women of Jerusalem that is all the more slashing for being so choice a specimen of his literary genius:

Moreover, the LORD saith, Because the daughters of Zion are haughty, and walk with stretched forth necks and wanton eyes, walking and mincing as they go, and making a tinkling with their feet: Therefore the LORD will smite with a scab the crown of the head of the daughters of Zion, and the LORD will discover their secret parts. In that day the LORD will take away the bravery of their tinkling ornaments about their feet, and their cauls, and their round tires like the moon, The chains, and the bracelets, and the mufflers, The bonnets, and the ornaments of the legs, and the headbands, and the tablets, and the earrings, The rings, and nose jewels, The changeable suits of apparel, and the mantles, and the wimples, and the crisping pins, The glasses, and the fine linen, and the hoods, and the vails. And it shall come to pass, that instead

---

*The modern translations give a better sense of what the word "judge" means in rendering it as "do justice" (NJPS) or "be just" (JB). For the last two lines, AB has "defend the rights of the orphan,/plead the widow's cause." And KJV's "rewards" are best understood as "bribes."

†NJPS has: "The LORD stands up to plead a cause,/He rises to champion peoples./The LORD will bring this charge ... etc." And, in common with other modern translations, it renders "ancients" as "elders."

of sweet smell there shall be stink; and instead of a girdle a rent; and
instead of well set hair baldness; and instead of a stomacher a girding of
sackcloth; and burning instead of beauty.*

Then there is a passage that makes conditions in the South seem even more
like those described by Amos, and casts even more serious doubt on the Albright
thesis about the different effects of prosperity on the two kingdoms. Having
sung " . . . a song of my beloved touching his vineyard . . . ," God, through the
mouth of the First Isaiah, translates the parable into an angry lament over the
expropriation of small landholdings by the owners of large estates:

> For the vineyard of the LORD of hosts is the house of Israel, and the
> men of Judah his pleasant plant: and he looked for judgment, but
> behold oppression; for righteousness, but behold a cry. Woe unto them
> that join house to house, that lay field to field, till there be no place, that
> they may be placed alone in the midst of the earth!†

And yet again, in the tradition of Amos, the First Isaiah declares in the name
of God:

> Woe unto them that decree unrighteous decrees, and that write griev-
> ances which they have prescribed; To turn aside the needy from judg-
> ment, and to take away the right from the poor of my people, that
> widows may be their prey, and that they may rob the fatherless!‡

Finally and perhaps most important, along with Amos, too, the First Isaiah
(comparing Jerusalem to Sodom and Gomorrah) violently denies that sacrifices
can wipe away, or serve as a cover for, moral evil abetted by judicial corruption:

> Hear the word of the LORD, ye rulers of Sodom; give ear unto the law
> of our God, ye people of Gomorrah. To what purpose is the multitude
> of your sacrifices unto me? saith the LORD: I am full of the burnt

---

*As NJPS frankly acknowledges, "Many of the articles named in vv. 18–24 cannot be identified
with certainty." I will therefore skip the various alternative guesses made by the modern translations as not necessarily more accurate, let alone more evocative, than KJV's.

†As usual, "judgment" in KJV means "justice." This passage also is an example of the wordplay
Isaiah loves to engage in and that cannot be captured in translation. Son: "Instead of *mishpat* (justice) there is *mispach* (violence [KJV's "oppression"]), instead of *tsedakah* (righteousness) there is
tse'akah (a cry).

‡NJPS has "compose iniquitous documents" instead of KJV's rather obscure "write grievances
which they have prescribed."

offerings of rams, and the fat of fed beasts; and I delight not in the blood
of bullocks, or of lambs, or of he goats. When ye come to appear before
me, who hath required this of your hand, to tread my courts? Bring me
no more vain oblations; incense is an abomination unto me. . . .

Nor is the First Isaiah communicating God's disgust only with animal sacrifice. He even rejects religious observances such as the Sabbath and the gatherings
for prayer:

Your new moons and your appointed feasts my soul hateth: they are a
trouble unto me; I am weary to bear them. And when ye spread forth
your hands, I will hide mine eyes from you: yea, when ye make many
prayers, I will not hear. . . .*

These verses provide striking evidence for anyone—which is to say, practically everyone—who believes that what distinguishes the prophets of the eighth
century B.C.E. is the primacy they accord to the ethical over the ritual. Yet as
with similar statements in Amos (and the famous one in Micah), the First Isaiah's
are often given a meaning that, as a man of his time, he neither does nor could
conceivably intend.

THIS BECOMES OBVIOUS if one of the verses I have just quoted in part is
read within its frequently ignored context. That context is supplied when God
explains His disgust with sacrifices and the rituals offered to Him: "And when ye
spread forth your hands, I will hide mine eyes from you: yea, when ye make
many prayers, I will not hear: your hands are full of blood."

Playing on the image of hands dripping with the blood of humans, God says
that they cannot be washed clean by "the blood of bullocks." The people can
obtain forgiveness for their sins and crimes only by repenting of the evil they are
doing and turning back to righteousness. And sin is not, as we might expect,
black, but red: red as the blood-stained hands of murderers: "Come now, and let
us reason together, saith the LORD: though your sins be as scarlet, they shall be
white as snow; though they be red like crimson, they shall be as wool."

If the people refuse this gracious invitation, and continue to rebel, God will
have to put them through a process of purgation:

And I will turn my hand upon thee, and purely purge away thy dross,
and take away all thy tin: And I will restore thy judges as at the first, and

---

*"Trouble" is less accurate than "burden," which is the word chosen by several of the modern
translations.

thy counsellors as at the beginning: afterward thou shalt be called, The city of righteousness, the faithful city.

Thus cleansed, the whore into which Jerusalem has transformed herself will again become "faithful," and the city that used to be full of "justice" and the habitat of "righteousness" until it was taken over by "murderers" will be restored to its former condition. *Then* the Temple will once again become a place in which animal sacrifice—the traditionally prescribed means for offering thanks to God and pleading for His mercies and blessings—will be acceptable to Him instead of being an abomination or a burden.

For most of us today, including plenty of professional biblical scholars, animal sacrifice is so primitive, so barbaric, so repellent that it takes a very arduous exertion of the historical imagination to acquire even a dim comprehension of how it could have been essential to religion at all, let alone a higher religion like that of ancient Israel. This is partly why the prophets of the eighth century B.C.E. who are assumed to have dismissed animal sacrifice altogether are so congenial to the modern sensibility. But in a book on the prophets (with whose central thesis I happen strongly to disagree), Abraham Joshua Heschel makes the necessary imaginative effort, and it sheds so much light on this issue that it is worth quoting at some length:

> One cannot doubt the sacred authority of the cult. It had a place and a procedure of its own, a sacred nimbus, a mysterious glory. It differed from all other pursuits; exceptional, striking, set apart, it conferred unique blessings. In the sacrificial acts something happened, something sacred was evoked, conjured up, initiated; something was released or cast away. The person was transformed, a communion vital to man and precious to God established. In the sacrifice of homage, God was a participant; in the sacrifice of expiation, God was a recipient. The sacrificial act was a form of personal association with God, a way of entering into communion with Him. In offering an animal, a person was offering himself vicariously. It had the power of atonement.

In this "unmistakably holy" sphere, Heschel continues, there was

> a spirituality that had both form and substance, that was concrete and inspiring, an atmosphere overwhelming the believer—pageantry, scenery, mystery, spectacle, fragrance, song, and exaltation. . . . The sanctuary was holiness in perpetuity, a miracle in continuity; the divine was mirrored in the air, sowing blessing, closing gaps between the here and the beyond. In offering a sacrifice, man mingled with mystery, reached the summit of significance: sin was consumed, self abandoned, satisfac-

tion was bestowed upon divinity. Is it possible for us today to conceive of the solemn joy of those whose offering was placed on the altar?

Heschel's intent in this description is to convey how shocking it must have been to the people of the time when the prophets said that God despised their sacrifices. Ultimately, however, he himself comes around to the Kaufmann position that the "prophetic polemic" could not have represented "a radical rejection of the cult," but only of the abuse or absolutization of it.

In more prosaic language, Jon D. Levenson goes even further than Heschel in illuminating the meaning of the cult in biblical thought. Basing himself on the first chapter of Genesis, Levenson proposes that the "creative ordering of the world has become something that humanity can not only witness and celebrate, but something in which it can also take part." And the way it takes part is, precisely, "through the cult." What follows from Levenson's persuasively argued view is that *any* misuse or corruption of the cult constitutes nothing less than an assault on the kingship of God and on the good ordering of creation itself.

Levenson is not referring here specifically to Isaiah, but his analysis adds another dimension to our understanding of the war against idolatry. Which brings up the most frequently overlooked factor in commentaries on the First Isaiah. It comes at the end of Chapter 1, capping what has gone before:

> And the destruction of the transgressors and of the sinners shall be together, and they that forsake the LORD shall be consumed. For they shall be ashamed of the oaks which ye have desired, and ye shall be confounded for the gardens that ye have chosen. For ye shall be as an oak whose leaf fadeth, and as a garden that hath no water.*

This is a reference to nature worship, one of the forms of idolatry prevalent in the North in those days and, we now learn, within Judah itself.

Here we have Isaiah announcing his enlistment in the war against idolatry. And by directly associating the abolition of idolatry with the restoration of righteousness, he simultaneously makes the obverse assumption that idolatry is the source, or even (in the spirit of Hosea) the equivalent, of Jerusalem's whoredom—that is, infidelity to God. Constituting a violation of the First Commandment, it is the cause of all the moral sins enumerated by the other commandments and by the laws to which they give rise.

---

*KJV's "oak," as all the modern translations recognize, should be "terebrinth," a species of tree involved in the type of idolatry the prophet goes on to describe. I was surprised that JB should have appended a note to this passage alleging that it is "One of the rare oracles in which Isaiah attacks pagan practice." But as we shall see, there are numerous attacks on idolatry in this book (though, often through circular reasoning, they are almost all taken to be later interpolations, which is perhaps why JB can call this one "rare").

With respect to those commandments and laws, in connection with Amos, I have already registered my agreement with the Andersen–Freedman opinion that the prophets of the eighth century B.C.E. are preaching out of a living religious culture that will later become codified and canonized in the Pentateuch. Therefore, when these prophets speak of such matters as justice and righteousness and sin, the people they are addressing know what they are talking about, even though they need constant reminding, further instruction, and exhortation.

The war against idolatry as it is further pursued by the First Isaiah, then, is inseparable (no less than it is for Amos and Micah) from his conception that an inextricable relation exists between the moral and the ritual. And no passage of the entire book sheds more light on this much-vexed question than the second chapter, which opens with one of the major eschatological visions in the Book of Isaiah. Having quoted it in full once in the very similar form in which it is reproduced in Micah,* I will not do so again. But I do want to make a few observations about it before examining the concluding half of the same chapter that is always conveniently overlooked whenever the first part is paraded before us.

FOR A START, the end of war (the beating of swords into plowshares, and so on) "in the last days" is seen by Isaiah as coming about through submission by "all nations" to the "ways" and the "paths" and the "law" and the "word of the LORD" emanating from "the house of the God of Jacob" in Jerusalem— namely, the Temple. But since the main purpose of the Temple is to serve as the locus of the sacrificial offerings and solemn assemblies that God supposedly rejects in the previous chapter, His disgust cannot be with the those offerings and assemblies in themselves. What God rejects—to emphasize it once more—is the idea that the blood on the hands of murderers can be washed clean by the blood of sacrificed bullocks, or that the red stain of sin and crime in general can become as white as snow through prayer and observance of the Sabbath and celebration of the festivals.

The corollary is *not* the abolition of these rituals, it is the extirpation of idolatry, which must (as always with the classical prophets) begin with an uprooting of it within the souls of the children of Israel themselves:

> Therefore thou hast forsaken thy people the house of Jacob, because they be replenished from the east, and are soothsayers like the Philistines. . . . Their land also is full of idols; they worship the work of their own hands, that which their own fingers have made: And the

---

*See Chapter 8, p. 168.

mean man boweth down, and the great man humbleth himself: therefore forgive them not. . . . For the day of the LORD of hosts shall be
upon every one that is proud and lofty, and upon every one that is lifted
up; and he shall be brought low: . . . and the LORD alone shall be
exalted in that day. And the idols he shall utterly abolish. . . . In that day
a man shall cast his idols of silver, and his idols of gold, which they made
each one for himself to worship, to the moles to the bats. . . .

Interspersed among these verses are castigations of the self-aggrandizement
represented by wealth and luxury, the weapons of war, and the instruments of
commerce (" . . . the ships of Tarshish . . ."). But it is not only the pride and arrogance of men that will be brought low on "that day." In a daring trope that may
well have influenced the metaphorical leaps or "conceits" of the English metaphysical poets of the seventeenth century (some of whom, like John Donne,
were Christian clergymen), we are told that the same humbling power of God
will even strike at the natural world—" . . . upon all the cedars of Lebanon, that
are high and lifted up, and upon all the oaks of Bashan, And upon all the high
mountains, And upon all the hills that are lifted up."

This alone should put paid to the notion that the First Isaiah gives primacy
to morals over ritual. What he—like all his fellow prophets, pre-classical as well
as classical—gives primacy to is the war against idolatry.

The long passage from which I have just been quoting takes us deep into the
nature of idolatry. Starting with the practice of sorcery and necromancy
imported from the Philistines—forbidden, as we have been taught before, precisely because of its association with idolatry—Isaiah moves to an incisive definition of what it means for man to worship the work of his own hands which he
has made with his own fingers and with the gold and silver he has accumulated.
It means, paradoxically, that bowing low in a posture of humility becomes a way
of expressing his overweening pride and his haughtiness. For it is toward *himself*
that he assumes this posture, and that is why God will bring him truly low. So
will the mountains and trees be brought low, as a sign that they are not to be
worshiped or exalted either, since they too have been created by God and owe
their majesty to Him and to Him alone.

At the "End of Days"—when all the nations of the world will cast away their
idols and their graven images and acknowledge the sovereignty of the one true
God—the prescribed laws for worshiping him, the ritual as well as the moral,
will be binding on everyone. In the meantime, as we have also been taught
before, they apply only to the children of Israel. But *to* the children of Israel, they
apply absolutely, without reservation or qualification; hence violations will be
punished with the utmost severity. (Amos again: "You only have I known of all
the families of the earth: therefore I will punish you for all your iniquities.") If
the children of Israel continue in their sinful ways, they will be struck with

curses of every kind: famine and drought and fire; conquest by other nations; exile from their homes and their land and dispersal among the heathens. All these calamities are described by Isaiah in harrowing detail, culminating in the picture of starving men eating their own flesh.

For the sake of His own name, however, and because of the promise He has made to their forefathers and then to King David, God will ensure that a remnant of His people will always survive such devastations. As a sign of this, he orders Isaiah to give his firstborn son the name Shear-jashub ("a remnant will return").

Which brings me to a theme that the great German sociologist of the early twentieth century, Max Weber, took to be the most important preoccupation of the Hebrew prophets:

> [It] must not be forgotten that in the motivation of the Israelite prophets . . . social reforms were only a means to an end. Their primary concern was with foreign politics, chiefly because it constituted the theater of their god's activity. The Israelite prophets were concerned with social and other types of injustice as a violation of the Mosaic code primarily in order to explain God's wrath, and not in order to institute a program of social reform.

Weber is closer to the truth than the critics who stress social reform as the primary concern of the prophets. Though his own analysis goes too far, he forces us to attend more closely to an element of classical prophecy that is almost always neglected (and that will also lead us, albeit a bit circuitously, to the Christological readings of Isaiah).

In 734 B.C.E., during the reign in Judah of King Ahaz, a member of the Davidic dynasty, Syria and the Northern Kingdom of Israel (often called Ephraim by the prophets, as it is here) join forces against the Assyrian empire, and they seek to enlist Judah in this alliance. But when, for whatever reason, Ahaz refuses, they attack Judah in the hope of toppling him and putting on the throne in Jerusalem a puppet of their own who will cooperate in their undertaking. Under siege, Ahaz applies to Assyria for protection, the price of which is turning Judah into a vassal state.

Historians once thought that it was Assyrian policy to force its religion on its vassals, but apparently this was not the case. Yet (as we read in the Second Book of Kings, though curiously there is no mention of it here), Ahaz winds up paying tribute not only in the form of treasure but also in the form of obeisance to the Assyrian gods. (As we also know from Kings, and as I mentioned in discussing Micah, such obeisance will even come to involve child sacrifice and that Ahaz himself will practice it.)

Before this plan has been acted upon, God commands the First Isaiah to meet with Ahaz for the purpose of persuading him that it is on Him the "house of David" should rely, and not on Assyria. Besides, there is nothing to fear from the Syrian–Ephraimite coalition. The attack on Judah by these two nations will fail ("Thus saith the LORD GOD, It shall not stand, neither shall it come to pass"*); and their rebellion against Assyria will also fail, with dreadful consequences for them, up to and including their extinction as nations. "Moreover the LORD spake again unto Ahaz, saying, Ask thee a sign of the LORD thy God; ask it either in the depth, or in the height above. But Ahaz said, I will not ask, neither will I tempt the LORD." To this the First Isaiah himself retorts in his own voice: " . . . Hear ye now, O house of David; Is it a small thing for you to weary men, but will ye weary my God also? Therefore the LORD himself shall give you a sign. . . ."

It is with this sign that we arrive at the first of the many verses that have been claimed by Christians as prophecies of the birth of Jesus, and that to them have made the Book of Isaiah, as the major herald of Christianity, the greatest in the entire prophetic corpus.

Before embarking on this discussion, I wish strongly to disavow any intention of engaging in a dispute with anyone who believes that Jesus was the Messiah (albeit in a different sense from the one Jews have always understood by that term); that he was the son of God born to a virgin; and that in being crucified he took upon himself, and atoned for, the sins of all mankind—or at least that portion of it which accepted all this as true. As a Jew, I am by definition not among that portion, but the last thing in the world I want to do is challenge its faith. What I do feel it necessary to challenge, however, is the idea held by many pious Christians throughout the past two millennia that the Book of Isaiah foretells the coming of their faith.

THE CONTENTION OVER THIS IDEA begins with the sign God gives to King Ahaz: the imminent birth of a boy whose name will be Immanuel (a transliteration of the Hebrew for "God-with-us"). So far, there is nothing to argue about, but endless debates have been conducted over the nature of the female now, or about to become, pregnant with this baby. In Hebrew she is *"ha-almah,"* which means "the young woman," but which has until very recently been understood by all Christian translators, including the King James Version, as

*I have often wondered whether England's then prime minister, Margaret Thatcher, knew that she was quoting Isaiah when she declared of the Iraqi invasion of Kuwait in 1991, "It shall not stand," or whether then President George Bush, in quoting the phrase, was aware of where it came from. His son, President George W. Bush, also used the same phrase repeatedly in expressing his determination to win the war against terrorism after the attack on the World Trade Center and the Pentagon on September 11, 2001.

"a virgin." " . . . Behold, a virgin shall conceive, and bear a son, and shall call his name Immanuel." The problem is that the word for virgin in Hebrew is *b'tulah,* and since that very word appears twice within the first thirty-nine chapters of Isaiah (and twice more in Chapters 40–66), it seems highly unlikely that the author or editor of 7:14, whoever he may have been, would not have used it here if what he had wanted to say was "virgin."*

An equivalent level of dispute has centered on the identity of Immanuel. Again until relatively recent times, Christians have assumed that he is Jesus, but few if any biblical scholars, even those who are devout Christians, still hold to that belief. The most popular candidate is Hezekiah, the son of Ahaz, who will succeed his father on the throne of Judah in 715 B.C.E. It is Hezekiah as well who has come to be accepted by most commentators as the king of whom Isaiah rhapsodizes (in a verse familiar from Handel's "Messiah" to many who do not know the Bible): "For unto us a child is born, unto us a son is given: and the government shall be upon his shoulder: and his name shall be called Wonderful, Counsellor, The mighty God, The everlasting Father, The Prince of Peace."†

The extreme hopes that the First Isaiah, as a Davidic "legitimist," voices here for the young Hezekiah must have been produced by his disgust with and rage against Ahaz. But it seems probable that in the second of the two utopian (or eschatological) prophecies for which the First Isaiah is best known, he is thinking not of Hezekiah but of some future Davidic king. If the first of these two prophecies—the one that also appears in Micah—envisages a day when all nations will stream to the Temple in Jerusalem and accept the sovereignty of the God of Israel, the second ties that day to an infinitely more secure establishment of the Davidic monarchy than Hezekiah can or will ever achieve.

It is a day that will come, however, only after much suffering has been endured as a result of Ahaz's submission to Assyria—an act of policy that to Isaiah constitutes an abandonment of God. The Northern Kingdom will have been utterly destroyed, and Judah itself will be afflicted by no end of grisly curses. But God will then set about to punish Assyria for its arrogance in failing to understand that it has been nothing more than His instrument, the "rod" He has used to chastise His own sinful people:

---

*The Septuagint translators who, in rendering the Bible into Greek, worked from an older Hebrew text than any now extant, chose a term (*he parthenos*) that has been taken to mean "virgin." But I gather from Blenkinsopp (who happens to be a Roman Catholic) that it is not even well established that this is what the Greek word actually signifies. In any event, the Septuagint is not generally regarded by critical scholars as a more reliable guide to the Hebrew than the Masoretic Text, where the word is *ha-almah.*

†The other most important passages that have been taken by Christians as prefigurings of Jesus, but that few biblical scholars still do, concern the "Suffering Servant" in the second half of the book. I will deal with those passages when I get to the Second Isaiah in Chapter 13.

Wherefore it shall come to pass, that when the LORD hath performed
his whole work upon mount Zion and on Jerusalem, I will punish the
fruit of the stout heart of the king of Assyria, and the glory of his high
looks. For he saith, By the strength of my hand I have done it, and by
my wisdom. . . . Shall the axe boast itself against him that heweth therewith? or shall the saw magnify itself against him that shaketh it? as if the
rod should shake itself against them that lift it up, or as if the staff lift up
itself, as if it were no wood.

The devastation of Assyria having been accomplished, and Judah liberated
from its ungodly and tyrannical grasp, a faithful "remnant" of "the house of
Jacob" will return to God. Conditions will then be ripe for the enthronement of
a true scion of the house of David the son of Jesse:

And there shall come forth a rod out of the stem of Jesse, and a Branch
shall grow out of his roots: And the spirit of the LORD shall rest upon
him, the spirit of wisdom and understanding, the spirit of counsel and
might, the spirit of knowledge and of the fear of the LORD; And shall
make him of quick understanding in the fear of the LORD: and he
shall not judge after the sight of his eyes, neither reprove after the hearing of his ears: But with righteousness shall he judge the poor, and
reprove with equity for the meek of the earth: and he shall smite the
earth with the rod of his mouth, and with the breath of his lips shall he
slay the wicked. And righteousness shall be the girdle of his loins, and
faithfulness the girdle of his reins.*

But this messianic† kingdom will not only bring justice to men; it will also
usher in an order of peace and harmony in the natural world such as has not
existed since the Garden of Eden:

The wolf also shall dwell with the lamb, and the leopard shall lie down
with the kid; and the calf and the young lion and the fatling together;
and a little child shall lead them. And the cow and the bear shall feed;
their young ones shall lie down together: and the lion shall eat straw like
the ox. And the suckling child shall play on the hole of the asp, and the
weaned child shall put his hand on the cockatrice' den. They shall not
hurt nor destroy in all my holy mountain: for the earth shall be full of
the knowledge of the LORD, as the waters cover the sea.

---

*For "reins," NJPS has "waist," and JB opts for "hips."

†The First Isaiah never uses the words "messiah" or "messianic," but the idea as it would subsequently develop is clearly implicit in these prophecies.

The First Isaiah then takes care to merge this vision into the one describing the conversion of the whole world to the religion of Israel: "And in that day there shall be a root of Jesse, which shall stand for an ensign of the people; to it shall the Gentiles seek, and his rest shall be glorious."* Everything is then rounded out with the promise that the Israelites will come home from the various countries to which they have been exiled; that the separated Kingdoms of Judah and Israel will be united once again into a single nation; and that their former oppressors will now become their subjects.

WHAT ALL THIS ADDS UP TO is that the messianic era in the First Isaiah's conception of it, both here and in the first vision of the End of Days, is a time of triumph for God over all the world. But it is simultaneously a triumph for the chosen people of God, who will be ruled by His law under the king of His choice and who will extend that rule to all the earth. The idea is entirely worldly, even political, and so little does it entail any new "testament" or religion that it can easily be reconciled with the words of Jesus:

Think not that I am come to destroy the law, or the prophets: I am not come to destroy, but to fulfill. For verily I say unto you, Till heaven and earth pass, one jot or one tittle shall in no wise pass from the law, till all be fulfilled. Whosoever therefore shall break one of these least commandments, and shall teach men so, he shall be called the least in the kingdom of heaven: but whosoever shall do and teach them, the same shall be called great in the kingdom of heaven.

But if the attitude of Jesus toward the Law is consistent with the First Isaiah's, there is no way to make peace between Isaiah's vision of the utopian future and the messianism of early Christianity, as fashioned not by Jesus but by St. Paul. This new messianism requires an *abrogation* of the old Law, which Paul identifies with death, not its perfect fulfillment, and still less its extension to the Gentiles (just the opposite, in fact). The only thing the First Isaiah's conception has in common with this infinitely more radical view is the touch of the mystical in his vision of peace and harmony in the animal kingdom.

On the other hand, the First Isaiah's conception has almost everything in common with what I have described as the *pax Israelitica* envisioned by Micah. "Almost" because Micah's is achieved by the military victories of the children of

---

*Both NJPS and JB make this verse a little less opaque. NJPS: "In that day,/The stock of Jesse that has remained standing/Shall become a standard to peoples—/Nations shall seek his counsel,/And his abode shall be honored." And JB: "That day, the root of Jesse/shall stand as a signal to the peoples./It will be sought out by the nations/and its home will be glorious."

Israel, whereas Isaiah's is brought about not by arms but by the actions of God. The First Isaiah is consistently against any reliance by his people on the force of arms, whether their own or anyone else's:

> Woe to them that go down to Egypt for help; and stay on horses, and trust in chariots, because they are many; and in horsemen, because they are very strong; but they look not unto the Holy One of Israel, neither seek the LORD!

Hence, as the First Isaiah opposes Ahaz's appeal to Assyria for protection against the Syrian-Ephraimite coalition in 734 B.C.E., and as at God's bidding he goes around naked and barefoot for three years to dramatize in his own person what will happen to the Egyptians at the hands of the Assyrians under Sargon in 711 B.C.E.*—so at the very end of his prophetic career in 701 B.C.E., with the Assyrians under Sennacherib having overrun much of Judah and having now laid siege to Jerusalem, the prophet opposes the effort of Ahaz's son Hezekiah to seek help from Egypt.† The frightened king prays to God, and his answer comes in a message from the First Isaiah:

> Then Isaiah the son of Amoz sent unto Hezekiah saying, Thus saith the LORD God of Israel, Whereas thou hast prayed to me against Sennacherib king of Assyria: This is the word which the LORD hath spoken concerning him; The virgin, the daughter of Zion, hath despised thee, and laughed thee to scorn; the daughter of Jerusalem hath shaken her head at thee. . . . Therefore thus saith the LORD concerning the king of Assyria, He shall not come into this city, nor shoot an arrow there, nor come before it with shields, nor cast a bank against it. . . . For I will defend this city for mine own sake, and for my servant David's sake.‡

Sure enough, on that very night,

---

*Blenkinsopp thinks it more likely that Isaiah did this in 701 B.C.E. rather than during a campaign of Assyria against the Philistine city of Ashdod. Perhaps. He—and others—also thinks that Isaiah did not literally go around naked and barefoot, "but merely paraded at *intervals* . . . in the guise of a prisoner of war." Still, "naked and barefoot" (*arom v'yakhef*) is what the Hebrew text says.

†This entire story, which occupies Chapters 36–39 of Isaiah, also appears, with some variations, in the Second Book of Kings (18–19), from which many scholars think it was borrowed. Many scholars also think that the Isaiah of these chapters is not the same person as the Isaiah of the oracles that are attributed to him. But even if that is true, the theo-political attitudes expressed by the figure called Isaiah the son of Amoz in the story seem entirely characteristic of the First Isaiah.

‡"Cast a bank" means build a siege ramp or mound.

... the angel of the LORD went forth, and smote in the camp of the Assyrians, a hundred and fourscore and five thousand: and when they arose early in the morning, behold, they were all dead corpses. So Sennacherib, king of Assyria departed, and went and returned, and dwelt at Nineveh.

In historical fact, whether through the agency of an angel or not, the Assyrians did depart (some sort of plague may even have swept through their ranks), and Jerusalem was spared.

Thus is the First Isaiah vindicated in his conviction that Judah can only "... triumph by stillness and quiet; Your victory shall come about Through calm and confidence."* And lest the children of Israel persist in forgetting what should by now be absolutely clear, the First Isaiah has all along been hammering it into them that the renunciation of idolatry is a precondition of their triumph:

Turn ye unto him from whom the children of Israel have deeply revolted. For in that day every man shall cast away his idols of silver, and his idols of gold, which your own hands have made unto you for a sin. Then shall the Assyrian fall with the sword, not of a mighty man...."†

And further:

Ye shall defile also the covering of thy graven images of silver, and the ornaments of thy molten images of gold: thou shalt cast them away as a menstruous cloth; thou shalt say unto it, Get thee hence. . . . [Then] through the voice of the LORD shall the Assyrian be beaten down....

IN THE LIGHT OF THESE VERSES, it becomes clear that the First Isaiah is what we would today categorize as a neutralist or a quietist or perhaps an isolationist. In the international conditions under which Judah is trying to avoid the fate of the Northern Kingdom, neutralism or quietism may or may not be the wisest possible policy. Certainly there are activists in Jerusalem who think that, in preaching such a doctrine, the First Isaiah is a dangerous demagogue. He tells them, always speaking in the name of God, that " . . . Their strength is to sit still," and they tell him to get lost. To which he counters, again in the name of God:

---

*I have deserted KJV here, whose translation is almost impossible to understand, in favor of NJPS, although *g'vuratkhem* might possibly be rendered as "strength" rather than "victory."

†The modern translations understand the last verse as meaning that the Assyrians will fall not by a human but by a divine sword.

> Now go, write it before them in a table, and note it in a book, that it
> may be for the time to come for ever and ever: That this is a rebellious
> people, lying children, children that will not hear the law of the LORD:
> Which say to the seers, See not; and to the prophets, Prophesy not unto
> us right things, speak unto us smooth things, prophesy deceits: Get you
> out of the way, turn aside out of the path, cause the Holy One of Israel
> to cease before us.*

Yet I cannot see how the First Isaiah's conviction that Judah should refrain
from getting itself entangled in foreign alliances makes him (as Yehezkel Kaufmann and many others assert) more of a "universalist" than Micah. It is true that
in a series of chapters containing Oracles against the Nations (like those with
which the Book of Amos opens), the fulminations and prophecies of doom are
interrupted from time to time by expressions of compassion (though some critics have interpreted these as intended sarcastically). But then there is the mysterious reversal that concludes a vituperative denunciation of Egypt:

> And the LORD shall be known to Egypt, and the Egyptians shall know
> the LORD in that day, and shall do sacrifice and oblation; yea, they shall
> vow a vow unto the LORD, and perform it. And the LORD shall smite
> Egypt: he shall smite and heal it: and they shall return even to the
> LORD, and he shall be intreated of them, and shall heal them. In that
> day shall there be a highway out of Egypt to Assyria, and the Assyrian
> shall come into Egypt, and the Egyptian into Assyria, and the Egyptians
> shall serve with the Assyrians. In that day shall Israel be the third with
> Egypt and with Assyria, even a blessing in the midst of the land: Whom
> the LORD of hosts shall bless, saying, Blessed be Egypt my people, and
> Assyria the work of my hands, and Israel mine inheritance.

This passage has been cited by commentators as a mark of the First Isaiah's
"universalism," but to me it seems of a piece with his other visions of conversion
"in that day" by the heathen nations to the God of Israel, all of whom will
acknowledge His sovereignty and worship Him (with, be it well noted, "sacrifice
and oblation"). To the First Isaiah, as to Micah, it is through the *particular* agency
of Israel (still "mine inheritance")—an Israel faithful to God and to His commandments—that strife, and war, and crime, and oppression will eventually
come to an end for everyone in the world.

---

*KJV is faithful enough to the Hebrew at the end of this passage, but NJPS's translation clarifies
the verse: "Let us hear no more/About the Holy One of Israel." Incidentally, this is one of the
passages adduced by scholars who think that many of the classical prophets wrote down their
own oracles.

What can be extracted from all this is what I previously concluded about Micah: that no more than an opposition exists in the First Isaiah between morality and ritual does any conflict arise in his mind between "particularism" and "universalism." And underlying everything is the continuing war of words waged by the classical prophets against idolatry and its abominations—words that in the case of the First Isaiah are both magnificent in themselves and as deadly in their sharpness as the sword that God wields against the Assyrians.

But the First Isaiah's words, even at their most polemically warlike, also reflect something more exalted. Blenkinsopp captures this quality well:

> What, in the last analysis, is most characteristic of [the First] Isaiah and perhaps most difficult for us to comprehend, is his overwhelming sense of divine reality. The attribution of holiness to God (the Holy One of Israel, the Holy God) implies not so much the ethical character of Yahweh, which is not a major concern for Isaiah, as absolute, transcendent otherness. . . . The power of divine reality at work in the world follows from this intuition of divine essence, and so Isaiah is able to communicate with remarkable immediacy the sense of this power acting on the world, and therefore also the reality of judgment.

To which I can only shout a very loud Amen.

CHAPTER TEN

UP FROM UNDERGROUND

FTER 701 B.C.E., when the First Isaiah disappeared from view, not a single prophetic voice was heard in Judah—at least any that has survived—for between fifty and seventy-five years. It seems unlikely—even impossible—that no prophets, or aspirants to prophecy, were in existence during all that time. The reason must therefore be that, fearing for their lives, they went underground, much as the prophets did when Ahab and Jezebel reigned in the now defunct Northern Kingdom. Actually, there is a strong parallel between the situation created by Ahab and Jezebel in the North and the one that developed in the South with the death of Hezekiah in the early part of the seventh century B.C.E., and the ascension of his son Manasseh to the throne of Judah.*

The parallel is even drawn in the Second Book of Kings itself. First Hezekiah launches a campaign to centralize all worship in the Temple in Jerusalem, which involves getting rid of the idolatrous altars and high places and sacred groves that have sprung up under his father Ahaz. But then Manasseh rebels against his father's reforms and returns with a vengeance to the path of his grandfather:

> And he did that which was evil in the sight of the LORD, after the abominations of the heathen. . . . For he built up again the high places

---

*The exact dates are difficult to pin down, since the authorities differ. If Hezekiah really did get another fifteen years of life after his miraculous recovery, Manasseh would have become king in 686 B.C.E., and if he remained on the throne for fifty-five years (as, according to the Second Book of Kings, he did), his reign would have ended in 631 B.C.E. But other, apparently more reliable, calculations make him king from 698 to 642 B.C.E.; or from 692 to 638 B.C.E.; or from 687 to 642 B.C.E.

which Hezekiah his father had destroyed; and he reared up altars for Baal, and made a grove, as did Ahab king of Israel; and worshipped all the host of heaven, and served them. And he built altars in the house of the LORD, of which the LORD said, In Jerusalem will I put my name. . . . And he made his son pass through the fire, . . . and used enchantments, and dealt with familiar spirits and wizards. . . . And he set a graven image of the grove that he had made in the house [of the LORD]. . . . Moreover Manasseh shed innocent blood very much, till he had filled Jerusalem from one end to another; beside his sin where-with he made Judah to sin, in doing that which was evil in the sight of the LORD.

The "innocent blood" shed by Manasseh is often taken to be that of prophets who have been protesting against these "abominations"—a view that may spring from, or perhaps is the origin of, a talmudic legend about the martyrdom of Isaiah at the wicked king's hands some time after the death of Hezekiah:

> . . . For as soon as Manasseh brought the idol into the Temple, Isaiah began prophesying to Israel. . . . "Behold, Nebuchadnezzar will come and destroy [the Temple], and exile you." At once Manasseh was enraged at Isaiah and said [to his servants], "Seize him." They ran after him to seize him. But he fled into a forest where, on his pronouncing the Name [of God], a cedar opened up and took him in. Still, the fringes of his garments remained visible outside the tree. So the servants returned and reported it to Manasseh, who brought carpenters and had them saw into the cedar until Isaiah's blood flowed forth. . . .

Legendary though this story is, it could well be based on an old tradition of Manasseh's treatment of the prophets of his time. If so, it would account for the prophetic silence during so long a stretch of the seventh century B.C.E.

There are, however, scholarly apologists for this king who come up with a different explanation. They maintain "that the absence of prophecy during Manasseh's reign was 'in part because there were no major crises nor any real options in foreign policy for the prophets to preach about.'" In this theory, Max Weber's idea that the main concern of the prophets was always foreign policy is carried to absurd lengths. And the irony is that it may not even be true that, as a loyal vassal of Assyria, the most powerful empire of the time, Manasseh played the hand he was dealt and thereby averted major crises.

We are told by the Second Book of Chronicles that Manasseh was hauled off at some point to face charges by the Assyrian authorities. The reason, it seems, is that he was suspected of participating in one of the rebellions against Assyrian domination that broke out during his reign. But either he was exonerated of the charge or he renewed his oath of allegiance fervently enough to save his life. In any event, he was allowed to return to Jerusalem.

Another piece of apologetics for Manasseh holds that in Assyrianizing religious life in Judah, the king did "what he had to do." But as previously indicated, scholars have discarded the old idea that the Assyrians forced vassal states to worship their gods. Newer evidence has shown that only provincial territories of the Assyrian empire were obliged to adopt the imperial religion. By contrast, vassal states like Judah were left to their own religious devices, required only to pay tribute in the form of treasure and to swear allegiance to Assyria. In his apostasy, therefore, Manasseh was not acting under foreign duress (though he may have been motivated by complicated domestic political considerations that need not concern us here).

Yet even if there really were no major crises in foreign policy in the time of Manasseh, the notion that the king's sponsorship of paganism and idolatry in such extreme forms and on so vast a scale gave prophets nothing "to preach about" would still reveal a total incomprehension of prophecy in Israel. During World War II, George Orwell once wrote of certain of his fellow Englishmen—who thought that America had intervened "not to fight the Germans but to crush an English revolution"—that one had "to belong to the intelligentsia to believe things like that," since "no ordinary man could be such a fool." Substitute "scholar" for "intellectual" and the remark applies to the even greater delusion that there was nothing for prophets to do during the reign of a king whose capitulation to idolatry presented them with so poisonously ripe a target. The only reasonable assumption is that prophecy was indeed suppressed by force during Manasseh's lifetime and went underground.

Hence not long after his death, it erupted with a pent-up force obversely commensurate with the spirit in which he had carried out his own apostasies. Manasseh was succeeded by his son Amon, who followed in his father's footsteps, only to die (apparently by assassination) two years later. This brought Amon's eight-year-old son Josiah to the throne. There he remained from 640 until 609 B.C.E., in the course of which time he launched the fierce campaign to rid the land of the abominations encouraged by his grandfather that I have mentioned before and will revisit in greater detail in the next chapter. It was also during those three decades that four new prophets became active: Zephaniah, Habakkuk, Nahum, and—the most important of them all—Jeremiah.

As with so many of the classical prophets, hardly any biographical information has been uncovered about the first three of these except that they showed up while Josiah was king, though even this (I wearily report) is under dispute in the case of one or another chapter of their books. But even when it is agreed that they all belonged to the late seventh century B.C.E., the usual quarrels break out among the experts as to precisely when each of them arrived on or departed from the scene.

• • •

UNLIKE THE OTHERS, Zephaniah is introduced with a superscription that sets him squarely in the days of Josiah. (Not that this has prevented the speculation that the book might have been written a century or more later by some anonymous person and placed in Josiah's reign.) He is also identified as the great-great-grandson of one Hezekiah. (It seems unlikely—to me, if not to others—that this is King Hezekiah, Josiah's great-grandfather: surely if it were, the text would have said so.)

Anyhow, most scholars accord Zephaniah chronological priority over Habakkuk and Nahum because of the ferocious prophecies with which his book begins. The reasoning is that such prophecies seem more appropriate to the early years of Josiah's reign, before the new king has launched his reform campaign, and when the religious policy adopted by his grandfather and left in place by his father is still defiling the land. But now that Manassah and Amon are gone and the coast is clear, Zephaniah is emerging from underground to rage against the situation they left behind them.*

In the first of the three chapters of this short book (which together add up to only fifty-three verses), Zephaniah shows himself to be one of the more zealous of all warriors against idolatry by presenting perhaps the most radical and fearsome picture in the classical prophetic literature of the coming "day of wrath" that is the "Day of the LORD." In the popular conception, we recall again, this will be a day when God vindicates Israel by pouring His blazing anger upon the nations. But then, as we also recall, along came Amos, who was the first to warn that when God was done punishing the nations, He would turn with equal fury on the people of Israel, though where they were concerned, a "remnant" would remain. The same theme was then subsequently picked up by the First Isaiah in preaching to Judah.

Now, about a century later, Zephaniah goes beyond Amos in turning the popular conception over by declaring that God will *begin* with Judah and Jerusalem because they have been so thoroughly infected by idolatry of every kind—Baalism, astral worship, and child sacrifice dedicated to the god Molech. Because of all this, and before he even gets to the Oracles Against the Nations that are becoming a familiar feature of classical prophecy, he proclaims that dire punishment will descend not merely on Jerusalem and Judah, but—it takes the breath away—upon the whole of creation:

---

*Others argue that Zephaniah's prophecies might also fit with the end of Josiah's reign, and might express the same disappointment that Jeremiah (as we shall see in the next chapter) will feel with the failure of the reforms to have taken hold. My own intuition is that the vehemence of the first chapter points to the pre- rather than post-Josianic campaign.

I will utterly consume all things from off the land, saith the LORD. I
will consume man and beast; I will consume the fowls of the heaven,
and the fishes of the sea, and the stumbling blocks with the wicked; and
I will cut off man from off the land, saith the LORD.

What Zephaniah is saying, as Adele Berlin paraphrases it in her edition of
the book, is that "the religious failure of Judah means the end of the world
order." More specifically, it means the revocation of the promise God made to
Noah after the flood that never again would He destroy what He Himself had
created. And Berlin then explains that to Zephaniah this failure lies precisely in
the area of ritual practice (or the "cult"), which the prophets before him in the
eighth century B.C.E. supposedly demoted to second place after morality and
social justice:

> The specific failure that the prophet criticizes is syncretistic prac-
> tices. . . . There is no suggestion that the Judeans ever abandoned wor-
> ship of the LORD totally; only that they combined it with all manner
> of foreign practices.

It is thus the *corruption* of sacrifice and other rituals and the "slide toward
paganism" to which Zephaniah accords an importance that the prophets of the
eighth century B.C.E. are widely alleged to have denied the cultic practices in
general. But after giving us one of the more harrowing descriptions in the
prophetic literature of the great Day of Wrath that is hastening toward the world,
Zephaniah backs down a bit to offer a way out for the children of Israel themselves:

> Gather yourselves together, yea, gather together . . .; Before the decree
> bring forth, before the day pass as the chaff, before the fierce anger of
> the LORD come upon you, before the day of the LORD's anger come
> upon you. Seek ye the LORD, all ye meek of the earth, which have
> wrought his judgment; seek righteousness, seek meekness: it may be ye
> shall be hid in the day of the LORD's anger.*

It seems that not even when this ferocious prophetic warrior against idolatry
envisages God's repudiation of the universal covenant He made with Noah after

---

*The modern translations render "meek" as "humble," and they come closer to the sense of the
Hebrew than KJV's "which have wrought his judgment" in translating it as "who have fulfilled
His Law" (NJPS) or "who obey his commands" (JB) or "who have performed his command"
(AB).

the flood—and not even when, on top of this, he foresees a revocation of the particular covenant into which God entered with the children of Israel—not even then can Zephaniah resist believing that a righteous remnant of Israel will survive the universal devastation.

What is more, after the nations that " . . . have reproached my people, and magnified themselves against their border" are laid waste, this remnant of His " . . . people shall possess them"—that is, reclaim territory that has been lost by force of arms. Nor can Zephaniah resist believing—in the tradition of the First Isaiah and Micah—that there will even be survivors among the pagan nations at the End of Days who will cast away their idols and worship the one true God, " . . . every one from his place, even all the isles of the heathen."

But in what has become the obligatory rhythm of the classical prophets, Zephaniah jerks back to denunciation. Having offered hope to his people (including the prophecy, soon to be fulfilled in reality, of the destruction of Assyria and the transformation of its capital city Nineveh into " . . . a desolation, a place for beasts to lie down in! . . ."), Zephaniah turns again on Jerusalem. If my guess about his dates is correct, the Jerusalem he now attacks is the one that was defiled by Manasseh and that has yet to be cleaned up by Josiah, whose reforms Zephaniah does not anticipate. Or so I would infer from this passage:

Woe to her that is filthy and polluted, to the oppressing city! She obeyed not the voice; she received not correction; she trusted not in the LORD; she drew not near to her God. Her princes within her are roaring lions; her judges are evening wolves; they gnaw not the bones till the morrow. Her prophets are light and treacherous persons: her priests have polluted the sanctuary; they have done violence to the law.*

But if Zephaniah does not anticipate Josiah's reforms, he does have a very ambitious eschatological vision of the far future, when the evildoers will be punished and when the proud and the haughty will be purged by the consuming fire of God's "jealousy." When the fire dies down, all that will be left in Jerusalem will be " . . . an afflicted and poor people, and they shall trust in the name of the LORD."† This " . . . remnant of Israel shall not do iniquity, nor speak lies; neither shall a deceitful tongue be found in their mouth: for they shall feed and lie

---

*There are wide divergences between KJV and the modern translations (which also differ among themselves) in the rendering of several phrases in this passage whose meaning is unclear. KJV's "oppressing city" becomes the "overbearing city" (NJPS and AB) or the "tyrannical city" (JB), while NJPS suggests that the term may actually mean "harlot city." So, too, with several other phrases. For KJV's "Her prophets are light," NJPS has "Her prophets are reckless," AB opts for "audacious," and JB for "braggarts" and "impostors." Still, as so often when details in the prophetic literature are obscure, the general idea is clear enough.

down, and none shall make them afraid." They will then be joined by the nations who, also purified by the fire of a jealous God, will come from the four corners of the earth to bring Him offerings.

This little book, which begins with a vision of nothing less than the end of the world, now ends with a joyous hymn to Jerusalem, whose sins are forgiven, whose enemies are no more, and whose exiles are brought back home. "The creation which was to have been swept away," comments Adele Berlin, "is reaffirmed"—but largely, I myself would add, because the war against idolatry has finally been won, first within the house of Israel itself and then, because of its victory at home, throughout the whole world.

IF ZEPHANIAH, in the tradition of Amos, turns the popular conception of the Day of the LORD around, Nahum turns it back again to where it once was. The origins and identity of this prophet, too, are shrouded in a dense historical mist (as is Elkosh, the town from which the superscription tells us he comes). But of the many speculations surrounding Nahum, the one that strikes me as most plausible is that he probably does his preaching shortly before, during, or immediately after the fall of the Assyrian capital of Nineveh in 612 B.C.E., which leads within two years to the complete collapse of the Assyrian empire as foretold by Zephaniah perhaps two or three decades earlier. That enormous event (which Adele Berlin appositely compares to the disintegration of the Soviet empire in our time) is the main—really the only—theme of this little book, whose length is about the same as Zephaniah's.

Nahum has been treated harshly by biblical critics, especially (but not exclusively) Christian ones; he has even been denied the title of prophet. What they dislike about him is the unalloyed joy he takes in the fall of Assyria.

We know that many other classical prophets—including Christian favorites like Amos and the First Isaiah—deliver diatribes against the nations (the tally one scholar has made of such oracles runs to a total of fifty throughout the classical-prophetic corpus). But these are more often than not accompanied by harsh words about the sins of the children of Israel as well.

Not in Nahum. All he does is celebrate God as a God of vengeance, and he gives himself entirely over to exultation—expressed through a torrent of gory images—over the destruction of the Assyrian oppressors of his people. Against Judah and its sins, however, not a syllable of reproach or rebuke escapes from the mouth of this "nationalist," as Nahum has derisively been dismissed by those who fancy that the mark of a true prophet is mainly to castigate the children of

†(See page 207.) Instead of KJV's "afflicted poor," the modern translations all choose some variant of "poor and humble" (NJPS and AB) or "humble and lowly."

Israel, even if the harshness is invariably mitigated by the holding out of hope for the future, and even if he attacks the idolatrous pagans as well.

What manner of prophet is this, then, who in speaking to his people, offers no castigation, only hope; no reproof, only consolation? He never evens calls for repentance as a condition of God's mercy:

> Thus saith the LORD. . . . Though I have afflicted thee, I will afflict thee no more. For now will I break his yoke from off thee, and will burst thy bonds in sunder. . . . Behold upon the mountains the feet of him that bringeth good tidings, that publisheth peace! O Judah, keep thy solemn feasts, perform thy vows: for the wicked shall no more pass through thee; he is utterly cut off.

As for Assyria, nothing will be left of it:" . . . out of the house of thy gods will I cut off the graven image and the molten image: I will make thy grave; for thou art vile." And here is Nahum's parting shot at Assyria: "There is no healing of thy bruise; thy wound is grievous: all that hear the bruit of thee shall clap the hands over thee: for upon whom hath not thy wickedness passed continuously?"

Certain pious Jewish critics who have their own troubles in defending Nahum's claim to the status of a prophet take comfort from the notion that his book "indirectly depicts God's moral government of the world: He is the Avenger of wrongdoers and the sole security to those who trust in Him." Yet all the palpable uneasiness about Nahum makes me wonder whether the decision to include his book among the classical prophets was one of those instances in which aesthetic considerations prevailed over religious or theological doubts.

As even the Roman Catholic editors of the Jerusalem Bible recognize, Nahum (who in my own opinion possesses an imagination of disaster second to none in its blazing heat and pellucid clarity), is "one of the great poets of Israel." Along with their counterparts among traditionalist Jews, the editors of the Jerusalem Bible bend over backward to acknowledge that running through Nahum's "violent nationalism" are "the ideals of justice and faith; the fall of Nineveh is a judgment of God, who punishes those who oppose his holy purpose, . . . the oppressors of Israel, . . . and of all the nations." But their real feelings come through when they then go on to deplore the fact that "The book pulsates with the hatred of Israel against the people of Assyria," and to shake their heads with disapproval over its "violent nationalism, where there is no anticipation of the gospel whatever, or even of the worldwide outlook of the second part of Isaiah."

THE BOOK OF OBADIAH also stands accused of being an expression of Israelite "hate literature" or "xenophobia." Since this prophet is yet another of those about whom we get no biographical information, speculation has run rampant over him as well. As I remarked in the Introduction, the book bearing his name, the shortest in the entire Hebrew Bible—it consists of a single chapter of only twenty-one verses—has been split up by some exegetes into no fewer than seven parts, which they think may or may not have been the words of Obadiah (whoever he was). It has also been assigned to periods as far apart as the ninth and sixth centuries B.C.E.

But for a variety of reasons, the argument constructed in his edition by Paul R. Raabe for the later date, and more precisely the first decades after the fall of Jerusalem to the Babylonians in 586 B.C.E., seems most convincing. So, too, does the argument Raabe develops for treating this little book as a unity and setting it in Judah (which was not entirely depopulated by the deportations following the fall).

In discussing Obadiah here, then, I may be vaulting chronologically ahead of our story. But I have decided to do it anyway because there is an interesting connection between Obadiah and Nahum. Like Nahum, Obadiah unleashes his prophetic indignation not at his own people but at another nation. Yet it is not Babylon, the nation that has actually devastated Judah and sacked Jerusalem, that Obadiah attacks. His target is Edom, which has rejoiced in Judah's downfall and also joined in the looting of Jerusalem, cut off refugees, and turned them over to the Babylonian invaders. And what makes it all even worse is that Edom is descended from Esau, the brother of Jacob. (This may be one reason that Edom figures more frequently than any other of Israel's neighbors in the many Oracles Against the Nations delivered by the classical prophets. It is attacked in the Books of Isaiah, Jeremiah, Ezekiel, Joel, Amos, and Malachi. But there must have been other reasons, too, since at different periods in the history of Israel, the enmity felt toward Edom had causes besides a presumed consanguinity.)

Obadiah resembles Nahum, too, in having nothing to say against Judah. On the contrary, he soothes the people still living there (and perhaps—Raabe thinks—also the exiles) with words of consolation for their present disasters and of sweet revenge for the future. "Esau" is doomed to destruction for its sins against "Jacob":

> But upon mount Zion shall be deliverance, and there shall be holiness; and the house of Jacob shall possess their possessions. And the house of Jacob shall be a fire, and the house of Joseph a flame, and the house of Esau for stubble, and they shall kindle in them, and devour them; and there shall not be any remaining of the house of Esau; for the LORD hath spoken it.

And like Nahum, too, Obadiah does not even make the repentance of the house of Jacob and the house of Joseph (that is, the scattered Israelites of the old Northern Kingdom who will be gathered up and reunited with the Judahites of

the South) a condition of this deliverance. Raabe: "The prophet simply proclaims unconditionally Israel's future restoration. It has no other basis than Yahweh's undeserved commitment and faithfulness to Jacob and Zion."

Raabe here travels some distance beyond the text of Obadiah, which contains nothing about God's commitment being "undeserved." In doing so, this
scholar (who otherwise tries commendably to defend the book against "some
readers [who] might be inclined to criticize Obadiah for his harsh language and
his pro-Israelite zeal or to dismiss his theological perspective as simply political
propaganda") reveals that he is not entirely immune from what he himself calls
such "anachronistic . . . contemporary Western views and sentiments."

But there is also a less up-to-date uneasiness with Obadiah, which is more
Christian than liberal, and is reflected in the comment by the Roman Catholic
editors of the Jerusalem Bible:

> This passionate appeal for national vengeance is in sharp contrast to the
> internationalism of the second part of Isaiah, for instance. But it . . . must
> not be isolated from the whole prophetic movement, of which it repre-
> sents no more than a fleeting moment and the most old-fashioned
> approach.

A SIMILAR UNEASINESS among Jews may conceivably provide a clue to the
riddle of how and why the Book of Jonah came to be included among the classical prophets, and possibly even to its placement right after Obadiah in the
order of the Twelve Minor Prophets. I am not denying—no one could—that
Jonah wonderfully tells a wonderful tale, and fully deserves on that account and
others, too, to have been canonized. But (as I also remarked in the Introduction)
it differs from the other fourteen books with which it is grouped in the Hebrew
Bible in being almost entirely a narrative *about* a prophet rather than a collection
of his oracles. As such, it bears a much closer resemblance to the Former than to
the Latter Prophets.

Of course, the section that Jewish tradition came to designate the Former
Prophets provides a historical account of the period from Joshua to the fall of
Jerusalem. This would leave no natural spot there for Jonah, which was probably
written two hundred or so years later, in the fourth century B.C.E. (though the
rabbis who fixed the canon might well have relegated him to the Writings, as
they did the Book of Daniel).

But may it not be that Jonah was chosen precisely as a mitigating counter-
point to Nahum? Consider the plot. The prophet Jonah is commanded by God
to go to Nineveh in order to warn the city of the disaster it faces. Jonah tries
very hard to escape from this mission. Yet nothing avails, not even being swal-
lowed up en route by " . . . a great fish . . ." (never specified as the whale of pop-

ular lore), and he winds up in Nineveh. There, to his great chagrin, the city takes heed of his warnings, repents of its sins, prays to the God of Israel, and is forgiven. Instead of rejoicing, Jonah is full of bitterness and wishes to die. But to teach Jonah a lesson, God stages an obscure parable involving the withering of a gourd beneath which the prophet has taken shelter, and the book ends with one of the more charming verses in the Hebrew Bible, spoken by God Himself: "And should I not spare Nineveh, that great city, wherein are more than sixscore thousand persons that cannot discern between their right hand and their left hand; and also much cattle?"

The comment of the editors of the Jerusalem Bible is again very instructive. Also placing Jonah in the fourth century B.C.E.,* they point out correctly that "There is no trace in Assyrian or biblical documents of a conversion of the king of Nineveh with all his people to the God of Israel" at any time. Then, without mentioning Nahum but pretty clearly using him as a foil, they anachronistically proceed to praise the author of Jonah for "rejecting . . . narrow racialism [*sic!*]" in favor of "an astonishingly broadminded catholicity. . . . The lesson of humility and sincere repentance comes to the Chosen People from their bitterest foes." If in Nahum, the Jerusalem Bible detects no anticipation of Christianity, in Jonah, it says, "We are on the threshold of the gospel."

A not dissimilar estimate—with the invidious comparison between the Chosen People and the gospel subtracted—comes from a traditionalist Jewish source. "The essential teaching is that the Gentiles *should not be grudged* God's love, care and forgiveness. It is this grudging [on Jonah's part] which is so superbly rebuked throughout the Book."

BUT WHETHER OR NOT I am right about the relation of Jonah to Obadiah and Nahum, it is hard not to perceive a challenge to the vindictive triumphalism of those two prophets in Habakkuk.

This book, like those of Zephaniah and Nahum, consists only of three chapters. About Habakkuk himself we are vouchsafed even less information than we get about Nahum: nothing but his name (though there are indications that he is a Levite who sings in the Temple choir and plays on stringed instruments). Nor do the scholars all agree that he lived and preached in the waning years of the Assyrian empire. But since he speaks so vividly of the coming of the Chaldeans (who in the prophetic literature, and other parts of the Bible as well, are the

*Others estimate that it was written a century earlier, but no one is sure of anything. Even those who think that the Jonah of this book is supposed to be the prophet Jonah the son of Amittai, who is mentioned in passing in the Second Book of Kings as living in the first half of the eighth century B.C.E., do not imagine that he could have been the author of the book bearing his name.

Babylonians*), many historians have concluded that he witnessed the rise of the "neo-Babylonian" empire led by Nebuchadnezzar, which was on the brink of replacing Assyria as the dominant power in the region. Moreover, since there is nothing in Habakkuk about Nebuchadnezzar's conquest of Judah and the despoliation of Jerusalem, the historians have tended to set his prophecies somewhere between the date of that calamity (586 B.C.E.) and the finishing off of Assyria in 610 B.C.E.

Habakkuk does not differ from Nahum in concentrating his fire upon the oppressors of his people rather than on their own sins. But he does take much less comfort than Nahum does in the idea that the Assyrian empire will eventually be smashed. He tremulously confronts God with the question of why the wicked so often prosper and why the righteous suffer, sometimes directly at the hands of the wicked (or, in Habakkuk's own words, " . . . when the wicked devoureth the man that is more righteous than he?").

Neither in Habakkuk, nor in any of the other books in which it comes up, does the Hebrew Bible censor this most fundamental of all questions concerning the justice of God. Nor is anyone punished or seriously rebuked for asking the question. On the other hand, neither does anyone get what most moderns would regard as a satisfactory answer. In the present instance, the question is posed by Habakkuk in terms of the individual's lot:

> O LORD, how long shall I cry, and thou wilt not hear! even cry out unto thee of violence, and thou wilt not save! Why dost thou shew me iniquity, and cause me to behold grievance? for spoiling and violence are before me: and there are that raise up strife and contention. Therefore the law is slacked, and judgment doth never go forth: for the wicked doth compass about the righteous; therefore wrong judgment proceedeth.†

God is more responsive to the question here than He will be when Jeremiah asks it (let alone when Job, who is not among the prophets, does). Yet His answer is framed in collective national terms rather than in terms of the individual fate that concerns Habakkuk. God tells the prophet that He is about to unleash the Chaldeans—" . . . that bitter and hasty nation, which shall march through the

---

*Although they were originally two separate peoples, the Chaldeans had by the end of the eighth century B.C.E. merged with the Babylonians to the extent of becoming indistinguishable from them: hence the term "neo-Babylonian empire."

†As always, the modern translations use "justice" instead of the KJV's "judgment." And rather than "wrong judgment proceedeth," they come up with "justice is perverted" or "distorted."

breadth of the land, to possess the dwellingplaces that are not theirs. They are terrible and dreadful. . . ."

These, then, are the instrument God has chosen to punish the doers of evil whose success so bothers Habakkuk. (Along with Kaufmann and others, I take these doers of evil to be the Assyrians, themselves the rod of His wrath in the past, who, as the First Isaiah taught, made the mistake of arrogantly attributing their conquests to their own power and wisdom). God also gives Habakkuk to understand that the Chaldeans will in turn be punished in much the same way and for much the same reason as the Assyrians before them.

Nevertheless, the prophet remains troubled. Why should other peoples, less evil than the Chaldeans,* suffer at their ruthless hands in the process? And in appointing one idolatrous people to punish another, is not God allowing the victor to impute " . . . his power unto his god"? But again God reassures him with a vision, one that he is commanded to write down. Out of this vision Habakkuk first speaks the best-known words in this book: " . . . the just shall live by his faith,"† and then delivers himself of an oracle against idolatry:

> What profiteth the graven image that the maker thereof hath graven it; the molten image, and a teacher of lies, that the maker of his work trusteth therein, to make dumb idols? Woe unto him that saith to the wood, Awake; to the dumb stone, Arise, it shall teach! Behold, it is laid over with gold and silver, and there is no breath at all in the midst of it.

Eventually, " . . . the earth shall be filled with the knowledge of the glory of God . . . ," but according to Kaufmann's highly suggestive reading, the vision of Habakkuk suggests that this—the complete defeat of idolatry—need not wait upon the End of Days. It may tarry, and for the moment, paganism may have triumphed in the political area, but "behind the clash of political forces [lies] a more primary issue: the one God versus the idols." And in this war, not all the horses and chariots and arrows of the pagan powers can or will avail against the vision that will be realized in its appointed time.

This is a "faith" that will be tested to the limit within only about twenty

---

*Some commentators see a reference to Judah in the "other peoples" who are "less evil than the Chaldeans," but I am not alone in feeling that even a passing swipe at his own people is contrary to the spirit of Habakkuk.

†Famous though these words are in KJV's translation (and even though it was in that sense—also found in the Septuagint—that they were given enormous historical importance by St. Paul, who would use them as the basis of the doctrine of justification by faith), the Hebrew *v'tzaddik b'e-munato yikhyeh* is more accurately rendered as "the righteous man will live by his faithfulness" (or "fidelity") rather than his "faith." But since such faithfulness or fidelity is equivalent in the Hebrew Bible to observance of the law, the verse ironically lends more support to the opposite doctrine of "justification by works."

years, when the very Babylonians whose demise Habakkuk confidently foretells will lay waste to Judah and Jerusalem. They will even burn down the holy Temple itself in which the prophet sees God sitting, " . . . the God of my salvation" to whose awesome power he sings with " . . . my stringed instruments" the psalm— filled at once with fear and joy—that forms the concluding chapter of this book.

It is in the face of this impending and most terrible calamity that another and greater prophet than Habakkuk will, while carrying the war against idolatry to new heights, also relate it directly to the catastrophe. But in the course of discharging this mission—one he resists, but for which God informs him he was chosen even while still in his mother's womb—Jeremiah will be forced to torment himself and his people by telling them what he cannot bear to say and they cannot bear to hear.

CHAPTER ELEVEN

JEREMIAH:
THE RELUCTANT PROPHET

FROM THE ADVENT OF AMOS and up to point we have reached in our story (the last decades of the seventh century B.C.E.), it is the classical prophets who have been charged with conducting the war against idolatry, and with doing so by means of words rather than through the sword. But with the accession of Josiah to the throne of Judah in 640 B.C.E., a large share of the responsibility for carrying on this war shifts for the moment from the prophets to a king. In that shift, the sword does not replace the word altogether, but it inevitably comes to play a greater part than it has since the days of Elijah.

Josiah is only a child of eight when he becomes the king. It is now over fifty years since his grandfather Manasseh introduced, encouraged, and supported the idolatrous "abominations" within Judah, and even within the Temple itself, that Josiah will dedicate himself to extirpating. In the version of the story based upon the Second Book of Kings that we have already glanced at briefly, it is not until 622 B.C.E. that Josiah—by then in his twenties—embarks on his great campaign of religious reform. To recapitulate: during repairs to the Temple, the Book of Deuteronomy (either in part or some sections of it) is discovered and brought to the king. Josiah, upon reading it, tears his clothes as a sign of grief and penitence. He then sends inquiries to the prophetess Hulda, who authenticates the scroll, but informs him that the doom of the nation has already been sealed by the unforgivable sins of Manasseh (though Josiah himself will be spared the sight of the disaster to come).

In spite of Hulda's prophecy, the king orders that the scroll be read to the people, who are as deeply impressed—and presumably as frightened—as he has been. And so he and all the people

...made a covenant before the LORD, to walk after the LORD, and to keep his commandments and his testimonies and his statutes with all their heart and all their soul, to perform the words of this covenant that were written in this book.
                                                                      ת

Now, no one in Judah really needs Deuteronomy to learn that idolatry is the most grievous of all violations of God's "commandments and his testimonies and his statutes." But some people have either forgotten or have never understood that putting other gods *beside* God is as bad as putting other gods *before* Him. That is, "syncretism," which has been prevalent in Judah, and which, it would appear, has been naively or ignorantly practiced with a good conscience by many, also runs counter to the First of the Ten Commandments. Those Commandments, originally promulgated in Exodus, are repeated in Deuteronomy with a few variations, and the First in particular serves as a potent reminder that syncretism is no better than outright apostasy.

Deuteronomy also goes over much else that in the future will be (or conceivably to some extent already has been) written down in the four books that will eventually be placed before it to make up the Pentateuch. But Deuteronomy also contains several new things. The most disturbing of these to Josiah and his audience is this series of verses:

Ye shall utterly destroy all the places, wherein the nations which ye shall possess served their gods, upon the high mountains, and upon the hills, and under every green tree: And ye shall overthrow their altars, and break their pillars, and burn their groves with fire; and ye shall hew down the graven images of their gods, and destroy the names of them out of that place. . . . But unto the place which the LORD your God shall choose out of all your tribes to put his name there, even unto his habitation shall ye seek, and thither thou shalt come: And thither ye shall bring your burnt offerings, and your sacrifices, and your tithes, and heave offerings of your hand, and your vows, and your freewill offerings, and the firstlings of your herds and of your flocks. . . . Ye shall not do after all the things that we do here this day, every man whatsoever is right in his own eyes.

Reading or hearing these verses, Josiah and the people can only conclude that "the place" where God has chosen to put His name is the Temple built by Solomon in Jerusalem, and that they are forbidden to offer sacrifices anywhere else.

The reason this comes as so great a shock is that nowhere is there even the remotest hint of such a prohibition either in the traditions out of which the stories and the laws in Genesis, Exodus, Leviticus, and Numbers will come (assuming they still have not been written down), or in the sermons and oracles of the prophets, or in the living religious culture of the children of Israel. On the contrary: the people of Judah are aware that their ancestors from Abraham on down built altars and shrines in many places to which no objection has ever before been raised—not by God Himself nor by any of His appointed spokesmen.

For all that, Josiah is convinced by Deuteronomy that even the altars and the shrines that have been dedicated to the God of Israel—including the most ancient—but that stand outside the Temple in Jerusalem must be destroyed along with all those serving other gods. But putting first things first, the king begins by ridding the Temple itself—where God has chosen "to put His name"—of the Assyrian cultic objects brought or erected there by Manasseh. Only then does he institute a purge of all altars and sanctuaries of every kind outside the Temple itself.

Fortunately, this is a period when the Assyrian empire, in an early sign of its impending decline, is too preoccupied with challenges from the newly rising power of the Babylonians and the ever-troublesome Egyptians to pay much attention to tiny Judah. Testing the waters by daring to desecrate what is sacred to the Assyrians and getting away with it, Josiah is emboldened to retake large swatches of territory that had been lost to the pagan empire.

Among the territories he reclaims is a segment of the old Northern Kingdom. This gives him an opportunity to extend his purge even unto the ancient altar dedicated to the God of Israel at Beth-el, as well as the "high places" scattered throughout the North where pagan rituals have been enacted; in the process—unsheathing the sword—he massacres many of the priests who have presided over these shrines. From hereon in, there will be no sacrificing and no celebration of such festivals as Passover anywhere except in the Temple in Jerusalem—now, thanks to Josiah's irredentist conquests, the capital of a kingdom almost as large as the one that existed before the death of Solomon and the subsequent secession of the North more than three centuries earlier.

In general, this picture of Josiah's program still holds among the historians, except that most of them have come to reject the idea that his religious reforms began only with the discovery in 622 B.C.E. of Deuteronomy. The prevailing view now is that Josiah, young as he was but guided by older advisers, initiated this campaign long before that date. Indeed, the repairs to the Temple fabric during which the scroll was presumably discovered are themselves now thought to have been a stage in the already ongoing job of cleaning up after Manasseh.

Lending credibility to this new version is the fact that (as we have already seen) Hezekiah, the great-grandfather of Josiah, preceded him in a campaign to centralize all worship in the Temple. From which it can be deduced that Deuteronomy itself, or the traditions out of which it was compiled, must already have been familiar for a long time (even if, as some scholars think, Hezekiah's motives were more political than religious in wishing to assert his power over the cult and the priesthood). But more telling evidence that Deuteronomy was not suddenly unearthed in 622 B.C.E., or newly composed out of whole cloth, is the thorough familiarity with the book shown by the young Jeremiah.

ALTHOUGH WRITING A PROPER "Life and Times of Jeremiah" would no more be possible than doing a similar job on Isaiah, the scholars, mercifully, have left us with only one Jeremiah. What plagues them—and us—here is the authenticity or the authorship of this or that chapter of the text.* Still, Jeremiah differs in one important respect from Isaiah or the other books of the classical prophets who came before him. Whereas they are all very stingy with biographical information, Jeremiah's is full of details about him and his life, and many of his oracles are precisely dated as well. Much of the biographical and autobiographical material is scattered and out of chronological order, but it can be sorted out with the help of sources outside the Hebrew Bible. Yet even on its own, this material supplies us with a fairly good basis for sketching a fuller portrait of this most human of the prophets than we can of any other.

We know, to begin with, that Jeremiah was born in the village of Anathoth near Jerusalem around 640 B.C.E. (making him about eight years younger than Josiah). We know that he came from a relatively prosperous priestly family whose ancestral roots were in the North (where the traditions underlying the book of Deuteronomy, or the book itself, may very well have originated and then been brought South by refugees after the fall of the Northern Kingdom in 722 B.C.E.). We know that (like Samuel) Jeremiah was called to be a prophet while still a boy of twelve or thirteen. We know that he later acquired a secretary or amanuensis, Baruch the son of Neriah, to whom he would dictate many of his prophecies and who would write them down.

As to his familiarity with Deuteronomy, we know—or can confidently infer—something about that, too. This was still a period when priests were not only cultic functionaries, but were also trained to be custodians and teachers of the law (in Hosea's phrase, "the knowledge of God"). Judging from his earliest prophecies, the young Jeremiah was already steeped in Deuteronomy by the time he began preaching, and it continued to be the major influence on his thinking, as witness the more than two hundred citations from it in his own book. Yehezkel Kaufmann:

---

*Of the two main versions we have, the Greek of the Septuagint is one-eighth shorter than the Masoretic Hebrew, which is the longest of the three major prophetic books in MT. There are also many discrepancies between the two versions, and this has naturally provided much fodder for unresolved debates. For whatever it may be worth, I am with those who believe that the Septuagint deliberately cut repetitions, either because the translators thought they were errors of transmission or to make the book more palatable to the Greek-speaking audience. I also think that most of these repetitions accord perfectly well with Jeremiah's literary style.

The inaugural vision of the young Jeremiah [in 627 B.C.E.] antedates the discovery of the book in the Temple, yet it is pervaded by the figures and language of Deuteronomy. The book must have been an element in Jeremiah's education; he studied it in his youth in the priestly school of Anathoth and absorbed its language and spirit. To him the book was "the Torah of God," and he regarded it thus to the end of his days.

There has been much dispute over Jeremiah's attitude toward the Josianic reforms. This is another issue on which I am disinclined to swell an already overcrowded field of speculations. To me, however, it seems almost inconceivable in the light of his relation to Deuteronomy that Jeremiah can have been anything less than enthusiastic about Josiah's efforts to do what "the Torah of God" commanded.

But then how do we explain Jeremiah's relentless denunciations of the results of these efforts? Or the position he takes on the political crises into which, he prophesies, his nation is shortly to be plunged as a punishment for sins that seem more characteristic of Manasseh's than Josiah's reign?

One much-favored theory is that Jeremiah is responding to a post-Josianic regression. Yet as will soon become clear, even during Josiah's lifetime the prophet is already out there warning about an unnamed menace from the north that will sweep all before it in a rampage of destruction. However, not until some five years after the death of Josiah at the Battle of Megiddo in 609 B.C.E. does the menace acquire a local habitation and a name in Jeremiah's prophecies.

The threat that worried Josiah was an Egypt bent on exploiting the weakening condition of Assyria (thanks to which condition Judah was enjoying a brief period of independence). This is probably why—at the cost of his life—he went to fight at Megiddo on the side of Assyria against Egypt. All in vain: the Egyptians won, and just as Josiah had feared, Judah became its vassal. But only for a short while. By 605 B.C.E., when the dust had settled over these imperial rivalries, the Babylonians replaced the Egyptians as the dominant power of the region—and as the masters of Judah.

Unlike Nahum, Jeremiah takes no delight in the fall of Assyria, and unlike Habakkuk, he does not regard the Babylonians as an even worse alternative. Jeremiah even goes around proclaiming to all and sundry—including Josiah's two main successors on the throne of Judah, Jehoiakim and Zedekiah—that they should submit without resistance to the Babylonian king Nebuchadnezzar. Otherwise they will bring destruction on their heads. And when Jeremiah speaks of destruction, he does not, in contrast to the First Isaiah, spare Jerusalem, or even the Temple, "the house of God." Neither of these, he says (just as Micah did before him in relation to Assyria a century before), is inviolate: if Judah provokes Nebuchadnezzar, both the city and the Temple will be set ablaze and the people will be exiled to a foreign land.

There are two major political crises during which Jeremiah spreads this mes-

sage around—a message that is understandably condemned as seditious by elements of the population who, together with many prophets and priests, believe
that under the right circumstances Judah can regain full independence. Worse
yet, Jeremiah's prophecies are considered blasphemous because they call into
question the still regnant belief that God's covenants both with the children of
Israel and with the Davidic dynasty are unconditional and irrevocable.

The first of these two crises occurs during Jehoiakim's reign. When we come
to Ezekiel in the next chapter of our story, it will be necessary to go into
Jehoiakim's policies in more detail. But for the present, we can skip over the
dynastic and other complications, and merely record that Jehoiakim was originally put on the throne in 608 B.C.E. as a vassal of Egypt during its brief rule over
Judah following the death of Josiah. However, Jehoiakim then became a vassal of
Babylon after its ascendancy over Egypt in 605 B.C.E. Subsequently—and again
I am deferring the details until we reach Ezekiel—around 600 B.C.E., Jehoiakim
decided to rebel against Nebuchadnezzar, and after some hesitation, the Babylonian king responded by sending in overwhelming force against Judah.

Before the conclusion of this episode, Jehoiakim died and was replaced by
his son Jehoiachin. But the new king held out for only three months before surrendering to Nebuchadnezzar. Acting with greater leniency than Jeremiah had
expected, Nebuchadnezzar did not destroy the city. Instead (in 598 B.C.E.), he
contented himself with carting off the sacred vessels of the Temple and the treasures of the royal palace. He also deported King Jehoiachin and most of Judah's
leading citizens to Babylon. But he did not depopulate Judah, which he left to be
ruled by Zedekiah, another of Josiah's sons.

EVEN BEFORE THIS relatively mild preview of what twelve years later, in 586
B.C.E., will be the complete fulfillment of his most dire and violent prophecies,
Jeremiah suffers harassment and persecution to a much greater extent than any
of the classical prophets before him. He is arrested; he is flogged; he is made to
spend a night in the stocks; he is mocked; he is put on trial for his life. Even
members of his own family join in conspiracies hatched by residents of his
birthplace of Anathoth not only to silence but to kill him.

Driven to despair, and complaining all the while to God, Jeremiah is still
incapable of desisting from speaking the words he is commanded to speak. On
orders from God, he even writes to the deportees in Babylon after 598 B.C.E.
telling them not to listen to those who promise a speedy return to Judah. They
are to strike roots in exile, to marry and make lives for themselves there, and even
to " . . . seek the peace of the city whither I have caused you to be carried away
captives, and pray unto the LORD for it: for in the peace thereof shall ye have
peace." News of this letter reaches Jerusalem, and the exiles demand that the
"madman" who wrote it be imprisoned or executed.

On another occasion—during a conference hosted by Jehoiachin's successor, King Zedekiah, of several fellow vassal states of Babylon to plot a joint effort to achieve independence—Jeremiah parades the streets of Jerusalem with an ox-yoke on his neck (much as the First Isaiah went around naked and barefoot) to symbolize the only course of action that can save them all from utter destruction. And in yet one more mimetic act, he refrains from marrying as a sign of what is in store for the country:

> The word of the LORD came also unto me, saying, Thou shalt not take thee a wife, neither shalt thou have sons or daughters in this place. For thus saith the LORD concerning the sons and concerning the daughters that are born in this place, and concerning their mothers that bare them, and concerning their fathers that begat them in this land; They shall die of grievous deaths; they shall not be lamented; neither shall they be buried; but they shall be as dung upon the face of the earth: and they shall be consumed by the sword, and by famine; and their carcases shall be meat for the fowls of heaven, and for the beasts of the earth.

Around 589 B.C.E., Zedekiah, responding to the hopes aroused by the prophets whom Jeremiah has all along denounced as false, and relying on the prospect of support from Egypt (which will prove to be the same "broken reed" it was in the time of the First Isaiah), makes a bid for independence from Babylon. Nebuchadnezzar dispatches his troops to put the rebellion down, but—again for complicated reasons that need not detain us here—there is a short respite of a year or two from the siege of Jerusalem.

During that interval, Jeremiah, accused of collaboration with the enemy and of subverting the morale of the people, is flung into a dungeon, and then transferred to a prison cell, after which he is thrown down a deep muddy pit where he is left to die until an Ethiopian court eunuch (with the complicity of the king) rescues him. Kept under guard in the palace compound, the prophet is secretly consulted again and again by Zedekiah, who hopes against hope that Jeremiah will bring him the same assurances from God about the inviolability of Jerusalem that the First Isaiah gave to Hezekiah. But no such luck. Although Jeremiah, at God's command, has just purchased a field in Anathoth from his cousin as a sign that the time will come when the land will again be restored to His people, it must first be conquered and made desolate. And so all the king can wring out of the prophet is the same old advice to surrender.

Finally, in 586 B.C.E., the long-besieged Jerusalem is taken by Babylonian forces, and this time there is no leniency. Zedekiah is brought to Nebuchadnezzar's encampment, where he is made to witness the execution of two of his sons, after which his own eyes are gouged out and he is dragged in chains to Babylon to die an ignominious death. Jerusalem is set to the torch, the Temple goes down in flames, and the contingent of Judahites deported to Babylon is much larger than it was twelve years before. Jeremiah, considered a friend by Nebuchadnezzar, is offered the choice of staying home or going to Babylon where, he is promised, he will be well treated. But he decides to stay. Two months later, however, Gedaliah, the puppet governor Nebuchadnezzar has left behind in Jerusalem, is assassinated along with many Babylonian retainers. Fearing reprisals, Jeremiah's sympathizers drag him with them against his will to Egypt.

Like the Book of the First Isaiah, the Book of Jeremiah ends with an appendix—a story drawn, with some additions but otherwise almost verbatim, from the Second Book of Kings (and a section of which also appears earlier in the Book of Jeremiah itself). In the First Isaiah the appendix is the story of how Jerusalem is saved from the Assyrians and how King Hezekiah is granted a reprieve from death; in Jeremiah, it is the opposite story of how Jerusalem is taken and destroyed by the Babylonians and how King Zedekiah is put to death.

But preceding the final chapter of Jeremiah is another appendix. It consists of a series of Oracles to the Nations, similar in kind to those we have come across in Amos and Isaiah and will meet with again in Ezekiel. The longest of the series in Jeremiah is a diatribe against Babylon, and though a few of the others seem to have been written at a later date by someone other than Jeremiah himself, a good part of the anti-Babylon tirade has his stylistic mark on it. And so vehemently vengeful are these sentiments that they should silence any and all doubts about whether Jeremiah is at all sympathetic to the imperial power whose strictly political interests he willy-nilly serves in demanding submission to it.

I come back, then, to the problem of how we are to account for the counsel of submission to Nebuchadnezzar that gives Jeremiah so much grief practically from the beginning of his long prophetic career to its very end.

In quest of a solution to this problem, we can turn for guidance to a precedent in the First Isaiah. Just as to Isaiah Assyria was the "rod" God was using to punish Judah, so to Jeremiah Nebuchadnezzar is God's "servant" who is being sent on the same mission. And as Isaiah declared that the Assyrians would later be punished both for the evil they had done and for their arrogance in thinking that it was through their own power and cunning that their victories had been achieved, so Jeremiah predicts a similar fate for Babylon. Jeremiah himself draws the parallel: "Therefore thus saith the LORD of hosts, the God of Israel; Behold, I will punish the king of Babylon and his land, as I have punished the king of Assyria."

Nor is this the only indication of an equivalence in Jeremiah's mind between Assyria then and Babylon now. For one thing, there is a verse earlier in the book in which God promises Jeremiah that He " . . . will punish the king of Babylon, and that nation, . . . for their iniquity, and the land of the Chaldeans, and will make it perpetual desolations." For another thing, at the conclusion of the oracle against Babylon, there is a third-person narrative telling how in

593–94 B.C.E. King Zedekiah goes to Babylon accompanied by an entourage that includes Seraiah, the brother of Jeremiah's amanuensis Baruch. Before they leave, Jeremiah

> . . . wrote in a book all the evil that should come upon Babylon, even all these words that are written against Babylon. And Jeremiah said to Seraiah, When thou comest to Babylon, . . . and shalt read all these words; Then shalt thou say, O LORD, thou has spoken against this place, to cut it off, that none shall remain in it, neither man nor beast, but that it shall be desolate for ever. And it shall be, when thou hast made an end of reading this book, that thou shalt bind a stone to it, and cast it into the midst of Euphrates: And thou shalt say, Thus shall Babylon sink, and shall not rise from the evil that I will bring upon her. . . .

According to *The Anchor Bible Dictionary,* Seraiah (as evidenced by an archaeological find) makes a duplicate copy before throwing the scroll into the river.

In short, even if all the words of the anti-Babylon diatribe are not the words of Jeremiah, we are entitled to postulate (along with John Bright in his edition of the book) that some of them are, and that all the sentiments they express are his.

YET ANOTHER PUZZLE REMAINS: if Jerusalem under a virtuous king like Hezekiah was spared from the Assyrian "rod," why should Jeremiah proclaim that God will now permit the city and the Temple to be destroyed by Babylon when Josiah, an even more virtuous king, has rededicated himself and his people to His laws and his commandments? The only persuasive solution to this puzzle is that Jeremiah believes Josiah's purge has failed so dismally that Judah is worse than the Northern Kingdom was in its time.

True, Josiah has undone many of his grandfather's worst abominations, and he has faithfully executed the commandment of Deuteronomy to destroy both the shrines to idolatry all over the land and those dedicated to God outside the precincts of the Temple in Jerusalem. But even during Josiah's own lifetime, idolatry either has been proving impossible to uproot or is insidiously seeping back in. This is what Jeremiah declares in a passage that harmonizes strains of Hosea with allusions to Deuteronomy:

> The LORD said also unto me in the days of Josiah the king, Hast thou seen that which backsliding Israel hath done? she is gone up upon every high mountain and under every green tree, and there hath played the harlot. And I said after she had done all these things, Turn thou unto me. But she returned not. And her treacherous sister Judah saw it. And I saw, when for all the causes whereby backsliding Israel committed adultery I

had put her away, and given her a bill of divorce; yet her treacherous sister Judah feared not, but went and played the harlot also. And it came to pass through the lightness of her whoredom, that she defiled the land, and committed adultery with stones and with stocks. And yet for all this her treacherous sister Judah hath not turned unto me with her whole heart, but feignedly, saith the LORD. And the LORD said unto me, The backsliding Israel hath justified herself more than treacherous Judah.

A host of commentators, mainly Protestant, but also Jewish, have read this grave charge as an indication that Jeremiah, like the prophets of the eighth century B.C.E. before him, is opposed to ritual and sacrifice. That is, they interpret Jeremiah as saying that the Josianic reform has involved only the "cult" and has not been accompanied by the sincere repentance that would show itself in the moral sphere rather than only in the realm of ritual.

In support of this interpretation, the phrase "her whole heart" is cited as well as other verses that denigrate sacrifice, such as: "To what purpose cometh there incense to me from Sheba, and the sweet cane from a far country? your burnt offerings are not acceptable, nor your sacrifices sweet unto me." Or, more radically: "For I spake not unto your fathers, nor commanded them in the day that I brought them out of the land of Egypt, concerning burnt offerings or sacrifices." But I agree entirely with Kaufmann that when Jeremiah

> says that God did not command them on the day of the Exodus concerning sacrifices . . . , he does not intend thereby to deny the divine origin of the sacrificial laws, but, like Amos, he wishes only to emphasize that the cult has no absolute value.

An additional, and more serious, objection to the notion that Jeremiah wants to eliminate the sacrificial cult, however, is that it ignores the passages in which the prophet himself says exactly the opposite:

> And it shall come to pass, if ye diligently hearken unto me, saith the LORD, to . . . hallow the sabbath day, to do no work therein; Then shall there . . . come [people] from the cities of Judah, and from the places about Jerusalem, and from the land of Benjamin, and from the plain, and from the mountains, and from the south, bringing burnt offerings, and sacrifices, and meat offerings, and incense, and bringing sacrifices of praise, unto the house of the LORD.

Then, too, in another of his prophecies of consolation (about which more later), where he envisages an ingathering of the exiles and the return of righteousness and joy to Jerusalem and the cities of Judah, Jeremiah includes two

promises: that there will never be an end to the Davidic dynasty, and that there
will never be lacking descendants of the priests and levites " . . . to offer burnt
offerings, and to kindle meat offerings, and to do sacrifice continually."

All this makes nonsense of the notion that Jeremiah is in favor of the abolition of sacrifice and other ritual observances.

But what of the frequently quoted verses that allegedly show him at one
with his predecessors of the eighth century B.C.E. in awarding "primacy" to
ethics over ritual, as well as in his outrage over the rich, who are in his description of them no better than they were in the time of Amos and the First Isaiah?
Does Jeremiah not exclaim: "They are waxen fat, they shine: . . . they judge not
the cause of the fatherless, yet they prosper; and the right of the needy they do
not judge"? And what of a verse like this?:

> Thus saith the LORD; Execute ye judgment and righteousness, and
> deliver the spoiled out of the hand of the oppressor: and do no wrong,
> do no violence to the stranger, the fatherless, nor the widow, neither
> shed innocent blood in this place.

Finally, what of the principal exhibit usually entered into evidence on this
matter—the sermon Jeremiah gives in the precincts of the Temple itself, when
he denies that worshiping there can "deliver" the people from punishment for
their moral "abominations"?

> Trust ye not in lying words, saying, The temple of the LORD, The tem-
> ple of the LORD, The temple of the LORD. . . . For if ye thoroughly
> amend your ways and your doings; if ye thoroughly execute judgment
> between a man and his neighbor; If ye oppress not the stranger, the
> fatherless, and the widow, and shed not innocent blood in this place. . . .
> Then will I cause you to dwell in this place, in the land that I gave to
> your fathers, for ever and ever.

But, God goes on through the prophet's voice, if " . . . ye steal, murder, and commit adultery, and swear falsely," do you imagine that I will allow you to turn my
house into " . . . a den of robbers . . . ?"

Jeremiah certainly says all these things. But the difficulty is that standing by
themselves they distort and oversimplify his attitude by omitting—as, for purposes of illustration, I myself have deliberately done in quoting these very passages—his conviction that the moral sins he is condemning stem directly from
idolatry and are inextricably connected with it.

This becomes especially vivid in the Temple sermon, where oppressing the
powerless and shedding innocent blood are immediately associated with
"walk[ing] after other gods to your hurt," and where the violations of several of

the Ten Commandments he then brings up are connected with "burn[ing] incense unto Baal, and walk[ing] after other gods whom ye know not."

So, too, with Jeremiah's declaration that when God brought the children of Israel out of Egypt, He never commanded them to perform sacrifices. This he instantly caps (or glosses) with a suggestion (which is repeated elsewhere in the book) that the people have been misled by false prophets and lying priests to think that God actually wants them to sacrifice their own children to Him:

> For the children of Judah have done evil in my sight, saith the LORD: . . . they have built the high places of Tophet, which is in the valley of the son of Hinnom, to burn their sons and daughters in the fire; which I commanded them not, neither came it into my heart.*

That God finds it necessary to repudiate this unthinkable suggestion ("neither came it into my heart") indicates that it must still be as prevalent as it was a century before in Micah's day.

THE PLAIN TRUTH is that Jeremiah returns so often to the sin of idolatry that he deserves to be remembered as one of the most valiant warriors against it among the prophets. It is idolatry, and nothing else, that to him is the cause of the catastrophe looming ahead:

> And I will make Jerusalem heaps, and a den of dragons; and I will make the cities of Judah desolate, without an inhabitant. Who is the wise man, that may understand this? and who is he to whom the mouth of the LORD hath spoken, that he may declare it, for what the land perisheth and is burned up like a wilderness, that none passeth through? And the LORD saith, Because they have forsaken my law which I set before them, and have not obeyed my voice, neither walked therein; But have walked after the imagination of their own heart, and after Baalim, which their fathers taught them.

The same note is struck in another great oracle:

> For thus saith the LORD of hosts, the God of Israel; Behold, I will cause to cease out of this place in your eyes, and in your days, the voice of mirth, and the voice of gladness, the voice of the bridegroom, and

---

*The valley of the son of Hinnom passed into English as Gehenna and would in later centuries become a symbol of Hell.

the voice of the bride. And it shall come to pass, when thou shalt shew this people all these words, and they shall say unto thee, Wherefore hath the LORD pronounced all this great evil against us? or what is our iniquity? or what is our sin that we have committed against the LORD our God? Then shalt thou say unto them, Because your fathers have forsaken me, saith the LORD, and have walked after other gods, and have served them, and have worshipped them, and have forsaken me, and have not kept my law; And ye have done worse than your fathers; for, behold, ye walk every one after the imagination of his evil heart. . . . Therefore will I cast you out of this land into a land that ye know not, neither ye nor your fathers; and there shall ye serve other gods day and night; where I will not shew you favor.

Yet, says God, it was not ever thus:

. . . I remember thee, the kindness of thy youth, the love of thine espousals, when thou wentest after me in the wilderness, in a land that was not sown. Israel was holiness unto the LORD, and the firstfruits of his increase: all that devour him shall offend; evil shall come upon them. . . .*

Obviously, like the idealized picture we get from Amos of the relation between God and Israel in the early days of their "marriage," Jeremiah's leaves out the incessant complaints of the "bride" about the hardships her "husband" forces her to undergo. We ourselves have seen how in the Pentateuch she demonstrates no "lovingkindness," or even gratitude to her "husband" and His servant Moses for having led her out of bondage in Egypt. Whining about the food with which she is miraculously provided, she even declares that her life was better in Egypt, slavery and all, and wonders whether she ought to go back. And as for fidelity, it is she who demands that an idol—the golden calf—be fashioned out of the precious metals that her "husband" has conspired with her to steal from her former slavemasters. Therefore He loses patience with her, threatening "divorce" and worse, and the "marriage" is saved only by the pleas of His servant Moses.

Jeremiah ignores all this, and only accuses her of having recently gone astray and become a "whore." But the poetic effect of the idealization is to highlight how disgusting this once devoted young bride has become in the present when,

---

*The simile used by Jeremiah here plays on the law (Ex 23:19; Num 18:12 f.) reserving the first fruits of the harvest to God, which in practice meant that they went to the priests and that anyone else who partook of them was guilty of sin.

as Jeremiah, addressing her directly, spits out with loathing, " . . . upon every high hill and under every green tree, *you bend, whore.*"*

The metaphor of the whore plying her trade in these particular haunts of nature worship and fertility cults makes for a very rich synthesis, especially pitted against the lingering memory of the faithful young bride. In one densely packed image, we get a pulsating embodiment of the idea that idolatry, being an act of infidelity to God, is both a great sin against Him and a breeder of degeneracy in the sinner.

Jeremiah is mystified. How, he asks, can such an incredible metamorphosis have been effected? How can God's people have chosen to trade everything in exchange for nothing at all? How can they have thrown away life, and chosen sterility in its place?

> Hath a nation changed their gods, which are yet no gods? but my people have changed their glory for that which doth not profit. Be astonished, O ye heavens, at this, and be horribly afraid, be ye very desolate, saith the LORD. For my people have committed two evils; they have forsaken me the fountain of living waters, and hewed them out cisterns, broken cisterns, that can hold no water.

But soon the metaphor of the whore comes back in an unstoppable rush of images of wild animals in heat:

> How canst thou say, I am not polluted, I have not gone after Baalim? see thy way in the valley, know what thou hast done: thou art a swift dromedary traversing her ways; A wild ass used to the wilderness, that snuffeth up the wind at her pleasure; in her occasion who can turn her away? all that seek her will not weary themselves; in her month they shall find her.†

Thanks to such passages (and the mistaken attribution to him of the Book of Lamentations) Jeremiah's name—like Cassandra's to the ancient Greeks—has become a byword for gloom and forebodings of disaster. Moreover, he has even been accused by some critics of lacking love for his own people. Here is a man, they charge, who never stops preaching submission by God's chosen people to a pagan enemy, and who seems to take a positive relish in using his literary powers

---

*In the italicized words, I have presumed to do my own translation because none of the versions I have consulted, not even KJV, seems to me to capture either the force or the precise sense of the Hebrew words *at tzoah zonah*.

†For KJV's "occasion," NJPS gives us "season." And "in her month" means when she is in heat.

to describe the horrors that will befall them if—as he fully expects—they should fail to adopt so repugnant a course.

It is not surprising, then, that Jeremiah excites the wrath of the leaders of Judah—from kings to priests and other prophets: not prophets of Baal, but prophets like Hananiah speaking in the name of God of Israel. It is not surprising that they look upon Jeremiah as a traitor to their country and a blasphemer against their God. It is not surprising that they keep asking what they have done to bring the wrath of God down upon them, even to the unimaginable extent of withdrawing protection from His own "house," and from the city in which He has placed His name, and consigning them to the flames of a marauding pagan empire. They themselves might have agreed that the royally sanctioned idolatry and the pollution of the Temple under Manasseh would merit such a fate. But why now, when all that has been abolished, and the only idolatry left in the land is being practiced in private?

Yet (as Jeremiah well knows) Deuteronomy is no less harsh on private than on public idolatry:

> If thy brother, the son of thy mother, or thy son, or thy daughter, or the wife of thy bosom, or thy friend, which is as thine own soul, entice thee secretly, saying, Let us go and serve other gods. . . . Thou shalt not consent unto him, nor hearken unto him; neither shall thine eye pity him, neither shalt thou spare, neither shalt thou conceal him: But thou shalt surely kill him; thine hand shall be first upon him to put him to death, and afterwards the hand of all the people. And thou shalt stone him with stones, that he die; because he hath sought to thrust thee away from the LORD thy God. . . .

Even with this passage from Deuteronomy ringing (as we may suppose) in his ears, Jeremiah does not call for the people of Judah to kill the sinners in their midst. What he keeps insisting is that God has appointed Nebuchadnezzar to administer the punishment, and that subjection to Babylon is His will. Hence, refusing to submit will only make the punishment worse. It is this lesson that his direst prophecies are intended to teach.

YET TO LEAVE IT AT THAT is to do a great injustice to Jeremiah. It requires turning a blind eye to his reluctance to deliver such a message—a reluctance so great that it sometimes spills over into outright rebellion against God. From the very beginning, when he is just a boy and God announces that he is destined to be a prophet, he protests:

Then the word of the LORD came unto me, saying, Before I formed
thee in the belly I knew thee; and before thou camest forth out of the
womb I sanctified thee, and I ordained thee a prophet unto the nations.
Then said I, Ah, LORD God! behold, I cannot speak: for I am a child.
But the LORD said unto me, Say not, I am a child: for thou shalt go to
all that I shall send thee, and whatsoever I command thee thou shalt
speak.

As the example of Moses himself demonstrates, there is nothing new or
unusual in this effort to avoid the burdens of prophecy. But compare the First
Isaiah. When he sees God sitting on His throne surrounded by six angels crying
to one another: " . . . Holy, holy, holy, is the LORD of hosts: the whole earth is
full of his glory," his first response is to moan, " . . . Woe is me! for I am undone;
because I am a man of unclean lips, and I dwell in the midst of a people of
unclean lips. . . ." But after one of the angels puts a burning coal from the altar on
his lips and tells him that his sin is now purged, he immediately responds to
God's question, " . . . Whom shall I send, and who will go for us?," with an eager
" . . . Here am I; send me." God then informs the First Isaiah that his mission will
be thankless. He is even instructed to *ensure* that it will be thankless:

Make the heart of this people fat, and make their ears heavy, and shut
their eyes; lest they see with their eyes, and hear with their ears, and
understand with their heart, and convert, and be healed. Then said I,
LORD, how long? And he answered, Until the cities be wasted without
inhabitant, and the houses without man, and the land be utterly desolate, And the LORD have removed men far away, and there be a great
forsaking in the midst of the land.

This mission would seem to be the very opposite of what a prophet is supposed to do—namely, to urge repentance—and yet the staunch and somewhat
aloof First Isaiah does not shrink from it, not now and not ever. His question
"how long?" is a sign of anguish and perhaps even a plea that God have mercy
on His people. Yet he accepts without demurring that it is too late for repentance
and that extreme punishment has become the only way back to forgiveness.

God does not make this as clear to Jeremiah as He did to the First Isaiah, but
Jeremiah senses that his mission will be no less thankless than Isaiah's was.
Though there is no burning coal in the scene of Jeremiah's consecration, God
Himself, touching the boy's lips, puts His words into his mouth. And the first two
visions given to the newly commissioned prophet are not only similar in content
to God's revelation to the First Isaiah but almost as inexorable:

> For, lo, I will call all the families of the kingdoms of the north, saith the
> LORD; and they shall come, and they shall set every one his throne at the
> entering gates of Jerusalem, and against the walls thereof round about, and
> against all the cities of Judah. And I will utter my judgments against them
> touching all their wickedness, who have forsaken me, and have burned in-
> cense unto other gods, and worshipped the work of their own hands.

There is nothing here about getting the people of Judah to repent as a means
of escaping these judgments. There is only God's assurance that Jeremiah will prevail " . . . against the kings of Judah, against the princes thereof, against the priests
thereof, and against the people of the land," who will fight him tooth and nail.

Still, like the First Isaiah before him, Jeremiah is promised by God that His
people will never be utterly destroyed, and that there will be a remnant out of
which a new and purified nation will arise. In common with the First Isaiah
before him, Jeremiah, too, cannot resist calling repeatedly for repentance. But
even less than the First Isaiah does he truly expect it ("Can the Ethiopian change
his skin, or the leopards his spots? then may ye also do good, that are accustomed
to do evil"), and if he ever does begin to entertain hopes, they are immediately
dashed. Only a few years after God has spoken to him for the first time, Jeremiah
concludes that the Josianic reform is failing to accomplish all that he once
expected. Nothing is now left but the chastisement of which Nebuchadnezzar
has been nominated by God to be the instrument.

FAR FROM TAKING SATISFACTION in what God forces him to see and
preach, it breaks Jeremiah's heart:

> My bowels, my bowels! I am pained at my very heart; my heart maketh
> a noise in me; I cannot hold my peace, because thou hast heard, O my
> soul, the sound of the trumpet, the alarm of war. Destruction upon
> destruction is cried; for the whole land is spoiled. . . . How long shall I
> see the standard, and hear the sound of the trumpet?*

There are many other instances of a like tenor, of which the following is
only one:

> When I would comfort myself against sorrow, my heart is faint in
> me. . . . For the hurt of the daughter of my people am I hurt; I am black;
> astonishment hath taken hold on me. Is there no balm in Gilead; is there

---

*The bowels were thought in those days to be the seat of the emotions.

no physician there? why then is not the health of the daughter of my people recovered? Oh that my head were waters, and mine eyes a fountain of tears, that I might weep day and night for the slain of the daughter of my people!

Feeling as he does, he tries to pray for the people, and is repeatedly forbidden by God to continue, on the ground that it will do no good. To which he retorts on one such occasion with an astonishingly brazen accusation: the people are not at fault, since the prophets who come to them with oracles of reassurance speak in the name of God: "Then said I, Ah, LORD God! behold, the prophets say unto them, Ye shall not see the sword, neither shall ye have famine; but I will give you assured peace in this place." But it is cold comfort to Jeremiah when God answers that He has not sent those prophets, that they are liars, and that they will perish by famine and the sword along with the people to whom they are prophesying falsely.

Hence the case or lawsuit against God that Jeremiah brings. I alluded to this passage in connection with Habakkuk, but here, in its local setting, it applies not to life in general, but to Jeremiah's own situation as against that of his enemies: " . . . Wherefore doth the way of the wicked prosper? wherefore are all they happy that deal treacherously? . . . But thou, O LORD, knowest me: thou has seen me, and tried mine heart toward thee. . . ." Cold comfort, too, is God's answer, which amounts to asking Jeremiah how he will be able to cope with worse in the future when he is having so much difficulty with relatively little trouble in the present.

But what Jeremiah wants is revenge (" . . . pull them out like sheep for the slaughter, and prepare them for the day of slaughter"). He wants revenge for his people ("Pour out thy fury upon the heathen that know thee not, and upon the families that call not on thy name: for they have eaten up Jacob, and devoured him, and consumed him, and have made his habitation desolate"); and he wants revenge, along with vindication, for himself:

Heal me, O LORD, and I shall be healed; save me, and I shall be saved. . . . Behold, they say unto me, Where is the word of the LORD? let it come now. As for me, I have not . . . desired the woeful day; thou knowest: that which came out of my lips was right before thee. Be not a terror unto me: thou art my hope in the day of evil. Let them be confounded that persecute me, but let not me be confounded: let them be dismayed, but let not me be dismayed: bring upon them the day of evil, and destroy them with double destruction.

God, Jeremiah insists, owes him this, having seduced or enticed him into this predicament:

O LORD, . . . thou art stronger than I, and hast prevailed: I am in derision daily, every one mocketh me. For since I spake, I cried out, I cried
violence and spoil; because the word of the LORD was made a
reproach unto me, and a derision, daily. Then I said, I will not make
mention of him, nor speak any more in his name. But his word was in
mine heart as a burning fire shut up in my bones, and I was weary with
forebearing, and I could not stay.*

There is even a moment when Jeremiah seems to tell God that he is resigning:

O LORD, thou knowest: remember me, and visit me, and revenge me
of my persecutors; take me not away in thy longsuffering: know that for
thy sake I have suffered rebuke. Thy words were found, and I did eat
them. . . . I sat not in the assembly of the mockers, nor rejoiced; I sat
alone because of thy hand: for thou hast filled me with indignation.
Why is my pain perpetual, and my wound incurable, which refuseth to
be healed? wilt thou be altogether unto me as a liar, and as waters that
fail?

God forgives him for this fantastic outburst (he calls God a "liar" and will
later exclaim: "Oh LORD, thou hast deceived me, and I was deceived . . ."!) and
lures him back into prophetic service (" . . . If thou return, then will I bring thee
again . . ."). He also promises Jeremiah that he will be saved from his enemies. Yet
Jeremiah still fails to get the revenge he so desperately craves, and falls into utter
despair:

Cursed be the day wherein I was born: let not the day wherein my
mother bare me be blessed. Cursed be the man who brought tidings to
my father, saying, A man child is born unto thee; making him very glad.
And let that man be as the cities which the LORD overthrew, and
repented not: and let him hear the cry in the morning, and the shouting
at noontide; Because he slew me not from the womb; or that my
mother might have been my grave, and her womb to be always great
with me. Wherefore came I forth out of the womb to see labor and sor-
row, that my days should be consumed with shame?

Reading this passage—the dimensions of whose anguish may even exceed a
similar outcry in the Book of Job—we cannot help remembering that it was

---

*Instead of "I was weary with forebearing, and I could not stay," the modern translations give us
"I could not hold it in. I was helpless" (NJPS) or "The effort to restrain it wearied me,/I could
not bear it" (JB), both of which convey a better idea of the meaning of the Hebrew.

precisely in the womb and before he was born that God chose Jeremiah to be a prophet; and this is what makes his repudiation of his prophetic vocation all the more daring and all the more shattering in its violence. When we come to the Second Isaiah, we will meet the mysterious "Suffering Servant" who is " . . . a man of sorrows and acquainted with grief. . . ." But the description fits Jeremiah to perfection.

NEVERTHELESS, and in spite of everything, Jeremiah persists with a courage that is all the greater for being wrested from so stubbornly powerful an inner resistance. For this God rewards him with the dream of a glorious future when, after seventy years of captivity, all will be forgiven, and the children of Israel, both North and South, will be brought home to live together under a righteous monarch descended from the line of David. No doubt because of his own ancestral connections with the old Northern Kingdom, he experiences a special joy in the prospect of the return of "Ephraim" to the fold, and contemplating this eventuality elicits some of his most beautiful verses:

> The LORD hath appeared of old unto me, saying, Yea, I have loved thee with an everlasting love: therefore with lovingkindness have I drawn thee. . . . Behold, I will bring them from the north country, and gather them from the coasts of the earth, and with them the blind and the lame, the woman with child and her that travaileth with child together: a great company shall return thither.

And it keeps getting better:

> . . . for I am a father to Israel, and Ephraim is my firstborn. Hear the word of the LORD, O ye nations, and declare it in the isles afar off, and say, He that scattered Israel will gather him, and keep him. . . . Then shall the virgin rejoice in the dance, both young men and old together: for I will turn their mourning into joy, and will comfort them, and make them rejoice from their sorrow.

And better:

> Thus saith the LORD; A voice was heard in Ramah, lamentation, and bitter weeping; Rachel weeping for her children refused to be comforted for her children, because they were not. Thus saith the LORD; Refrain thy voice from weeping, and thine eyes from tears: for thy work shall be rewarded, saith the LORD; and they shall come again from the land of the enemy.

And better still:

> Is Ephraim my dear son? is he a pleasant child? for since I spake against
> him, I do earnestly remember him still: therefore my bowels are trou-
> bled for him; I will surely have mercy upon him, saith the LORD.*

The consolations of Jeremiah are all summed up in the two declarations by
God that He would as soon abrogate the laws governing the physical world He
created as He would permit the children of Israel to disappear altogether:

> Thus saith the LORD, which giveth the sun for a light by day, and the
> ordinances of the moon and of the stars for a light by night, which
> divideth the sea when the waves thereof roar; The LORD of hosts is his
> name: If those ordinances depart from before me, saith the LORD, then
> the seed of Israel shall cease from being a nation before me for ever.

In the second such declaration, an even more explicit identification is made
between the laws of nature and God's covenant with the house of David (and in
the reference to priests and Levites, incidentally, we hit upon another bit of evidence that Jeremiah is not an opponent of the Temple cult):

> Thus saith the LORD; If ye can break my covenant of the day, and my
> covenant of the night, and that there should not be day and night in
> their season; Then may also my covenant be broken with David my ser-
> vant, that he should not have a son to reign upon his throne; and with
> the Levites the priests, my ministers. . . . Thus saith the LORD; If my
> covenant be not with day and night, and if I have not appointed the
> ordinances of heaven and earth; Then will I cast away the seed of Jacob,
> and David my servant, so that I will not take any of his seed to be rulers
> over the seed of Abraham, Isaac, and Jacob: for I will cause their captiv-
> ity to return, and have mercy on them.

But even as the old laws of the covenant will always remain in force, God is
preparing a new form of this covenant that will be written not on tablets or in
books but in the hearts of a reunited people:

---

*One last time, I want to offer my own translation of a phrase I especially love whose sense and
feel are not conveyed by the KJV or any of the other versions I have seen. The phrase in Hebrew
is *ha-ven yakir li Ephraim im yeled sha-ashuim,* which I would render as: "A precious son is
Ephraim to me, a child of delights." The rest of the verse is more satisfactorily translated by NJPS
than by KJV: "Whenever I have spoken against him,/My thoughts would dwell on him
still./That is why my heart yearns for him;/I will receive him back in love."

> Behold, the days come, saith the LORD, that I will make a new covenant with the house of Israel, and with the house of Judah.... After those days, saith the LORD, I will put my law in their inward parts, and write it in their hearts....

As a result, no longer will any need exist for people to teach one another to " ... Know the LORD: for they shall all know me, from the least of them unto the greatest of them...." This is the ultimate promise made in Jeremiah by God, but it is made to Israel and to Israel alone: " ... [I] will be their God, and they shall be my people."

Does Jeremiah, then, have nothing to say to the other peoples of the earth? He most emphatically does. Appointed by God from the outset to be "a prophet unto the nations," and not just to Israel, he is true to this mission—and never more so than in the new attitude he adopts toward idolatry.

Here it is necessary to remind ourselves yet again that idolatry is still regarded as a sin only among the children of Israel. Other nations are not a party to the covenant forbidding the worship of other gods, and therefore cannot be held accountable for it. At the End of Days—so the First Isaiah and Micah have prophesied—they will come to see the error of their ways and submit to the God of Israel. But until that time, they are under no requirement to abandon their idols and they will not be punished for idolatry itself (though they will be accountable for their crimes and cruelties).

Habakkuk has already moved toward a different position, but Jeremiah pushes the envelope:

> Thus saith the LORD against all mine evil neighbors.... Behold, I will pluck them out of their land.... And it shall come to pass, if they will diligently learn the ways of my people, to swear by my name, The LORD liveth; as they taught my people to swear by Baal; then shall they be built in the midst of my people. But if they will not obey, I will utterly pluck up and destroy that nation, saith the LORD.

In his letter to the exiles of 598 B.C.E., Jeremiah also instructs them to teach the idolators among whom they are now living that " ... the LORD is the true God, he is the living God, and an everlasting king: at his wrath the earth shall tremble, and the nations shall not be able to abide his indignation." Then, suddenly switching from Hebrew to Aramaic (the language of Babylon), and thereby emphasizing that this message is directed straight at the idolators, Jeremiah continues: "Thus shall ye say unto them, The gods that have not made the heavens and the earth, even they shall perish from the earth, and from under these heavens." "For the first time," writes Kaufmann,

and not in vision but in reality, a message on idolatry is addressed "to
them." ... Jeremiah carries the war against idolatry into its own territory.... Isaiah had heralded the end of idolatry in an eschatological act
of God; Jeremiah charges Israel with the task of carrying this message to
the nations and thus take part in bringing them back to God.

Even as he stresses the "practical universalism" of Jeremiah, however, Kaufmann rightly warns against interpreting the idea of the new covenant as awaiting
its fulfillment in Christianity, since the new religion will "nullif[y] the law and
commandments." And quite apart from the error of thinking that Jeremiah or the
other classical prophets are against sacrifice, there is the further consideration
raised by Kaufmann that what those prophets demand is "not a particular doctrine, but a particular reality" expressing itself primarily in obedience to the law.

THIS MISUNDERSTANDING OF the new covenant as an incomplete prelude
to the New Testament has made it possible for many Christian commentators to
revere Jeremiah as a "great thinker" and forerunner. But otherwise he tends to be
patronized. This man, who was without doubt one of the greatest poets ever to
walk the earth, is even denied eminent literary standing. "While it is generally
agreed that Jeremiah ranks as one of the truly great thinkers in the Old Testament," reports Jack R. Lundbom, "his language and style have not always won
high acclaim."

Lundbom traces this lack of acclaim all the way back to one of the early
Fathers of the Church, Jerome, who translated the Bible into Latin in the fourth
century C.E. In his *Prologue to Jeremiah,* Jerome remarks that "Jeremiah the
prophet ... is seen to be more rustic in language than Isaiah and Hosea and certain other prophets among the Hebrews, but equal in thought." Since Jerome,
Lundbom goes on, "it has been agreed that Jeremiah suffers when compared to
Isaiah," and he gives as an example a commentator, S. R. Driver, who, writing
some fifteen centuries after Jerome, still finds Jeremiah's style "essentially artless."
Yet even Lundbom himself, who wishes to defend Jeremiah against these philistine judgments, can come up with nothing stronger than a tepid dissent: "Upon
close inspection, Jeremiah is seen to be a skillful poet, someone well trained in
the rhetoric of his day.... His poetry is generally well balanced."

Similarly with other of Jeremiah's qualities. Besides being one of the greatest
poets ever to walk the earth, he was one of the bravest of all men in overcoming
the inner reluctance and the resentments that plagued him all his life, and in
never yielding to the intolerable pressures put upon him to soften the message
he had been sent by God to bring. And yet he is charged—in John Bright's
recital of the indictment—with being "a weakling, a quitter, a small-spirited man
whose faith was not great enough to endure the testing that was imposed upon

it." Bright sets out to refute these preposterous slanders, and he says all the right things along the way:

> [Jeremiah] was driven by his calling to exhibit a strength that was not by nature his. More than this, Jeremiah seems himself to have understood that his complaints and recriminations were unworthy of him . . . [and] he struggled to purge himself of this weakness of his character.

Yet so defensive in tone is this defense that it almost leaves the charges standing.

It is the same with Jeremiah's prophecies of consolation. Never mind that these are among the most tender and sublime ever offered to his people: even the Talmud concurs with the reductive and simplistic view that "Jeremiah is all doom." In fact, his consolatory oracles are thought by some modern scholars to be so alien to his true spirit that they are assigned to the Second Isaiah. Here, again, the rabbis, evidently overlooking as much of the Book of Isaiah as they do the Book of Jeremiah, concur: "Isaiah," the same talmudic passage adds, "is all consolation." On this issue, John Bright is less defensive in arguing that there is no good reason to rob Jeremiah of much of the soothing material that has been credited to others.

The book as we have it, however, ends with the Jeremiah who is "all doom." In the first appendix—the Oracles Against the Nations—he is a prophet of consolation only to the extent of envisaging punishment of the pagan peoples who have oppressed the children of Israel. This is the Jeremiah we last hear (and I am continuing to assume along with Bright that at least parts of the final chapters are in his voice).

But the Jeremiah we last see (in a third-person narrative, presumably written by Baruch, about the aging prophet's arrival in Egypt) is not in the business of consolation either. The minute he sets foot in Egypt, he discovers that the Israelites who are already living there have been practicing idolatry, and this instantly sets him to railing against them and threatening the direst of punishments. But instead of taking heed, they respond to his chastisements by attributing all their misfortunes to the very fact that for a time they had stopped sacrificing to the Queen of Heaven. And so the story ends as it began: with Jeremiah forced to sally forth yet again into the war against idolatry among his people, and yet again being repulsed and jeered at by them, even in exile.

There is no sign of what then happened to him, but chances are that he met his death in Egypt shortly thereafter, when in his sixties. With his departure, the tradition that—for all his reluctance and resistance—he so magnificently upheld and so valiantly advanced will now be passed on to and carried forward on the foreign soil of Babylon by two more of Israel's greatest prophets: Ezekiel and the Second Isaiah.

CHAPTER TWELVE

EZEKIEL AND THE JEALOUS GOD

T O SAY THAT THE PROPHETIC TORCH was passed from Jeremiah to Ezekiel is fair enough, but it would be more precise to think of this transmission as taking place in space rather than time. By which I mean that the concluding phase of Jeremiah's ministry in Jerusalem—before the destruction of the Temple and before his flight to Egypt—overlapped with the early prophetic activity of Ezekiel.

It is possible to calculate from the text that Ezekiel was about fifteen or so years younger than Jeremiah, which fixes his date of birth in the late 620s B.C.E., just about when, or shortly after, the older prophet received his call. Beyond that, we are informed that Ezekiel was, like Jeremiah, a priest, and it is pretty widely agreed that he grew up in Judah and perhaps in Jerusalem. There he in all likelihood received as thorough a grounding in the traditions of the so-called Priestly Code that would find their way mainly into Leviticus as Jeremiah was given in Deuteronomy (by which Ezekiel too was strongly influenced).

Assuming that this estimate of his date of birth is correct—though, like practically everything else of this nature, it is under scholarly dispute—Ezekiel lived through the tail end of King Josiah's purge, and was by then just old enough to retain memories of Judah's religious condition under Manasseh. And he was also old enough to see what happened after the death of Josiah at the battle of Megiddo in 609 B.C.E. What happened—going now, as I promised, into greater detail than I did in discussing Jeremiah but still hewing to the essentials—was this:

After Josiah's death, the reform party around him placed his son Jehoahaz on the throne. But in very short order—and to the dismay of Jeremiah—the temporarily victorious Egyptians deposed Jehoahaz and replaced him with his half-brother Jehoiakim. The new king paid a huge tribute to the Egyptians (which, in the way of these things, was exacted from the people). About five years later, however, the Babylonian king Nebuchadnezzar, flexing the muscles of his own rising imperial power, drove the Egyptians back at the battle of Carchemish (605 B.C.E.). At this point Jehoiakim prudently submitted to Babylonian suzerainty.

While engaging in these maneuvers in foreign policy—of which more were in store—Jehoiakim faced the problem at home of his father's great religious reform. Again, as with so much else in our story, the scholars disagree over Jehoiakim's attitude toward Josiah's policy. One group maintains that he reversed the reform; another that he slowed it down; and yet another that he more or less let it be. Something like a synthesis of the three positions on this hotly disputed issue comes from Walther Eichrodt in his edition of Ezekiel:

> In the religious sphere, [Jehoiakim] returned to the syncretism of Man-asseh, which had barely been suppressed. True, he did not make any state enactment to repeal the covenant pledged by his father; the strict prohi-bitions against the worship of foreign gods still stood on paper, but in actual practice the way was left open for heathen cults to spring up in such a way that Jeremiah could speak of a conspiracy against Yahweh, which turned its back on the nation's true LORD while cloaking itself in the mantle of legal fidelity to the covenant.

Before expanding on the situation that developed in the religious sphere in the years after Josiah's death, I also want to delve into Jehoiakim's foreign policy in greater detail than before, because it has so much to do with Ezekiel's fate. It may be useful as well to rehearse (at least in simplified form) the complicated history of those years over which I skated lightly in relation to Jeremiah.

So: the Egyptians, though having suffered a defeat at the hands of the Baby-lonians in 605 B.C.E., were by no means finished off, and in 601 B.C.E., they sal-lied forth for another encounter in which they fared so much better that Nebuchadnezzar waited more than a decade before tangling with them again. Apparently this demonstration that Nebuchadnezzar was not invincible led Jehoiakim to believe that the time was ripe for him to rebel against his Babylon-ian masters. Which he proceeded to do. At first, Nebuchadnezzar tried to put down the rebellion through other vassal states in the immediate area. But when that strategy dragged on unsuccessfully for a few years, he himself finally took matters into his own hands.

As Nebuchadnezzar's own army advanced to besiege Jerusalem, Jehoiakim died (either by assassination, by the sword, or from the illness Jeremiah once pre-dicted for him). After only three months, his son and successor Jehoiachin sur-rendered (in 598 B.C.E.). We have already seen that Nebuchadnezzar did not sack Jerusalem. This surprising forbearance, it has been suggested, was a reward for Jehoiachin's decision not to give him a hard time. In any case, as we have also seen, all Nebuchadnezzar did (besides removing valuable objects from the Temple and from the royal palace as booty, while putting another of Josiah's sons, Zedekiah, on the throne as his vassal) was deport Jehoiachin to Babylon along with eight thousand leading citizens of Judah. Among these citizens was the young priest Ezekiel, the son of Buzi.

Having gone easy on Jerusalem, Nebuchadnezzar followed the same policy toward the exile community in Babylon. Jehoaichin himself was lodged in the royal palace, and the people were given a considerable degree of autonomy. Governed by their own Elders, they were also left free to practice their own religion. Of course, practicing their religion was possible only to a limited extent: now that a commitment had been made to the laws enunciated in Deuteronomy, they were not permitted to offer sacrifices anywhere except in the Temple in Jerusalem. But they were comforted by the expectation that their exile would be short and that they would return home soon—an expectation that was fostered by prophets who arose among them in Babylon, and others who (provoking Jeremiah's ire) were taking the same position in Jerusalem.

IT IS UNDER SUCH CONDITIONS that Ezekiel lives for five years, though we are completely in the dark as to what he may have been doing during that period. But then one day in the year 594 B.C.E., when (as some scholars controversially figure) he has reached the age of thirty, he is sitting by himself on the banks of the River Chebar near the exile settlement of Tel-abib. Given what we will learn about him, the chances are that he has by now reached the conclusion that his fellow exiles and their optimistic prophets are wrong in believing that they will soon be returning home, and that he has gone to the river to get away from a community from which he has already alienated himself.

Though there is no evidence in the text to back me up, I would imagine that he may also be brooding about the ultimately abortive conspiracy to rebel against Babylon being hatched just about then in Jerusalem between King Zedekiah and other Babylonian vassals—the one that drives Jeremiah into tying a yoke around his neck as a sign that their only hope of avoiding total destruction is to continue submitting to Nebuchadnezzar. But then, suddenly and with no warning, the heavens are opened and a wondrous vision is vouchsafed to Ezekiel:

> And I looked, and, behold, a whirlwind came out of the north, a great
> cloud, and a fire infolding itself, and a brightness was about it, and out
> of the midst thereof as the color of amber, out of the midst of the fire.

He then sees four creatures with something like human shapes, except that each of them has four wings and four faces: one of a man in front, one of a lion on the right, one of an ox on the left, and one of an eagle on the back. Beside each of these creatures is a wheel, and within that wheel is another wheel, both with eyes all around their rims:

> And when the living creatures went, the wheels went by them: and when the living creatures were lifted up from the earth, the wheels were lifted up.... And when they went, I heard the noise of their wings, like the noise of great waters, as the voice of the Almighty, the voice of speech, as the noise of an host....

This (as it were) chariot rises to the firmament, and from above it Ezekiel hears a voice and sees " ... the likeness of a throne ... and upon the likeness of the throne was the likeness as the appearance of a man above upon it"—all suffused and enclosed in radiance and fire and brightness." ...This was the appearance of the likeness of the glory of the LORD. And when I saw it, I fell upon my face, and I heard a voice of one that spake."

I have left out many details in describing this extraordinary vision, every single one of which will give rise in future centuries to endless mystical speculation among both Jews and Christians. Where Jews are concerned, the chariot (*merkabah* in Hebrew) will become a main focus of such speculation. But mystical speculation will always worry the rabbis of the Talmud, who will try to keep people from engaging in it because of the dangers it poses to the balance of an ordinary mind. There is even a story about four of the leading sages of the first century C.E. venturing into this territory, only one of whom—Akivah, the greatest of his generation—emerges with his sanity intact.

Nor is this the sole element of the Book of Ezekiel that will bother the talmudic sages to come. Because alien soil is characterized as "impure" or "unclean" by many prophets themselves, the rabbis will also be afflicted with doubts as to whether the call to prophecy that follows the chariot vision can really have come to Ezekiel in Babylon. Hence, they take the position that Ezekiel must have received his call while still in Jerusalem, and that he must have begun prophesying before being exiled.*

Curiously, some modern critical scholars have made common cause across the centuries with these rabbis. It goes without saying this is not because the modern scholars share the theological scruples of the early Jewish commentators. The main reason is that the critics have been unable to imagine how someone living hundreds of miles away could, in those days, have addressed himself, as Ezekiel does, mainly to Jerusalem.

Thus Ezekiel, who for a long time "escaped the heavy hand dealt to the books of Isaiah and Jeremiah that questioned their unity and their authorship,"

---

*The rabbis were troubled by several additional problems with this book that I will touch upon in the proper place.

began being subjected to this very treatment by, among others, the same C. C. Torrey who once complained of the "hatchet" that was hacking the Second Isaiah into "hopeless chunks." Torrey himself did not dismember the book, but he interpreted it as a fictional (or "pseudepigraphic")* work originating in the third century B.C.E. Various other theories were developed arguing that Ezekiel never lived in Babylon at all, or that the book was actually the product not of a much later but of a much earlier period, or that only a very small part of it could be assigned to Ezekiel himself.

To my mind, Moshe Greenberg, in his edition of Ezekiel, disposes of such theories very convincingly, and I will be adopting—or perhaps I should say adapting—his "holistic" approach here (without necessarily accepting all his interpretations). That approach, as he describes it, is grounded in

> the working assumption that the present Book of Ezekiel is the product of art and intelligent design. . . . The persuasion grows on one as piece after piece falls into the established patterns and ideas that a coherent world of vision is emerging, contemporary with the sixth-century prophet [active between 594 and 571 B.C.E.] and decisively shaped by him, if not the very words of Ezekiel himself.

Going along, then, with the view that it is actually a man named Ezekiel to whom a vision comes while he is sitting on the banks of a river in Babylon in the year 594 B.C.E., we can return to the words he reports hearing after falling on his face at "the appearance of the likeness of the glory of God."

THESE WORDS ARE Ezekiel's commission as a prophet, and in many aspects they resemble the calls issued to other prophets like the First Isaiah and Jeremiah. But there are fascinating differences as well. One is that Ezekiel is the only prophet God addresses as *"ben-adam,"* a term that literally means "son of man," but the idiomatic sense of which is simply "man" or "mortal." When God speaks to Abraham or Samuel or Amos or Jeremiah and uses their names, a feeling of intimacy is instantly established between the divine and the human. But in referring to this prophet (about a hundred times) only as "son of man,"† and never as "Ezekiel," God seems to be emphasizing the distance between Himself and the human.

---

*Like "apocrypha," "pseudepigra" is a Greek word. It denotes books that pretend to have been written by someone, usually eminent, of an earlier time, either to escape censorship or to claim greater authority than the true author possessed.

†This is how KJV translates the term. All the modern translations (except JB) drop it in favor of "man" or "mortal," and though they are technically correct, "son of man" sounds better to my ear, and I will accordingly use it here throughout.

This impression is entirely consonant with the conception of God that gradually emerges from the book and that is expressed in the first chariot vision: a
conception that emphasizes not the divine attribute of mercy nor even the
attribute of justice (though both show themselves now and then, especially in
the second half of the book) but rather His "jealousy." Nowhere else in the
prophetic literature is this attribute of God, announced in the first of the Ten
Commandments, so vividly revealed. And it is in speaking the words of the God
who manifests Himself mainly through this quality that Ezekiel develops into
perhaps the fiercest warrior yet among the classical prophets against the idolatrous practices of his own people—the most extreme, I would judge, since the
pre-classical Elijah. But in doing so, Ezekiel also sheds new light on the meaning
of God's jealousy and its great importance in His relation to the children of
Israel.

However, all this becomes apparent not at once but gradually, coming out
with ever increasing saliency only after God's inaugural description of Ezekiel's
mission and after the newly commissioned prophet has performed various acts
that dramatize the more specific message that Jerusalem is doomed. The call
itself, like the one to Jeremiah, commands Ezekiel to speak what God tells him
to speak. He is not to be intimidated by the opposition his words will arouse
because God will make him strong enough to withstand " . . . a rebellious nation
that hath rebelled against me: they and their fathers have transgressed against me,
even unto this very day." God does not go as far with Ezekiel as He did with the
First Isaiah, whom He shockingly directed to make sure that the people would
not listen to his prophecies. To Ezekiel He only says that there is no chance that
they will listen, but that he must speak anyway, so that they will at least " . . .
know that there hath been a prophet among them."

All of which more or less parallels the encouragement given by God to Jeremiah despite the certain prospect that the people of Jerusalem will reject his
message. The encouragement to Jeremiah was reinforced by the fact that the
words of the message themselves were put by God into the prophet's mouth:
they were God's words, not his, and it therefore did not matter that Jeremiah,
hoping to get off the hook, claimed to be inarticulate.

Ezekiel makes no such claim, but as we get to know him, we realize that he
has a strong tendency to withdraw into silence. Perhaps this is why, when it
comes to having God's words put into their mouths, Ezekiel is subjected to an
ordeal the like of which Jeremiah was never asked to undergo. "Then the
LORD put forth his hand, and touched my mouth," Jeremiah told us. "And the
LORD said unto me, Behold, I have put my words in thy mouth." Nothing hard
about that. As for the First Isaiah, in the scene describing his call, an angel
touched his lips with a burning coal, but the purpose was not to put words into
his mouth; it was to cleanse him of the iniquity he felt that he shared with an
iniquitous people. Here, by contrast, is what Ezekiel has to do:

But thou, son of man, hear what I say unto thee; . . . open thy mouth, and eat that I give thee. And when I looked, behold, an hand was sent unto me; and lo, a roll of a book was therein; And he spread it before me; and it was written within and without: and there was written therein lamentations, and mourning and woe. Moreover he said unto me, Son of man, eat that thou findest; eat this roll, and go speak unto the house of Israel. So I opened my mouth, and he caused me to eat that roll. And he said unto me, Son of man, cause thy belly to eat, and fill thy bowels with this roll that I give thee. . . .

Jeremiah might well have protested at such a command before submitting to it, but Ezekiel is neither " . . . rebellious like that rebellious house [of Israel] . . ." nor inclined like his older contemporary in Jerusalem to enter into disputations with God. Without even a second's hesitation, he does with the scroll exactly as he has been told to do, and instead of the parchment's causing him to gag, " . . . it was in my mouth as honey for sweetness." (At a much later stage in his career, Jeremiah, too, ate the words of God, but only metaphorically: "Thy words were found, and I did eat them; and thy word was unto me the joy and rejoicing of mine heart . . .").

The additional trials God has in store for Ezekiel as part of his initiation, however, partake not of the sweet taste of the scroll, but of the lamentations and mourning and woe written on it. Returning to Tel-abib, the fledgling prophet is full of bitterness. The text gives us no idea of what he is bitter about. It may be over his mission, or over the dashing of any lingering dream he may previously have entertained that Jerusalem will survive and that the exile will come to a quick end. All we are told is that instead of beginning to preach—which we expect him to do from the commission God has just given him—he sits among his fellow exiles in complete silence for seven days, as though struck dumb by the shattering experience he has just had.

At the end of the seven days, the word of God comes to him again. Now he is informed that he has been made " . . . a watchman over the house of Israel . . . ," and that this carries an awesome responsibility. If he conveys God's warnings to the wicked, or to the righteous who have strayed, and they do not mend their ways, they will surely die, but their blood will not be on the prophet's hand. Yet if he fails to communicate these warnings, the wicked and the formerly righteous (whose virtuous deeds of the past will now count for nothing) will perish, but their " . . . blood will I require at thine hand."

THIS VISITATION READS like a kind of interlude in the story of the ordeals Ezekiel is to go through in becoming a prophet. But it strikes two distinctive notes of great significance. The first is to express the possible efficacy of repentance—a possibility that is not only at most a minor motif in the rest of this book, but one that will have very little to do with what we learn as we go along about the nature of God and of His designs for "the house of Israel."

The other unusual note is the heavy stress placed on the individual rather than the nation. Later, we will encounter an extraordinary chapter that underlines this emphasis even more heavily in seeming to repudiate the idea (also stated in the Ten Commandments) that the sins of the fathers are visited upon the children. Jeremiah, too, attacks the same idea in the proverbial form it has taken among the populace: " . . . The fathers have eaten a sour grape and the children's teeth are set on edge." But in Jeremiah, the abrogation of this rule is to herald the ushering in of a new era at the End of Days. That is when God will make the "new covenant" with Israel that will be inscribed upon the heart of every individual so that he will know even without instruction what the law is and will therefore obey it, in effect, instinctively.

In Ezekiel, the idea is also attacked in its popular proverbial form:

> What mean ye, that ye use this proverb concerning the land of Israel, saying, The fathers have eaten sour grapes, and the children's teeth are set on edge? As I live, saith the LORD God, ye shall not have occasion any more to use this proverb in Israel. Behold, all souls are mine; as the soul of the father, so also the soul of the son is mine: the soul that sinneth, it shall die. But if a man be just, and do that which is lawful and right. . . . Hath walked in my statutes, and hath kept my judgments, to deal truly; he is just, he shall surely live, saith the LORD God.

If the sons will not be punished for the sins of their fathers, neither, conversely, will they be rewarded for the merits of their fathers. Nor—in spite of the fact that God long ago yielded to Abraham's argument about Sodom and Gomorrah on this very point—will the presence of a few righteous men in a sinful city save it:

> Son of man, when the land sinneth against me by trespassing grievously, then will I stretch out mine hand upon it. . . . Though these three men, Noah, Daniel, and Job, were in it, they should deliver but their own souls by their righteousness, saith the LORD God. . . . they shall deliver neither sons nor daughters, but they shall only be delivered themselves.

As in Jeremiah, too, God in Ezekiel brings up the idea of " . . . a new heart. . . ." But in Jeremiah's eschatological vision—and in one of the prophecies of consolation that will dominate Ezekiel's oracles after the fall of Jerusalem in 586 B.C.E.—it is God who will make such a heart for Israel in the future. Here, though, it is the individual who is supposed to make it for himself, and to do it now, in the present:

Therefore I will judge you, O house of Israel, every one according to
his ways, saith the LORD God. Repent, and turn yourselves from all
your transgressions; so iniquity shall not be your ruin. Cast away from
you all your transgressions, whereby ye have transgressed; and make you
a new heart and a new spirit: for why will ye die, O house of Israel? For
I have no pleasure in the death of him that dieth, saith the LORD God:
wherefore turn yourselves, and live ye.

This doctrine of individual responsibility, combined with the suggestion of
the efficacy of repentance, will have tremendous influence on later generations.
But I say again that it strikes a discordant, and even a contradictory, note in
Ezekiel. In this book, God's actions, whether punitive or merciful, are mainly or
even entirely unrelated to what the people do or fail to do. So far as the residents
of Judah and Jerusalem are concerned, it is already (six years before the fall) too
late, and even if they now repent, it will do them no good. Their fate is sealed, as
we are made aware by the next ordeal through which Ezekiel is put and the
accompanying symbolic actions God commands him to take.

At the end of his seven days of silence, Ezekiel is again summoned, this time
to the plain outside Tel-abib, where he again falls on his face before an experience of the glory of God. Again we expect that he will be sent forth to preach.
But no:

Then the spirit entered into me, and set me upon my feet, and spake
with me, and said unto me, Go, shut thyself within thine house. . . . and
thou shalt not go out among them: And I will make thy tongue cleave
to the roof of thy mouth, that thou shalt be dumb, and shalt not be to
them a reprover: for they are a rebellious house.

Instead of preaching through words, Ezekiel is (and by no means for the last
time) to enact the prophetic message on his own person. After constructing a
kind of model of the siege of Jerusalem, he is to be tied up (whether by his
neighbors or by God is unclear). Thus bound, he is to lie first on his left side for
390 days, each day corresponding to a year of the iniquity of the Northern
Kingdom. Having accomplished that task, he is to turn around and lie on his
right side for forty days, each of these representing a year of the iniquity of
Judah. During the whole sixty-one weeks, he is to eat nothing but sparse siege
rations of bread baked on dung and to drink only small quantities of water.

One wonders how, after all this, he still has enough strength to carry out the
next of the symbolic acts he performs. It consists of taking a knife and a razor
and cutting off clumps of his hair, which he is then to weigh on a scale, so that
he can divide them into thirds, each to be disposed of in a way that represents a
different aspect of the catastrophe approaching Judah and Jerusalem. Rarely, if

ever, in the prophetic literature does the punishment to be meted out seem so cruel and unyielding—and (as in Hosea) it is God Himself, not some pagan nation used as His instrument, who will mete it out:

> Therefore thus saith the LORD God; Behold, I, even I, am against thee, and will execute judgments in the midst of thee in the sight of the nations. And I will do in thee that which I have not done, and where-unto I will not do any more the like, because of all thy abominations. . . . and I will execute judgments in thee, and the whole remnant of thee will I scatter into all the winds. Wherefore, as I live, saith the LORD God; Surely, because thou hast defiled my sanctuary with all thy detestable things, and with all thine abominations, therefore will I also diminish thee; neither shall mine eye spare, neither will I have any pity.*

On and on it pounds away without letup—much along the same lines of the curses in Leviticus and Deuteronomy and in the darkest visions of Jeremiah—with pestilence and the sword and wild beasts being sent by God to wreak almost unimaginable pain and destruction, and with a famine so severe that " . . . the fathers shall eat the sons in the midst of thee, and the sons shall eat their fathers. . . ."

Will there then be no remnant such as is promised by all the other prophets of doom, from Amos to Jeremiah? Yes; but this will not be a remnant out of which the nation will be regenerated or from which a new shoot of the house of Jesse will spring:

> Yet will I leave a remnant, that ye may have some that shall escape the sword among the nations, when ye shall be scattered through the coun-tries. And they that escape of you shall remember me among the nations whither they shall be carried captives, because I am broken with their whorish heart, which hath departed from me, and with their eyes, which go a whoring after their idols: and they shall lothe themselves for the evils which they have committed in all their abominations.

The next mention of a remnant is a comfort only to the degree that the mis-erable moral condition of the survivors will show the previously exiled commu-nities to which they flee that God is just in the "evil" He will visit upon Judah and Jerusalem:

---

*Instead of KJV's "I, even I, am against Thee," AB gives us the more vivid "I am coming at you, I. . . ."

Yet, behold, therein shall be left a remnant that shall be brought forth, both sons and daughters: behold, they shall come forth unto you, and ye shall see their way and their doings: and ye shall be comforted concerning the evil that I have brought upon Jerusalem. . . . and ye shall know that I have not done without cause all that I have done in it, saith the LORD God.

Those awesome curses are hurled at Judah by God through Ezekiel, whose tongue no longer cleaves to the roof of his mouth. Later he will preach to his fellow exiles, but not now:

And the word of the LORD came unto me, saying, Son of man, set thy face toward the mountains of Israel, and prophesy against them, And say, Ye mountains of Israel, hear the word of the LORD God; Thus saith the LORD God to the mountains, and to the hills, to the rivers, and to the valleys; Behold, I, even I, will bring a sword upon you, and I will destroy your high places. And your altars shall be desolate, and your images shall be broken: and I will cast down your slain men before your idols. And I will lay the dead carcases of the children of Israel before their idols; and I will scatter your bones around your altars. In all your dwellingplaces the cities shall be laid waste, and the high places shall be desolate; that your altars may be laid waste and made desolate, and your idols may be broken and cease, and your images may be cut down, and your works may be abolished.*

MUCH MORE OF THE SAME is ahead. But it is already clear, and will become even clearer as we move on, that idolatry is the prime and overriding and all-embracing sin for which the Kingdom of Judah, like the Kingdom of Israel before it, must be so drastically punished:

Then shall ye know that I am the LORD, when their slain men shall be among their idols round about their altars, upon every high hill, in all the tops of the mountains, and under every green tree, and under every thick oak, the place where they did offer sweet savor to all their idols.

As often with Ezekiel, in the imagery of this passage—the high hills, the green trees, and the other idolatrous shrines and locales—we see traces of Jeremiah (and Deuteronomy). Soon whoredom as a metaphor for chasing after strange gods, already alluded to in passing, will be reintroduced with a very loud

---

*Israel, of course, here refers not to the defunct Northern Kingdom but to Judah.

bang, and will resound in Ezekiel more powerfully than it does even in Hosea.

But before it returns, the almost obsessive stress on idolatry is intensified by an explicit vision, neither metaphorical nor symbolic, that is given to Ezekiel of the Temple in Jerusalem. God Himself, seizing the prophet by a lock of his hair, transports him through the air from Babylon to the Temple in order that he may see with his own eyes the abominations that are rampant there. In each room or chamber to which he is taken, a different idolatrous practice is going on, and after each one, God says, " . . . Son of man, seest thou what they do? even the great abominations that the house of Israel committeth here . . . ? but turn thee yet again, and thou shalt see greater abominations."

In the course of this visionary tour, angels in the form of men are summoned to "Slay utterly old and young, both maids, and little children, and women . . . ," sparing only the few they have found in the city " . . . that sigh and that cry for all the abominations that be done in the midst thereof." This is too much even for the normally docile Ezekiel, who tries to intervene:

> And it came to pass, while they were slaying them, and I was left, that I fell upon my face, and cried, and said, Ah LORD God! wilt thou destroy all the residue of Israel in thy pouring out of thy fury upon Jerusalem?

But like Jeremiah, when he tried to plead for the people through prayer, Ezekiel is rebuffed by God.

A few moments later, however, when Ezekiel intercedes once more with a similar plea—" . . . Ah LORD God! Wilt thou make a full end of the remnant of Israel?"—he is given a different answer. This time, in a foreshadowing of the consolations that will dominate the second half of the book, God promises the prophet that the people already in exile, to whom He has been " . . . a little sanctuary . . ." in the absence of a Temple, will one day be gathered together from the pagan lands to which He has dispersed them and that they will be brought back to the Temple in Jerusalem.

In this, and in what will follow, we detect another trace of Jeremiah. It is of the older prophet's belief that the Jerusalemites are "evil" figs and the exiles of 598 B.C.E. are " . . . good figs . . ." Jeremiah has prophesied that these "good figs" will in the end inherit the land and will be endowed—as the gift of God, not as a product of their own actions—with the new heart and the new spirit of the new covenant. Here is the comparable prophecy in Ezekiel:

> And they shall come hither, and they shall take away all the detestable things thereof and all the abominations thereof from thence. And I will give them one heart, and I will put a new spirit within you; and I will take the stony heart out of their flesh, and will give them an heart of

flesh: That they may walk in my statutes and keep mine ordinances, and
do them: and they shall be my people, and I will be their God.

With this, the divine chariot, of which Ezekiel has just had a final glimpse,
leaves the Temple and flies to a mountain on the east side of the city with the
glory of God radiating above it. Ezekiel remains behind, but the spirit then transports him back to Babylon, where he reveals everything he has seen to his fellow
exiles there.

Though he can attract an audience even before he has been vindicated as a
prophet by the fall of Jerusalem, the people do not believe what he says. As God
will later explain, they come not because they mean to act on what he tells them;
it is only because he is " ... unto them as a very lovely song of one that hath a
pleasant voice, and can play well on an instrument. . . ." (Somehow the idea of
Ezekiel possessing a melodious voice—and being treated, in the coinage of one
commentator, as an "entertainer"—comes as a great surprise.) God therefore decides once more that Ezekiel's most effective means for communicating to these
people (who, in language the Hebrew Bible often uses of idols, " ... have eyes to
see, and see not ..." and " ... ears to hear, and hear not ...") is to stage a dramatic
demonstration of what he has been trying in vain to get across in words.

Ezekiel thus acts out the process by which the Jerusalemites (led by the king)
will escape the sacking of the city. But they will be spared " ... from the sword,
from the famine, and from the pestilence ..." and will go into exile only " ... that
they may declare all their abominations among the heathens whither they come;
and they shall know that I am the LORD." Furthermore, the time is fast
approaching when this will occur:

> And the word of the LORD came unto me, saying, Son of man, what is
> that proverb that ye have in the land of Israel, saying, The days are pro-
> longed and every vision faileth? Tell them, therefore, Thus saith the
> LORD God; I will make this proverb to cease. ... I will speak, and the
> word that I shall speak shall come to pass; it shall be no more pro-
> longed. ...

Then, in what seems more of a quotation from than an echo of Jeremiah's
denunciation of those who cry " ... Peace, peace; when there is no peace ... ,"
Ezekiel excoriates the false prophets, both men and women, " ... which prophesy concerning Jerusalem, and which see visions of peace for her, and there is no
peace, saith the LORD God."

After the prophets comes the turn of the Elders to be excoriated. For some
unspecified reason, these Elders consult with Ezekiel who, in accordance with
God's command, denies them whatever advice they are seeking. Obviously they
are not the "good figs" to whom the future belongs, although the fact that they

make inquiries of Ezekiel indicates that they have not altogether abandoned God. But what they have done is " . . . set up their idols in their heart, . . ." and consequently they will get no guidance from God through the prophet:

> Therefore speak unto them, and say unto them, Thus saith the LORD God; Every man of the house of Israel that setteth up his idols in his heart, . . . and cometh to the prophet; I the LORD will answer him that cometh according to the multitude of his idols; . . . because they are all estranged from me through their idols. . . . And I will set my face against that man, and will make him a sign and a proverb, and I will cut him off from the midst of my people; and ye shall know that I am the LORD.

WHETHER THROUGH A VISIONARY TOUR of the Temple in Jerusalem or an actual look at the exile community in Babylon, then, everywhere Ezekiel takes us we see virtually nothing but idolatry. Nor is it only in the present generation that this greatest of sins, and the source and fount of all others, the one that most arouses God's wrath, pollutes and befouls His people wherever they live and even contaminates His own house in Jerusalem. The past, too, is implicated. Ezekiel composes a darker account of the history of the children of Israel than any other prophet, and in drawing it, he for once diverges from Jeremiah even while resorting to much the same imagery.

In the sharpest possible contrast to Jeremiah's roseate portrait of the early days of God's "marriage" to Israel, Ezekiel's is unmitigatedly black. In Jeremiah we are beguiled by the picture of a loving and devoted youthful bride who has now become a whore. But in Ezekiel, Israel, like Hosea's wife Gomer, has been a whore from the very beginning.

There are two distinct but equally seething versions of this parable in Ezekiel. The first has God adopting a newborn baby abandoned in an open field and wallowing in her own postnatal blood. "And when I passed by thee, and saw thee polluted in thine own blood, I said unto thee when thou wast in thy blood, Live; yea, I said unto thee when thou wast in thy blood, Live." God cares for her tenderly and raises her until she reaches marriageable age. "Now when I passed by thee, and looked upon thee, behold, thy time was the time of love; and . . . I sware unto thee, and entered into a covenant with thee, saith the LORD God, and thou becamest mine." She has grown up to be a very beautiful young woman, with full breasts and long hair, and he enhances His new wife's beauty by clothing her with the most luxurious fabrics and bedecking her with jewels and ornaments of gold and silver and feeding her with " . . . fine flour, and honey, and oil. . . ."

Neither grateful nor loving in return, she immediately begins fornicating with " . . . every one that passed by. . . ." The fine garments He has given her she now uses to decorate the " . . . high places . . ." to which she goes for trysts with her lovers. She even takes the " . . . fair jewels of my gold and of my silver, which I had given thee, and madest to thyself images of men, and didst commit whoredom with them." But we have not yet been plunged down to the nadir:

> Moreover thou hast taken thy sons and thy daughters, whom thou hast borne unto me, and these hast thou sacrificed unto them to be devoured. Is this of thy whoredoms a small matter, That thou hast slain my children, and delivered them to cause them to pass through the fire for them?

We can feel the escalating fury of the cuckolded husband, unable to stop even after having just charged his wife with murdering their own children for the sake of her paramours:

> And in all thine abominations and thy whoredoms thou hast not remembered the days of thy youth, when thou wast naked and bare, and wast polluted in thy blood. And it came to pass after all thy wickedness, (woe, woe unto thee! saith the LORD God). . . . Thou hast built thy high place at every head of the way, and hast made thy beauty to be abhorred, and hast opened thy feet to every one that passed by, and multiplied thy whoredoms.

So insatiable is this nymphomaniacal creature that no amount of fornication can satisfy her. Nor is it even for the "rewards" that she behaves in this way. An ordinary whore (like Hosea's Gomer) plies her trade for money, but she does the opposite: "They give gifts to all whores: but thou givest thy gifts to all thy lovers, and hirest them, that they may come unto thee on every side for thy whoredom."

In the course of this diatribe, God accuses her of being even worse than her "sisters," Sodom [!] and Samaria (the Northern Kingdom of which this city was one of the capitals). But the idea awaits fuller development in the second of the two parables on the same subject that Ezekiel will deliver. In between the two, the marriage motif is dropped and (among other things) a direct assault is launched in plain language against the whole house of Israel.

Here, in a version of the early history that is no less inconsistent with the Pentateuch's than Jeremiah's, though from the opposite direction, God accuses the Israelites of carrying idol worship with them out of Egypt:

> Then said I unto them, Cast ye away every man the abominations of his eyes, and defile not yourselves with the idols of Egypt: I am the LORD your God. But they rebelled against me, and would not hearken unto

me: they did not every man cast away the abominations of their eyes, neither did they forsake the idols of Egypt. . . .

Despite repeated forgiveness, so it has been ever since, generation after generation until the present moment:

> Wherefore say unto the house of Israel, Thus saith the LORD God; Are ye polluted after the manner of your fathers? . . . For when ye offer your gifts, when ye make your sons to pass through the fire, ye pollute yourselves with all your idols, even unto this day. . . .

The end result is to be hideous punishment, though as we know by now is common in the classical prophets, even these prophecies of doom can culminate in passages envisioning future redemption. Conversely, when being transformed largely into a comforter after Jerusalem falls, Ezekiel will mix the sweet with the bitter, throwing in denunciations and threats whenever the spirit moves him. But before the transformation takes place, Ezekiel is dragged back to the adulterous wife as the most fully realized metaphor for idolatry.

This time (in still one more reminiscence of Jeremiah that is darker than the older prophet's vision), the parable Ezekiel offers is of two sisters, Aholah and Aholiba,* both married to God (and openly identified by Ezekiel as representing the Northern and Southern Kingdoms). Again he charges that " . . . they committed whoredoms in Egypt; they committed whoredoms in their youth. . . ." The detail in this passage is so much more graphic than before that (though rather tame by the standards of today) it has been felt by some to be pornographic. Twice, for example, Ezekiel dwells on the rough fondling of the virginal breasts of the sisters by their first lovers (" . . . there were their breasts pressed, and there they bruised the teats of their virginity").

He also accuses the younger one (Judah) of doting on paramours with very large penises and abundant seminal emissions.† For her part, the older one, Aholah/Samaria, is especially attracted to the handsome young Assyrian soldiers with their gorgeous uniforms, " . . . and with all on whom she doted: with all their idols she defiled herself." God therefore delivers her into their hands, and (in a reference to the destruction of the Northern Kingdom) they promptly put her sons and daughters to the sword.

Yet instead of learning the lesson of her older sister's fate, Aholibah/Judah

---

*Thus KJV, but transliterated as Oholah and Oholiba in most other versions.

†KJV, relying on the Hebrew euphemism, translates this verse (23:20) as "whose flesh is as the flesh of asses, and whose issue is like the issue of horses." But AB captures the sense behind the euphemisms: "She lusted after concubinage to them, whose members were like those of asses and whose discharge was like that of horses."

becomes an even more wanton whore than ever. For this she will suffer the same fate at the hands of her Babylonian lovers as her sister did from the Assyrians. Both sisters

> ... have committed adultery, and blood is in their hands, and with their idols have they committed adultery, and have also caused their sons, whom they bare unto me, to pass for them through the fire, to devour them. Moreover this they have done unto me: they have defiled my sanctuary on the same day, and have profaned my sabbaths. For when they had slain their children to their idols, then they came the same day into my sanctuary to profane it; and, lo, thus have they done in the midst of mine house.

In mentioning Judah's Babylonian lovers, Ezekiel says that she has come to hate them. This must be an allusion to Zedekiah's revolt (which Ezekiel has already attacked in veiled terms in an earlier chapter). On the strictly political issue, Ezekiel is wholly at one with Jeremiah, who has been saying that rebellion against Nebuchadnezzar is a rebellion against God because He has decreed that seventy years of captivity in Babylon are necessary to the purgation of Judah's sins. Ezekiel, taking much the same position, adds to it the peculiar wrinkle that in betraying his oath of vassalage to Nebuchadnezzar, Zedekiah has betrayed God as well, since it was in God's name that the oath was made.

Just when God gives Ezekiel the news that Jerusalem is about to fall, He also delivers another piece of news to the prophet—that his wife, the delight of his eyes (of whose existence we have not previously been apprised), is to die suddenly the next day. Ezekiel, however, is forbidden to mourn, and this is to be a sign for the exiles that they too are forbidden to mourn the loss of the Temple.

BUT NOW COMES a typically abrupt prophetic switch from condemnation to consolation. Ezekiel is commanded to deliver one of those sets of Oracles Against the Nations that are a staple of classical prophecy. Here the nations are mainly condemned either for oppressing the house of Israel or for rejoicing in the downfall of Judah—for which, one after another, they will be plunged into the netherworld and be forgotten entirely or reduced to insignificance. Conversely, God will raise up the entire house of Israel, gathering the "sheep" who have strayed into faraway places, bringing the North and the South together again into one kingdom under another David.

This new kingdom will flourish in every way, throwing off the sins of its past and willingly and fully obeying the laws and the commandments of God, who will make an " ... everlasting covenant ..." with its people. No fortifications or arms will be needed because there will be peace and security. Even when the wicked King Gog of Magog, tempted by an easy prey, sets out on an attack from (more shades of Jeremiah) the north, God Himself will intercept and defeat him with a rain of hail, fire, and brimstone.

Like Ezekiel's vision of the divine chariot, this prophecy of the defeat of the mythical Gog will become the source of endless mystical and apocalyptic speculation (in which Magog will eventually get transformed from a country into Gog's partner in evil). But of the various passages in which Ezekiel's vision of Israel's rebirth as a nation is spelled out, the greatest, and the most memorable, is the one of the dry bones.

Intended to refute a popular saying among the exiles in their moments of despair, it is worth quoting in full, both for its own sake and as a demonstration of how much Ezekiel can pack into a mere fourteen verses:

> The hand of the LORD was upon me, and carried me out in the spirit of the LORD, and set me down in the midst of the valley which was full of bones, And caused me to pass by them round about: and, behold, there were very many in the open valley; and, lo, they were very dry. And he said unto me, Son of man, can these bones live? And I answered, O LORD God, thou knowest. Again he said unto me, Prophesy upon these bones, and say unto them, O ye dry bones, hear the word of the LORD. Thus saith the LORD God unto these bones; Behold, I will cause breath to enter into you, and ye shall live: And I will lay sinews upon you, and will bring up flesh upon you, and cover you with skin, and put breath in you, and ye shall live; and ye shall know that I am the LORD. So I prophesied as I was commanded: and as I prophesied, there was a noise, and behold a shaking, and the bones came together, bone to his bone. And when I beheld, lo, the sinews and the flesh came up upon them, and the skin covered them above; but there was no breath in them. Then said he unto me, Prophesy unto the wind, prophesy, Son of man, and say to the wind, Thus saith the LORD God; Come from the four winds, O breath, and breathe upon these slain, that they may live. So I prophesied as he commanded me, and the breath came into them, and they lived, and stood up upon their feet, an exceeding great army. Then he said unto me, Son of man, these bones are the whole house of Israel: behold, they say, Our bones are dried, and our hope is lost: we are cut off for our parts. Therefore prophesy and say unto them, Thus saith the LORD God; Behold, O my people, I will open your graves, and cause you to come up out of your graves, and bring you into the land of Israel. And ye shall know that I am the LORD, when I have opened your graves, O my people, and brought you up out of your graves, And shall put my spirit in you, and ye shall live, and I shall place you in your own land: then shall ye know that I the LORD have spoken it, and performed it, saith the LORD.

"In view of the vivid metaphors and powerful rhetoric of this passage," writes Moshe Greenberg, "it is no wonder that it was understood literally by interpreters living in an age when the doctrine of a future resurrection had (on other grounds) taken hold in the Jewish and Christian communities." But other interpreters, both ancient and modern, have understood the passage (as, with Greenberg, I myself do) more narrowly as having to do only with national redemption.

Ezekiel's glimpses into the future are capped by yet one more vision. It consists of a minutely detailed blueprint of the new Temple that will be rebuilt when the reunited people of Israel are resettled in the land; along with this description come very detailed instructions as to the rites that will be performed there and who will be empowered to perform them.

Here is another element of Ezekiel that will bother the sages of the Talmud. In addition to their concern that this book will unleash dangerous waves of mystical speculation, and on top of their doubts as to whether God can have appointed a prophet on "impure" foreign soil, they will be deeply troubled by the many contradictions between the Book of Leviticus and Ezekiel's plans and prescriptions for the new Temple. According to a story in the Talmud, Rabbi Haninah ben Hezekiah works so long into the night at reconciling Ezekiel with Leviticus that he has to burn three hundred jars of oil in his lamp in order to finish the job. Even then questions are left over whose answers will, Rabbi Haninah says, have to await the coming of the Messiah. If not for Rabbi Haninah's ardent championship, the Book of Ezekiel might have been withdrawn from circulation.

I THINK WE ALL OWE Rabbi Haninah a great debt for saving a treasure that could otherwise have faded away. Yet I would be less than honest if I pretended that my high estimate of this book is universally shared. The fact is that the talmudic sages against whom Rabbi Haninah would have to defend Ezekiel were not the only group that came to raise serious questions about his stature as compared with the other classical prophets. The attack—and I do not think this is too strong a word—has centered on a number of different though overlapping issues.

One is literary. Unlike most of classical prophecy, the Book of Ezekiel is almost entirely in prose. And whereas most of the other classical prophets are acknowledged as being among the great poets of world literature, Ezekiel's prose (except in a few visions like the valley of the bones) seems to some critics more didactic than inspirational, more convoluted than direct, and repetitive to the point of tiresomeness.

Yet in my judgment, Ezekiel's style has a unique greatness of its own. It constantly moves and shakes the reader into a fresh awareness of old ideas, while the repetitions that weary others most often strike me not as interpolations, or mistakes in transcription, but as the conscious technique of an artist who knows exactly what he is doing. There are many examples in the passages I have already quoted, but let me choose one where repetition is used to create a rhythmically driving prose that makes an all too familiar prophetic threat of destruction into something newly dreadful:

> Also, thou son of man, thus saith the LORD God unto the land of Israel; An end, the end is come upon the four corners of the land. Now is the end come upon thee, and I will send mine anger upon thee, and will judge thee according to thy ways, and will recompense upon thee all thine abominations. And mine eye shall not spare thee, neither will I have pity: but I will recompense thy ways upon thee, and thine abominations shall be in the midst of thee: and ye shall know that I am the LORD.

The main theme having been stated, a bridge follows that is itself full of repetition and that leads into a new theme:

> Thus saith the LORD God; An evil, an only evil, behold, is come. An end is come, the end is come: it watcheth for thee; behold, it is come. The morning is come unto thee, O thou that dwellest in the land: the time is come, the day of trouble is near, and not the sounding again of the mountains.

Having caught his breath, Ezekiel then resumes with the original rhythm, and by using almost the same words as before, he pounds them into our very souls:

> Now will I shortly pour out my fury upon thee, and accomplish mine anger upon thee: and I will judge thee according to thy ways, and will recompense thee for all thine abominations. And mine eye shall not spare, neither will I have pity: I will recompense thee according to thy ways and thine abominations that are in the midst of thee; and ye shall know that I am the LORD that smiteth. Behold the day, behold, it is come: the morning is gone forth; the rod hath blossomed, pride hath budded. Violence is risen up into a rod of wickedness: none of them shall remain, nor of their multitude, nor of any of theirs: neither shall there be wailing for them. The time is come, the day draweth near....

This is the writing of a great religious genius.

Another item in the bill of indictment against Ezekiel is that he has many affinities with the pre-classical prophets, the implication being that he is more primitive than the other classical prophets. Thus, although he never performs any miracles, miracles are performed on him. He also goes into ecstatic trances, and when he describes the extraordinary visions he experiences, he often draws on the kind of language used of Elisha and Elijah (as when he is seized by "the hand of God" or feels the "spirit of God" rushing in upon him).

Moreover, the dramatic representations Ezekiel puts on to illustrate his message seem to many readers bizarre to the point of pathology. Even Maimonides, the greatest of all medieval Jewish philosophers, considers some of the things Ezekiel does (such as lying on his side for 390 days) as too "crazy" to have been ordered by God, and therefore he interprets them as visions rather than actual happenings. And if a devout medieval rabbi like Maimonides—to whom every word of the Bible is of divine origin—can treat suspicions about Ezekiel's sanity seriously enough to explain them away, it is no wonder that the twentieth-century German philosopher Karl Jaspers can confidently diagnose the prophet as a schizophrenic with paranoid tendencies.

Now, I myself confess to sniffing symptoms of clinical depression in Ezekiel's strange periods of silence and withdrawal. But I would say the same about scores of great artists, secular as well as religious. And I must also confess that within the context of classical prophecy I see nothing any crazier in his mimetic representations of his message than the First Isaiah walking around Jerusalem naked and barefoot for three years, or Jeremiah tying a yoke around his neck, or Hosea marrying a whore. To be sure, Ezekiel holds the record for the number of such symbolic actions, and it is also true that Jewish sages of a rationalist bent like Maimonides feel the same need to explain the others away too as visions rather than actual behavior. But only Ezekiel's have been taken as the signs of a psychologically disordered mind.

There are, however, scholars like Lawrence Boadt who argue that through his putative primitivism and insanity Ezekiel was "consciously reinstitut[ing] some archaic prophetic signs of divine inspiration and authority, perhaps to bolster faith in the prophetic word when people were doubting its power during the crises of 593–586 B.C.E." That rings right to me, as does Boadt's waving away of the notion that Ezekiel's vivid descriptions of Jerusalem show either that he had abnormal parapsychic powers or that he did not really live in Babylon.

On the other hand, Yehezkel Kaufmann and Moshe Greenberg, who do not doubt that Ezekiel lived in Babylon, come close to ridiculing those "vivid descriptions" of Jerusalem that other scholars accept at face value. The Kaufmann-Greenberg contention is that the idolatrous abominations by which Ezekiel is so shocked in his visionary visit to the Temple have long since been cleaned out by the Josianic purge, and that the prophet is in this instance being haunted by memories of Manasseh's reign left over from his childhood. Yet even supposing this contention to be correct, it tells us only that Ezekiel is a bad reporter, and says nothing about the crucial role of idolatry in his thought—or, for that matter, in the thought of Jeremiah.

I revert to Jeremiah here because Kaufmann also dismisses *his* diatribes against idolatry, interpreting them as stemming not from what he actually sees as he walks the streets of Jerusalem, or enters the Temple, but from the gap between prophetic idealism and reality. People, says Kaufmann, are never perfect, in either their moral or their religious conduct. They violate ethical norms, and in Jeremiah's Jerusalem some old women may even hold privately on to a vestigial "fetishism" (which is in Kaufmann's scheme of things not even truly or fully idolatrous because it is never accompanied by a belief in pagan myths). This the prophet cannot abide, and he exaggerates the degree of it in order to make it seem commensurate with his outrage (rather like a poet creating what T. S. Eliot—not in one of his own poems but in a critical essay—calls the "objective correlative" of an emotion).

It is the same in Babylon, where, Kaufmann passionately argues, the exiles are nothing short of heroic in maintaining their faith under conditions that radically challenge it, and in resisting the pressures to worship strange gods. (They even, he rightly observes, manage to make converts among the Babylonians.) The long and short of Kaufmann's argument is that Ezekiel overstates the sinfulness of the exiles as much as Jeremiah does of the residents of Jerusalem.

This assessment stems from an effort to defend the people against what Kaufmann and Greenberg believe to be unfair charges, and as such I think their work is laudable.* But in my opinion, measuring both Jeremiah and Ezekiel against the concrete historical circumstances under which they deliver their prophecies also obscures the more general significance of what the two prophets are intent on communicating.

LIKE JEREMIAH, Ezekiel absolves God of any blame for the fall of Jerusalem. It is the people who have broken their covenant with God, not God who has broken His covenant with them. But Ezekiel's justification of God is not the same as Jeremiah's—or that of the other classical prophets—and this difference may supply the real, if unacknowledged, reason for the uneasiness over him that expresses itself in speculations about his sanity or in denigrations of his literary worth.

In Ezekiel, God is portrayed as more concerned about His name—or, as we might say today, His reputation—among the pagans than about anything else. Time and again, He refrains from destroying the incorrigibly rebellious people He has chosen only because of " . . . my name's sake, that it should not be polluted before the heathen, among whom they were, in whose sight I made myself known unto them. . . ." From one generation to the next, the children of Israel have gone on profaning and polluting His holy name by refusing to obey His laws and His commandments, and by whoring after strange gods instead. And

---

*This is another subject about which I will have more to say below, in the concluding chapter.

when He has punished their apostasies by scattering them to the winds, matters have only been made worse, since the nations have seen in this punishment not a humiliation of the children of Israel but rather a defeat of their supposedly all-powerful God.

Therefore, when He gathers the exiles and establishes the new reunited kingdom of David, it will not be out of love or mercy for Israel but out of "pity" for His own name. And when, in this new kingdom, the people finally walk in His ways, it will not be through genuine repentance but because *He* will fashion a new heart for them. (Note again in the following passage—a small part of which I quoted above—the power generated by the repetitious style that bothers so many overly fastidious readers.)

> Son of man, when the house of Israel dwelt in their own land, they defiled it by their own way and their own doings. . . . Wherefore I poured my fury upon them for the blood they had shed upon the land, and for the idols wherewith they had polluted it: And I scattered them among the heathen, and they were dispersed through the countries: according to their way and according to their doings I judged them. And when they entered unto the heathen, whither they went, they profaned my holy name, when they said to them, Those are the people of the LORD, and are gone forth out of his land. But I had pity for mine own holy name, which the house of Israel had profaned among the heathen, whither they went. Therefore say unto the house of Israel, Thus saith the LORD God; I do not this for your sakes, O house of Israel, but for mine holy name's sake, which ye have profaned among the heathen, whither ye went. And I will sanctify my great name, which was profaned among the heathen, which ye have profaned in the midst of them; and the heathen shall know that I am the LORD, saith the LORD God, when I shall be sanctified in you before their eyes. For I will take you from among the heathen, and gather you out of all countries, and will bring you into your own land. Then will I sprinkle clean water upon you, and ye shall be clean: from all your filthiness, and from all your idols, will I cleanse you. A new heart also will I give you, and a new spirit will I put within you: and I will take away the stony heart out of your flesh, and I will give you an heart of flesh. And I will put my spirit within you, and cause you to walk in my statutes, and ye shall keep my judgments, and do them. And ye shall dwell in the land that I gave to your fathers; and ye shall be my people, and I will be your God.

And a little later, He declares again: "Not for your sakes do I do this, saith the LORD God, be it known unto you. . . ."

To eyes that can see and are willing to look, and ears that can hear and are willing to listen, it all comes together in this passage with such great force and with such incandescent clarity that we modern readers, unlike Rabbi Haninah, have no need to burn gallons of midnight oil or to wait for the Messiah's arrival to answer the questions that are bound to arise for people like us. With Ezekiel's help, we can penetrate more fully and deeply than before into the connection between the war declared by God against idolatry when He revealed Himself to Israel as a jealous God, and the role Israel agreed to play in that war.

"How odd of God/To choose the Jews," quipped an otherwise unknown British wag of the twentieth century named William Norman Ewer in a little jingle (often mistakenly attributed to the writer Hilaire Belloc). There have also been those (like the Protestant theologian Friedrich Schleiermacher in nineteenth-century Germany) to whom it was more than odd that God should have bestowed His special favor upon *any* single people, let alone the Jews: they called it a scandal, "the scandal of particularity."

Nevertheless, odd as I myself would agree it seems to Reason, and scandalous as it must indeed strike Theology, this is what the Hebrew Bible tells us God decided to do. The Hebrew Bible also tells us that the people of Israel submitted to that odd and scandalous choice and took upon itself the responsibilities—and the *burden*—accompanying the covenant at Sinai. The believer, whether Jewish or Christian, has no choice but to accept this and go on from there; and the non-believer who wishes to understand the story has no choice but (vaulting ahead to the late nineteenth century and borrowing from Henry James, a great critic as well as a great novelist) to "grant the artist his subject, his idea, his *donnée.*"

Either way, we learn afresh what we have been taught by earlier prophets: that the children of Israel are the instrument through which God's Law will gradually be revealed to all the nations of the world. Hence any attempt to throw that responsibility off, or to shrink from it, amounts to a betrayal of God Himself. Bad as this is in its own right, what is worse is that it undermines or sabotages the very purpose for which the children of Israel have been chosen. Instead of bravely waging the war against idolatry within themselves, they make a mockery of His name by going over to the enemy, and instead of acting to spread the knowledge of and the glory of God, they strengthen the forces of evil—epitomized most egregiously in child sacrifice—that are the poisoned fruits of worshiping other gods.

ALL THE CLASSICAL PROPHETS preach much the same doctrine. But they are easier to take than Ezekiel because they can be read (or rather misread) as looking forward to a time when the "scandal of particularity" will be overcome—a time when all peoples will be as one, serving God not through ritual but through an elevated moral code that has supposedly been weighed down by the primitivism of the ancient religion of Israel.

No such idea emerges from Ezekiel. So far as the relation between ritual and morality is concerned, if demoting the former to a lower status than the latter is the mark of the classical prophet, then Ezekiel can definitely be seen as harking back in substance as well as in style to the pre-classical line. In his eyes, perhaps even less than in those of the much-misunderstood prophets of the eighth century B.C.E., no invidious distinction can be drawn between morality and ritual: they are equally important parts of the laws and the statutes and the ordinances of God, and they are to be observed with equal fervor, scrupulousness, and devotion.

Nor is there any invidious distinction in Ezekiel between the "particular" and the "universal." God, being the one true God, is by definition the God of all, and at the same time, Israel is His chosen people. To Ezekiel there is no contradiction here, because—to say again what cannot be stressed too often—God's whole point in choosing Israel is to use this one people as a vehicle for the ultimate recognition by the other nations of His sovereignty over them. In the meantime, in their self-satisfaction, and through their mockery of Him, these nations will be plunged, one by one, into the pit of Sheol, while Israel will continue to live, even if it be in a diminished condition.

Which brings me right up against what is perhaps the hardest pill of all for a modern reader of Ezekiel to swallow: the harping on God's jealousy and on the repute of His name. But Ezekiel makes—or should make—the pill easier to swallow by showing that this divine attribute is inseparable from, and absolutely necessary to, the war against idolatry. It is a war that will only be won in the world at large when Israel, the people He has chosen to fight it, finally purge themselves of the idolatrous abominations they have no more been able to resist than an adulteress in a state of perpetual heat can resist bedding more and more lovers. Yet because punishing, let alone destroying, Israel (which He has often been tempted to do) will only lead to further profanations of His name, and thus retard the progress of the war against idolatry, He Himself will have to step in and give His chosen people the means they have always lacked to fulfill their mission: a "new heart" and a "new spirit."

It is, I strongly suspect, because Ezekiel is so scandalously "particular" that he has always been the least admired of the major classical prophets. But reading him reminds us of a truth the modern mind tends to forget: that the only road to the universal is through the particular—and not only in religion but in all spheres of life.*

_____

*This subject, too, will be elaborated upon in the concluding chapter.

CHAPTER THIRTEEN

THE SECOND ISAIAH AND "UNIVERSALISM"

INTERNAL EVIDENCE combined with extra-biblical sources have made it possible for scholars to achieve unusual certainty in fixing the date of Ezekiel's last prophecy at 541 B.C.E. But for the twenty years or so leading up to that moment, he fell into another long silence, coming out of "retirement" only to correct a mistaken prediction he had once made about the conquest of Tyre by Nebuchadnezzar. Nor was this his only lapse of political prescience. Most spectacularly, he never anticipated that Babylon's days were numbered, and that its empire would be taken over in a very short time (539 B.C.E.) by Cyrus of Persia.

It was no different in the religious, or religio-political, sphere. Ezekiel was right all along in his conviction that the exiles in Babylon (or anyway many of them) would return to Jerusalem, but wrong in thinking that the two kingdoms of Judah and Israel would be reunited under a new David. The Northerners were by now gone from the house of Israel forever, presumably having disappeared through assimilation into the pagan world to which they had been dispersed nearly two centuries before; never would they be heard from again except in legends about the "Ten Lost Tribes." So, too, with Ezekiel's vision of the new Temple in Jerusalem. A Second Temple would indeed arise in Jerusalem (in 515 B.C.E.), but as a physical structure it would not remotely correspond to Ezekiel's visionary blueprint, and neither would the regulations under which or the persons by whom its rites would be conducted.

Clearly, then, one of the two criteria laid out by Moses in Deuteronomy and invoked by Jeremiah and others for distinguishing between true and false prophets—that the former's oracles come true and the latter's do not—never took hold. Apart from the insuperable problem it presented to the prophet's au-

dience itself of deciding what would happen in the future, it was trumped by
the other criterion enunciated in Deuteronomy. As God says there through
Moses, one who claims to be a prophet may perform "wonders" and still be a
false prophet whom God has sent to test the people's faith. (This could be so
tough a test to pass that Jeremiah, as we have heard, even dared to reproach God
for misleading the people with it.) Conversely, when a prophet enlists in the
war against idolatry by elucidating and reiterating the meaning and the ramifications of Israel's covenant with God, he might still be a true prophet even—as
I would argue, we are entitled to infer—if his "signs and wonders" do not
"come to pass."

Such was the case with Ezekiel. Such was also the case with Jeremiah, whose
prediction that the exiles would return home only after seventy years of captivity in Babylonia was about two decades too long. Jeremiah, too, like Ezekiel, was
wrong about the ingathering of the deportees from the North.

But the most serious failure of all the prophetic predictions was the assurance given to King Hezekiah in 701 B.C.E. by the First Isaiah that Jerusalem
would never fall. Pious commentators have interpreted this assurance as applying
only to the Assyrian siege of the city under Sennacherib. But even if they are
right, the First Isaiah's influence must have reinforced what had already become
a popular article of faith: the inviolability of Jerusalem and of the Temple.

Inevitably, then, their destruction by Nebuchadnezzar in 586 B.C.E. created a
very great spiritual crisis. Which was why it had to be justified so vehemently on
the spot by Jeremiah, and by Ezekiel from afar, not as the result of God's violation of His covenant with David, but—exactly like the fate that had been suffered by the Northern Kingdom before it—as the consequence of the
unquenchable lust for other gods that had driven Judah into one infidelity to
God after another.

The oracles of the First Isaiah were thereby saved from being discredited by
the future fall of Jerusalem, and kept alive by a school of his disciples. In discussing him, I accepted Joseph Blenkinsopp's theory that these disciples, in trans-
mitting the master's words down through the generations, put them through a
steady process of "recycling," updating, and interpolating—always, however, in
the belief that their work was consistent with the spirit of the master.

The number of such transmitters remains, and will probably always remain,
in doubt. So will the questions of exactly what they did to the original words of
Isaiah, when they did it, and how many (or how many parts) of the first thirty-
nine chapters of the Book of Isaiah—even aside from the two third-person narratives they contain—can be assigned to them rather than to him.

But (again with the exception of strict fundamentalists) practically everyone
who has studied these matters agrees on one point. This is that it was not until
the 540s B.C.E.—about a century and a half after the First Isaiah himself ceased
hearing the word of God or just died (or was murdered by King Manasseh)—

that the greatest of his disciples came along. And it was in Babylon, not in Jerusalem, that he appeared, some twenty years after his fellow exile Ezekiel had departed from the scene.

IS IT BY DESIGN that this new prophet never identifies himself by name? Does he himself—or some future editor—append his oracles to those of Isaiah the son of Amoz in order to give them greater authority than they might have acquired if they were standing on their own? Or is it the other way around? Is this new prophet humbly producing what he considers nothing more than an extrapolation of the words of his master? Or—a third possibility—is this how he is seen by the editor who eventually ties the two together and treats them as one?

There is no way we can answer any of these questions. But of one thing we can be sure: the anonymous prophet who has come to be known as Deutero-Isaiah, or the Second Isaiah, or Isaiah of the Exile, is thoroughly familiar with the First Isaiah. Not only does the Second Isaiah often relimn the visions of the First, but he almost seems to be engaged in a deliberate effort to dispel any doubts that the fall of Jerusalem may have stirred up about the master.

In my analysis of the First Isaiah, I said that I have never been persuaded by the theory that the last eleven chapters of the book emanate from a Third or "Trito"-Isaiah. I also said that I am even less inclined to accept the "new paradigm," which splits what used to be only one Trito-Isaiah into a whole school of "pseudo-Isaiahs." As this latest theory would have it, these "pseudo-Isaiahs" were never deported. Rather, they were already living in Jerusalem, when Cyrus—in accordance with his imperial policy of granting a considerable degree of local autonomy to the provinces he had wrested from the Babylonians—issued his decree in 538 B.C.E. giving the exiles from Judah permission to return to Jerusalem and even granting them a subsidy with which to rebuild their Temple. The oracles of the "pseudo-Isaiahs" in Jerusalem were in this theory tacked onto the prophecies of the Second in Babylon, just as his were appended to those of the First.

What is the poor layman to do in the face of all this? I would suggest that, in the absence of a definitive consensus, and once his head stops spinning from a review of the competing "paradigms," the lay reader is free—even compelled—to make his own choice. Mine is eclectic, composed of elements derived from three different groups of scholars, each of which disagrees with the others and would regard my approach as lacking consistency (which it may well do).

Thus, I side with the scholars who still stubbornly hold out for only two Isaiahs. On the other hand, I go along with the critics who think that the last eleven chapters are set in Jerusalem, not in Babylon. But—with yet a third school—I do not take this shift of locale to Jerusalem as evidence that there are three Isaiahs, or fifty or seventy. And lest these large numbers sound like a flip exaggeration, consider the following summary by Isaac Avishur:

Gunkel, who originated the method of "form criticism," ... maintained
that the prophetic books are composed of small units of separate "oracles" which were joined together by editors. ... Gressman applied this
method of Gunkel to Deutero-Isaiah, and ... attempted to prove that
chapters 40–55 are composed of 49 small independent units. ...
Koehler distinguished 70 units in chapters 40–55, ... while Begrich
pointed to the existence of more than 70 units.

In opposition to this fissiparous analysis, I find it hard to resist the conclusion that the Second Isaiah was in the first wave of exiles who went back
home. This is only a guess, based on the supposition that he would feel it
incumbent upon him to do what he himself was passionately urging his fellow
exiles to do: "Go ye forth of Babylon, flee ye from the Chaldeans, with a voice
of singing declare ye, tell this, utter it even to the end of the earth; say ye, The
LORD hath redeemed his servant Jacob." If not a concrete piece of evidence,
a verse like this—and there are others—makes a strong psychological case for
the Second Isaiah's return. "The great prophet," declares John Bright, "would
surely have made the return—had he been able so much as to crawl!" I think
so, too.

Finally, I agree with the critics who think that the Second Isaiah continued
prophesying after returning to Jerusalem. That a marked difference in the pre-
dominant tone and content can be detected between the Babylonian and the
Jerusalem oracles is what led in the first place to the positing of a Third Isaiah.
But in the opinion of some scholars, the change may equally reflect the Second
Isaiah's disappointment in the hopes aroused by Cyrus. The prophet seems to
have anticipated that the Persian king would go over to the God of Israel; instead
he embraced Marduk, the god of Babylon. Nor did Cyrus, for all the benevo-
lence of his policies, restore Judah to full sovereignty; while enjoying a certain
degree of autonomy, it remained a province of his empire. Nor did the Babylonian exiles flock to Jerusalem in droves, and those who did return failed to get on
with the rebuilding of the Temple, and—most embittering of all—even began
reverting to idolatry. There was more than enough cause in all this to enrage the
Second Isaiah, and more than enough reason for the reverberations we hear now
of the angry prophecies of the First.

Yet we also get the obverse: pictures of an eschatological future that are virtually quotations from the First Isaiah's vision of peace among men and even
among wild beasts. To pick only one example, we read in the penultimate chapter of the book (65) that "The wolf and the lamb shall feed together, and the lion
shall eat straw like the bullock: and dust shall be the serpent's meat...."

Given all this, it seems to me humanly and dramatically right that the Second Isaiah, having returned home after many years—or, if he was born in Babylon, having set foot in Jerusalem for the first time—should also have come full

circle in a spiritual sense, undergoing a virtual metamorphosis into a latter-day version of his master, Isaiah the son of Amoz.

BUT HAVING VAULTED so far ahead of our story, let me return to the Second Isaiah while he is still in Babylon—the Isaiah who is universally held up as the supreme prophet of consolation. It is often forgotten that, like all the other classical prophets, this one is prone to sudden shifts of mood, so that there is more rebuke and anger in the early chapters than is allowed for by his reputation. Still, at the very beginning* the prevailing winds are fair, carrying with them words of such sweetness that to Jews they will become the most beloved verses in the prophetic literature, and perhaps even in the whole of the Hebrew Bible:

> Comfort ye, comfort ye, my people, saith your God. Speak ye comfortably to Jerusalem, and cry unto her, that her warfare is accomplished, that her iniquity is pardoned: for she hath received of the LORD's hand double for all her sins.†

The prophet continues in this vein, mostly quoting the words of an unidentified "voice" that calls out to him—a voice that seems to be God's (though some have identified it as coming from an angel). This voice then commands the prophet to repeat the same good news and to bring more and more of it to his fellow captives. Not only have they been forgiven, but they will soon leave Babylon and go home to Judah, where the ruined cities will be rebuilt and a new Jerusalem will arise out of the ashes.

There is nothing here about Jeremiah, according to whom God condemned the exiles to seventy years in Babylon, nor is there any reference to Ezekiel, whose vision of the ingathering and the rebuilding of Jerusalem was set in an unspecified eschatological future. But the new prophet's audience must understand what he is telling them. He is telling them that God has commuted their

---

*By "the very beginning," I mean Chapter 40, which has for long been accepted as the first prophecy of the Second Isaiah. But most scholars detach Chapters 34 and 35 from the First Isaiah, and some assign them to the second and/or third sections of the book. Others credit them to Jeremiah, and still others give only 35 to Deutero- and/or Trito-Isaiah, leaving 34 out in the cold as a nameless orphan.

†NJPS has "tenderly" instead of "comfortably," AB gives us "kindly," and Son opts for "Bid Jerusalem take heart." Judging KJV's "Her warfare is accomplished" to be overly literal, NJPS renders the Hebrew *ki mal'ah ts'va-ah* as "term of service" and AB as "her sentence is served." JB's translation of the passage differs most radically from the others: "'Console my people, console them'/says your God./'Speak to the heart of Jerusalem/and call to her/that her time of service is ended,/that her sin is atoned for,/that she has received from the hand of Yahweh/double punishment for all her crimes.'"

sentence. They do not have to wait another twenty years, and certainly not until the End of Days: the time is *now*. God has appointed Cyrus, king of the Persians, as their liberator from the Babylonians.* We remember—and the prophet's audience probably does, too, without being reminded—that the First Isaiah characterized Assyria as the rod of God's anger, the instrument by which He punished a sinful and rebellious Israel. But now, with Cyrus, He is employing a pagan empire to play the opposite role in His scheme of things. Hence no political obstacle will stand in the way of the return to Judah.

But neither will there by any physical obstacles on the journey through difficult terrain. God will prepare a highway for Himself, along which the exiles will travel with Him, and He will even transform the landscape to make it easy to traverse:

> The voice of him that crieth in the wilderness, Prepare ye the way of the LORD, make straight in the desert a highway for our God. Every valley shall be exalted, and every mountain and hill shall be made low: and the crooked shall be made straight, and the rough places plain.†

God will also provide the homebound exiles with sustenance, just as He did to their ancestors when they fled from Egypt. Indeed, this new Exodus will be even more miraculous than the first:

> Remember ye not the former things, neither consider the things of old. Behold, I will do a new thing; now it shall spring forth; shall ye not know it? I will even make a way in the wilderness, and rivers in the desert. The beast of the field shall honor me, the dragons and the owls: because I give waters in the wilderness and rivers in the desert, to give drink to my people, my chosen.‡

---

*Cyrus is mentioned twice by name. The first time he is described as a "shepherd" and the second as *"m'shikhi,"* or "my anointed one." It does not, however, signify that Cyrus is being heralded as the Messiah—a concept that does not yet exist, and that will in the future only be applied to a monarch descended from David.

†Here is what I singled out in the Introduction as the most famous error in the King James Version. In accordance with the rules of parallelism that are among those governing ancient Hebrew poetry, the verse (using KJV's own language) should read: "A voice crieth: In the wilderness prepare ye the way of the LORD. . . ." The modern translations also make the purpose of these changes in the landscape clearer. Thus NJPS: "A voice rings out:/ Clear in the desert/ A road for the LORD!/ Level in the wilderness/ A highway for our God!/ Let every valley be raised,/ Every hill and mount made low./ Let the rugged ground become level/ And the ridges become a plain."

‡All the modern translations I have consulted give us "jackals and ostriches" rather than KJV's "the dragons and the owls."

Clearly there are skeptics among those the prophet is addressing, because God takes pains to answer them when they express doubt as to whether all this can really be so:

> But thou, Israel, art my servant, Jacob whom I have chosen, the seed of Abraham my friend. Thou whom I have taken from the ends of the earth, and called thee from the chief men thereof, and said unto thee, Thou art my servant; I have chosen thee, and not cast thee away. Fear thou not; for I am with thee: be not dismayed; for I am thy God: I will strengthen thee; yea, I will help thee; yea, I will uphold thee with the right hand of my righteousness.*

As though further to still the doubts of the skeptics and to strengthen the credibility of this lyrical reassurance, it is accompanied by repeated assertions of God's power. He, and He alone, created the universe and rules over everything in it from the heavens to the earth. His ways are not the ways of man and His thoughts are not the thoughts of man. Nor is there anything in the world, whether natural or human, that can stand against Him:

> All nations before him are as nothing; and they are counted to him less than nothing, and vanity. . . . It is he that sitteth upon the circle of the earth, and the inhabitants thereof are as grasshoppers; that stretcheth out the heavens as a curtain, and spreadeth them out as a tent to dwell in: That bringeth the princes to nothing; he maketh the judges as vanity. . . . Hast thou not known? hast thou not heard, that the everlasting God, the LORD, the Creator of the ends of the earth, fainteth not, neither is weary? there is no searching of his understanding.†

THIS AND SEVERAL OTHER PASSAGES in the Second Isaiah are similar to the voice from the whirlwind in the Book of Job that also evokes God's absolute power and the inability of the puny human mind to comprehend Him. Yet the awe reverberating through these verses in the Second Isaiah, wonderfully phrased though it may be, is neither singular nor novel in the prophetic literature, and Job is not the only non-prophetic book of the Bible that expresses the

---

*KJV's "chief men thereof" is a mistranslation, which the modern versions correct with some variant of NJPS's "its far corners." All the modern versions also correct the "right hand of my righteousness," rendering the phrase as "my victorious right hand."

†For the obscure "sitteth upon the circle of the earth," NJPS has "enthroned upon the vault of the earth" and AB gives us "he sits upon the dome of the earth."

same sense of God. Nor is there anything new in the *idea* of God put forward
here. He is, as always, the one and only true God, the creator of all things, while
the gods of the idolators are no gods at all:

> Thus saith the LORD the King of Israel, and his redeemer the LORD
> of hosts; I am the first, and I am the last; and beside me there is no
> God. . . . Fear ye not, neither be afraid: have not I told thee from that
> time, and have declared it? ye are even my witnesses. Is there a God
> besides me? yea, there is no God; I know not any.*

All this is also fairly standard in the classical prophetic tradition, and the
Hebrew Bible in general. Yet John L. McKenzie, in his edition, informs us that
"Second Isaiah has often been called the most explicit spokesman of monothe-
ism up to his time."

McKenzie himself, while gingerly offering a few pallid qualifications, shares
in this assessment. But the only evidence he provides for it is that "no earlier
prophet so often confronts Yahweh and false gods." Admittedly, I have not done
a statistical analysis of the number of attacks launched on idolatry in the earlier
prophets, and it may be true (though I doubt it) that more of them appear in the
Second Isaiah than in any of his predecessors. Yet it should be obvious by now
that the Second Isaiah is not diverging from or advancing beyond precedent in
this respect. He is, on the contrary, joining the legion of his predecessors in the
war against idolatry. And in doing so, he shows that he is aware of how long ago
that war began, and why—in the absence of a definitive written text of the
Law—prophets have been sent to serve as a living Torah.

Significantly, the personage the Second Isaiah brings up is not Amos, the first
of the classical prophets, but Abraham, the first of *all* the prophets—Abraham,
who turned away from the alien gods served by his fathers and entered into a
covenant with the one true God. Then there is the *pre*-classical prophet Elijah,
whom the Second Isaiah never actually names. But when he portrays God as
challenging the worshipers of idols to stand up and make their case, what springs
immediately to mind is the contest that Elijah conducted with the 450 prophets
of Baal.

Like Elijah, the Second Isaiah, speaking in the voice of God, mocks the idols
and those who fashion and worship them:

> They that make a graven image are all of them vanity; and their delec-
> table things shall not profit; and they are their own witnesses; they see

---

*All the modern translations agree that the word "God" in the very last of these verses should be
"rock."

not, nor know; that they may be ashamed. Who hath formed a god, or molten a graven image that is profitable for nothing? . . . He heweth him down cedars, and taketh the cypress and the oak. . . . Then shall it be for a man to burn: for he will take thereof, and warm himself; yea, he kindleth it, and baketh bread; yea, he maketh a god, and worshippeth it; he maketh a graven image, and falleth down thereto. He burneth part thereof in the fire; with part he eateth flesh, he roasteth roast, and is satisfied. . . . And the residue thereof he maketh a god, even his graven image: he falleth down unto it, and worshippeth it, and prayeth unto it, and saith Deliver me; for thou art my god. . . . He feedeth on ashes: a deceived heart hath turned him aside, that he cannot deliver his soul, nor say, Is there not a lie in my right hand?

If a "new thing" (in the phrase often used in this part of the book) really has entered into the oracles of the Second Isaiah concerning the contention between God and the idols, it is not a more fully adumbrated statement of, or a higher stage in, the evolution of monotheism. No: what emerges in the Second Isaiah is an especially keen awareness by this prophet of his connection with the various phases in the long war against idolatry as enjoined from the start upon the whole people of Israel and as led by the prophets before him.

To be more specific: in the sense that the Second Isaiah directs his fire *both* against the idolatry of other peoples and against its seductive appeal to the people of Israel, his oracles represent a synthesis of the pre-classical tradition of the Judges and Elijah (when the primary task was to discredit the surrounding idolatrous cultures in the eyes of the Israelites) and the classical tradition (when the target became Israel's faithlessness to God as expressed by its *own* idolatrous practices). McKenzie himself comes close to grasping as much:

> The Israelites had known mighty nations and their gods before Babylon, but for the first time they knew a people and gods who had defeated Judah utterly. Second Isaiah addressed those who had been transported to a foreign country, where the wealth and success of the nation was attributed to the gods whose temples they could see and whose cult they could observe.

In this situation "The Israelites of Babylon could well have said, in a modern phrase, that Yahweh was dead." Hence "a mere restatement of earlier belief was not enough."

However, such a "mere restatement," as the Second Isaiah understands (and as Ezekiel did before him), is exactly what the people require. But he also understands that it can only be effective if it is infused with the absolute confidence that Babylon is about to fall. Like Assyria before it, Babylon was selected by God

as the rod of His anger against Israel ("I was wroth with my people, I have polluted mine inheritance, and given them into thine hand . . ."). But as He formerly sent the Babylonians to requite the Assyrians, now He is sending Cyrus to
make the Babylonians themselves suffer the consequences of their cruelty and
their trust in idols, which, being the work of their own hands, are nothing more
than a reflection of their own arrogant self-regard:

> Therefore hear now this, . . . that sayest in thine heart, I am, and none
> else beside me. . . . For thou hast trusted in thy wickedness: thou hast
> said, None seeth me. Thy wisdom and thy knowledge, it hath perverted
> thee; . . . and desolation shall come upon thee suddenly, which thou
> shalt not know. Stand now with thine enchantments, and with the mul-
> titude of thy sorceries, . . . if so be thou mayest prevail. . . . Let now the
> astrologers, the stargazers, the monthly prognosticators, stand up, and
> save thee from these things that shall come upon thee.

ANOTHER, RELATED, CLAIM endorsed by McKenzie (albeit again with a
certain hesitancy) is that the "universalism of outlook in Second Isaiah . . . has no
real antecedent in earlier books of the Old Testament." This claim logically flows
from the premise that the Second Isaiah's monotheism is more highly developed
than that of the earlier prophets. But since the premise is faulty, so is the conclusion. As with the condemnation of idolatry, the conception in the Second Isaiah
of God's sovereignty over all nations (which is McKenzie's definition of "universalism") is not—and cannot be—new. If only one God exists, then it is axiomatic
that He is the God of all people. There is no problem here: it constitutes a self-
evident proposition. A question arises only because God has entered into a special relation with one people alone, the people of Israel.

With this question, we are back to the "scandal of particularity." But I would
deny that the Second Isaiah's answer is any different, or any more highly evolved,
than the one given by Ezekiel or the other classical prophets.

Along with them—to go over ground one is forced by the standard misconceptions to traverse again and again—he affirms that for inscrutable reasons of
His own, God has chosen the children of Israel as the human instrument
through which to reveal Himself and to promulgate His laws and His commandments. But in order to spread those laws and those commandments
throughout the world, the people of Israel first have to fight against their own
attraction to idolatry, which is always standing in the way of their divinely
ordained mission. It is an attraction so strong—and they are so incorrigibly
rebellious—that not even the wonders shown them by God are able to wipe it
out:

I have declared the former things from the beginning; and they went forth out of my mouth, and I shewed them; I did them suddenly, and they came to pass. Because I knew that thou art obstinate, and thy neck is an iron sinew, and thy brow brass; I have even from the beginning declared it to thee; before it came to pass I shewed it thee: lest thou shouldest say, Mine idol hath done them, and my graven image, and my molten image, hath commanded them. . . . Yea, thou heardest not; yea, thou knewest not; yea, from that time that thine ear was not opened: for I knew that thou wouldest deal very treacherously; and wast called a transgressor from the womb.*

In this the Second Isaiah again joins hands with his immediate predecessor Ezekiel, the other great prophet of the exile, tracing the sinfulness of Israel to the very beginning of its birth as a people. He also follows Ezekiel in declaring that God has forgiven them not because they have repented, or because they deserve it, but because, having chosen them to be His "witnesses," He has tied His own honor to their regeneration and their survival:

For my name's sake will I defer mine anger, and for my praise will I refrain for thee, that I cut thee not off. . . . For mine own sake, even for mine own sake, will I do it: for how should my name be polluted? and I will not give my glory unto another.

But what the Second Isaiah communicates from God is indeed a "new thing" as compared with what He said through Ezekiel. For in reaffirming that He will never cut Israel off, He has now also decided to bring the redemption forward from the far-distant to the immediate future. With the imminent advent of Cyrus, the exiles will return home, and Judah and Jerusalem will in their restored state become more glorious than ever before. Then all the other nations, finally recognizing that their idols are not gods, and that there is no God but God, will come to worship Him:

I have sworn by myself . . . That unto me every knee shall bow, every tongue shall swear. Surely, shall one say, in the LORD have I righteous-ness and strength: even to him shall men come; and all that are incensed against him shall be ashamed.†

---

*Most of the modern translations think that "rebel" is more accurate than "transgressor" here.

†Some modern translators think that KJV is wrong in translating *ts'dakot* as "righteousness" and that it means "victory." Others (myself included) think KJV is right.

But to this prophecy a concluding note is attached that casts a bright light on the "scandal of particularity": "In the LORD shall all the seed of Israel be justified, and shall glory."

Many partisans of "universalism" ignore or dismiss the implications of this verse because they assume that the message the Second Isaiah wishes to convey is that the children of Israel will no longer be special to God. In McKenzie's words, "The position of Israel does not mean that it receives blessings Yahweh does not give to other peoples; its position is that of mediator of blessings." If McKenzie is saying that Israel, purged now of any trace of inner idolatry, will at last be capable of bearing full and proper witness to the knowledge of God throughout the world, so that all the pagan nations will come to recognize that they too are ruled by Him, then there can be no disagreement. But there is more to it than that.

To be sure, as the First Isaiah, speaking for God, promises that His word will issue forth from Jerusalem to " . . . many people . . ." who will go up to the holy mountain to hear it, so in different words does the Second:

> Behold my servant, whom I uphold; mine elect, in whom my soul delighteth; I have put my spirit upon him: he shall bring forth judgment to the Gentiles. . . . He shall not fail nor be discouraged, till he have set judgment in the earth: and the isles shall wait for his law.

Yet in an even stronger echo of the First Isaiah (with an allusion to Jeremiah thrown in, together with a merciful retraction of the harsh judgment of Ezekiel about the birth of Israel that the Second Isaiah endorsed earlier), we get this:

> Listen, O isles, unto me; and hearken, ye people, from far; The LORD hath called me from the womb; from the bowels of my mother hath he made mention of my name. . . . And he said unto me, Thou art my servant, O Israel, in whom I will be glorified. . . . And he said, It is a light thing that thou shouldest be my servant to raise up the tribes of Jacob, and to restore the preserved of Israel: I will also give thee for a light to the Gentiles, that thou mayest be my salvation unto the end of the earth.

Israel, then, is not to be merely a "mediator of blessings": it is to be the *teacher* of God's law. Therefore the potentates to whom Israel was formerly enslaved will be subject to it—and not merely in a spiritual sense:

> Thus saith the LORD God, Behold, I will lift up mine hand to the Gentiles, and set up my standard to the people: and they shall bring thy sons in their arms, and thy daughters shall be carried upon their shoul-

ders. And kings shall be thy nursing fathers, and their queens thy nursing mothers: they shall bow down to thee with their face to the earth, and lick up the dust of thy feet. . . .

Such images cannot be considered the picture of an Israel that is only "a mediator of blessings." And still less can the furious verses that conclude this triumphalist prophecy be read as restricting Israel to so modest or pacific a role:

But thus saith the LORD, . . . I will contend with him that contendeth with thee, and I will save thy children. And I will feed them that oppress thee with their own flesh; and they shall be drunken with their own blood, as with sweet wine: and all flesh shall know that I the LORD am thy Savior and thy Redeemer, the mighty One of Jacob.

Then we have these verses as well:

Thus saith the LORD, the Redeemer of Israel, and his Holy One, to him whom man despiseth, to him whom the nation abhorreth, to a servant of rulers, Kings shall see and arise, princes also shall worship, because of the LORD that is faithful, and the Holy One of Israel, and he shall choose thee. Thus saith the LORD, In an acceptable time have I heard thee, and in a day of salvation I have helped thee: and I will preserve thee, and give thee for a covenant of the people, to establish the earth, to cause to inherit the desolate heritages.

Perhaps the most potent such oracle of all is addressed to Jerusalem. It is from a chapter that is usually attributed to the Third or some other Isaiah, but is consistent in tone and substance with the other verses I have just quoted, and no more or less eschatological than the vision of the First Isaiah that also appears in Micah:

Arise, shine; for thy light is come, and the glory of the LORD is risen upon thee. . . . And the Gentiles shall come to thy light, and kings to the brightness of thy rising. . . . Then thou shalt see . . . the abundance of the sea shall be converted unto thee, the forces of the Gentiles shall come unto thee. . . . they shall bring gold and incense; and they shall shew forth the praises of the LORD. All the flocks of Kedar shall be gathered together unto thee, the rams of Nebaioth shall minister unto thee: they shall come up with acceptance on mine altar, and I will glorify the house of my glory. . . . Surely the isles shall . . . bring thy sons from afar, their silver and their gold with them, unto the name of the LORD thy God, and to the Holy One of Israel, because he hath glorified thee.

But it is not only wealth that will pour into Jerusalem: there will be other forms of tribute from the nations, too:

> And the sons of strangers shall build up thy walls, and their kings shall minister unto thee: for in my wrath I smote thee, but in my favor have I had mercy on thee. . . . For the nation and kingdom that will not serve thee shall perish; yea, those nations shall be utterly wasted. . . . The sons also of them that afflicted thee shall come bending unto thee; and all they that despised thee shall bow themselves down at the soles of thy feet; and they shall call thee, The city of the LORD, the Zion of the Holy One of Israel.

Kaufmann may be right when he denies that the Second Isaiah looks forward to an Israelite "imperium" in the normal politico-military sense of that term. But surely when this Isaiah—like the First, if not entirely like the warlike Micah—envisages a *spiritual* imperium, it is one that brings with it material benefits, together with the religious vindication that (the children of Israel being human) is not entirely free of the taste of revenge:

> And strangers shall stand and feed your flocks, and the sons of the alien shall be your plowmen and your vinedressers. But ye shall be named the Priests of the LORD: men shall call you the Ministers of our God: ye shall eat the riches of the Gentiles, and in their glory shall ye boast yourselves.

THE MAIN ARGUMENT I am intent on getting across, however, is that the universalism of the Second Isaiah falls well within the bounds of the tradition of classical prophecy: it is a universalism arrived at through particularity—and in two senses. First, he no more gives priority to the ethical (conventionally identified with universalism) over the ritual (just as conventionally associated with particularism) than any of the other classical prophets allegedly do. Obviously, living in exile after the Temple has been destroyed, the Second Isaiah has no cause to insist, as does the First, that God rejects sacrifices and the observance of festivals if they are used as a cover for immoral behavior in the social realm. Yet there are several clear indications that the Second Isaiah is no enemy of the sacrificial cult.

The strongest of these is in one of the passages of rebuke that sometimes interrupt the flow of consolation:

> This people have I formed for myself; they shew forth my praise. But thou hast not called upon me, O Jacob; but thou hast been weary of me,

O Israel. Thou hast not brought me the small cattle of thy burnt offerings; neither hast thou honored me with thy sacrifices. . . . Thou hast
brought me no sweet cane with money, neither hast thou filled me with
the fat of thy sacrifices: but thou hast made me to serve with thy sins,
thou hast wearied me with thy iniquities.*

Reading this, one rubs one's eyes: can God really be rebuking the exiles for
failing to perform sacrifices even though—in this post-Deuteronomy era—they
are forbidden by His own law to do so anywhere but in the Temple in Jerusalem,
which no longer even exists? So bewildering is this rebuke that many a fancy
exegetical dance has been executed around it. Yet for all the rationalizations that
have been developed to explain the passage away, there it stands as vivid testimony to the Second Isaiah's positive attitude toward sacrifice.

Another very telling example can be drawn from a chapter supposedly
belonging to the Third Isaiah (or to one of the indeterminate number of
"pseudo-Isaiahs" who have been replacing him in scholarly favor). It concerns
the Babylonians who have converted to the religion of Israel and the young
exiles from Judah who have been castrated and forced to serve as court eunuchs.

Both groups doubt that they can return to Zion as full members of the community—the converts because they were not born to the people of Israel, and
the eunuchs because it is written in Deuteronomy that "He that is wounded in
the stones, or hath his privy member cut off, shall not enter into the congregation of the LORD." Yet the Second Isaiah has this to say to them in the name of
God (who with respect to the eunuchs contradicts His own edict again, but now
in love and mercy rather than in reproof):

Neither let the son of the stranger, that hath joined himself to the
LORD, speak, saying, The LORD hath utterly separated me from his
people: neither let the eunuch say, Behold, I am a dry tree. For thus saith
the LORD unto the eunuchs that keep my sabbaths, and choose the
things that please me, and take hold of my covenant; Even unto them
will I give in mine house and within my walls a place and a name better than of sons and daughters: I will give them an everlasting name, that
shall not be cut off.

These converts and eunuchs, in short, will be brought by God to His "holy
mountain" where they will be full members of the congregation of Israel. And

---

*NJPS has "you have burdened Me with your sins" instead of "thou hast made me to serve with
thy sins." So, too, several of the other modern translations.

what will this mean? It will mean that " . . . their burnt offerings and their sacrifices shall be accepted upon mine altar. . . ."

The Second Isaiah emphasizes keeping of the Sabbath because it is the main
form of ritual that can lawfully be practiced in exile; prayer, fasting, and the
observance of certain festivals are also permitted. (In fact, the rudiments of the
new institution of the synagogue—which will become the substitute for a temple after the second one is destroyed by the Romans in 70 C.E.—are evidently
already present in Babylon in the days of the Second Isaiah.)

In spite of all this, the Second Isaiah is still alleged to give priority to the ethical even over this type of ritual, as the First Isaiah supposedly does in his attack
on sacrifice. Reaching into what many consider "Trito" territory, they cite the
complaint directed there at God by people who look upon themselves as righteous: "Wherefore have we fasted, say they, and thou seest not? wherefore have
we afflicted our soul, and thou takest no knowledge? . . ." To which God replies
that fasting is not acceptable to Him when it is accompanied by strife and contention, by the doing of business, and by the oppression of laborers. This is not
the fast He desires. The fast He requires must be tied to deeds of mercy and
kindness:

> Is not this the fast that I have chosen? to loose the bands of wickedness,
> to undo the heavy burdens, and to let the oppressed go free, and that ye
> break every yoke? Is it not to deal thy bread to the hungry, and that
> thou bring the poor that are cast out to thy house? when thou seest the
> naked, that thou cover him . . .?

With words like that before our eyes, we would have to be blind not to perceive that the Second Isaiah (like the other classical prophets) rejects the idea
that the obligations of the Israelite religion begin and end with the ritual commandments. Nor is it possible to deny that the classical prophets often take pains
to remind us of the commandments governing the relations between man and
man. But neither can there be any denying that they attach equal sanctity to the
commandments governing the relations between man and God. Even the very
passage I have just quoted ends with a reminder of the supreme importance of
keeping the Sabbath:

> If thou turn away thy foot from the sabbath, from doing any pleasure on
> my holy day; and call the sabbath a delight, the holy of the LORD, hon-
> orable; and shalt honor him, not doing thine own ways, nor finding
> thine own pleasure, nor speaking thine own words: Then shalt thou
> delight thyself in the LORD; and I will cause thee to ride upon the
> high places of the earth, and feed thee with the heritage of Jacob thy
> father. . . .*

At some moments, one set of commandments is stressed; at some moments the other; and at some moments the two are brought together without distinction:

> Thus saith the LORD, Keep ye judgment, and do justice: for my salvation is near to come, and my righteousness to be revealed. Blessed is the man that doeth this, and the son of man that layeth hold on it; that keepeth the sabbath from polluting it, and keepeth his hand from doing any evil.

I have returned to the issue of ritual here because it is so closely connected to the "scandal of particularity" in the second of the two senses mentioned above. For when it is asserted that the Second Isaiah is even more radical than the First and the other prophets of the eighth century B.C.E. in his elevation of morality over the cult, the objective is to show that he is administering yet another cut in the umbilical cord tying the religion of ancient Israel to its "tribal" origins and giving it a mighty push toward something more "universal." From which it follows, conversely, that if he holds intransigently on to ritual, he is helping to perpetuate the "particularism" of the ancient religion and blocking the breadth of his own vision.

But my contention is that, like the earlier classical prophets, the Second Isaiah is doing both of these things simultaneously, and that in his eyes, as in theirs, no contradiction appears between the particular and the universal. To them it is a given that God has chosen Israel to be a light unto the nations, but that the light will shine with full radiance only when Israel, securely restored in Zion, rebuilds His "house" on His "holy mountain" and then obeys *all* His laws and statutes.

To reiterate the point yet another time: God depends upon the people of Israel to live in such a way as to create the conditions under which every knee will bend to Him and all will acknowledge His sovereignty. This—as distinguished from preaching to the pagan nations and trying to convert them—is the mission He has chosen them to perform.

The theological conundrum such a conception presents is indeed very real: why should an omnipotent God have mortgaged His honor or His reputation or His glory to the behavior of a single nation—and a "stiff-necked" one at that, in constant need of punishment? (So it will be that downtrodden Jews in the Diaspora of the future centuries will wryly pray: "Dear God, please choose someone

---

*KJV's translation of the first verse here is literally accurate, but NJPS gives a better idea of the meaning with "refrain from trampling." Also, where KJV twice uses "pleasure," NJPS opts more precisely for "affairs" (i.e., business), and it has "strike bargains" instead of "speaking thine own words."

else for a change.") Why should it bother Him when punishment intended to purge His chosen people of their sins should be interpreted by the pagan nations as a sign that their gods are stronger than He is? Correlatively, why should the redemption of this people in Zion be a necessary precondition of His triumph over idolatry throughout the whole world?

I have never heard any fully satisfactory responses to these questions (which are perhaps raised even more sharply by a reading of Ezekiel than of the Second Isaiah). But believers, whether Jewish or Christian, are permanently saddled with them because—to paraphrase the old song—the Bible tells them so. For that matter, even wholly secularist historians have had trouble coming up with convincing rational explanations for the survival of the Jews against all odds, when the mighty empires, both ancient and modern, which conquered and dispersed and oppressed them have disappeared one by one into the pit of "Sheol."

Even so, the idea that "universalism" is reachable only through "particularism" has always bothered Christians, and since the nineteenth century, it has been bothering Jews as well. (One modern Jewish movement, Reconstructionism, has actually eliminated from the liturgy all reference to the idea of chosenness.) Strong tremors of that disturbance are evident to this day in many commentaries on both parts of the Book of Isaiah, where (as in McKenzie's on the Second) the "highest" stage of "universalism" in the Hebrew Bible has long been imagined to reside.

FOR MANY CHRISTIANS, however, "universalism" is too general a term, and not in itself the main point. What they see—or used to see—in the Isaiahs is the most graphic prophetic vision of the advent of Jesus. Yes, there are tantalizing hints in Jeremiah's "new covenant," and also in Ezekiel's idea of a "new heart" (and there will be others in the last of the classical prophets). But in a Christological reading, the Book of Isaiah does more than hint: it even supplies crucial details of the short career of Jesus on earth. Some of these details I examined when I went through the chapters now assigned to the First Isaiah—the most important being the birth of the son Immanuel to a "virgin." But others that seem even more startling appear in the latter part (or parts) of the book.

Specifically, they are located in four separate passages to which scholars have given the collective title the "Songs of the Servant of the LORD."* Except in being regarded as a unit whose elements have been scattered throughout the text, everything about the Songs is in hot dispute, so much so that I doubt that anything in the Hebrew Bible has generated more controversy.

---

*The passages are: 42:1–4; 49:1–6; 50:4–9; and 52:13–53:12. I have already quoted above from two of these.

At a minimum, four sets of questions about these passages are under constant debate. The first concerns the author of the Songs: is it the Second Isaiah himself, or a later editor? The second issue is what, if anything, can be learned from the placement of the Songs in different contexts. The third is directed at the identity of the servant: is he the personification of a group, and if so, which?; or is he an individual, and if so, who? The fourth revolves around his mission: is it "particularistic" (in which case God has sent him to Israel alone), or "universalistic" (in which case God has sent him to all the nations)?

Of these four sets of questions, the first two belong to the province of the professional scholars and exegetes. I will consequently give them a pass, except to report that the exercise of plucking the Songs out and repeatedly reading them together has failed to persuade me that they actually constitute a single unit of their own. The relation of each passage to the other three is so very far from clear—in one of them, the word "servant" never even appears—that I am puzzled as to why and how the idea of the Songs as a unit has won over almost every scholar in the field when nothing else about them has succeeded in doing so.

That aside, the other two questions, about which there is nothing approaching a consensus, are of enough general interest to warrant a bit of discussion.

As to the servant's identity, the leading candidate among the collectivist interpretations has always been Israel, here personified as an individual and there spoken of as a people, either in its historical reality or in some idealized state. True, in the first Song (42: 1–4), where God says He has chosen the servant and put His spirit upon him, Israel is not named. But only two chapters later (though in a verse not considered to be part of the Songs), the very same words are applied openly to Israel: "Yet now hear, O Jacob my servant; and Israel, whom I have chosen," and God adds that He will pour His spirit upon the servant's descendants. Moreover, in the second Song (49:1–6), Israel *is* named as the servant (" . . . Thou art my servant, O Israel . . ."), while in the third (50:4–9), there is no reference either to a servant or to Israel. Finally, in the fourth (52:13–53:12), a servant does appear, but not Israel.

The nominees put forward by those who believe that the servant is an individual have ranged from Moses to the Second Isaiah himself to one of his disciples to the (earthly) Jewish Messiah, with many others in between. However, the leading candidate by far has been not the Jewish but the Christian Messiah, Jesus.

Thus, in the first two Songs, the fact that the servant's mission extends beyond Israel itself—to "bring forth judgment to the Gentiles"; to " . . . set judgment in the earth . . ."; and to be " . . . a light to the Gentiles, that thou mayest be my salvation unto the end of the earth"—has been read as a prophecy of the future spread of Christianity. In the third Song, where (to repeat) no servant is mentioned at all, someone (who to my ear is the prophet himself and not some interpolated character) declares: "I gave my back to the smiters, and my cheeks to them that plucked off the hair: I hid not my face from shame and spitting." This has been understood as a prediction of the fate of Jesus before and/or during the crucifixion. But it is the fourth Song that has probably been the most powerful "prooftext" in the entire Christological interpretation of the "Old Testament."

Understandably so, since to those who have diligently sought for, and found, foreshadowings and anticipations of the coming of Jesus, no other passage in the Hebrew Bible fits better with the New Testament gospels than the fourth Song. Here the servant is described as " . . . despised and rejected of men; a man of sorrows and acquainted with grief. . . ." More strikingly, he suffers vicariously for our sins:

> Surely he hath borne our griefs, and carried our sorrows: . . . But he was wounded for our transgressions, he was bruised for our iniquities: . . . and with his stripes we are healed. . . . and the LORD hath laid on him the iniquity of us all. . . . for the transgression of my people was he stricken. . . . it pleased the LORD to bruise him; he hath put him to grief: . . . [and made] his soul an offering for sin. . . . by his knowledge shall my righteous servant justify many; for he shall bear their iniquities. . . . because he hath poured out his soul unto death: and he was numbered with the transgressors; and he bare the sin of many, and made intercession for the transgressors.

McKenzie, a Catholic priest, sums up the contemporary view that now prevails among believing Christians about these Songs as compared with what it was in past centuries:

> [It] is the venerable belief in the Christian church that the Servant poems, in particular the fourth, are predictions of Jesus Christ. In this form the opinion is defended by no one today except in a few fundamentalist circles. This type of predictive prophecy does not appear in the Old Testament.

On the other hand, McKenzie continues:

> It is another question whether the person and mission of Jesus Christ are interpreted in the New Testament in terms of the Servant poems: that is, whether Jesus or his disciples or both identified him with the Servant of Yahweh.

McKenzie then states that it is his "personal opinion that Jesus was identified with the Servant in the primitive church, and that this identification goes back to Jesus himself." But he emphasizes that "this does not imply that the poems are a prediction of Jesus Christ in the literal sense of the term." He also convincingly argues that the servant cannot be the Jewish Messiah either, and opts instead for "an ideal who reflects the genuine character of all Israel."

Yet supposing that the servant does represent Israel, we are left with three more problems. One is how to place the fourth Song into the picture. In grappling with that problem, I turn for help, as I so often have done even in disagreement, to Yehezkel Kaufmann. I am on his side in believing that there are only two Isaiahs, and against his view that the Second never went back to Jerusalem, but when it comes to the servant Songs, I am with him all the way.

As he interprets them, these passages are not (as one theory has it) interpolations but rather part of the book of the Second Isaiah. He also reads the fourth allegorically to mean that just as the righteous of Israel have been punished by exile because of the sins of their wicked brethren, so it will be through their merit that all Israel will be redeemed. The evidence Kaufmann piles up for this interpretation beautifully reconciles the fourth Song with the thinking of the Hebrew Bible—where, as he irrefutably demonstrates, there is collective punishment, but no trace of vicarious atonement in the Christian sense.

WITH THIS OUT OF THE WAY, the two additional problems that remain to be addressed are whether the Second Isaiah expresses a purer and higher stage of monotheism than any other classical prophet ever achieved, and whether as a result he envisages a more "universalistic" mission for Israel than anyone before him.

Many pages back, I indicated that I cannot accept Kaufmann's thesis that all Israelites—the masses as well as the elites—were fully monotheistic from the beginning. If that were so, it would not have been necessary to wage so fierce a war against idolatry over the centuries. But even Kaufmann recognizes that the Second Isaiah, in turning from consolation to rebuke in the mode of the First, blames the dashing of his hopes for an immediate redemption on the relapse into, or persistence in, idolatry, up to and including child sacrifice, the greatest of its abominations. How could he not when the prophet tells him so several times?

> . . . are ye not children of transgression, a seed of falsehood, Enflaming yourselves with idols under every green tree, slaying the children in the valleys under the cliffs of the rocks? . . . Upon a lofty and high mountain hast thou set thy bed: even thither wentest thou up to offer sacrifice. Behind the doors also and the posts hast thou set up thy remembrance: for thou hast discovered thyself to another than me, and art gone up; . . . and made thee a covenant with them. . . .

In another such passage, where the Second Isaiah's indictment stretches all the way from the present into the past, he sounds more like the early Ezekiel than his own early self:

A people that provoketh me to anger continually to my face; that sacri-
ficeth in gardens, and burneth incense upon altars of brick. . . . Your
iniquities, and the iniquities of your fathers together, saith the LORD,
which have burned incense upon the mountains, and blasphemed me
upon the hills. . . .

Since Kaufmann takes the position that the Second Isaiah remained in Babylon, he ascribes the condemned practices—together with others mentioned by
the prophet, like eating the flesh of swine—to certain elements of the exile community rather than to the returnees, or to the people who remained in Judah all
along.

In this way, Kaufmann rescues his profound conviction that there was in
Israel a fully developed monotheism from the start and fights off the notion of an
evolutionary advance from a tribalistic "monolatrous" worship of YHVH to a
new understanding of Him as the God of all. But these are not the only alternatives. To restate it for the tenth—or is it the hundredth?—time, the notion of an
evolutionary advance rests on a distinction between the "particular" and the
"universal" that is altogether alien to the Hebrew Bible. As such, it is equally foreign to the classical prophets. Each of the prophets, in his own way, and with an
eye on the concrete circumstances of the moment, comes not to innovate or
"improve," but to elucidate over and over and over the ramifications of the revolutionary idea that there is only one true God ruling over the world; to remind
the people of Israel that His inexplicable choice of them carries with it special
demands and responsibilities; and to explain how fulfilling these demands and
responsibilities will ultimately bring all other peoples to acknowledge His sovereignty over them as well.

On *this* issue, I believe Kaufmann puts his finger in exactly the right place.
The true universalism of the Second Isaiah, he says, does not reside mainly in his
vision of the bowing of all knees to the one true God at the End of Days (when
He will " . . . create new heavens and a new earth . . ."). It comes out in the present reality of the reassurance this prophet gives to the converts made in Babylonia who are worried about the status they will have when they arrive in
Jerusalem:

Here, for the first time, the concept of religious conversion is adumbrated, the institution which . . . would make possible the spread of
monotheism throughout the world. . . . The requirement that the pros-
elyte accept the entire complex of Israel's commandments . . . in no way
[connotes] narrowness and separatism; rather it is the supreme universalism. It assumes that all the commandments, even those which are dis-
tinctly "Israelite," were given for all men, that every man is able to keep
them, even he who is not of the nation Israel.

In this formulation, we see clearly how the "scandal of particularity" loses all touch of the scandalous in a proper conception of the relation between chosenness and universality. To wit: that even though God decided to reveal the Law to Israel and through Israel, He does not intend it for Israel alone. Nor is the ability to follow the Law confined to Israel alone: it is a power that resides in all human beings.

But this two-sided truth will not prevail in the centuries ahead even after the realization of the prophetic vision of the triumph over idolatry. For it will turn out that even though the commandments are given for all, very few will be ready to shoulder so heavy a burden, or (like St. Paul in the New Testament) will admit to possessing the power to carry it. In the war against idolatry, the monotheistic religion of Israel will ultimately prove victorious throughout much of the then "known world." But it will also prove itself unable to compete against the new religion that will be born out of its own womb and will base itself precisely on a rebellion against the Law.

In Deuteronomy, in a passage I have quoted before and will quote again, God says through Moses that the law is a "blessing" and a giver of "life," and that it is neither "hidden" nor "far off" nor beyond the human capacity to obey: rather, it " . . . is very nigh unto thee, in thy mouth, and in thy heart, that thou mayest do it." In another passage I have quoted before, Jesus will later ringingly reaffirm all this:

> Think not that I am come to destroy the law, or the prophets: I am not come to destroy, but to fulfill. For verily I say unto you, Till heaven and earth pass, one jot or one tittle shall in no wise pass from the law, till all be fulfilled.

Yet through the voice of St. Paul, who will ingeniously turn these words upside down without seeming to do so, the new religion—mystically identifying the fulfillment of the law with its abolition—will proclaim that the commandments have been superseded or abrogated. Inverting Deuteronomy, it will deny that carnal beings have it in them to obey the Law, which it will accordingly denounce not as a blessing but as a "curse," and not as the giver of life but as the bringer of death.

CHAPTER FOURTEEN

THE END OF THE LINE

WHETHER, AS I BELIEVE, the Second Isaiah returned to Jerusalem soon after the edict of Cyrus in 538 B.C.E.; or whether it was "Trito"-Isaiah who declaimed the oracles comprising the last eleven chapters of the book; or whether (as Joseph Blenkinsopp thinks) those chapters emanated from many members of a whole Isaianic school, the "new thing" envisaged both in them and in earlier chapters of the book did not materialize.

Far from it. In Judah, the conditions that greeted the first wave of returnees— a paltry number, since the exiles had been living relatively well in Babylon— showed not the slightest sign of any glorious restoration. Jerusalem was still a ruin of a city, and the economic situation throughout the country as a whole (its territory reduced and its name changed by the Persians to the province of Yehud*) was very bad.

To make matters worse, almost immediately, the newcomers became embroiled in bitter conflicts—religious, economic, social—with the people who had been allowed to remain behind in 586 B.C.E. Trouble also soon developed with the Samaritans. These were descendants of the Assyrians sent to colonize the Northern Kingdom (or Samaria, as it was occasionally called after its sometime capital city) when it had been conquered and the indigenous Israelites deported. Some of the new inhabitants had subsequently adopted the religion of Israel, and were now practicing it. But their manner of observance was looked upon as improper by the returnees, who saw themselves as the keepers of the true way. The exiles wanted nothing to do with the Samaritans (and this rebuff,

---

*It is from this name that *Yehudi*, the Hebrew word for Jew, derives (as opposed to Judahite, meaning a subject of the Southern Kingdom, or Judean, from what the Romans will call the same province). See also the footnote on p. 296.

complicated by political rivalries, eventually led to a complete split between the two communities).

The Second Isaiah was sorely let down by all this. But in the true tradition of classical prophecy, he moved from denunciations of the present to exultant visions of the future. The "new heavens and a new earth" he had thought imminent before leaving Babylon would still be created by God, but this, and everything it implied, was now deferred to the indefinite future. For even though God had forgiven the sins of the past, abominations both novel and familiar were cropping up again that needed to be uprooted, punished, and purged before the new order of life could be brought to birth. Yet brought to birth it would assuredly be.

In the meantime, the Temple had to be rebuilt. But for a variety of reasons, after the laying of the foundation stone, nothing further was done for eighteen years (by which time the Second Isaiah had died or lapsed into silence). It was in response to the long neglect of this overriding imperative that in 520 B.C.E., within months of each other, two new prophets, both probably returnees from Babylon, now appeared in Jerusalem. Their names were Haggai and Zechariah the son of Berechiah, and their primary mission was to stir up enthusiasm for the rebuilding of the Temple.

HAGGAI ADDRESSES HIMSELF directly to the two leading officials appointed by the Persians to administer the civil and religious affairs of Yehud—the governor Zerubbabel and the High Priest Joshua. He admonishes them in the name of God that the time has come to get to work on the Temple. In an image similar to the one King David used in telling the prophet Nathan why he wanted to build the First Temple, Haggai says that the people have housed themselves comfortably while allowing the house of the LORD to " . . . lie waste." It is for this that they are now being punished:

> Ye have sown much, and bring in little; ye eat, but ye have not enough;
> ye drink, but ye are not filled with drink; ye clothe you, but there is
> none warm; and he that earneth wages, earneth wages to put it into a
> bag with holes.

Amazingly, the prophet's admonitions have an immediate effect. Within weeks an extraordinary amount of progress is made on the building—enough so that what it will look like in its completed state is already being invidiously compared to Solomon's Temple by those old enough to remember. But Haggai now returns to lift their spirits:

> Who is left among you that saw this house in her first glory? and how
> do ye see it now? is it not in your eyes in comparison of it as nothing?

> Yet now be strong . . . and work: for I am with you, saith the LORD of
> hosts. . . . The glory of this latter house shall be greater than of the for-
> mer. . . .

God then promises through Haggai that if the people purify themselves and
punctiliously observe the Law, they will be blessed with prosperity and with
peace. However, this peace, and the glory of the Temple, are to be preceded in
" . . . a little while . . ." by a cataclysm, in which God " . . . will shake the heavens,
and the earth, and the sea, and the dry land; And . . . all nations, and the desire of
all nations shall come. . . ."*

But this very short book—the second shortest in the Bible, after Obadiah—
concludes with yet one more promise. It is made to the governor Zerubbabel,
the grandson of Jehoiachin (the king who had been deported to Babylon by
Nebuchadnezzar in 598 B.C.E.) and hence a descendant of David:

> And I will overthrow the throne of kingdoms, and I will destroy the
> strength of the kingdoms of the heathen; and I will overthrow the char-
> iots, and those that ride in them; and the horses and their riders shall
> come down, every one by the sword of his brother. In that day, saith the
> LORD of hosts, will I take thee, O Zerubbabel, my servant, . . . saith the
> LORD, and will make thee as a signet: for I have chosen thee. . . .

Much debate has been triggered by these verses. Some have seen in them a
prediction of the downfall of the Persian empire, and an identification of Zerubbabel as the Messiah in the sense of that term that is nascent or perhaps has
already become prevalent in the late sixth century: an earthly liberator who will
be anointed king of a great new united monarchy like the one ruled over by
David. Others have argued that this is an eschatological prophecy—that Haggai
envisages such a state of affairs as occurring only at the End of Days.

But the plain sense of the text gives more support to the first interpretation
than the second. Not that Haggai imagines that the enthronement of Zerubbabel and the subjugation of the nations to the God of Israel can be achieved
through force of arms. Judah, or Yehud, is too small and too weak militarily, and
there is no prospect that this will change. Therefore, God Himself will have to do
the necessary fighting—as in Ezekiel's vision of the war against Gog of Magog
(with which Haggai must have been familiar and by which he might well have
been inspired).

A similar declaration is made at almost exactly the same time by Haggai's
slightly younger (or so the scholars calculate) contemporary and virtual collabo-

*For KJV's "desire," Son has "the choicest things," and AB gives us "riches."

rator, Zechariah the son of Berechiah. This prophet is also known as the First Zechariah, since it is very widely agreed that only the first eight chapters of the book bearing his name can be ascribed to him. The last six (9–14) used to be credited to an anonymous prophet, Deutero-Zechariah, but as with Isaiah, the Second Zechariah begat a Third, and now the latest tendency of his scholarly fathers is to assign these chapters to a whole school of prophets working in the tradition of Zechariah the son of Berechiah.

Unlike the First Zechariah (and Haggai), whose dates are among the easiest to determine of all the classical prophets, thanks to both internal and extra-biblical signposts, the last six chapters of the book give no clue whatever as to when they might have been spoken and/or written. But in their editions of Haggai and the Zechariahs, Carol L. Meyers and Eric M. Meyers submit a very solid brief for setting them in the early-to-mid fifth century (anywhere from twenty-five to fifty years after 518 B.C.E, which is when the First Zechariah departs from the prophetic scene).

Persuaded by their case, I am postponing my discussion of the last half of the book until we arrive at that stage in our story. For now, then, I will return to Zechariah the son of Berechiah, and the question of whether he and Haggai anticipate the imminent enthronement of Zerubbabel as the king of a great and glorious new united kingdom.

THE FIRST ZECHARIAH shows up at the Temple site about a month after Haggai's initial visit, and he describes a series of cryptic visions he has had, each of which is interpreted for him by an angel as bearing on some aspect of the renewed glory of Judah and Jerusalem. One of these involves Zerubbabel and it culminates in the most frequently quoted verse in the Book of Zechariah: " . . . This is the word of the LORD unto Zerubbabel, saying, Not by might, nor by power, but by my Spirit, saith the LORD of hosts." And even before being informed by God that there will be no need for Zerubbabel to wage war in order to triumph, Zechariah has been instructed through another vision that Jerusalem will have no need of walls (i.e., fortifications) to protect herself from attack, "For I, saith the LORD, will be unto her a wall of fire round about. . . ."

Because so much of the First Zechariah consists of visions of the future, Chapters 1–8 of the book certainly have a more eschatological feel than Haggai, even though Zechariah has enough of an eye on the present to use Zerubbabel's name and to speak of him in messianic terms. (In an obscure verse—6:12—it is, I believe, Zerubbabel, and not, as some think, the High Priest Joshua, who is the "Branch" God is preparing to send: an image that can only be understood by the prophet's audience as referring to a descendant of David.*) Yet if the two prophets actually imagine that governor will soon become king, they are sorely mistaken. Zerubbabel shortly disappears so completely from history that no one has ever found out what became of him.

On the other hand, both Haggai and Zechariah are right in recognizing that, with the rebuilding of the Temple, the High Priest, and the priesthood in general, will now become more important than they may ever have been before. Thus, Haggai is commanded by God to summon the priests for answers to questions of law, and although these are strictly ritual questions, they seem to stand in for the entire range of the commandments.

More saliently, Zechariah has a vision resolving doubts that have apparently been raised about the fitness of Joshua, who has lived in an "unclean" land, to serve as High Priest in the new Temple. In the presence of the heavenly host, Joshua is cleansed of sin by the removal of the filthy garments he is wearing, and a crown is placed on his head. Furthermore, God tells him, if he walks in His ways and judges righteously, he will not only be one of God's " . . . two anointed ones . . . ," but will even be admitted to the company of the angels.

No doubt this elevation of the High Priest reflects the political realities of Persian imperial policy under Darius I, who is now king of the Persians. Like Cyrus before him, Darius encourages the provinces under his rule to worship their own gods, seeing this as a force for stability. But if theocratic rule is desirable so far as the Persians are concerned, secular monarchs are another matter. They can be a potential source of rebellion (and in all likelihood it is precisely because a movement has grown up to make Zerubbabel king that he is whisked away and perhaps executed).

Carol L. Meyers and Eric M. Meyers suggest that Haggai and the First Zechariah are political realists as well as prophets who are trying to keep hope alive by, in effect, populating the far-distant eschatological future with characters from the present. This is an ingenious interpretation, but I doubt that it will do much to rescue these two prophets, and the three still to come, from the denigration to which they have often been subjected because of their passionate concern with the Temple.

In opposition to this denigration, Joseph Blenkinsopp argues against the "misunderstanding [that] has arisen from the once commonly accepted assumption that for all practical purposes prophecy came to an end with the Babylonian exile"—that is, before the return to Judah (or Yehud) and the subsequent advent in those post-exilic times of Haggai, Zechariah, Joel, Malachi, and the Second Zechariah, who will be the last five representatives of the classical line. The Meyers team also takes strong issue with that assumption:

---

*(See page 291.) The entire verse (6:12) reads: "And speak unto him, saying, Thus speaketh the LORD of hosts, saying, Behold the man whose name is The BRANCH; and he shall grow up out of his place, and he shall build the temple of the LORD."

The beginning of the Second Temple period in 515 B.C.E. has all too frequently been viewed as a period of decline in Israelite religion. It is a period that has been said to have encompassed the demise of prophecy, as well as a narrowing of religious concerns and a concomitant overemphasis on the Temple and its ritual.

The source of this negative attitude, the Meyers team says, is the Higher Criticism of the nineteenth century, and especially the work of a scholar we have encountered before in these pages, Julius Wellhausen. Along with his colleagues and disciples, Wellhausen contrasted

Israel's supposedly ever-increasing commitment to law, narrowly conceived after the Exile, in contrast to the prominence of prophecy as the supposed high point of all biblical religion in the preexilic and exilic periods.

In this conception, the Judaism that in later centuries will grow out of the ancient Israelite religion of the Hebrew Bible is beginning to show the whites of its eyes as rigidly legalistic and "Pharisaic." Such distortions and misrepresentations of rabbinic Judaism, originating in the polemics of the New Testament, and brought up to date by the Wellhausen school, are said to have provoked the early twentieth-century Jewish scholar Solomon Schechter into dismissing the Higher Criticism as the "Higher Anti-Semitism."

Yet Jews themselves were anything but immune to the same distortions and misrepresentations, which in religious circles came to be extended to the other antitheses on which I have been casting a cold eye throughout the preceding pages and which I have been doing my best to discredit as foreign to prophetic thought—morality versus ritual, and "universalism" versus "particularism."

In our own day, the same antitheses also keep popping up in secular guise. For example, I learn from the Meyers team that a biblical scholar has emerged from the 1960s who affixes to Haggai and the First Zechariah the label of "hierocrats," by which I suppose he means lackeys of the priesthood. The same scholar has accused the two prophets and their followers of "selling out [*sic!*] to the Persian-supported government." Besides being swaddled in anachronistic language, it is an accusation difficult to reconcile with the messianic imagery in which both Haggai and the First Zechariah drape Zerubbabel, or the hints by Haggai that God is planning to wipe out the Persian empire.

The roots of *this* type of denigration are not in the varieties of ancient Christian polemics against Judaism that have by now been almost entirely abandoned by most Christian scholars themselves. They lie, rather, in a combination of Marxist presuppositions and the idea of an opposition between priest and prophet that Max Weber did much to spread. Here the priest represents what in our day has come to be vilified as the "Establishment" and the prophet is the radical critic, or (in that previously cited unfortunate term adopted by the usually more reliable Blenkinsopp) a "dissident intellectual."

But Weber and his disciples are wrong. The attacks by prophets like the First Isaiah, Hosea, and Jeremiah on the priests of their times are no more passionate than their attacks on rival prophets. The object of the attack, whenever it is launched in the prophetic literature, is always the corruption of office or mission—the failure to teach the people Hosea's "the knowledge of God"—not of the office itself. The prophet-priest antinomy stems from the usual inability or unwillingness to appreciate the mentality of the prophets and of the biblical worldview they all share. Like the classical prophets in whose tradition they self-consciously take their place, Haggai and the First Zechariah cannot conceive of any conflict between prophet and priest, or between morality and ritual, or between "universalism" and "particularism": between God as the God of all and His choice of the children of Israel to be His people, and the Temple in Jerusalem to be His "house."

ALL THIS IS CLEAR ENOUGH in both of these post-exilic prophets, but the First Zechariah, a longer book, contains more detail more explicitly spelled out. It is because the joint mission of the two prophets is primarily to goad the leaders and the people to complete the rebuilding of the Temple that the First Zechariah accords a very exalted status to Joshua, the High Priest—*provided* that he performs his ritual duties in accordance with the will of God. But at the same time, the people are exhorted by God through the First Zechariah to obey " . . . my words and my statutes, which I commanded my servants the prophets. . . ." When these "words and statutes" are later specified, they include both moral and ritual injunctions. On the one hand,

> Thus speaketh the LORD of hosts, saying, Execute true judgment, and shew mercy and compassions every man to his brother: And oppress not the widow, nor the fatherless, the stranger, nor the poor; and let none of you imagine evil against his brother in your heart.

But on the other hand,

> Thus saith the LORD of hosts; Let your hands be strong, ye that hear in these days these words by the mouth of the prophets, which were in the day that the foundation of the house of the LORD of hosts was laid, that the temple might be built.

There is no separation here between morality and ritual, or between prophet and priest: it is the prophet who urges the building of the Temple in which the priest presides. And as to the relation of "universalism" and "particularism," the First Zechariah could hardly be more oblivious of any distinction between them:

> Sing and rejoice, O daughter of Zion: for, lo, I come, and I will dwell in the midst of thee, saith the LORD. And many nations shall be joined to the LORD in that day, and shall be my people: and I will dwell in the midst of thee. . . .

Many nations will be His people, but Zion will still be His chosen habitation, and the children of Israel His chosen people. Listen to this lovingly lyrical effusion:

> Thus saith the LORD; I am returned unto Zion, and will dwell in the midst of Jerusalem: and Jerusalem shall be called a city of truth; and the mountain of the LORD of hosts the holy mountain. Thus saith the LORD of hosts; There shall yet old men and old women dwell in the streets of Jerusalem, and every man with his staff in his hand for very age. And the streets of the city shall be full of boys and girls playing in the streets thereof. . . . Thus saith the LORD of hosts; Behold, I will save my people from the east country, and from the west country; And I will bring them, and they shall dwell in the midst of Jerusalem: and they shall be my people, and I will be their God, in truth and righteousness.

But it is the last words of the First Zechariah's book that stand as a perfect encapsulation of how "all flesh" will eventually accept the God who has chosen Israel:

> Thus saith the LORD of hosts; It shall yet come to pass, that there shall come people, and the inhabitants of many cities: And the inhabitants of one city shall go to another, saying, Let us go speedily to pray before the LORD, and to seek the LORD of hosts: I will go also. Yea, many people and strong nations shall come to seek the LORD of hosts in Jerusalem, and to pray before the LORD.

And the "scandal of particularity"?

> Thus saith the LORD of hosts; In those days it shall come to pass, that ten men shall take hold out of all languages of the nations, even shall

take hold of the skirt of him that is a Jew, saying, We will go with you: for we have heard that God is with you.*

WE HAVE NOW REACHED the last three of the classical prophets, but not the last of the disagreements among the scholars. Here the main issue is who followed whom. Did Joel precede Malachi? And where does the Second Zechariah (or the school of prophets brought together under that name) belong?

In the section of the Hebrew Bible devoted to the Latter Prophets, Joel comes fifth, Zechariah is fourteenth, and Malachi is last. But chronological sequence was not the major consideration in the canonical ordering of the prophetic books by the rabbis, whereas hardly anything is more important to modern biblical scholars. In picking my way through several different sources containing highly complicated technical analyses, I have wound up in the company of those that fix the order of the last three classical prophets as Joel, Malachi, and the Second Zechariah.

In his edition of the Book of Joel, James L. Crenshaw expresses a healthy skepticism about the ability of scholars to date biblical texts, but his own examination of the historical and linguistic evidence leads him to the well-informed guess that Joel best fits the period between the late sixth century B.C.E. and the early fifth. Andrew E. Hill, after an even more painstaking analysis (aided by computers), concludes in his edition of Malachi that this prophet belongs roughly to the year 500 B.C.E. If these estimates are correct, Joel follows shortly after Haggai and the First Zechariah, and overlaps with Malachi.

Then there is the Second Zechariah, whom the Meyers team, after the most painstaking analysis of all, locates in the first half of the fifth century B.C.E. (with the whole book being edited into its final canonical form in 450). If the Second Zechariah is in fact another of those "anthologies" we keep being presented with in the scholarly literature on the prophets, the earliest parts of it must also overlap with Joel and Malachi, with the rest coming later. This makes him (or them), rather than Malachi, the last of the Hebrew prophets.

IN ENTERING INTO the final phase of our story, therefore, I will begin with Joel, another of the many prophets about whom nothing beyond his name and that of his father (Pethuel) has ever been determined. If Crenshaw is right, how-

---

*The word "Jew" (yehudi) has been used before in various connections, but in this passage we find one of the first indications that it will become the name of the people previously always known as Israel (or, more rarely, Hebrews).

ever, Joel is speaking from Jerusalem after 515 B.C.E., when the Second Temple
has already been dedicated, but when the promises that Haggai and the First
Zechariah made of the material prosperity that would ensue are failing to materialize.

The book begins with a brilliantly vivid description of a plague of locusts
exacerbated by a drought: "That which the palmerworm hath left hath the
locust eaten; and that which the locust hath left hath the cankerworm eaten; and
that which the cankerworm hath left hath the caterpillar eaten."

Because Joel likens the locusts to an invading army, the plague has been
interpreted as an allegory of the relatively recent past (the Babylonian invasion).
But with the imagery shifting back and forth between the ravages of insects and
the soldiers, it becomes very hard to tell whether an actual plague is in progress,
or whether the prophet is reminding his audience of the disasters brought about
by their sins when the First Temple still stood, and warning of similar disasters
that are already following the building of the Second Temple, or are about to follow as the terrible Day of the Lord approaches. Possibly all of the above are
involved, and if they are juxtaposed in what strikes us as arbitrary logic, this
would be no barrier to understanding by Joel's audience.

The nature of the sin for which the people are now being punished is never
specified, but from the form of repentance Joel prescribes, we can conclude that
it has to do with the failure to offer prescribed sacrifices now that a Temple exists
again:

> Gird yourselves, and lament, ye priests: howl, ye ministers of the altar:
> come, lie all night in sackcloth, ye ministers of my God: for the meat
> offering and the drink offering is withholden from the house of your
> God.

But it is not only the priests who need to turn to God for mercy; the people too
are summoned by the prophet:

> Therefore also now, saith the LORD, turn ye even to me with all your
> heart, and with fasting, and with weeping, and with mourning: And
> rend your heart, and not your garments, and turn unto the LORD your
> God: for he is gracious and merciful, slow to anger, and of great kind-
> ness, and repenteth him of the evil. Who knoweth if he will return and
> repent, and leave a blessing behind him . . . ?

Then back the prophet turns to the priests:

> Let the priests, the ministers of the LORD, weep between the porch

and the altar, and let them say, Spare thy people, O LORD, and give not thine heritage to reproach, that the heathen should rule over them: wherefore should they say among the people, Where is their God?

Like Haggai's, these exhortations are taken to heart, and they have the desired effect. With a sudden twist, God answers and says that all will be well. Everything the locusts have eaten will be restored, there will be abundance of rain and food and drink in the land, and He will show Himself through great wonders. He will pour His spirit upon everyone, young and old, all of whom will become prophets. The terrible Day of the LORD is still coming, when "The sun shall be turned into darkness, and the moon into blood, . . ." but in that day " . . . whosoever shall call on the name of the LORD shall be delivered: for in mount Zion and in Jerusalem shall be deliverance. . . ."

Not so, however, the nations that have oppressed Israel and Judah, who have scattered them and " . . . have cast lots for my people; and have given a boy for an harlot, and sold a girl for wine, that they might drink." These nations will all be gathered into the valley of Jehoshaphat—"Multitudes, multitudes in the valley of decision . . ."—where they will be judged for their crimes and where they will be recompensed by like treatment.

God invites them—with an irony reminiscent of Elijah's challenge to the prophets of Baal—to muster their armies. And having inverted Amos's inversion of the popular conception of the Day of the Lord, Joel executes a much more startling inversion—this one of the famous utopian vision of the First Isaiah (and Micah)—when He reports God as advising the nations to "Beat your plowshares into swords, and your pruninghooks into spears. . . ." Not that this will save them from His wrath:

> Egypt shall be a desolation, and Edom shall be a desolate wilderness, for the violence against the children of Judah, because they have shed inno-cent blood in their land. But Judah shall dwell for ever, and Jerusalem from generation to generation. For I will cleanse their blood that I have not cleansed: for the LORD dwelleth in Zion.

This is how the book of Joel ends. Because its first two chapters contain many frightful rebukes of God's chosen people, Joel has in the past generally been exempted from the near-contempt that has so often been suffered by Nahum and Obadiah for sparing Israel and attacking only other nations. But if Crenshaw's commentary in his edition of the book is any indication, attitudes toward Joel may be on a downward trajectory.

For instance, Crenshaw compares Joel's "fondness for the cult and external aspects of worship," invidiously with "the prophetic activity of the eighth- or seventh-century reformers (Amos, Isaiah, Micah, Jeremiah)." Perhaps, he says, throwing his cards on the table, "priestly interest in Joel prompted him to prefer texts from Ezekiel and Zechariah over the exquisite images" in Hosea, Isaiah, and Micah.

More damning in Crenshaw's scheme of things is Joel's excessive concern for his own people, and his correlative lack of sympathy for others. Crenshaw characterizes this as the product of a "particularistic cult," but "particularistic" clearly seems to him an insufficiently pejorative term. He therefore also uses another: "The book's xenophobia comes closest to that of Haggai, Zechariah, Obadiah, and . . . farthest from Jonah."

One wonders why Nahum is omitted from this roll of dishonor, and the inclusion of Haggai and Zechariah is even stranger. But Crenshaw can hardly restrain his animus against the "restricted vision" of Joel, who

> never achieved the broader notion of YHWH's compassion for all creatures on earth that enabled the . . . author of the book of Jonah to indict the sulking prophet. . . . Instead of expanding the breadth of YHWH's compassion to embrace all humankind and animals, Joel restricts the blessing and spirit to citizens of Judah and particularly residents of Jerusalem.

Crenshaw is even offended by the satirical play on what is clearly his favorite passage in the classical prophetic literature. So shaken up is he by this act of impiety that it overrides what to his grudging approval accompanies it: "Joel does think in terms of universal judgment ushering in an era of peace, but he reverses the sentiment about beating swords into plow tips and spears into pruning shears."

Behind this line of criticism is a standard of judgment that is at once Christological and political. If a prophet can be read as building a bridge to Christianity, or transcending the putative limitations of Israelite "xenophobia," he is esteemed; otherwise, he is downgraded as religiously and morally retrograde (or, in the more delicately tactful language the Jerusalem Bible uses of Obadiah, "old-fashioned"). Nowhere does Crenshaw give the slightest indication of having grasped that the destruction of the pagan nations and the vindication of God's chosen people are the necessary precondition for realizing the "big dreams" (his phrase) of Isaiah, Micah, and the other prophets he admires, or that this is axiomatic to these same prophets themselves.

MALACHI, LIKE JOEL, is still another of the prophets about whom nothing is known except his name, and some doubt that we even know that much. That "Malachi" is the Hebrew word for "my messenger" or "my angel" has led to the speculation that it may not even be a proper name at all, or that the whole book may have been split off from the end of Zechariah. But while accepting that it is anonymous, I propose to treat it as a book in its own right.

As such, it might be considered even worse than Joel—if, that is, "a fondness for the cult and external aspects of worship" is one of the principal signs that the prophets of the Second Temple constitute a slide into decadence of the great tradition they have inherited. And, in fact, there are, writes Andrew E. Hill in his edition, "Those who contend that Malachi only appreciates the cultic and legalistic aspects of Israelite religion."

Hill mounts a defense of Malachi against this assessment. But I must admit that the disparagers have a lot going for them in the text, where God repeatedly accuses the priests of insulting Him by the way they are doing things in the Temple. The sacrifices offered to Him are—contrary to the laws of Leviticus—so blemished by disease and imperfection that " . . . The table of the LORD is polluted; and the fruit thereof, even his meat, is contemptible." God refuses such offerings, and threatens the priests that unless they mend their ways, He will curse them and their " . . . seed, and spread dung upon your faces, even the dung of your solemn feasts. . . ." In addition to breaking the covenant He made with their forefather Levi (who here represents the whole priestly caste), they have betrayed the duty entrusted to them as teachers of the Law:

> For the priest's lips should keep knowledge, and they [the people] should seek the law at his mouth: for he is the messenger of the LORD of hosts. But ye are departed out of the way; ye have caused many to stumble at the law; ye have corrupted the covenant of Levi, saith the LORD of hosts.

In defining the nature of this stumbling, Malachi provides what is considered the second most serious sign of how low the mighty prophetic tradition has fallen: his "xenophobia," or what some—with an even greater readiness to use anachronistic concepts than we found at work in the criticisms of Haggai and the First Zechariah—do not hesitate to call his "racism." In Malachi, the main victim of this imputed intolerance, narrowness, and exclusivism is not other nations (though some of that, too, comes in earlier in God's declaration that He has always " . . . hated Esau . . ." [Edom]): it is, rather, the marrying by the people of " . . . the daughter[s] of a strange god."

The people defend themselves by an appeal to what certainly seems on the surface the "universalism" of God: "Have we not all one father? Hath not one God created us? . . ." But God is not moved. If anything, He becomes even angrier, denouncing intermarriage as treachery and an " . . . abomination . . ." and a profanation of His " . . . holiness . . ." that He will punish by cutting off " . . . the man that doeth this, the master and the scholar, out of the tabernacles of Jacob, and him that offereth an offering unto the LORD of hosts." Not content even with that, God—though His laws have never included a prohibition against divorce—just as strongly condemns the men of Judah (or Yehud) for exacerbating the abomination of marrying foreign women by discarding the wives of their youth.

As if, in the view of his critics, such rigid ethnic exclusivism, tied to an excessive "fondness" for the cult, were not enough to prove that Malachi is no Amos or Isaiah, this prophet is so preoccupied with the Temple that he has God stooping even lower—down to the crass issue of *tithes:*

> Will a man rob God? Yet ye have robbed me. But ye say, Wherein have we robbed thee? In tithes and offerings. Ye are cursed with a curse: for ye have robbed me, even this whole nation. Bring ye all the tithes into the storehouse, that there may be meat in mine house, and prove me now herewith, saith the LORD of hosts, if I will not open you the windows of heaven, and pour you out a blessing. . . .

The materials for an indictment of Malachi, then, are all in plain sight. However, to the eyes of this prophet, as—yet again I am forced to say it—with all the classical prophets in whose wake he travels, so invisible is the line between the stereotyped modern antitheses that he can move from one to another and back again with no sense of incongruity or contradiction.

In introducing the theme of the tithes, for example, Malachi begins naturally enough with the Temple:

> Behold, I will send my messenger, and he shall prepare the way before me: and the LORD, whom ye seek, shall suddenly come to his temple, even the messenger of the covenant, whom ye delight in: behold, he shall come, saith the LORD of hosts. But who may abide the day of his coming? and who shall stand when he appeareth? for he is like a refiner's fire, and like fullers' soap: and he shall sit as a refiner and purifier of silver: and he shall purify the sons of Levi, and purge them as gold and silver, that they may offer unto the LORD an offering in righteousness.

Then, without a break, and with no transition, He shifts into the moral realm:

> And I will come near to you to judgment; and I will be a swift witness against the sorcerers, and against the adulterers, and against false swearers, and against those that oppress the hireling in his wages, the widow, and the fatherless, and that turn aside the stranger from his right, and fear not me, saith the LORD of hosts.

Now the fierce complaint enters about being "robbed" of tithes, hard upon which there is a restatement of the deepest question haunting the Hebrew Bible:

> Your words have been stout against me, saith the LORD. Yet ye say, What have we spoken so much against thee? Ye have said, It is vain to serve God: and what profit is it that we have kept his ordinance, and that we have walked mournfully before the LORD of hosts? And now we call the proud happy; yea, they that work wickedness are set up; yea, they that tempt God are even delivered.

God's response (which seems more humanly satisfying than those He gives to Jeremiah or Habakkuk or Job) is that

> . . . the day cometh, that shall burn as an oven; and all the proud, yea, and all that do wickedly, shall be stubble; and the day that cometh shall burn them up, saith the LORD of hosts, that it shall leave them neither root nor branch. But unto you that fear my name shall the Sun of righteousness arise with healing in his wings. . . .

But just as it is impossible to separate the "universal" from the "particular" in Malachi's vision of the Day of Judgment, so is it inconceivable to this prophet that, for the nations of the world, there is any way to God other than through a purified Israel. The last verses are taken by most commentators as two later interpolations, but there they are:

> Remember ye the law of Moses my servant, which I commanded unto him in Horeb for all Israel, with the statutes and judgments. Behold, I will send you Elijah the prophet before the coming of the great and dreadful day of the LORD: And he shall turn the heart of the fathers to the children, and the heart of the children to their fathers, lest I come and smite the earth with a curse.

These two "appendices," which look back to the pre-classical prophetic era and forward to a messianic future, are a beautifully fitting conclusion not only to Malachi himself but to the entire corpus of classical prophecy that closes in the Hebrew Bible (and in the Catholic and Protestant canons as well) with this book.

FITTING CONCLUSION though it is, Malachi is almost certainly not in historical fact the last of the classical prophets. If the Meyers team is, as I think, right, the line that begins with Amos around 750 B.C.E. actually ends almost exactly three hundred years later, in 450 B.C.E., when the oracles of the Second Zechariah (or a group of the First Zechariah's disciples) are collected and attached to the Book of Zechariah to become Chapters 9–14.

So enigmatic are these chapters that several key passages in them have been rated (against stiff competition from verses in Job, Hosea, and Micah) as the most obscure in the Hebrew Bible. Thus, in striving to identify the famous shepherds, good and bad, who keep moving into and out of these prophecies, exegetes have burned as much or more oil than Rabbi Hananiah ben Hezekiah did in trying to reconcile the contradictions between Ezekiel and Leviticus.

Obviously the shepherds are a symbol of rulers of some kind, but why is the presumably good one as cruel to his flock as the bad ones ("Then said I, I will not feed you: that that dieth, let it die; and that that is to be cut off, let it be cut off; and let the rest eat every one the flesh of another")? The same kind of difficulty bedevils the question of why, at another point, Judah is aligned with an unnamed enemy in a war against Jerusalem. And many other equally perplexing and unsolved problems could be cited as well.

Still, the general outlines of the vision that emerges from the Second Zechariah can be discerned through the dense foliage of the impenetrable details. It is the vision of a future age, which will be preceded by great suffering, and worse, of the kind already undergone both by the defunct Northern Kingdom and by the people of Judah. There will be oppression by evil leaders. There will be bloody battles in which God Himself will participate. Horrible plagues will afflict " . . . all the people that have fought against Jerusalem; Their flesh shall consume away while they stand upon their feet, and their eyes shall consume away in their holes, and their tongue shall consume away in their mouth." Two-thirds (or, alternatively, one-half) of God's people will be decimated in these battles, leaving a remnant that has emerged purified from being put " . . . through the fire. . . ." But the land lost to the pagan nations by the house of Israel will be reclaimed (by the remaining third?), and the two halves of the old monarchy will be reunited under a Davidic king. Then, at last, " . . . the LORD shall be king over all the earth: in that day shall there be one LORD, and his name one."

Curiously, the only mention of idolatry in the last group of classical prophets occurs in the Second Zechariah. Does this mean that the war the prophets have for so long been waging against it from within has finally resulted in victory? If so, it would help us understand why, despite all the hopes that have been dashed after the rebuilding of the Temple, and why, despite the fact that the prophecies of imminent prosperity uttered by Haggai and the First Zechariah have never come true, the Second Zechariah can still believe so confidently in the triumph over idolatry throughout the world.

The same consideration may also clarify another of the mysterious passages in this last outburst of classical prophecy—the one in which the extirpation of idolatry within Israel is linked to a strange condemnation of prophecy itself:

And it shall come to pass in that day, saith the LORD of hosts, that I
will cut off the names of the idols out of the land, and they shall no
more be remembered: and also I will cause the prophets and the
unclean spirits to pass out of the land. And it shall come to pass, that
when any shall yet prophesy, then his father and his mother that begat
him shall say unto him, Thou shalt not live; for thou speakest lies in the
name of the LORD: and his father and his mother that begat him shall
thrust him through when he prophesieth.

In these verses the subject is clearly false prophets who encourage idolatry:
such prophets are condemned to death in Deuteronomy (though there the elders of the community or even close relatives, but not their own parents, are the
designated executioners). But the prophets in the following verses seem to be
different:

And it shall come to pass in that day, that the prophets shall be ashamed
every one of his vision, when he hath prophesied; neither shall they
wear a rough garment to deceive: But he shall say, I am no prophet, I am
an husbandman; for man taught me to keep cattle from my youth.

Yet it was Elijah, and not any false prophet, who wore a rough garment (the
hairy mantle that he passed on to his disciple Elisha), and it was Amos who
denied being a prophet—in almost exactly the phraseology used here—when
the High Priest Amaziah accused him of prophesying for money. To deepen the
mystery, the good shepherd, who seems to be the Second Zechariah himself,
solicits and accepts money for the job he has done, just as though he were one of
the professional seers from whom Amos so angrily dissociated himself.*

Can it be that the Second Zechariah is including true prophets, along with
false ones, in this vision of the new era, when God will have no further need of
them to communicate His word and His laws (possibly because the formerly
rebellious people of Israel have, as in Joel, all become prophets)? If so, and if the
mark of the true prophet is (to invoke again the dubious criterion in Deuteronomy) that the things he prophesies come to pass, then the Second Zechariah, in
proclaiming the abolition of the office to which he has been appointed, turns
out to be a true prophet indeed.

Joseph Blenkinsopp even speculates that the last of the prophets (or, more
precisely, those who add words of their own to the Book of Zechariah and oth-

---

*The Meyers team interprets the shepherd's demand for payment as an ironic gesture intended
to implicate the people in the bad things he has done in order to dramatize a point God wishes
him to make. But this seems to me a rather convoluted reading.

ers) may not regard themselves as prophets at all, but men through whom God continues to speak by means of the insight He gives them into the meaning of already existing prophetic texts. While claiming for themselves "an inspiration comparable to that of the prophets," they "probably [think] of genuine prophecy as a phenomenon belonging either to the past or to the new age that God [is] even then preparing to usher in."

But what is this new age? And what role does the tradition of prophecy play in it?

CHAPTER FIFTEEN

CODA

I N EMBARKING ON the story of prophecy in ancient Israel, I said that the classical prophets did not come out of nowhere. But in sketching the ancestral "clouds of glory" they all trailed, I hurried over the issue of why they should have appeared just when they did. Now, with the whole story behind us, I want to take that issue up a little more fully. I also want to expand, if only briefly, on the statement I made at the very outset that they did not simply vanish into thin air three hundred years later, and that there was something mysterious about the entire phenomenon of classical prophecy, both in its beginning and in its end.

Why then did they appear when they did, and why did they disappear when they did?

To the first question, the most common response—and the one to which I assented at the conclusion of Part One (Chapter 5)—is that, in the words of Shalom Paul, "classical prophecy arose and reached its zenith during the rise and fall of world empires." In the period of the pre-classical prophets, "the political-historical horizon was of limited local significance" in the sense that "the enemies of those days—Ammonites, Moabites, Edomites, Philistines, and Arameans—did not strive for world dominion." But the late eighth century B.C.E. witnessed the formation of great empires, in whose ambitions and rivalries the two kingdoms of Israel in the North and Judah in the South were caught, subjected, and finally destroyed. The mission of the classical prophets was to explain, as Professor Paul puts it, "the 'why' of destruction and the 'how' of restoration."

In general, this is a good account, but we are now in a position to recognize that it requires a bit of supplementing and qualifying. For when, in the middle of the eighth century B.C.E., Amos and Hosea first started warning the Northern Kingdom of impending disaster, there were no clear signs of any such thing on the horizon. The Northern Kingdom was enjoying one of the most prosperous and powerful periods in its history, while Assyria was not yet on the move. There lies the mystery. How did Amos and Hosea know with such certainty that they were right in what must have seemed ridiculous warnings to the people they excoriated—and to rival prophets as well?

What made them so sure, of course, was the absolute conviction that it was not they but God who was expressing these warnings through them: with every fiber of their beings, they believed that He had appointed them to proclaim what they were proclaiming. Now, to anyone who has taken what the great nineteenth-century Danish theologian Søren Kierkegaard called "the leap of faith," there is no mystery here—or if there is, it gets quickly dissolved in straightforward agreement with what the classical prophets themselves believed. But to a modern skeptic, they can just as readily be written off as delusional, subject to auditory and visual hallucinations, and we have seen several of the classical prophets dismissed as madmen even in their own day. Yet I wonder how even the skeptic can, down deep, fail to be uneasily impressed by the uncanny feel these men had for the connection between the religious condition of the people and their political fate.

It was that feel—and not any special prescience about the coming shape of international affairs—that drove them to speak out. And what they said when they did speak out was that national calamity would inevitably result from the corruption and degeneration of the religion the people of Israel had been chosen by God to uphold.

It took only a few decades—until 722 B.C.E.—for Amos and Hosea to be proved right by the Assyrian conquest of the Northern Kingdom and the dispersal of its entire Israelite population. Then, a little more than a century later, the turn of the Southern Kingdom came at the hands of the Babylonians. The principal classical prophets who succeeded Amos and Hosea in the South (Micah, the First Isaiah, and Jeremiah—along with Ezekiel in Babylon) had been confident that this would happen because, they kept insisting in scorching words, the people of Judah were being faithless to God by putting other gods before Him, or beside Him, or both, and failing to keep His laws and walk in His ways.

At the same time, first in the North and then in the South, they kept preaching (not always with complete consistency or conviction) that the worst might still be averted by repentance. Yet even if it were not averted, the children of Israel would remain God's chosen people and He would eventually take pity on them (even if they did not deserve it). In the end, a remnant of them would always be brought back to Zion, their enemies and oppressors would be destroyed, and God Himself would be vindicated among all who had blindly clung to their useless idols and refused to acknowledge His sovereignty over the whole world.

•   •   •

IF CONVEYING THIS MESSAGE was the mission of the classical prophets, why should they have stopped delivering it around 450 B.C.E.? Or, posing the question another way: why should no more such prophets have appeared after that date? Without pretending entirely to dispel the element of mystery here, we can perhaps rest relatively content with the partial answer that emerges from the relation between the last of the classical prophets—the five with whom our story has just ended—and their pre-exilic and exilic predecessors.

Students of the post-exilic prophets of the late sixth and early-to-mid-fifth centuries B.C.E. have been able to show that all of them—Haggai, the two Zechariahs, Joel, and Malachi—knew the oracles of their predecessors very well. Their books are so full of echoes and allusions and even direct quotations from those predecessors that written texts must already have been accessible to them. Hence, as early as the late sixth century B.C.E., and perhaps even before that, a goodly part of what would in due course become the section of the Hebrew Bible devoted to the classical (or "Latter") prophets must already have been there for the reading.

Blenkinsopp elaborates on the implications of this fact:

> Once prophecies delivered in an earlier epoch were available in writing, the emphasis would tend to be less on direct inspired utterance and more on the inspired interpretation of past prophecy. . . . What it amounted to was a much stronger conviction that, at least in the normal course of events, God does not communicate directly but has revealed his will and purpose in past communications whose bearing on the present situation remains to be elucidated.

This being the case, the main task now became exegesis, or the clarification of the word of God that was there before one's eyes for pondering and studying. Indeed, already in what the Meyers team rather inelegantly calls the "intertextual dependency" of the last of the classical prophets—that is, their liberal drawing upon oracles of the past—we get a foretaste of the new emphasis on exegesis that, beginning three hundred years down the road and continuing for another six or seven centuries, will reach its apogee with the rabbis of the Talmud.

It is as though the last of the prophets thought that their role—their divinely appointed role—was to show how the word of God, as it had been communicated to a different age, could be applied to the new problems of the present. They also wanted to show that the word of God could provide guidelines to the future as well (a future that, though they themselves did not envisage it in concrete terms, would bring new imperial powers—the Greeks, the Seleucids, and the Romans—to affect the destiny of the people of Israel, as had the Assyrians, the Babylonians, and the Persians before them).

Blenkinsopp, as a Roman Catholic, remarks that his fellow Christian scholars have "routinely" regarded this transformation as a symptom of religious decline, or the drying up of inspiration, or "the triumph of the letter over the spirit." He, too, like the Meyers team, traces this pejorative view back to our old "friend" Julius Wellhausen, and like them, he will have none of it. A contemporary example he cites of the persistent influence of the Wellhausen view is the statement that "the fate of prophecy was sealed when, side by side with the living word of the messenger of Yahweh, there appeared a new authority, that of the written word."

In my judgment, Blenkinsopp is entirely right in dismissing this downgrading of the "written word" as compared with "the living word." So is the Meyers team. They even more passionately express a similar attitude in discussing the Second Zechariah:

> Insofar as Zechariah 9–14 represents an extraordinary concentration of inner biblical exegesis, it both demonstrates the vitality of biblical prophecy in its own time and, as a kind of proto-midrash, provides a prototype for the flourishing of cultural modes that were to sustain the spiritual and moral life of the community in the post-biblical period.

But as the Meyers team recognizes, the prophetic impulse simultaneously would take a second course after it had "departed from Israel" in its original form. If the first course would lead into the intensive study and explication of the written Law that would become the major activity of the rabbis of the Talmud, the second would move in what might be considered the opposite direction. This other direction would be toward the "apocalyptic" literature (typified by the Book of Daniel) that would flourish among Jews in the last two centuries before the beginning of the common era, and that would give more than a small push to the birth of Christianity.

But the influence of apocalyptic thinking on the development of Christianity out of Judaism is a very long and complicated subject, and beyond the scope of the story I have been telling here. That story closes with the cessation of classical prophecy in the mid–fifth century B.C.E. (just when—in another touch of mystery?—Socrates and Plato and Aristotle and many other giants of Greek culture are becoming prominent in Athens), and it remains for me only to expand slightly on the analysis of Blenkinsopp and the Meyers team as to why this should have happened when it did.

IF, AS THEY ARGUE, it was a definitive written corpus of history and law that finally deprived classical prophecy of the positive function it had performed in communicating God's word and will to His people in the absence or the lack of easy accessibility of such a corpus, what happened to the complementary nega-

tive mission of the prophets—the war God had sent them to wage against idolatry? I doubt that John Bright's explanation can be improved upon:

> The prophetic polemic against idols bore its fruit. . . . Judging from the
> literature of the period of the Second Temple, idolatry . . . ceased to be
> a problem within the Jewish community. . . . Pagan cults were not
> allowed in restoration Judah; Israelites who participated in them were
> not recognized as Jews. Jews might dabble in astrology, or believe in
> magic—but worship idols, never! Indeed, by the time idolatry once
> more became a problem, with the Seleucid persecutions [of the second
> century B.C.E.], one can say that the battle had already been internally
> won. Though individual Jews might apostatize, Judaism could not itself
> temporize with idols as the official religion of old Israel on occasion
> did; the bitterness with which it resisted Antiochus [IV] is evidence of
> this. Jewish monotheism was uncompromising.

Classical prophecy came to an end, then, because after three hundred years it
had fulfilled its dual mission. The classical prophets had kept the will of the invisible God alive and fresh through speaking His words before they were all at hand
in written form; and simultaneously they had battled against the great force and
enticements of pagan idolatry that had always stood as the main obstacle to a
complete acceptance and an unambiguous understanding by the people of Israel
of what those words entailed.

Having won that seemingly endless war against idolatry from within—and
having in this way contributed mightily to the growth of the Israelites into "a
kingdom of priests, and an holy nation"—the classical prophets helped to create,
just as God had promised, the precondition for the victory of monotheism over
paganism in those parts of the world where the battle had been joined.

But little did they realize, nor would they ever have expected (since their
prophetic powers did not extend to actual prescience about such matters any
more than they did to geopolitical affairs), that the spoils of the spiritual triumph
they had done so much to bring about would be reaped not by Judaism but by
the new religion that would spring from it under the name of Christianity.

"Wondrous," writes Kaufmann of this phenomenon, "is the career of ideas."
So indeed it is. And that it also contains an element of mystery in its own right
we will now have a further opportunity to discover, as we conclude by exploring the impact the classical prophets have had over the centuries that followed,
and as we try to determine what their ideas may still have to say to us today.

PART THREE

Aftershocks

CHAPTER SIXTEEN

THE PROPHETS AND US

THE CENTRAL PART of the service held in the synagogue every Saturday and on all holidays is the reading aloud of a portion of the Pentateuch or the First Five Books of Moses—the books Jews call the Torah or the *Khumash.* This is followed by the *haftarah,* a supplementary reading from either the Former or the Latter (classical) prophets usually chosen because it links up thematically in some way to the Torah portion of that particular week. But while the system is designed to get the congregation through the entire Pentateuch in the course of a year, a smaller percent of the corpus of classical prophecy gets covered.

The result is that even if one regularly goes to services at the synagogue, and even if one pays close attention to the *haftarah* (which is often chanted by a boy celebrating his bar-mitzvah, or—a recent innovation—a girl celebrating her bat-mitzvah), one's acquaintance with the classical prophets will be limited unless one makes a special point of studying them on one's own.

I am far from a regular attendee at the synagogue, and until I started working on this book, it had been a long time since I had done more than dip occasionally into the prophetic literature. But over fifty years ago, while an undergraduate at Columbia, where I majored in English and eventually earned a B.A., I also spent two long nights a week and the whole of every Sunday afternoon working toward, and finally being awarded, the degree of Bachelor of Hebrew Literature (B.H.L.) at the College of Jewish Studies, which was then one of the divisions of the Jewish Theological Seminary.* It was there—where

---

*The seminary is the leading institution of the Conservative movement, one of the three main branches of Judaism in America, the other two being Orthodoxy on its right and Reform on its left. But it is conservative with respect to religious practice, not to secular politics. Like most American Jews, members of Conservative congregations—and their rabbis—tend to be liberals.

the approach was academic or "scientific" rather than religious or devotional—
that I first studied the classical prophets intensively, in Hebrew, and under the
tutelage of several professors who were eminent scholars and up-to-date on all
the latest theories and discoveries.*Yet time was limited and many other subjects
also had a place in the curriculum. So it was that we were assigned only bits and
pieces of the classical prophets. Naturally these tended to be either the juiciest or
the ones that were relatively easy for students who could understand Hebrew
but had a way to go in achieving mastery over the language.

Still, I learned a lot about the prophetic literature, and I fell in love with the
poetry of much of it, especially Jeremiah. When I was young and equipped with
a very good memory, I could quote long passages from the classical prophets, and
even before doing research for this book, when I had already reached the age of
seventy, with the fading memory that goes along with being a septuagenarian, I
could still manage to fish up long passages from Jeremiah or some of the others.
To my chagrin, I have found in revisiting them that not all the quotations I
recently prided myself on knowing by heart were exactly accurate. But even less
accurate, as I have also found—and with more shock than chagrin—were the
ideas about the classical prophets that I had carried away from my studies and
that had been sitting there placidly in my head ever since.

These ideas were the staples of modern biblical criticism, and they had
gained such widespread currency among Jews as well as Christians that there
would have been no reason for me to challenge them even if I had possessed the
knowledge and the intellectual equipment to do so. But studying the prophets
once again for the first time in half a century—and more intensively and exten-
sively than I did then—I could see that while some of the ideas I had been
taught about them in my student days had been superseded by later developments in the field, the main ones were still regnant in the scholarly literature.
And these kept striking me either as downright fallacious or drastically oversim-
plified, or both.

To offer one last summation of what a close reading of the texts revealed: the
classical prophets did *not* invent monotheism or carry it to a higher level than it
had reached among their ancestors; they did *not* elevate morality over ritual; they
did *not* constitute a party of the "spirit" in opposition to a rigidly legalistic
priestly "establishment"; and they did *not* feel or give expression to a "tension" (a
word that has become popular in modern-day discussions of this issue) between
"universalism" and "particularism."

Furthermore, the fact that the early Christians read back a forecast of the

---

*Among them were some who have turned up here—H. L. Ginsberg and Abraham Joshua Hes-
chel. Moshe Greenberg, who would join their scholarly company in years to come, was a contemporary and friend of mine, and it was he who introduced me to the work of Yehezkel
Kaufmann, which he would later abridge and translate from Hebrew into English.

career of Jesus, down even to small details, in some of the classical prophets did *not* make the prophets themselves premature Christians or heralds of Christianity. And if the "Christological" interpretation of the classical prophets was based on a religiously driven selective and distorted perception of the texts, there was just as much misrepresentation behind the politically driven "liberological" construal of them as the fathers of certain modern notions of social justice, or as protesters speaking "truth to power," or as "dissident intellectuals."

But suppose that my own latest interpretation of the classical prophets is right. Suppose that, instead of being all the things I have just said they were not, what they really were doing was fighting with all their might against idolatry in order to keep their people faithful to God because they believed with all their hearts and all their souls that He had, out of an inscrutable love, chosen the children of Israel as the instrument through which His Law would be revealed and ultimately accepted by every other people as well. What then? What difference would it make to anyone but a serious believer, either Jewish or Christian, or an antiquarian or a professional student of the Hebrew Bible? Except for these groups, have I perhaps cut the ground out from under the possibility that the classical prophets still have something important to say to the world of today? Have I perhaps turned them, in Jeremiah's image, from "a fountain of living waters" into "broken cisterns"—as obsolete to us as prophecy itself became some twenty-five hundred years ago?

I think this is a fair set of questions, and I hope that by confronting them now as candidly as I can, I will better be able to communicate what I believe the classical prophets, properly read, still have to say to us today. And by "us" I mean everyone—Christians, Jews, and non-believers—living in the civilization that no one disputes has been shaped to a huge extent by the influence of the Hebrew Bible.

"We" so defined have, of course, not been shaped by the Hebrew Bible alone. The twentieth-century philosopher Leo Strauss was obviously right when he located the roots of Western civilization in two ancient cities: Jerusalem and Athens. But as the centuries wore on, the originally disparate cultures of these two cities met and crossed and merged to the point where—to exaggerate slightly—they almost become one. Thus, in the twelfth century C.E., the great Jewish theologian Maimonides set out to reconcile the teachings of Judaism with those of Aristotle; then in the next century St. Thomas Aquinas dedicated himself to the same gigantic project as it applied to Christianity. And if we are speaking of the influences that have formed us, how can we omit the scientific worldview that in the seventeenth century C.E. began replacing the Bible (and Aristotle, too) for very large numbers of people as the main source of—and the best method for discovering—the truth?

Yet such qualifications having been admitted into the picture, it remains the case that, whether we know it or not, and whether or not we regard the Hebrew

Bible (in one sense or another) as divinely inspired, we of the West are all still liv-ing on the income of its moral and spiritual capital. Even those skeptics and rationalists among us who do not consider themselves creatures of God are— and to a far greater extent than some of them even begin to realize—creatures of the Hebrew Bible. And that means—also to a far greater extent than many of them, and the rest of us, too, recognize—the classical prophets.

Nevertheless, even assuming all that, it still fails to answer the question I posed a minute ago: what, if anything, is contained in the classical prophets that is relevant or applicable to us today? Today: when we live in times and places so remote from theirs, and with problems so radically different from those with which they grappled?

I say *what, if anything,* because the possibility must squarely be faced that the classical prophets may have nothing, or nothing much, to say to us at all. Indeed, there is a great paradox here: the more closely one studies the classical prophets, the more one comes to learn about the concrete historical circumstances in which they were embroiled, and the more one grasps the specifics of what they were saying to their contemporaries about *their* problems, the more likely one is to wonder how much of it has any connection with or relation to the span between the cradle and the grave that is allotted to us today.

THIS PARADOX HAS BEEN another of the other great surprises I have expe-rienced in studying the classical prophets with the indispensable help of the his-torians and the exegetes. Even though I have dipped into only a tiny sample of the innumerable commentaries on these books, and even though my grip on the history of the children of Israel from Abraham to Malachi and the Zechariahs still leaves much to be desired, I have been left with a new respect for the old cliché about the forest and the trees.

Modern biblical scholars, critics, and historians command a staggering range of learning. It goes without saying that they are complete masters of Hebrew. But they can also read all the cognate Semitic languages—Sumerian and Akka-dian and Aramaic and Syriac and Ugaritic—some of which have been discov-ered and deciphered only in the fairly recent past and have led to the understanding of many previously unintelligible Hebrew terms; and because these scholars often need to compare the Masoretic Hebrew text with the Sep-tuagint or the Vulgate, they also know Greek and Latin; and because so much of the scholarly work on the Hebrew Bible was originally written in German, they all read that language as well. On top of all this, they are intimately familiar with the cultures of the pagan peoples of the ancient Near East with which Israel came into contact, and they keep up with the ever-increasing number of archae-ological finds that simultaneously illuminate—or sometimes obfuscate—those cultures and the Hebrew Bible itself.

Nor is this even the whole of it. Many (most?) scholars and critics of the Hebrew Bible are experts on the Apocrypha, that collection of (depending on how they are divided) between thirteen and fifteen Jewish books or parts of books written between 200 B.C.E. or thereabouts and 70 C.E. in a Semitic language other than Hebrew (such as Aramaic), or in Greek. As I indicated in the Introduction, none of these books made it into the Jewish canon,* whereas all but a few were accepted as divinely inspired by Roman Catholics and integrated into their version of the "Old Testament." On the other hand, their status later came under dispute among Protestants, who either omitted them from their own editions or placed them just before or after the New Testament (another collection of books in which the scholars and critics of the Hebrew Bible— including the Jews among them—are at home in the original Greek). Finally, many or most of the scholars—this time including the Christians among them—can swim comfortably in the "ocean" of the Talmud in the original Aramaic, and in later rabbinic commentaries on the Hebrew Bible.

As we would expect, these scholarly polymaths bring all their knowledge to bear on the texts they edit and analyze, and to great effect. But the result is that to study the classical prophets under their guidance is to be led into thickets from which it is very hard to emerge and in which the classical prophets themselves virtually disappear.

In some instances, they literally disappear. For example, as we have seen, by the time one is through with the modern commentaries on Isaiah, one has the impression that no more than a mere handful of the original words of this reputedly greatest of all the classical prophets were left to us by his disciples and editors, and that these words amount to no more than something like "My name is Isaiah the son of Amoz. You are all wicked and deserve to be horribly punished. Farewell."

Short of disappearing completely, the classical prophets can seem reduced in stature once they are dug out of the scholarly thickets. I hasten to acknowledge that this is not always, or mainly, the fault of the commentators. It is the classical prophets themselves who are to blame, though I also hasten to acknowledge that if it is a question of blame, the truly guilty party may well be us, their latter-day readers.

What makes us guilty is that we tend to approach them with misplaced or excessive anticipations of uplift or spiritual exaltation in every verse—misplaced not because the classical prophets never satisfy such cravings (of course they often do) but because they are constantly mired in mundane issues. I have said that Max Weber goes much too far when he writes that all they really cared

---

*A great many American Jews would be surprised to discover that one of the most widely observed of their holidays, Hanukkah, is based on an event recounted in the First Book of Maccabees, which, written in Greek, is in the Apocrypha but not in the Hebrew Bible.

about was foreign policy. But it is unquestionable that every one of them was passionately involved in the politics of his time, both domestic and foreign; in the social conditions that prevailed; in the religious controversies that were always breaking out between one group and another, and between themselves and rival prophets also claiming to speak in the name of God. They took very strong positions on such matters; they intervened in local policy disputes, invoking the authority of God for one party and condemning the other for advocating courses contrary to His will; they told the people at large and their leaders and rulers what God wanted them to do and not to do.

Frequently the classical prophets were so allusive about these matters that it is impossible to figure out what they were talking about without resorting to the scholars who assiduously make it their business to uncover the long-forgotten details. "For who hath despised the day of small things? . . ." asks the First Zechariah. Well, things that seemed big in the distant past can look very small in the present, and how much more so things that seemed small even then. Thus when we learn that behind some cryptic set of suggestive images nothing more lies hidden than the prophet's polemic against an opponent requiring pages of complicated exegetical analysis to unravel, we are likely to feel let down, and perhaps also to feel that the prophet himself has been diminished.

Here is a passage from Ezekiel that I have selected at random as an illustration:

> . . . Thus saith the LORD God; Woe to the women that sew pillows to all armholes, and make kerchiefs upon the head of every stature [*sic*] to hunt souls! Will ye hunt the souls of my people, and will ye save the souls alive that come unto you? And will ye pollute me among my people for handfuls of barley and for pieces of bread, to slay the souls that should not die, and to save the souls alive that should not live, by your lying to my people that hear your lies? Wherefore thus saith the LORD God; Behold, I am against your pillows, wherewith ye there hunt the souls to make them fly, and I will tear them from your arms, and will let the souls go, even the souls that ye hunt to make them fly. Your kerchiefs also will I tear, and deliver my people out of your hand, and they shall be no more in your hand to be hunted; and ye shall know that I am the LORD.

Now here, much abridged, is Moshe Greenberg's commentary on these largely incomprehensible verses which, he begins by explaining, are about fortune tellers:

> On their arms and heads the women attached what the prophet scoffingly calls cushions and rags [the "pillows" and "kerchiefs" of KJV]; since it was by these that the folk were beguiled, . . . it may be surmised

that they were divinatory paraphernalia, amulets, which when worn (like the priestly garments) lent special sanctity and power to the wearer. . . . The grain items, used in a religious ritual in which God was invoked . . . , may have been either a means through which the divine decision (of life and death) was disclosed (say, by being strewn on water), or, as seems more likely, offerings accompanying the prayers and invocations of the women.

Greenberg rolls on for several more paragraphs, in which he cites the Talmud and various medieval and modern commentators in support of this or that fine point of interpretation. It is as brilliant as it is erudite, and it opens up what was closed before. Yet it also makes one's head ache, and rereading the passage from Ezekiel in its light, one's comprehension may be enhanced but one's spirit is not exactly bound to be uplifted.

For a somewhat different illustration, consider this from the First Isaiah (if it was in fact by him):

> Thus saith the LORD God of hosts, Go, get thee unto this treasurer, even unto Shebna, which is over the house, and say, What hast thou here? and whom hast thou here, that thou has hewed thee out a sepulcher here, as he that heweth him out a sepulcher on high, and that graveth an habitation for himself in a rock? Behold, the LORD will carry thee away with a mighty captivity, and will surely cover thee. He will surely violently turn and toss thee like a ball into a large country: there shalt thou die, and there the chariots of thy glory shall be the shame of thy lord's house.

Joseph Blenkinsopp's commentary on these few verses runs to almost four closely printed pages, from which I will pluck out only a few sentences:

> Since no sustained metrical regularity is detectable, we take [this passage] to be a straightforward prose appendix to 22:1–14, similar therefore to 20:1–6, appended to the preceding anti-Egyptian sayings. The connection would suggest an addition dictated by prophetic opposition to the pro-Egyptian and insurrectionist policy pursued by this Shebna prior to the campaign of 701 B.C.E. . . . It seems that Shebna was what the Assyrian annals call a "son of a nobody," and is consequently being put in his place as a social climber. . . . Even so, the punishment threatened seems to be quite disproportionate to the offense, and practically unintelligible except on the assumption that the text is silent about the real reason for the hostility it displays. This may well be Shebna's political agenda.

To which a modern reader might well respond, What is Shebna to me or I to him that I should care about his fate? And what is admirable, let alone spiritually inspiring, about such a political diatribe?

Abraham Joshua Heschel—whose book about the classical prophets sets forth the standard "liberological" view of them as "iconoclasts" and disturbers of the peace, but gives that view a rhapsodically mystical twist—raises the problem of "small things" even in connection with their great moral passions:

> A student of philosophy who turns from the discourses of the great metaphysicians to the orations of the prophets may feel as if he were going from the realm of the sublime to an area of trivialities. Instead of dealing with the timeless issues of being and becoming, of matter and form, of definitions and demonstrations, he is thrown into orations about widows and orphans, about the corruption of judges and affairs of the market place. . . . [The classical prophets] make much ado about paltry things, lavishing excessive language upon trifling subjects. What if somewhere in ancient Palestine poor people have not been treated properly by the rich? So what if some old women found pleasure and edification in worshiping "the Queen of Heaven"?

Heschel deploys this set of questions rhetorically, as a way of convincing us of our moral inferiority to the classical prophets. "We and the prophet have no language in common. To us the moral state of society, for all its stains and spots, seems fair and trim; to the prophet it is dreadful." But in praising the classical prophets by denying that we have a language in common with them, and by asserting that we are so complacent and obtuse that we cannot even take in their words (since they employ "notes one octave too high for our ears"), Heschel does not seem to realize that he is willy-nilly adding fuel to the fire of suspicion that they have nothing to say to us today. Beyond that, his generally rhapsodic style in describing the classical prophets is just the kind of approach that fosters the expectations of continuous uplift that can prevent us from appreciating the classical prophets for who they truly were and from learning what they still have to teach.

IN MY OPINION, as it happens, some of what the classical prophets have to say to us today is inherent precisely in the negative considerations that—playing the Devil's advocate—I have just brought up. To repeat, all these considerations flow from the fact that the classical prophets were incessantly preoccupied either with "small things" or with issues so archaic that they no longer command general interest. Yet from this very preoccupation alone—quite apart from the great sermons or oracles or prophecies that it could yield—there is a major lesson to be extracted. The lesson is this: that the highest spiritual and moral states to which human beings are capable of attaining can best—or possibly even only—be reached through engagement with the affairs of the world around one, emphatically including what seem to be, or even are, transient or petty or trivial.

William Blake, who besides being one of the great English Romantic poets, was something of a latter-day prophet himself (though a highly heterodox or even heretical one from the Christian point of view), wrote in 1815:" ...Art and Science cannot exist but in minutely organized particulars." Neither, as I have been insisting throughout this book, can religion. Which is only one reason that the classical prophets, for all the harsh words several of them hurled against sacrifice, could never have imagined the worship of God without it, and why they would have been mystified by the notion that ritual could be conducted without a meticulous attention to the minute particulars by which it was regulated at God's command.

What we have, then, in the classical prophets is a running response to the social, political, and historical realities of the world around them. Such realities can be as large and momentous as the clash of empires in which the fate of the nation is at stake. Or they can be as trivial as an improper deal between two anonymous traders in the marketplace. But caring about such things as they actually exist in their full concreteness, in the here and now, is of the essence of the prophet's nature.

This facet or aspect of classical prophecy can also be understood as a derivative instance—an epiphenomenon, if you like—of the "scandal of particularity." For just as, in the view of the prophets, the only road to the one God of all is through the revelation He mysteriously granted to one small and insignificant people, so does the apprehension of universal or "higher" truths depend upon a grasp of and an immersion in the realm of the mundane and in the dailiness of life. A well-known stanza from another of Blake's poems captures the point perfectly:

> To see a world in a grain of sand
> And a heaven in a wild flower,
> Hold infinity in the palm of your hand
> And eternity in an hour.

But where does all this leave the moral side of the prophetic tradition for which it is most often valued: the exhortations to justice, righteousness, compassion for the poor and the widow and the orphan and the stranger? I would say that it leaves them exactly where they are, so long as we look at them in the soil in which they are planted, and so long as we resist uprooting and turning them into abstractions hanging in the air or standing alone as self-sufficient unto themselves.

To reiterate what I have attempted to show throughout this book: when the classical prophets denounce sacrifice and other forms of ritual, and when they declare that what God primarily demands of us is morality, they are not undergoing a sudden metamorphosis into modern liberal Protestants or older-style Reform Jews for whom ritual is primitive or archaic or barbaric.* They are teaching that ritual—whether animal sacrifice or Sabbath observance or the singing of hymns—cannot be used as a cover for moral sin, or as a substitute for obedience to the moral commandments.

These days, we sometimes hear from the newspapers about outwardly pious people—among them Orthodox rabbis, Catholic priests, and Protestant ministers—who deal dishonestly in business, or are cruel to their families, or are incorrigible pedophiles, and yet who seem to believe that if they fulfill their ritual obligations, they are atoning adequately for these sins and have nothing to fear from the wrath of God. If we wish to translate the message of the classical prophets on the issue of ritual into contemporary terms, we can without distortion or misrepresentation read it as chastising such people. But we cannot, at least not without doing violence to the words of the prophets, read them as advocating the abolition of ritual, or use them to support a contemptuous attitude toward it.

Does this diminish the value of the ethical emphasis for which the classical prophets have always, and preeminently, been so highly esteemed? Any reader who has followed me this far will know that I for one do not think so—that, to my mind, separating the two realms of morality and ritual, or exalting the former over the latter, is yet another instance of the larger fallacy of setting up an invidious opposition between "universalism" and "particularism" that is totally foreign to the classical prophets and to the Hebrew Bible in general—not to mention the nature of life itself.

THE SECULAR WORLD has many rituals of its own. Some are ceremonies commemorating special public occasions like national holidays, or turning points in private life like graduation from school. But a less obvious functional equivalent of ritual in secular society is manners. To the modern American ear,

---

*The qualifier "older-style" is necessary because early in the twenty-first century, the Reform movement in America began showing a new interest in and respect for ritual, both in synagogue services and in the rules for conversion to Judaism. "Probably what we did," one Reform rabbi informed The New York Times in June 2001, "is we over-intellectualized religion, and we set aside so much of the emotional, affective side of religion—and that's what ritual is, the affective side." Another prominent Reform rabbi also told the Times that thirty years earlier in his congregation, "no one had a ritual circumcision" at birth. But now, instead of having circumcisions performed by doctors in hospitals as in the past, "all my families have the circumcisions on the eighth day" done by religious professionals (mohelim).

the word "manners" smacks of triviality or of snobbery, evoking an archaic world of ceremony that ill consorts with the easy informality of contemporary social intercourse. What we forget is the ethical dimension of the courtesy toward and the consideration for others that are the prime ingredients of good manners. We also forget the converse, which is the hurt, the rending of trust, and the damage to decent social relations that bad manners can and do cause. Not for nothing did the venerable English public school Winchester (and New College at Oxford) adopt the slogan "Manners Maketh Man."

All this is important and pertinent, but there is a deeper dimension, and it was once brought out very saliently by Lionel Trilling, one of the very best literary critics of the twentieth century. In an essay he wrote in the late 1940s entitled "Manners, Morals, and the Novel," Trilling argued that manners were inseparable from morality, and that because of this intertwining of the two, it was through the investigation of manners that the greatest novelists of the Western tradition were able to scale not merely aesthetic but also moral heights. These writers, Trilling concluded, attained to a "moral realism" that was being lost as a consequence of the declining interest in manners among modern novelists.

What is "moral realism"? I cannot here rehearse the complex symbiotic relations Trilling teases out between this concept and a concern with manners, so I will restrict myself to his short definition of it as "a perception of the dangers of the moral life itself." This fertile perception breeds the further awareness—subtle and very hard to grasp or hold on to—"that the moral passions are even more wilful and imperious and impatient than the self-seeking passions." It is because I agree with Trilling's very important observation about how dangerous the moral passions can be that I am unable to share in the reverence for the visions of perfect peace and harmony and justice throughout all of creation—even among wild animals—that to so many people constitute the greatest glory of classical prophecy.

We have already examined all, or most, of these visions. The two most famous ones are in the Book of Isaiah, and to them we may join a less familiar one from Hosea, on which the First Isaiah (and/or Micah) may have drawn and at which we have only glanced before in part:

> But I will have mercy upon the house of Judah, and will save them by the LORD their God, and will not save them by bow, nor by sword, nor by battle, nor by horsemen. . . . And in that day will I make a covenant for them with the beasts of the field, and with the fowls of heaven, and with the creeping things of the ground: and I will break the bow and the sword and the battle out of the earth, and will make them to lie down safely.

Eschatological visions like this assuredly provide total satisfaction for even the most extravagant desires for uplift and exaltation that are brought to the classical prophets by readers in quest of such emotions. What could be more sublime than the picture of a world in which the wolf feeds contentedly alongside the lamb, in which little children and even babies can play safely among lions and formerly poisonous snakes, and when, under new heavens and on a new earth, there will be no more weeping or crying among human beings? What could be more glorious than a day when war will become so inconceivable and weapons will therefore become so useless that swords will be beaten into ploughshares and spears into pruning hooks?

There is no measuring the influence of visions like this, but we can safely bet that it has been as great as anything in the Hebrew Bible, or possibly in any other book in the history of the Western world. In our civilization, these visions, in one form or another, are behind every utopian dream that has ever been dreamed. The air has been so pervaded by their spirit that they have inspired even many who may never have read the classical prophets themselves. They have generated within such people tumultuous moral and political ambitions that wipe out all doubt about their own virtue and about the wickedness of any who might be misled by "moral realism" into entertaining so much as a smidgen of skepticism.

But concerning the vision of a perfect world, I would say this: if one believes in God, one can—indeed must—accept that it *is* in His power to bring about so miraculous a transformation at the End of Days. But if one believes in God, one must by the same token also accept that it is *only* in His power to perform these miracles, and not in the power of mere mortals like ourselves.

In sharp contrast to the revolutionaries who have been influenced by their eschatological visions, the classical prophets were thoroughly imbued with this truth—a simple truth that is easy to understand and easier to forget.* That is why they kept fulminating against the alliances with this or that empire through which the political leaders of the Northern Kingdom of Israel and the Southern Kingdom of Judah tried to ensure their security or independence. From the prophetic perspective, not even these relatively limited maneuvers could succeed unless God was behind them. How, then, could a mere king, who had not been

---

And not only by atheists or secularists. One school of Jewish mystical thought, for example, holds that every commandment fulfilled by every Jew brings the day of messianic redemption closer, thereby endowing mortals with at least some share in the divine power to realize the eschatological visions of the prophets. But these extremely pious Jews—who adhere to various Hasidic sects influenced by the kabbalistic tradition that originated with Rabbi Isaac Luria ("Ha-ari"*) in the sixteenth century—were not and are not revolutionaries. Nevertheless, Gershom Scholem, the greatest twentieth-century scholar of Jewish mysticism, was able to trace a connection between the Lurianic kabbalists and the secular revolutionaries of later centuries.

sent by God for the purpose, create the conditions that would usher in the perfect world of the prophets' eschatological dreams?

On the other hand, a mere king could do the opposite. Manasseh might have managed to stay on the throne for fifty-five years by turning Judah into an obedient vassal of Assyria, but because he sponsored idolatry even within the Temple itself, the price of his political "success" would in the prophetic perspective eventually be the destruction of the country, the sacking of Jerusalem, and the exile of most of its population. To the prophets, not even the efforts of his grandson, Josiah, to undo the damage he did could avert the doom Manasseh had brought upon his country.

My intention is not to defend the quietism or neutralism or defeatism of the policies that the First Isaiah or Jeremiah urged upon the rulers of Judah in the eighth or the sixth centuries B.C.E. In retrospect, and from a strictly political angle, the classical prophets may have been right at some moments and wrong at others. But when it came to historical predictions other than general warnings that infidelity to God would lead to national catastrophe, they were so often wrong that if—harking back to that troublesome criterion in Deuteronomy—the mark of a true prophet were the ability to foresee future events, hardly a one of the classical prophets would qualify.

Reviewing the record, we can begin at the beginning, with Amos. He rightly foresaw the fall of the Northern Kingdom, but he was wrong in predicting that King Jeroboam II would die by the sword, and moreover he had no idea that the death blow to the kingdom would be struck by Assyria. Nor was his contemporary Hosea any more specific about who would administer the coup de grace to the Northern Kingdom.

Remaining in the eighth century B.C.E., but moving down to the Southern Kingdom of Judah, we come upon the First Isaiah, who did warn that Assyria would be the "rod of God's anger," but who never predicted that Assyria would in turn be conquered by Babylon. The same was true of the First Isaiah's contemporary, Micah (who, however, did not commit Isaiah's error about the inviolability of Jerusalem). Skipping from the eighth to the seventh and sixth centuries B.C.E., neither Zephaniah nor Nahum expected the rise of Persia. Nor did Habakkuk or Jeremiah know that the Persians would take over from the Babylonians. In his early years, Jeremiah could never even name the vague enemy from the north that was coming to destroy Judah, and only later—when it showed its own colors—did he identify it as Babylon. Nor did Ezekiel, prophesying the fall of Babylon, where he himself was living, have a clue that its conqueror would be Persia, and when that happened, the Second Isaiah, also living in Babylon, entertained wildly excessive, and mistaken, ideas about what Cyrus would do for Judah and its people. Haggai, the First Zechariah, and Malachi—like the Second Isaiah before them—all witnessed the rise of the Persian empire, but none of them suspected that the Greeks would succeed it.

I owe several of the items on this list to Yehezkel Kaufmann. He uses them as evidence that there was far less tinkering by future editors with the texts of the classical prophets than other scholars assume, since these editors would surely have tried to correct erroneous forecasts and to insert material that would demonstrate the prescience absent from the original prophecies.

I concur, but my purpose is a different one. It is to bolster the argument that there is no lesson for us—especially those of us living in a powerful nation like the United States—in the prophetic counsels to a tiny and weak country caught between rival empires which had a strategic interest in controlling it because it sat athwart vital trade routes.

However, there *is* a lesson of the very greatest importance to be learned from the conviction of the classical prophets that neither kings nor priests—nor, for that matter, prophets—could on their own build the utopia of their eschatological visions. The words so often quoted from the First Zechariah—"Not by might, nor by power, but by my spirit, saith the LORD of hosts"—are usually celebrated as an attack on militarism. But their most profound meaning is that *only God can bring about the messianic era.* Not believing in God, and therefore oblivious of that essential truth, revolutionaries of the modern era from Robespierre to Lenin, from Mao to Pol Pot, who set out to realize the utopian visions of a world of perfect justice, harmony, and brotherhood, felt justified in constructing totalitarian regimes and murdering as many millions as they thought it would take to create such a world.

And then there is the dream of peace. In the eschatology of the classical prophets, this dream almost always accompanies the other elements of their utopian visions. But it is never entertained by the prophets for the world as it bloodily exists in the present and as it will continue to exist until the End of Days. Like the eschatological utopia itself, its realization rests with God, and is beyond the power of human political maneuverings.

This the disarmers and treaty makers of the 1920s in Europe and the United States failed to grasp when they signed pieces of paper that they believed would put an end to war. Instead, these treaties had the opposite effect. But an ever surer path to war was marked out in the 1930s. With the horrors of the First World War still fresh in their minds, the French and British appeasers of Germany under Adolf Hitler in that period felt that nothing could be worse than another such war, and they were willing to pay almost any price to avoid it. In 1938, shortly before the British prime minister Neville Chamberlain traveled to a meeting at Munich where the policy of appeasement was consummated by handing over democratic Czechoslovakia to Nazi Germany, Winston Churchill, who was then a lonely and much vilified opponent of that policy, wrote: "[W]e seem to be very near the bleak choice between War and Shame. My feeling is that we shall choose Shame, and then have War thrown in a little later."

Chamberlain and the other appeasers might not have done what they did if they had remembered what may be the greatest warning against appeasement ever made: " . . . from the prophet to the priest every one dealeth falsely. They have healed also the hurt of the daughter of my people saying, Peace, peace, when there is no peace." Ironically, this was an inadvertent warning, since when Jeremiah (seconded by Ezekiel) issued it, in the early years of the sixth century B.C.E., he himself was a lonely and much vilified *opponent* of those who wished to choose honor and not shame by rebelling against Babylon. As we know, Jeremiah even went beyond supporting a policy of appeasement to advocating actual surrender and submission as the only alternative to the sacking of Jerusalem and the burning down of the Temple. He did this, however, not for political reasons but because God had told him that the Babylonian king Nebuchadnezzar—"my servant"—was the instrument through which He meant to punish Judah and purge it of its sins, and that rebellion could only make things worse.

In any event, Jeremiah's words blazingly articulated the dangers posed under *any* circumstances by the pursuit of peace when the reality is that peace is *not* at hand, and when the conditions for it are *not* present. It was a warning that would be ignored by his descendants in the modern state of Israel who—misunderstanding the nature of the prophetic utopianism subliminally egging on their conscious calculations—tried prematurely and unilaterally to make peace with an enemy who had not the slightest desire to make peace with them.

IN TANDEM WITH the eschatological utopianism of the classical prophets, their idealism, religious and moral, has always been held up as the second of the two main sources of their lasting value, above all to non-believers. Understanding why this should be so is not difficult. After all, idealism enjoys a reputation second to none among human virtues, and there is no doubt that it can smack of nobility.

Yet I must confess to feeling as uneasy about the secular influence of that side of the prophetic tradition as I do about how its visions of eternal peace and harmony have played themselves out historically. Here I am with Abraham Joshua Heschel (though, as I have indicated before, I disagree with his overall interpretation of the classical prophets) when he observes that

> If justice means giving every person what he deserves, the scope and severity of the accusations by the [classical] prophets of Israel hardly confirmed that principle. The [classical] prophets were unfair to the people of Israel. Their sweeping allegations, overstatements, and generalizations defied standards of accuracy. Some of the exaggerations reach the unbelievable.

Yehezkel Kaufmann, by whom Heschel seems to have been influenced on this matter, is more specific about Jeremiah's ferocious indictment of the people of Jerusalem of his day:

> Jeremiah lists public and private sins, the likes of which are prevalent in every age and every society: lying and deceit, treachery and slander, adultery, love of gain, fraud, and perversion of justice. . . . Jeremiah himself betrays his exaggeration. . . . The indictment . . . opens with the words, "Wicked men have been found among my people"; it closes with, "Shall my soul not take vengeance against such a nation!" Because "wicked men are found" among the people, they become "such a nation." . . . Jeremiah's indictment springs from the same source as that of his predecessors: religious-moral idealism, coupled with a deep disappointment at the realization of the gulf that separated ideal from reality.

By accusing the classical prophets of unfairness to Israel, neither Kaufmann nor Heschel—nor I, in agreeing with them—is invoking the old charge that the God of the Hebrew Bible, in whose name the classical prophets speak, is all justice and no mercy. Thus, Heschel rightly dwells at length on the love of Israel that invariably tempers the anger, and the forgiveness that God is always ready to bestow even when it is not earned by repentance. I fear that Heschel leaves me far behind when he translates this into something he calls the "divine pathos" and when he makes the shared experience of such pathos—on a human scale— the main mark of the prophet. But the more prosaic Kaufmannesque core of his analysis retains its validity.

In the light of the "moral realism" I share with Trilling, other dangers besides unfairness can also be detected lurking in the shadows of idealism. One is self-righteousness. Few who have the honorific of idealist bestowed upon them, or stake their own claim to it (usually by way of disingenuous denial), are as selfless as they or others may imagine. Like the political utopianism to which it bears a close family resemblance, and with which it often overlaps, moral idealism can conceal a lust for superiority over others that is more ruthless, because unrecognized, than an open and visible ambition for the same unlovely gratification.

In addition, there is little if any tolerance for human weakness in moral idealism. This lack of tolerance is the very quality for which—in another, decidedly non-Kaufmannesque, mood—Heschel praises the prophets (who, remember, speak "an octave too high" for our morally stuffed ears to hear). It demands a perfection that is unattainable by fallible mortal creatures, and in pressing for or pursuing such perfection, it is unrestrained by an appreciation of the inescapability, and even the desirability, of human limitations.

In an essay about the Indian leader Mahatma Gandhi, who was regarded as a saint by his admirers, George Orwell memorably began by announcing that

"Saints should always be judged guilty until they are proved innocent." In expanding on this proposition, Orwell explained:

> The essence of being human is that one does not seek perfection, that one is sometimes willing to commit sins for the sake of loyalty, . . . and that one is prepared in the end to be defeated and broken up by life, which is the inevitable price of fastening one's love upon other human individuals. . . . Many people genuinely do not wish to be saints, and it is probable that some who achieve or aspire to sainthood have never felt much temptation to be human beings.

As an outspoken, even aggressive, atheist, Orwell argued in the same essay that "the other-worldly, anti-humanist tendency of Gandhi's teachings" could not "be squared with the belief that our job is to make life worth living on this earth, which is the only earth we have." He did, however, concede that Gandhi's "sainthood" made sense "on the assumption that God exists." But this was to concede too much from the viewpoint of a religion like that of the classical prophets, for whom "the world of solid objects" was the polar antithesis of an "illusion to be escaped from" that it was to a devout Hindu like Gandhi.

To avoid any misunderstanding, let me state flat out that the classical prophets were almost by definition never self-righteous because, in speaking for God, more often than not against their own will, they no longer had a self. Personality might come through, but not self: except for Jeremiah and perhaps Ezekiel, they were all either anonymous or, if they had names, that was almost all they had. When, as I have remarked before, we get any biographical details (about Hosea's marriage, say, or the First Isaiah's children), these invariably turn out to represent non-verbal prophetic messages: the word of God dramatized in action rather than in speech.

My reservations about moral idealism, then, pertain less to the classical prophets themselves than to the example they set for others who—shall we say?—were less imbued, or not imbued at all, with the conviction that it was God, and not they, who was speaking: a category that would eliminate all but a very tiny handful of idealists. Even the "unfairness" of the classical prophets toward the people of Israel can be justified as following logically from the idea of chosenness. In this connection, Amos is worth citing yet again: "You only have I known of all the families of the earth: therefore I will punish you for all your iniquities."

FINALLY, there is the greatest problem of all: the absence from the classical prophets—who in this as in most other respects encapsulate the Hebrew Bible as a whole—of any firm idea of an afterlife in which the righteous are rewarded and the wicked are punished.

Some classical prophets, both early like Micah, and late like Joel, refuse to go along with Amos in overturning the original popular conception of the Day of the Lord as a day when God will judge the oppressors of all Israel, whose destruction will be a prelude to the triumph of His Law and His People. Instead they build on the popular conception in offering consolation and attempting to still doubt. Joel:

> Let the heathen be wakened, and come up to the valley of Jehoshaphat: for there will I sit to judge all the heathen round about. . . . Egypt shall be a desolation, and Edom shall be a desolate wilderness, for the violence against the children of Judah. . . . But Judah shall dwell for ever, and Jerusalem from generation to generation. . . . for the LORD dwelleth in Zion.

Yet even from a nationally optimistic eschatological prophecy like this one, something is missing.

It is no oversimplification to say that the books of the classical prophets—again mirroring the Hebrew Bible as a whole—constitute a "theodicy": an unstinting effort to do what John Milton averred was his aim in writing *Paradise Lost,* to "justify the ways of God to man."* Whatever goes wrong—from the expulsion of Adam and Eve from the Garden of Eden to the many calamities visited upon the children of Israel—flows from human disobedience to God's Law, and can never be blamed on Him or on the Law. The trouble is that, while the classical prophets are full of assurances like the one from Joel that a time is coming when justice will be meted out to all *nations,* there is hardly any sign of a correlative assurance to the *individual.*

Yes, God's promise is that those who obey His commandments will prosper and that their days will be lengthened in *this* life, while those who disobey will suffer all manner of curses, ending (so it is logically implied) in a premature death, or (as is graphically pictured innumerable times) an ignominious one, with their corpses exposed like dung to the scavenging beasts of earth and sky. Yet, as God is constantly being reminded by the prophets, the facts of experience belie this promise. To return to the words of Jeremiah I have quoted more than once before: " . . . Wherefore doth the way of the wicked prosper? wherefore are they all happy that deal very treacherously?"

I have always felt—and all the more so after having studied the prophets again—that the willingness to include this question, and not to censor it, is one of the glories of the Hebrew Bible. But I now also feel that what makes the

---

*Three hundred years later, in 1896, A. E. Houseman irreverently responded in *A Shropshire Lad:* "And malt does more than Milton can/To justify God's ways to man."

inclusion even more impressive, especially when we consider that the Hebrew Bible's overriding purpose is to justify the ways of God to man, is that never once does it show us God returning an answer that is satisfactory from the ordinary human point of view. Since Jeremiah in particular poses the question in the form of a lawsuit, it may not be overly impious to criticize God's explanations in the way a contemporary American judge might do, as "unresponsive."

Thus, all Jeremiah gets is a pep talk: "If thou hast run with the footmen, and they have wearied thee, then how canst thou contend with horses? . . ." Habakkuk, having more tremulously uttered a complaint very similar to Jeremiah's (" . . . wherefore lookest thou upon them that deal treacherously, and holdest thy tongue when the wicked devoureth the man that is more righteous than he?") is informed that " . . . the just shall live by his faith." And—reaching beyond the classical prophets themselves, but not beyond their own ideas—Job is hit with this:

> Then the LORD answered Job out of the whirlwind, and said, Who is this that darkeneth counsel by words without knowledge? Gird up now thy loins like a man; for I will demand of thee, and answer thou me. Where wast thou when I laid the foundations of the earth? declare, if thou hast understanding.

True, neither Job nor any other mortal was present when God created the world, and we may not be capable of grasping the awesome powers He goes on to invoke. But the reader of the first two chapters of the book knows full well that Job has been deprived of his children and his wealth, and also made to suffer greatly from horrendous illnesses and physical torments, as a result of nothing more incomprehensible to the human mind than a challenge to God from Satan (here conceived not as the Devil but as a kind of heavenly prosecutor). The only reason Job is so righteous, Satan declares, is that God has blessed him with many worldly goods; take them away, and Job will curse You.

God accepts the challenge, and as the afflictions pile up, Job's wife angrily urges him to " . . . curse God, and die." But Job refuses. He does come to curse the day he was born (as does Jeremiah), but never God: "Though He slay me, yet will I trust in him. . . ." Because Job passes the test, all his losses are made up at the end, when he gets " . . . more than his beginning: for he had fourteen thousand sheep, and six thousand camels, and a thousand yoke of oxen, and a thousand she asses. He also had seven sons and three daughters."* The recompense comes *here,*

---

*It should be noted that most scholars think—and on stylistic grounds alone, I agree—that the first two chapters about God and Satan, and the last, were an old folk tale on which the author built, and that his own book begins with Chapter 3 and ends with Chapter 41, in which neither the cause of Job's sufferings nor the recompense is mentioned.

on *earth*. Nothing is said about rewards bestowed in the form of an eternal life in Paradise.

So far as God's reply to Job goes, one might adapt the quip of a French general about the heroic but suicidal British charge of the Light Brigade at Balaclava in 1854: *C'est magnifique, mais ce ne pas la guerre* ("It is magnificent, but it is not war"). The words blasted from the whirlwind are also magnificent, but they are no better an answer to the anguished question of why the righteous suffer or why the wicked prosper than His retorts to Jeremiah and Habakkuk.

In Malachi, though, God is somewhat more responsive to the question, returning, if not exactly an answer, then at least a promise to the individual comparable to those He often makes to the entire people. Earlier, I quoted the conclusion to that answer, but now I will give it in full:

> Ye have said, It is vain to serve God: and what profit is it that we have kept his ordinance, and that we have walked mournfully before the LORD of hosts? And now we call the proud happy; yea, they that work wickedness are set up; yea, they that tempt God are even delivered. Then they that feared the LORD spake often one to another: and the LORD hearkened, and heard it, and a book of remembrance was written before him for them that feared the LORD, and that thought upon his name. And they shall be mine, saith the LORD of hosts, in that day when I make up my jewels; and I will spare them, as a man spareth his own son that serveth him. Then shall ye return, and discern between the righteous and the wicked, between him that serveth God and him that serveth him not. For, behold, the day cometh, that shall burn as an oven; and all the proud, yea, and all that do wickedly, shall be stubble: and that day that cometh shall burn them up, saith the LORD of hosts, that it shall leave them neither root nor branch. But unto you that fear my name shall the Sun of righteousness arise with healing in his wings; and ye shall go forth, and grow up as calves of the stall.

A hint might be detected in these beautiful verses of an afterlife in which all will be made well—in which the virtuous who have suffered in this life will be compensated and the wicked will be duly punished. But it is only a faint hint, and it gets very little backing from any of the other classical prophets. As they all understand it, the dead go down into a pitch-dark pit called Sheol (a word whose meaning no one knows) where they mostly sleep. They can be roused momentarily from this eternal sleep by the forbidden arts of necromancy (as when the witch of Endor summons up the ghost of Samuel at Saul's bidding), and they can even then forecast the future. Yet nothing in the nature of reward or punishment takes place in Sheol.

None of this means that there is no idea whatsoever of eternal life in the classical prophets. There is, but it applies *only* to the people of Israel *as* a people (even if, in the codicil the prophets tack on, Israel's disobedience and rebelliousness may reduce it to a small remnant rather than the great and mighty nation that was supposed to spring from the loins of Abraham whose numbers would be " . . . as the stars of the heaven, and as the sand which is upon the sea shore . . ."). But where individual human beings are concerned, the only immortality they can achieve is through their "seed."

In later centuries, the rabbis of the Talmud would develop a belief in "the world to come" that they would claim to have extracted from the Bible. But this claim would be based at best on the same species of "penumbras, formed by emanations" that Justice William O. Douglas of the American Supreme Court relied upon to dig rights out of the American Constitution that were never written into it. We may read in Genesis that " . . . Enoch walked with God: and he was not; for God took him." We also read in the Second Book of Kings that " . . . Elijah went up by a whirlwind into heaven" in a chariot of fire drawn by horses of fire. And there are a few straws—in one of the Psalms and in a single verse in the Book of Proverbs—at which the rabbis would eagerly grasp.

Yet in none of these instances, nor anywhere else, does the Hebrew Bible unmistakably and unambiguously hold out the prospect of an afterlife in which rights are wronged and wrongs are righted. When (in the Book of Isaiah) King Hezekiah prays for deliverance from his illness, this is how he pleads with God:

> For the grave cannot praise thee, death can not celebrate thee: they that
> go down into the pit cannot hope for thy truth. The living, the living,
> he shall praise thee, as I do this day: the father to the children shall make
> known thy truth.

Outside the prophetic literature, we come upon almost exactly the same sentiment in the Book of Psalms: "The dead praise not the LORD, neither any that go down into silence." An even more forceful expression of the same idea comes from Job:

> O remember that my life is wind: mine eye shall no more see good. The
> eye of him that hath seen me shall see me no more. . . . As the cloud is
> consumed and vanisheth away: so he that goeth down to the grave
> [Sheol] shall come up no more.

But what about resurrection of the dead? Like the afterlife, the belief in resurrection would become one of the major principles of faith in the Judaism freely extrapolated out of the Bible by the Talmud. Yet also like the afterlife, it is confined to vague hints in the Bible. There arose rabbinic commentators who would read Ezekiel's vision of the Valley of the Dry Bones as just such a parable.

But Moshe Greenberg is more convincing when he interprets it more narrowly as a prophecy of national renewal and the return from exile.

A passage that points more clearly to the concept of resurrection is in the "Little Apocalypse" that we are told was inserted into the First Isaiah: "Thy dead men shall live, together with my dead body shall they arise. Awake and sing, ye that dwell in dust: for . . . the earth shall cast out the dead." Yet even here we see nothing about reward and punishment.

The Book of Daniel is another matter. There we are presented with the only vision of resurrection that unambiguously combines it with reward and punishment.

> And many of them that sleep in the dust of the earth shall awake, some to everlasting life, and some to shame and everlasting contempt. And they that be wise shall shine as the brightness of the firmament; and they that turn many to righteousness as the stars for ever and ever.

George Foote Moore, in his classic three-volume work of the late 1920s, *Judaism in the First Centuries of the Christian Era,* attributes the birth of this new doctrine to the growing dissatisfaction with the traditional view—the one long since questioned by Jeremiah and Job and the others—that it is in *this* life that rewards and punishments are meted out by God. Like most scholars, Moore has no doubt that the Book of Daniel, prudently pretending to be set in the distant past, was actually written during the occupation of Judea by Antiochus IV in the second century B.C.E. (which may also be the date of the Isaian Apocalypse).

The triggering event was the infamous decree of 167 B.C.E. issued by Antiochus, a Seleucid monarch and a great devotee of Greek culture. Under its provisions, anyone caught with a copy of the Torah or circumcising a baby boy would be executed (and many were, including several of the leading rabbinical sages of the period). Antiochus then followed up this ruthless policy of Hellenization by rededicating the Temple in Jerusalem to Zeus and offering sacrifices to him there. "At this point," Moore comments, "the extension of divine retribution beyond the tomb came as a necessary corollary to the idea of God's justice and the assurance of his faithfulness in fulfilling his promise to the righteous."

In what is at once a gloss of Moore's observation and of the relevant verses from Daniel, Moshe Greenberg writes:

> Traditional theodicy, explaining national distress as the product of sin, was incapable of consoling the pious victims of Antiochus's agents, for this time it was precisely the righteous who died, while apostates flourished. The anguish of the moment was assuaged by the belief that in the coming deliverance the injustice perpetrated on earth would be recti-

fied by a judgment rendered to the deceased, called back to life on earth
for the purpose.

It was through this doctrine that the rabbis of the Talmud (those much misrepresented and maligned Pharisees of the New Testament) plugged up the gap-
ing hole in the biblical theodicy. But what astonishes is that it took so long for
the problem to be resolved in a religion based from its inception on the belief
that God is just. Centuries before Jeremiah and the others were agonizing over
it, Abraham, the first of the patriarchs and the first of the prophets, confronted
God when He was about to destroy the wicked cities of Sodom and Gomorrah:

> And Abraham drew near, and said, Wilt thou also destroy the righteous
> with the wicked? Peradventure there be fifty righteous within the city:
> wilt thou also destroy and not spare the place for the fifty righteous that
> are therein? That be far from thee to do after this manner. . . . Shall not
> the judge of all the earth do right?

It is a miracle—no milder word will do—that fidelity to the God of Israel
should have remained strong for nearly two thousand years amid so much evidence that the righteous were always being destroyed along with the wicked;
and, worse yet—as the classical prophets could not prevent themselves from
complaining to God—that in spite of His own promises to the contrary the
wicked so often even prospered. One suspects that this very unanswered question contributed mightily to the people's constant backsliding into idolatry.

GRANTED THAT, strictly construed, the oracles of the classical prophets are
lacking in any vision of an afterlife of reward and punishment, this alone would
seem to decide the issue of whether they have anything to say to us today. For if
the persecutions of Antiochus finally exposed the limitations of the traditional
theodicy, how much more so does the Holocaust, when two million innocent
children were slaughtered, and when countless Jews who were obedient to the
will of God, were incinerated side by side with rebels against His Law?

Explanations have been sought and found. To Orthodox Jews, for whom the
afterlife is a central article of faith, it will all be made right in the "world to
come"; and there are non-Orthodox Jews for whom the survival of a "remnant"
and its return to Zion seem an eerie confirmation of certain passages in the classical prophets that we ourselves have encountered throughout their story. But
my own conviction is that there can be no satisfactory answer in any alternative
to an afterlife, and that it is better to give up struggling to find one.

Later, I will try to explain why I think giving up this struggle is better. But
for now I would like to put forward the suggestion that if the classical prophets

had been at issue, the atheist Orwell—an honest man if there ever was one—could not have been so categorical in pronouncing, as he did in his essay on Gandhi, that "one must choose between God and Man." I am not asserting that the classical prophets can be "squared" with Orwell's contention that "man is the measure of all things" any more than Hinduism can. To the classical prophets, God is supreme, and man is as nothing beside Him (and yet, paradoxically, everything *to* Him). What I would assert, however, is that classical prophecy can be harmonized very smoothly with Orwell's "belief that . . . this earth . . . is the only earth we have."

To George Orwell, a socialist, the implication—following as the night the day—was that "our job is to make life worth living" on this, "the only earth we have." Being a socialist, he would have discovered much in Amos and the others that was highly congenial to the kind of egalitarian economic justice he favored (though unlike most of his fellow believers in socialism, he worried about its potential for limiting the political freedom to which he was also committed). Growing up in the early twentieth century in England—then still a culture in which, as Matthew Arnold said, everyone knew the Bible—he would almost certainly have drawn inspiration from the classical prophets, whether consciously or through the air he breathed.

Yet the socio-political views of these prophets seem to me the least important element of what they have to say to those today for whom, like Orwell, this is "the only earth we have." The most important thing is that, even if this is the only earth we have, it is still governed by moral and spiritual laws, and that these laws are as binding on human beings as the laws of physics are on the natural world. The difference is that the natural world is not free to violate the laws ordained in its creation, whereas we human beings can choose to break those that are ordained for us. But we deceive ourselves in one direction if we imagine that we can do so with impunity, and in another if, to paraphrase Malachi, we imagine there is no profit in obeying the Law.

The classical prophets assumed that it was the God of Israel who had promulgated these laws and that to obey them was—in contemporary usage—to live a rich and full life, as rich and full a life as it was possible for mortal beings to enjoy. They—and God Himself—described such a life in terms of material prosperity, health, and longevity. This may seem crass to some sensibilities, but surely it would be the sheerest cant to deny that the material goods of this life are blessings. Just as surely, however, only a fool would say that they are the only blessings available to us, or the most important.

Significantly, even though the rabbis of the Talmud recognized the demand and the need for the belief in an afterlife, and even though they did everything in their ingenious power to plug up this gap in the biblical theodicy, they also sought no less vigorously to make sure that *all* the blessings of *this* life would be appreciated at their proper worth. They did so by prescribing expressions of gratitude to God for virtually everything that swims into a person's ken, from the very first moment he arises from sleep and until the very last moment of his waking day. A pious Jew offers thanks for the rising of the sun and its setting; for every morsel of food he eats; and even—in a regulation that is at once comical and impressive in its robust and earthy attitude toward life—for the successful conclusion of the lowliest bodily functions.

In mandating *this* form of worship, I would maintain, the rabbis were not relying on emanations and penumbras. Here they were being "strict constructionists," true to the classical prophets who spoke most eloquently and authoritatively for the ancient religion of Israel until its laws were finally written down and organized into a collection of documents incorporating their own oracles and sermons. For these oracles are so thoroughly pervaded by a sense of wonder at the beauty of creation and a sense of awe at its glory that their words become blessings in themselves. Outside the classical-prophetic corpus, the only other books of the Hebrew Bible that contain equally great poems of celebration and gratitude are Psalms and Job.

The classical prophets (and the Psalmists, and even poor Job) were "God-intoxicated" men—to a much greater extent than the philosopher Baruch Spinoza, of whom this was once said (and who was excommunicated for his heretical pantheism by his fellow Jews of seventeenth-century Amsterdam). Is it, then, necessary to be drunk on the personal God of the classical prophets—the God who cares about every one of his creatures, " ... from the least of them even unto the greatest of them ... ," as Jeremiah put it—in order to understand and be instructed by what the classical prophets have to say?

Well, it certainly helps. To any believer in God, and most especially a believer who truly loves and reveres and stands in awe of Him, the classical prophets will inevitably resound with a force that hardly anything else in the Hebrew Bible can touch. They will articulate feelings for such a person that might otherwise be inexpressible, and they will evoke the majesty and the holiness to which they were uniquely privy among men. Through the classical prophets, the believer will hear what they heard: the voice of God Himself.

But the classical prophets have also spoken, and can still speak, to people like George Orwell, who have no faith at all. Or is Orwell an exception? Can the classical prophets have anything to say to less open-minded atheists or agnostics?

The old cliché has it that there are no atheists in foxholes, but all this tells us is that men are driven by fear at the onset of death into taking out a last-minute insurance policy. Yet outside of the foxhole, there is an idea in the classical prophets that I think has the greatest relevance to non-believers. This idea derives from the prophetic doctrine that great kings and emperors who attribute their successes to their own wisdom and cunning are in reality being manipulated by God. Let me recapitulate the main examples: to the First Isaiah, Assyria is an instrument God has chosen to punish Israel for its sins, the rod of His anger;

to Jeremiah, Babylon under Nebuchadnezzar, "my servant," has been assigned the same role; to the Second Isaiah, Persia under Cyrus, God's "anointed," is given the opposite job of sending the exiles back to Judah where they will rebuild the Temple destroyed by the Babylonians he has conquered.

What I am attempting to convey through a rehearsal of these examples is the inference that can be drawn from them that one can serve God without being aware that He exists; one can even do so (if, as with the ancient empires, it suits His plan) through wickedness. And if one can all unawares serve God through wickedness, how much more so can one serve Him through virtue—even while denying Him? If this is true of a king like Cyrus (" . . . I have surnamed thee, though thou hast not known me"), it must also be true by extension of all persons.

A MODERN INSTANCE of this strange and paradoxical truth concerns the early Zionist pioneers who migrated to Palestine a little less than a century ago. Most of these young people were also socialists and atheists who had rebelled against their strict religious upbringing. Their Orthodox parents and teachers, by contrast, tended to be anti-Zionist, on the premise that Jewish sovereignty in the Land of Israel had to await the coming of the Messiah. But Abraham Isaac Kook, the chief rabbi of the Jewish community in Palestine (the *yishuv*) in the 1920s and 1930s, was exceptional among his Orthodox fellows in embracing Zionism. Naturally he deplored the rejection of religion by these young pioneers who spat at so much of what he most cherished. Yet the story goes that Kook once said he kissed the ground on which they walked because, holy though it already was, it was made even holier by their footsteps. They might be atheists, and they might despise Judaism as nothing but an archaic collection of foolish superstitions. But to Kook, these young Jews were acting inadvertently in accordance with the will of God. They were to him fiery spirits who did not have the slightest idea what an important role they played in the scheme of Divine Providence: they were called but they did not know who was calling them.

Kook—who taught that there must be a synthesis between the holy and the profane—might well have agreed that a Gentile like George Orwell, who as a man of the left conducted a great fight against the totalitarianism of the left, was thereby serving God or doing the Lord's work. And there are millions upon millions of non-believers (non-believers, that is, in the depths of their hearts, if not in their answers to pollsters) who have no such great or extraordinary achievements to their credit as did Orwell, but who live what can fairly be considered godly lives.

Then there are those who are not atheists or agnostics but whose faith is abstract or pallid. Consider the Founding Fathers of the United States. They were by most accounts Deists—a rationalistic brand of religion that is not exactly conducive to the kind of passion that pours out of the classical prophets (and does not entail the expectations of an afterlife, even if it may at certain periods prudently try to conceal this).*

Yet when in the Declaration of Independence they stated with full conviction that they were staging a rebellion against the king of England in accordance with "the laws of Nature and Nature's God," the voice of classical prophecy could be heard speaking through them, loud and clear. And so it was too when, in the Preamble to the Constitution, the Founding Fathers with equal conviction proclaimed that one of their principal objectives in establishing this new nation was to secure "the blessings of liberty" to themselves and their posterity. But political liberty was not the only blessing they had in mind. In the Declaration of Independence, Thomas Jefferson's phrase "life, liberty, and the pursuit of happiness" was inspired by a similar one drawn from the English philosopher John Locke in which "property" was used rather than "happiness."

In other words, to the Founding Fathers, as to the classical prophets, the fact that this may have been the only earth we had did not preclude accepting that it was governed by a moral law. Nor did their diluted version of Christianity preclude accepting that this law derived its authority from a higher power ("Nature's God") than the "consent of the governed." Nor did it preclude accepting that by following this law, a man would bring blessings down upon his head and the heads of his children and their children—blessings defined in the first instance as the same material goods (many cattle, abundant crops, and so on) that are emphasized as much by the classical prophets as by the promises of God in other parts of the Hebrew Bible. Notwithstanding that the God being invoked by the Founding Fathers may not be the personal God of the Hebrew Bible, and notwithstanding their extreme sobriety and rationalism, when they wrote the Constitution, the voice of the classical prophets was heard yet again in the land. And it can and does still speak to us, their "posterity," the moment we open our ears.

I could cite many more such illustrations of the point I am working to get across, but I will permit myself just one. It is in the concluding paragraph of *Mr. Sammler's Planet,* a novel published in 1969 by the American writer Saul Bellow. The hero, keeping vigil at the bedside of a dying man, quietly intones a prayer for him:

> He was aware that he must meet, and he did meet—through all the confusion and degraded clowning of this life through which we are speeding—he did meet the terms of his contract. The terms which, in

---

*In his book *On Two Wings,* Michael Novak, however, makes a strong case that the Founding Fathers were not Deists but serious Christians. Even if he is right about them, this would not affect the general validity of my own view about Deism and other "abstract or pallid" forms of faith.

his inmost heart, each man knows. As I know mine. As all know. For that
is the truth of it—that we all know, God, that we know, that we know,
we know, we know.

Saul Bellow is a member of the Jewish people—which may account subliminally for his choice of the word "contract," with its echo of "covenant"—but he
is not religious as measured by observance of the *mitzvot,* or commandments, of
Judaism. He does not keep the Sabbath, or the dietary laws, or most of the hundreds of other rules that a pious Jew is required to follow. The God to whom his
protagonist Mr. Sammler prays is not the God of the classical prophets, any more
than Thomas Jefferson's was. And there is no sign in his books that he anticipates
an afterlife in which we would all be judged. One may safely conclude that for
Bellow, as for Orwell, this is the only earth we have or will ever have.

But is that why the classical prophets have so much to say to him about the
moral and spiritual dimension of *this* life and about the laws that tell us how to
live it? For I am certain they do, if on the basis of no other evidence than that
"The terms which, in his inmost heart, each man knows" is a formulation that
could easily be taken as the fulfillment of Jeremiah's prophecy. To quote that
prophecy a second time:

> But this shall be the covenant that I will make with the house of Israel;
> After those days, saith the LORD, I will put my law in their inward
> parts, and write it in their hearts. . . . And they shall teach no more every
> man his neighbor, and every man his brother, saying, Know the LORD:
> for they shall all know me, from the least of them unto the greatest of
> them, saith the LORD. . . .

In my heterodox opinion, then, one of the things the classical prophets have
to say to us today is that we need not believe in heaven and hell—or even, if it
comes to that, in God, let alone the God of the Hebrew Bible—in order to
accept that our lives are governed by laws whose "terms" we all know in our
"inmost hearts"; that people who obey those laws will be blessed; and that people who disobey them will be cursed.

YET THE MINUTE we are ready (if we are) to grant all this, we find our faces
rudely being rubbed again in the problem of why the innocent suffer while the
wicked prosper. I will not withdraw my acknowledgment that an afterlife is the
only fully adequate solution to this problem. But I am now ready to admit that
in thinking this issue through after a prolonged drenching in the classical
prophets—and even in the course of this very discussion—I have become

increasingly vulnerable to second thoughts about the "unresponsive" answers God keeps giving to them, and to Job, when they plead with Him, in fear and trembling, to explain.

These answers (even the one to Malachi) all boil down to what God says of Himself in another context to the Second Isaiah: "For my thoughts are not your thoughts, neither are your ways my ways, saith the LORD. For as the heavens are higher than the earth, so are my ways higher than your ways, and my thoughts than your thoughts." To a genuine believer in the God of the Hebrew Bible, that should be enough. How can a mere human being, who is by definition limited in understanding, know anything more about an omnipotent and omniscient God and His designs than God chooses to reveal to him? Under such a dispensation, there are mysteries that the human being cannot penetrate and never will, and if he has faith, he will have to live with these mysteries. This does not necessarily inoculate him with permanent immunity from attacks of doubt and despair, or ensure that God will never " . . . hide [His] face . . ." from him. Far from it. But in the end, he will bow his head, accept in all humility that there are questions he cannot and never will be able to answer, and he will rely on faith to carry him through.

To people of little faith or no faith, this will never do, and it may very well be that classical prophecy has nothing whatever to say to them—unless they happen to be of a literary bent. If they are, they might value the classical prophets as great poets and read them with the "willing suspension of disbelief for the moment" that one of the major English Romantic poets and critics, Samuel Taylor Coleridge, equated not with religious but with "poetic faith." Coleridge's younger contemporary, and a greater poet than he was, John Keats, similarly considered that the appreciation of literature—all literature—required the exercise of "Negative Capability, that is when man is capable of being in uncertainties, mysteries, doubts, without any irritable reaching after fact and reason." Ironically, Keats criticized Coleridge himself for being deficient in negative capability: "Coleridge, for instance, would let go by a fine isolated verisimilitude caught from the penetralium of mystery, from being incapable of remaining content with half knowledge." Yet Coleridge was a good Christian, and Keats was not.

If, however, poets are, or should be, "content with half knowledge," scientists never have been, and for much of the time during the last few centuries, they felt sure that they had hit upon a technique for dissolving all mysteries and resolving all doubts and uncertainties. So did many non-scientists. The prevailing attitude was expressed in the eighteenth century by another poet, Alexander Pope. Pope was a Roman Catholic, but nothing could be further from the way his Church had looked upon the threat science posed to religion only about a hundred years earlier (through the likes of Galileo) than this reverential couplet about the pre-eminent scientist of Pope's own day:

Nature, and Nature's laws, lay hid in night;
God said, "Let Newton be!" and all was light.

Yet in the twentieth century, the tremendous confidence in itself that science had enjoyed for several hundred years was shaken by the discovery—at first resisted but ultimately triumphant—that our universe had originated with a "big bang." This seemed so uncomfortably close to the account of creation in Genesis that the cosmologists angrily denounced the "vulgarity" of such an association. And yet the more imaginative of them were bothered by their inability to figure out what lay behind the big bang. One eminent member of the scientific fraternity, Robert Jastrow, was so bothered that in 1992 he wrote a book, *God and the Astronomers,* unhappily concluding (since he was a self-declared atheist) that "It is not a matter of another year, another decade of work, another measurement, or another theory; at this moment it seems as though science will never be able to raise the curtain on the mystery of creation."

Scientists, it appeared, even the atheists among them, were being tossed into the same boat as believers in God. The scientists too were stuck with impenetrable mysteries and questions that they might never be able to answer, and in an arena—the arena of physical nature—whose secrets they had always assumed the human mind possessed the power to uncover in full.

Perhaps, given the new humility that has been forced upon the scientists, the classical prophets will finally have something to say even to them. Such as:

Who hath measured the waters in the hollow of his hand, and meted out heaven with the span, and comprehended the dust of the earth in a measure, and weighed the mountains in scales, and the hills in a balance?

To supplement this verse from the Second Isaiah, I trespass once more beyond the strict boundaries of my subject and turn—where else?—to the Book of Job. For it is in Job that we have the *locus classicus* of God's response to the question of why the righteous suffer. Toward the end of that book, God, after reminding Job that he was not present when He "laid the foundations of the earth," spends four incomparable chapters (38–41) detailing much else of what Job neither knows nor understands:

Or who shut up the sea with doors, when it brake forth, as if it had issued out of the womb? When I made the cloud the garment thereof, and thick darkness a swaddling-band for it, And brake up for it my decreed place, and set bars and doors, And said, Hitherto shalt thou come, but no further: and here shall thy proud waves be stayed? Hast

thou commanded the morning since thy days; and caused the dayspring
to know his place?

As with the sea and the morning, so with everything else, of which I give
only a tiny sample:

Have the gates of death been opened unto thee? or hast thou seen the
doors of the shadow of death? . . . Where is the way where light
dwelleth? and as for darkness, where is the place thereof? . . . Knowest
thou it, because thou wast then born? or because the number of thy
days is great?

Pondering these verses, I thought of the concluding sentence of Jastrow's
book:

For the scientist who has lived by his faith in the power of reason, the
story ends like a bad dream. He has scaled the mountains of ignorance;
he is about to conquer the highest peak; as he pulls himself over the
final rock, he is greeted by a band of theologians who have been sitting
there for centuries.

It would more likely be a band of classical prophets than a band of theologians, but never mind: the point is unaffected. And it is, I repeat, that scientists are
now constrained to admit—just as the classical prophets and the Book of Job tell
us—that the natural world in its own fashion is as mysterious and impenetrable
as the human condition with all its attendant moral perplexities. As mortal
beings we are imprisoned within severe limits of knowledge and understanding.
Working within those limits, we can go very far, as indeed science has done in
the past four centuries, and will continue doing. But the limits will always be
there, and we will never have any choice other than to live with them and
within them as best we can.

In this regard, neither the Second Isaiah nor any other classical prophet nor
the Book of Job draws a distinction between the moral and physical spheres. As
we do not know how the world was created and can only glimpse the minuscule
portion of its secrets that our minds have been endowed by God to uncover, so
it is with the human moral condition. The Second Isaiah:

Who hath directed the Spirit of the LORD, or being his counselor hath
taught him? With whom took he counsel, and who instructed him, and
taught him in the path of judgment, and taught him knowledge, and
shewed to him the way of understanding?

And if " . . . there is no searching of his understanding," how then can we "command" Him "concerning the work of [His] hands"?

On this aspect of the prophetic teaching, in my opinion, Heschel's gloss gets it right. Living, he writes, with

> a divine wisdom which defies human understanding, those who question Him expect the Lord to adjust His thought to their thoughts, His design to their conceptions. The prophet maintains that those who question Him try to enlighten Him; that those who contend with Him presume to instruct Him in "the path of justice" [KJV's "judgment"]. . . .
> [But] the overwhelming grandeur of His wisdom as manifested in the realm of nature should inspire humility when reflecting about His ways in the realm of history.

Or, I would add, morality.

Rashi, the leading Jewish exegete of the Middle Ages, took the group of verses I have just quoted from the Second Isaiah as a sufficient explanation of why the righteous suffer and the wicked prosper. Having mischievously poked a little impious fun at the non-answer—the assertion that we are incapable of arriving at one—I will now reverse myself and announce that it has begun to satisfy me as well. Nor does the inability to solve the problem undermine my conviction that our moral lives are governed by law. Why should it, when the corresponding assumption about the physical universe made by science remains—and properly so—intact despite its own growing awareness that it will never uncover all the secrets of the physical universe?

I FULLY RECOGNIZE that the argument I have—through the agency of the classical prophets—been striving to develop about law is so general and so abstract that it tells us nothing about content. Nor does it provide any guidance whatever on the competing claims and demands of the religions stemming from the Hebrew Bible (let alone religions like Hinduism and Buddhism that do not). And it does not bear at all on the rationales by which the various denominations of each of these religions have gone about picking and choosing among the ordinances and statutes that the classical prophets exhort us to observe.

Yet even by itself the idea that the moral realm is governed by law becomes something more than an empty abstraction when placed against the background of a culture that has for all practical purposes denied or repudiated that idea. The technical term for the denial or repudiation of law is "antinomianism," and it is antinomianism by which, more than any other single force, our culture has been shaped for some time, and is still being shaped today. But there are other names for antinomianism. The one under which the classical prophets so relentlessly fought it was idolatry. The one the historians give it is paganism or polytheism. Today we know it as relativism.

To a degree, nothing could be simpler than the opposition between monotheism and polytheism—one God against many gods, or "traditional values" as opposed to "different strokes for different folks." But complexities proliferate here of which account must be taken.

So far as the ancient world is concerned, I am prepared to concede that the paganism of the Near East could be more formidable and more culturally sophisticated than the classical prophets, in their zealous polemics against it, were ever willing to admit. (Jon D. Levenson has remarked that using the Hebrew Bible as a source for learning about paganism is like trying to learn about Judaism from the New Testament, where the parent religion is comparably misrepresented by polemical zeal.) And even if that were not true of Mesopotamia, there would still be pagan civilizations like that of Greece in the fifth century B.C.E., or of China and India even earlier, to prove the point.

Nor was polytheism always as conducive to evil as the classical prophets made out: the ancient pagan world had its own highly advanced rules, of which the Code of Hammurabi is only the best-known, and it could also boast great literary achievements like the Babylonian epic of Gilgamesh. On the other hand, the practice of sacrificing children to the gods was enough in its own right to cancel out a multitude of virtues, while conversely, the fierce opposition to it by the God of Israel alone sufficed to establish the moral superiority of the religion of Israel.

Yet the main difference did not turn on this or that practice—not even one so horrendous as child sacrifice—or this or that ordinance. Indeed, we know that in their earliest days the Israelites syncretistically borrowed many things from the surrounding cultures that were not always strictly consonant with the will of God. But the borrowing they did must not be exaggerated either. Most of what the Israelites took was transformed and transmuted by assimilation into the revolutionary new religion of the one and only true God, who—in an even more radical innovation—was invisible and could not be pictured or represented in statues or other images.

Robert M. Seltzer, after compiling a long catalogue of such borrowings, concludes:

> Compared to the epics of other peoples, the biblical narratives underwent drastic reorientation. . . . Absent are myths of the birth of the gods, their rivalries and feuds, their sexual relations, their annual cycles of death and resurrection. . . . Biblical thought eliminates the notion, found in many pagan mythologies, of a primordial, inescapable Fate to which

man and gods are subject, a Fate that can, at times, be manipulated
through incantation, divination, and wisdom. Instead, the Bible is preoccupied with the moral condition of mankind. . . . Perhaps the overar-
ching theme of the Bible is the tension between God's will and
man's. . . . As a result, the basic theological conceptions of sin and faith,
holiness and redemption, justice and repentance are reworked and given
new significance.

But the main difference that flowed from the Israelites' revolutionary concept of God was the corollary that there was only one source of law rather than
many, or even only two: "I form the light, and create darkness: I make peace, and
create evil: I the LORD do all these things," God declares through the Second
Isaiah. Some commentators think that, living under the rule of Persia, the Second Isaiah was boldly giving the lie to its dualistic religion—according to which
there were two warring divinities, one of good and light (Ahura Mazda) and one
of evil and darkness (Ahriman); others interpret the verse as just another repudiation of all polytheistic religions.* But under either reading, the meaning is that
there can be no rival power to God.

The one true set of laws, having been revealed not merely to a special caste
of priests but to every Israelite, is—in the words of the key passage from
Deuteronomy to which I keep circling back—neither in the heavens above nor
beyond the sea; it is in the mouth and in the heart. And in Jeremiah's codicil to
this great and overriding and essential principle of the religion of Israel, it will
literally be inscribed in all our hearts, so that we will no longer have to learn it
by instruction from others or from books. The "we" here is Israel, but through
Israel, it will ultimately be inscribed in the hearts of all the peoples in all the
nations of the world.

In the language of today, this says that the moral law is instinctual (Bellow's
"we know, we know, we know"). We are still as free as ever to violate it, and most
of us do violate it in one way or another every day. But there are inexorable consequences, even if they are not always immediately apparent: the punishment is
not always directly traceable to the sin nor (by certain standards) does the punishment always fit the crime. Something—physical or spiritual or both—goes
wrong inside. This is what I think William Blake was expressing symbolically in
one of his greatest short poems:

---

*Whichever way it is taken, the verse is unpalatable to Orthodox Jews (and not them alone).
Son: "The term *evil* here denotes calamity and suffering. These serve as means of punishment for
the sins of man. Moral evil, on the other hand, does not proceed from God, but is the result of
man's actions. In the *Hebrew Prayer Book* . . . the phrase is changed to 'create all things.'"

O Rose, thou art sick:
The invisible worm
That flies in the night,
In the howling storm,
Has found out thy bed
Of crimson joy,
And his dark secret love
Does thy life destroy.

The antinomians or the relativists of today do not see life as the classical prophets did, or as Blake in his own highly idiosyncratic fashion also did (although he, alas, was not above flirting with antinomianism himself, which is why he could say that that "all true poets"—not just Milton in *Paradise Lost*—were of "the Devil's party").* The most radical among the antinomians among us now resemble those of the First Isaiah's own contemporaries about whom the prophet lamented: "Woe unto them that call evil good, and good evil; that put darkness for light, and light for darkness; that put bitter for sweet, and sweet for bitter!"

Inverting everything is the key to antinomianism, reflected among Christians, for example, in the black mass celebrated by worshipers of the Devil. This was an obscene parody of the Catholic Mass, in which everything was turned on its head—the Lord's prayer was read backward, the crucifix was hung upside down so that the figure of Christ was on the bottom rather than the top, and so on. The rites would also frequently involve sexual orgies that not only defied the law through indiscriminate coupling, but also featured anal intercourse, especially between men and women. Why? Because if the commandment of God was " . . . Be fruitful and multiply . . . ," the commandment of the Devil must be the opposite—"Be sterile and diminish." The way to fulfill this commandment to be sterile was through inverting the sexual act itself by directing it into the channel of excretion and waste, signifying death, instead of the channel of propagation and birth, signifying life. (A twentieth-century American writer, Norman Mailer, has traced the same line between anal intercourse and the Devil in some of his stories and novels.)

Possibly black masses are still being conducted in secret meeting places. But the desecration of Christian symbols need no longer be hidden away. It has come out into the open in mainstream museums and galleries where a crucifix can be shown floating in the artist's urine, or dung can be smeared over a painting of the Holy Family, or the Virgin Mary can be portrayed in a graphically erotic pose.

---

*But with at least equal plausibility, the tables could be turned on Blake. He may have written "Proverbs of Hell," but I would maintain that he, like Orwell or the early atheist Jewish pioneers to the Land of Israel, were of "God's party without knowing it."

Among Jews, an antinomian movement arose in the seventeenth century
C.E. after the disillusionment that set in when Sabbatai Zevi, who had been
acclaimed by millions as the Messiah, converted to Islam. Those who clung to
their faith in him in spite of his conversion believed that his advent had abrogated the old commandments and that the only way to observe the law was now
to break it. Sin became holiness, and holiness became sin. (As the greatest of all
antinomians in literature, Milton's Satan, declares in *Paradise Lost:* "Evil, be thou
my good!")

In the 1960s, another wave of naked antinomianism swept through the West,
but as was appropriate to the age, it burst out within the secular rather than the
religious world. Yet it had religious roots in that, under the name of the counterculture, it attempted to invert the moral order of "bourgeois" or middle-class
society which had itself grown out of the biblical tradition (not for nothing did
a song by the Rolling Stones entitled "Sympathy for the Devil" become one of
its signature anthems).

As a precondition for bringing that order down, the counterculture openly
declared that to live by the dictates of middle-class morality was to condemn
oneself to a walking death; to come alive (or, as it were, to be resurrected), it was
necessary to shake off responsibility—the shackles of work, marriage, and par-
enthood.

This new dispensation had its own prophets. There was Jack Kerouac, who
preached going—in the words that form the title of his most influential novel—
"on the road" in quest of endless sexual adventure. There was the poet Allen
Ginsberg, who exhorted his followers to "scatter ... semen freely to whomever
come who may." There was Timothy Leary (a former Harvard professor of psy-
chology), who called on the young to "drop out" of society and immerse themselves in psychedelic drugs.

In a related inversion, madness was glorified by Ginsberg, and in holding it
to be the true sanity as against the delusions of rationality, he was given professional backing by the psychiatrist R. D. Laing and many thousands of others. The
novelist William Seward Burroughs, one of Ginsberg's mentors, joined him in
proclaiming that homosexuality was superior to "straight" sex (women, Burroughs instructed Ginsberg, "were extraterrestrial agents sent by enemies to
weaken the male species"), and Ginsberg himself, though not so misogynistic,
sanctified homosexuality and beatified its practitioners in "Howl" and elsewhere
as "saints." And almost as though they were determined not to omit any of the
inversions decried by the First Isaiah, they all set about to redefine darkness as
light and light as darkness by celebrating drugs as the road not to hallucination
but to illumination and an expanded consciousness of the cosmos.

Confronted with an earlier and much milder wave of antinomianism that
swept through England in the two decades between the First and Second World
Wars, George Orwell (again demonstrating how a man who, like King Cyrus of

Persia, did not know God could still do His work) remarked: "The fact to which we have got to cling, as to a lifebelt, is that it is possible to be a normal decent person and yet to be fully alive." Orwell was also among the few who understood that Communist totalitarianism represented the incarnation of the antinomian principle of inversion in politics, as witness the slogans he invented for the Party in his novel *Nineteen Eighty-Four:* "WAR IS PEACE/FREEDOM IS SLAVERY/IGNORANCE IS STRENGTH."

This particular strain of the antinomian virus comes and goes, and the outbreak of the 1960s—leaving behind it a trail of destroyed lives, deep intellectual confusion, and gravely wounded institutions (notably the universities)—set off a powerful recoil. But while waiting for an opportunity to show itself in all its nakedness again, it remained active in subtler and more insidious guises.

As THE TWENTIETH CENTURY gave way to the twenty-first, the most prominent and pervasive of these guises was precisely the relativistic philosophy that—rather than brazenly calling evil good and good evil—professed to discern no basis at all for judging between them. There were, in this view, no absolutes, no constants, no fixed or unchanging points of moral reference. All "values" were derived from social conditioning, and they changed as conditions changed. What was a virtue yesterday could become a vice today, which meant that neither virtue nor vice could be taken as real. No society's conventional moral standards had any basis for asserting superiority over another's, and tolerance was therefore the only rational stance.

However, moral judgments being almost impossible to avoid in practice—and even in scrupulous philosophical discourse—the words "appropriate" and "inappropriate" came into wide currency as acceptable substitutes for "right" and "wrong" or "good" and "evil." But only among sincere relativists—usually well-intentioned and even kindly people, who performed the same function Lenin notoriously assigned to the liberal fellow-travelers of the Soviet Union. Not realizing the true character of what they were supporting, and helping to spread their own illusions about the Communist regime, these liberals were in Lenin's heartlessly icy gaze "useful idiots."

The "useful idiots" of the turn of the twentieth century were those who failed to grasp that the appeal to tolerance was only a means of further subverting whatever remnants of the traditional moral outlook had managed to survive the onslaught of the 1960s. The strategic objective of the new antinomians was to smuggle their own exactly contrary notions of good and evil into the culture and then to enthrone these inversions as a new and regnant orthodoxy.

Sometimes, however, they slipped, or were prematurely dragged, by the logic of this very process, into a more open display of their aims than was tactically prudent in a climate of opinion that—for all its deep confusions—had not yet reached a new stage of receptivity to open antinomianism such as had developed in the late 1950s.

As an indication that the culture was not yet fully prepared for another all-out onslaught, resistance began being mounted toward the end of the twentieth century to what was labeled "political correctness" or "PC." This was an imprecise designation, since most of the issues involved belonged more to the moral than to the political realm. But the label stuck. The new *soi-disant* champions of tolerance had tipped their hand, and what they were up to could no longer be convincingly concealed.

Why should this have happened? The reason was that the new antinomians had grown heady with success. Wherever their writ extended—the leading universities above all, but also the major media of information and entertainment—they had done very well in holding the line against many of the traditional attitudes and ideas that were threatening to rise up again from the ruins of the sixties: about the nature of women, about the qualities of men, about sexual freedom, and about marriage and family.

Not content with so large an achievement, they then impatiently pushed to delegitimize these traditional attitudes and ideas altogether. Students and professors who refused to toe the line were punished by suspension or sentenced to undergo "sensitivity training" that resembled nothing so much as a gentler version of the "reeducation camps" to which American prisoners of war had been sent in Korea and then Vietnam. "Incorrect" points of view on these matters were stigmatized as "hate speech," and for all practical purposes not only censured but censored. In some jurisdictions, they were even made a criminal offense.

So ugly was all this, and so "chilling" to the tolerance (and the freedom) the cultural commissars affected to cherish, that it provoked a backlash. Yet not even the bad odor exuded by "political correctness" prevented its spread through the institutionalization of its mandates by the courts and other agencies of government. It also got a little help from "voluntary" programs adopted under pressure by private organizations that were trying to fend off boycotts or lawsuits or punitive state action.

Nor did the derision of "PC" do much to slow the progress of "deconstructionism" and "multiculturalism," the two main weapons employed by the new antinomians. Deconstructionism was a slippery school of thought and difficult to define with precision, but its central aim was to deny the existence of what we normally consider objective reality or truth. Hence it served as the intellectual face of the new antinomianism. Multiculturalism, similarly, was the cultural face of the same tendency, since it based itself on the proposition that no standard existed by which, say, Aztec civilization could be judged inferior to the civilization of the West.

Here, too, however, the same hypocrisy was at work that escaped the notice of the "useful idiots" in other parts of the forest. While pretending to think that all cultures were equal, the multiculturalists were actually exempting our own from any such benevolent toleration. We preened ourselves on being advanced, they sneered, but in reality (an entity which, though in their theory non-existent, could be invoked at the polemical convenience of these putative disbelievers in it) we were racist and sexist and homophobic and despoilers of the environment.

The practical program flowing from multiculturalism (and constituting its political agenda) was "diversity." This sounded as though it meant ensuring, in the spirit of tolerance, that every sector of society be composed of a great variety of racial and ethnic groups. But on this issue, too, the antinomian cat was inadvertently and prematurely let out of the bag, as it became blatantly obvious that another inversion was being pulled off. For what "diversity" dictated in the realm of ideas or opinions or attitudes was its polar antithesis: complete uniformity. Even blacks or other minority groups were ruled out of the calculus of diversity if they were conservative, and the not altogether invisible sign hung out in the window read: the religious need not apply.

Then there was "environmentalism." No doubt many who supported this movement were moved by a desire to limit industrial pollution, to protect the untamed wilderness from being entirely exploited for human use, and to save animals in the wild from extinction. No doubt the movement even did some good (along with an equivalent or greater amount of harm by preventing various measures that would have resulted in greater supplies of much-needed energy).

But what mainly interests me in this context is not the politics or the economics of environmentalism. It is the spiritual element buried within this movement. This was in its own way as antinomian as the other legacies of the counterculture that successfully underwent mutations enabling them to survive in a less hospitable climate. In the case of environmentalism, the antinomian strain grew out of the counterculture's assault on technology with its contempt for the workings of man. To this it appended a kind of nature worship that even involved an attack on "speciesism," or the assumption that human beings were superior to animals. Here, in the repudiation of the dominion of man over the animals granted by God in the Book of Genesis, the religious—or rather the anti-religious—impulse reared its antinomian head.

BUT PROBABLY THE MOST IMPORTANT of all the legacies of the antinomianism of the counterculture was the women's movement. For prudential political purposes, "Women's Lib" presented itself in a sanitized version as nothing more radical than a demand for simple equality—equal rights, equal access to the world of work, equal pay, and so on. Millions of people, men and women alike, bought into this description of its agenda. On the surface it was almost impossible to oppose in principle and it seemed at a minimum reasonable and at best desirable.

What remained hidden to these millions was the antinomianism that lurked in the depths of the feminist movement. Here the antinomian impulse expressed itself in a determination to establish that the differences between the sexes were rooted not in the immutable laws of nature but in the changeable laws of society: they were "social constructs." That men and women had—as a congresswoman once said—different "plumbing" did not imply that they were designed for different "roles." Biology was not destiny.

Even if I were to allow that some part of this argument had some validity, and even if I were further to assent that the women's movement had some good to its credit, I would still insist that the antinomianism it did so much to further was in the long run far more significant and far more harmful. Through the unhappy confusion about the relations between men and women it—shall we say?—engendered, still more poison was injected into an already sufficiently poisonous situation. The movement also did damage to institutions like the military, forcing them to lower standards of training and discipline in order to accommodate the—dare I say?—natural inferiority in bodily strength of women to men.

More telling than any of this, however, was the plight of children under the feminist dispensation. Has there ever been a society or a culture—or any sector of the animal world so admired by the new antinomians—in which the needs of the very young were subordinated to those of their mothers? That this most radical of all possible inversions of the natural order of things should have been represented as good for the children only stoked the antinomian fire with yet more hypocrisy or self-delusion.

Like the other manifestations of antinomianism I am looking at here, the feminist one had its roots in the repudiation of a fundamental principle of the Hebrew Bible as enunciated in the Book of Genesis: " . . . male and female created He them." And something similar was at work in the deepest recesses of the gay-rights movement as well. Like the feminism by which it was politically preceded and encouraged, the gay-rights movement presented itself as a quest for simple equality, even to the point of demanding that homosexuals be permitted to marry. But like Women's Lib, too, the gay-rights movement was at bottom a rebellion against the same biblical verse that only yesterday seemed universally self-evident. Opponents jeered that "God created Adam and Eve, not Adam and Steve," but crude though it may have been, this crack got to the heart of the movement's sanitized claim. For if Women's Lib contended that the differences between men and women were a matter of social conditioning and not of natural law, the gay-rights movement vehemently insisted that being erotically attracted to members of one's own sex was also no less in accord with natural law than heterosexuality.

When it suited them, moreover, gay-rights activists (before AIDS put a damper on the promiscuity that had been rampant among male homosexuals) were wont to proclaim that "the joys of gay sex" were far greater than those available to "straights." Feminists, too, were perfectly capable of claiming that women were superior to men—more sensitive, less aggressive—while in the same breath asserting that all they wanted was to be recognized as equal and given equal treatment.

EXPLORING ALL THIS GROUND, we catch a glimpse of how the paganism of the ancient Near East against which the classical prophets fought so hard managed to stage a great comeback toward the end of the twentieth century—and in the very heartland of the civilization in which it seemed to have been vanquished for all time by the classical prophets so many centuries before.

Item: Paganism, with its multiplicity of gods, was by definition relativistic, and could sometimes be tolerant in action. But more often its relativism was just as capable as its latter-day descendant of turning into an orthodoxy to be forced on others, usually by the sword. To be sure, Christianity and Islam—both monotheistic religions—also did this, but when they did it, they never pretended to be relativistic or tolerant. As for the classical prophets, we have already noted that, with the tentative exceptions of Jeremiah and Habakkuk, they rarely made any effort to convert the pagan peoples, and certainly not by the sword. The typical attitude was shared even by the militant Micah: "For all people will walk every one in the name of his god, and we will walk in the name of the LORD our God for ever and ever."

Item: Paganism often (always?) involved the worship of nature: trees, mountains, the sea, and animals. Even when the Egyptian Pharaoh Akhenaton in the fourteenth century B.C.E. approached what some consider a monotheistic outlook, it was the sun that became the ruler of the divine pantheon.

Item: Paganism often (always?) sanctioned sexual promiscuity.

Item: Paganism often (always?) involved the readiness to sacrifice one's own children for one's own good.

In touching on this radioactively charged subject, I am not insinuating that parents today literally put their own young offspring "through the fire." But I cannot shake off the information pulled together by the social critic Mary Eberstadt about the condition of children in what (alluding to a highly popular film of the 1990s) she called "Home-Alone America."

What this information revealed was that as more and more mothers went off to their jobs (often *not* out of economic necessity but because they preferred being in the workplace to being at home with the kids), the children wound up paying the price. As William Damon, one student of adolescent behavior quoted by Eberstadt, observed in the mid-1990s: "Practically all the indicators of youth health and behavior have declined year by year for well over a generation. None has improved."

Damon was talking about poor performance in school, drug abuse, early sexual activity, sexually transmitted diseases, and the like. ("The litany," he said, "is now so well known that it is losing its power to shock.") But the most relevant statistic for us in tracking the revival of pagan practices is that between 1960 and 1990—a period not of poverty but of *prosperity*—the suicide rate among teenagers rose more than threefold. Breaking these numbers down: for girls aged ten to fourteen the suicide rate between 1979 and 1988 went up 27 percent, and for boys the number was a staggering 71 percent. Eberstadt also quoted another student of the subject, Robert D. Putnam: "Americans born and raised in the 1970's and 1980's were three to four times more likely to commit suicide as people that age had been at mid-century."

Eberstadt argued that there was a causative link between the abandonment of so many children to their own devices and the suicide rate among them. Seeing it as the sign of a revived paganism, I would say that instead of being put "through the fire" for the sake of their mothers' "needs," they were in effect putting themselves through the fire. This was not exactly a distinction without a difference, but it hovered on the brink.

While I am on the subject, I think I would be remiss—especially in a book about the struggle between monotheism and paganism in the ancient Near East—if I failed to mention a much more literal practice of child sacrifice that returned to plague modern Israel toward the end of the twentieth century and the beginning of the twenty-first.

In the war the Palestinian Arabs were conducting against the Jewish state, they adopted the tactic of sending their own children to provoke Israeli troops by throwing stones or molotov cocktails at them, in the expectation that these children would get killed by return fire under the gaze of television cameras. The motive of the Palestinians was to gain the sympathy of the world by exposing the Israelis as heartless murderers. But to put their own children "through the fire" for such a purpose was not only to offer them as a sacrifice to the idol of their own political dreams; it also—as the classical prophets always taught that idolatry did—flowed from and served an evil end: here, the destruction of the Jewish state. The irony is that some Palestinian parents committed this abomination in the name of Islam, which is, if anything, even more strictly monotheistic in its theology than Judaism, and even more hard-line in its prohibition of idolatry.

Another abomination committed in the name of Islam around the same time was a form of terrorism involving suicide bombing, the most spectacular example of which was the murderous attacks of September 11, 2001, on the World Trade Center in New York and the Pentagon in Washington. Following these attacks, strenuous efforts were made to represent such actions as contrary to the teaching of Islam. This may well have been true, at least in theory. Yet very far from every Muslim cleric or academic expert on Islam agreed even on that issue. And it was a plain fact that huge numbers of approving sermons were delivered from mosques throughout the vast Muslim world, while hordes of ordinary believers cheered and danced for joy in celebrating the terrorists as martyrs who would be rewarded with a special place in Paradise, complete with a harem of seventy-two "black-eyed virgins." Did the terrorists, then, have a legitimate right to speak and act in the name of Islam—as so many of their clerical supporters maintained—or were they "hijacking" a religion and distorting it for political purposes?

BECAUSE THE ANSWERS to these questions are beyond the scope of our discussion, let me now return to the classical prophets. As we know, their main target was not paganism as such: it was idolatry. The two were hard to separate, in that such "abominations" of paganism as child sacrifice were committed in the service of the gods before whose graven images their worshipers bowed. But to the classical prophets, idolatry was an evil in and of itself as well as in its practical consequences. Therefore, having surveyed the manifestations of pagan thought and practice in the contemporary world, I want now to peer at that world as the classical prophets did at theirs—through the lens of idolatry—in order to bring certain sectors of the picture more sharply into focus.

In those sectors, the terrain is less ideologically and emotionally treacherous, since many who would angrily reject much of what I have just been associating with a resurgence of paganism would on reflection probably, and perhaps even enthusiastically, embrace the proposition that idolatry is rampant in America today.

Sir Francis Bacon identified four classes of idols in the England of the seventeenth century. His were forces "which beset men's minds" and prevented clear thinking about nature. "To these . . . I have assigned names,—calling the first class *Idols of the Tribe;* the second, *Idols of the Cave;* the third, *Idols of the Marketplace,* the fourth, *Idols of the Theatre*" (italics in the original). Virtually all liberals, as well as many conservatives, would fix on an equivalent number in the America of the new millennium. Their four would of course be different from Bacon's. They would say that no matter how large a proportion of the American people may claim or imagine that they believe in the God of the Bible, or in Jesus, what they really worship are the gods of Money and Power and Celebrity and Status.

It would be hard to disagree that money and power and celebrity and status are of great importance to Americans (though whether they are more important to Americans than to anyone else is another matter). But it was not the desire for, or the possession of, things of this nature that the classical prophets were excoriating when they denounced idolatry. As Israelites infused by the ethos of the living traditions that later came in written form to comprise the Hebrew Bible, they never doubted that worldly goods were a blessing and a reward for fidelity to God's will.

To them an idol was something altogether different. Supposedly the image of a god, it actually was "dumb," an inanimate statue that men fashioned of stone or wood or precious metals with—in Habakkuk's words—" . . . no breath at all in the midst of it." Going more deeply into the same idea, the First Isaiah sneered that an idol was nothing more than " . . . the work of their own hands, that which their own fingers have made," and he marveled that it was to this that " . . . the mean man boweth down . . . ," and even " . . . the great man humbleth himself. . . ." A third theme was introduced by Jeremiah. Those who forsook God " . . . and served strange gods . . ." were " . . . foolish people, and without understanding; which have eyes, and see not; which have ears and hear not." Ezekiel picked up the same theme, in almost the same language: "Son of man, thou dwellest in the midst of a rebellious house, which have eyes to see, and see not; they have ears to hear, and hear not. . . ." It is an astonishing idea, this, that the makers of idols become *indistinguishable from the idols they have made.*

All the classical prophets composed variations on these three themes, sometimes poking fun at the absurdity of idol worship, sometimes shaking their heads in puzzlement at it, and sometimes recoiling in disgust. But it was the author of Psalm 115 who brought the three themes together and orchestrated them into a single great poem:

> Their idols are silver and gold, the work of men's hands. They have mouths but they speak not; eyes have they, but they see not: They have ears, but they hear not: noses have they but they smell not: They have hands, but they handle not: feet have they, but they walk not: neither speak they through their throat. *They that make them are like unto them; so is every one that trusteth in them.* [Italics added.]

As always in such passages, the contrast between the dead idol and the living God was underlined or reverberated whisperingly like the "still, small voice" that came to Elijah at Mt. Horeb/Sinai, and always those who trusted in Him were posed against those who trusted "in them," and became "like unto them." A brilliant example was the Second Isaiah's assemblage of all the images associated in the prophetic literature with the contest between idolatry and fidelity to God:

> And I will bring the blind by a way that they knew not; I will lead them in paths that they have not known: I will make darkness light before them, and crooked things straight. These things will I do unto them, and not forsake them.

But, he goes on, "they . . . that trust in graven images, that say to the molten images, Ye are our gods" will be "turned back" and will remain as deaf and blind as before.

Deaf and blind, that is, to life itself, and to the blessings available for the taking to eyes that could see and ears that could hear and legs that could walk. These blessings were denied to the worshipers of idols because (as we learned in studying the two Isaiahs) in bowing down to the work of their own hands, what they were worshiping was *themselves;* and in worshiping themselves, in trusting in themselves as though they were gods, they not only failed to acquire superhuman status, but they lost even such powers as were granted to human beings, becoming as dead to the world as the idols they constructed.

My thesis, in short, is that to the classical prophets idolatry amounted to self-deification, the delusion that we humans could become " . . . as gods." This was the same delusion that resulted in the expulsion from Eden. By disobeying God and eating from the tree of knowledge, Adam and Eve acquired the awareness of good and evil, and the price of that awareness, as God had warned, was that they, and the entire human race destined to stem from them, would become mortal.

In retelling the story John Milton wrote that he was singing

> *Of Man's First Disobedience, and the Fruit*
> *Of that Forbidden Tree whose mortal taste*
> *Brought Death into the World*
> *And all our woe. . . .*

Being an English Puritan of the seventeenth century with a strong feeling for the Old Testament, Milton adopted the same interpretation of the sin of Adam and Eve as Jews did: it was disobedience, not (as in the Roman Catholic view) pride. But being a Christian, Milton also looked forward to our restoration to Eden through "one greater Man" of whose advent he would later sing.

Yet while no such possibility of returning to Eden was offered by the classical prophets, neither did they attribute "all our woe" to the knowledge of good and evil. According to them, the human race, once possessed of the power to tell the difference between good and evil, was also endowed with the resources to act on this knowledge. To do good was to obey the Law ordained by God, which would bring us not woe but the blessings of life, even if that life must some day end. To do evil was to disobey or altogether deny the validity of His Law, and it was by thus reenacting the sin of Adam and Eve that we called down woe upon our heads, even if it might appear otherwise to the naked eye.

In the Ten Commandments, the primary violation of the law is idolatry ("I am the LORD thy God. . . . Thou shalt have no other gods before me. Thou shalt not make unto thee any graven image . . ."), and if I am right about the classical prophets, they are telling us that idolatry is the cult of self. In politics, as I have already observed, this species of idolatry has been the prime progenitor of the delusion that we humans are capable of creating a perfect world—a delusion out of which in the past century alone mountains of corpses have been amassed and oceans of blood have been spilled. But we are also taught by the classical prophets that the same form of idolatry is what robs us as individuals of the capacity to reap the blessings of life by deadening our senses and leaving us with eyes that are blind and ears that are deaf and noses into which no sweet scent can penetrate.

It was to this lesson that, in the heady days of the late 1800s, Walt Whitman, the self-appointed bard of a younger America, threw out a bold challenge: "I celebrate myself, and sing myself. . . . I dote on myself, there is that lot of me and all so luscious. . . . And nothing, not God, is greater to one than one's self is." It is here that we finally and definitively come to the true idol of the American tribe: not Money or Power or Celebrity or Status, but Self.

In the early twentieth century, the English novelist D. H. Lawrence compared the kind of infatuation with Self celebrated by Whitman to falling from the hands of God into a bottomless pit. (Though no believer in the Bible—in fact, he was attracted to certain forms of paganism—Lawrence was in this instance, like Blake and Orwell, but more deliberately, joining the party of God and doing His work.) And indeed, since Whitman let loose his "barbaric yawp," we have been exposed to the decidedly less "luscious" side of what the social critic Christopher Lasch, in the late twentieth century, characterized as a "culture of narcissism."

Narcissism: it is a word that derives not from monotheistic Israel but from polytheistic Greece. In the time of the classical prophets, these two cultures had very little if any contact. Yet if ancient Israel borrowed elements of the paganism of Mesopotamia and adapted them to its own purposes (a process the classical prophets never acknowledged, except where it bred infidelity to God), with Greece it was a matter not so much of influence as of perceptions that were sufficiently similar to eventuate in the merger that would later supply the foundations of Western civilization.

In the idea behind the story of Narcissus—the mythological figure who, having fallen in love with his own reflection in a pool, drowns while trying to capture it—we have one instance of such parallel perception. Another is the Greek concept of *hubris,* the overweening pride that resembles the self-deification that the classical prophets saw in idolatry. And there are many more examples, especially in the words of Socrates as recorded in the Dialogues of Plato, and in the philosophy of Aristotle. Socrates and Plato and Aristotle may have been pagans, but they were no antinomians, and I cannot help feeling that their entry onto the stage of history in the middle of the fifth century B.C.E., almost at the very moment that the classical prophets left it, was an uncanny coincidence.

IF, AS THE CLASSICAL PROPHETS ASSUMED, we are all now living the only life we will ever have, there is no need to belabor the abiding and overriding importance of what they have to say about the idolatry of self and how it deprives us of the chance or the ability to live that life to the full. But even on the assumption that another life awaits us when this one is done, what the classical prophets have to teach remains a superb pointer to the road from here to there. It is not the road that the voice ordered the Second Isaiah to build through the dark and dangerous wilderness separating Babylon from Zion. But I see no great incongruity in naming it after him. On, then, to the Isaian highway.

Alas, nowadays it will have to beat its path through those new fronts that have opened up in the war this anonymous prophet and his fellows waged against paganism and idolatry for three hundred glorious years. Now, as then, the battle will have to be fought first and foremost within ourselves and then in the world of ideas around us. And now as then, it will have to be conducted in the spirit in which the classical prophets themselves conducted it, and in which we are commanded by the book of Deuteronomy to love the Lord our God: with all our hearts, with all our souls, and with all our might.

And those among us for whom God does not exist? I presume to suggest that even, or indeed especially, they are called upon to answer the summons to battle sounded by the ancient prophetic trumpet of Israel. Because unless we all commit ourselves to the struggle for our own civilization, it will, like Jerusalem in the days of Jeremiah twenty-five hundred years ago, wind up being sapped from within by the insidious antinomian workings of the new paganism, and it will then become vulnerable to sacking from without.

At the same time, our own lives, and the lives of our children, and the lives of our children's children (unto the fourth generation?), will be sacrificed—yes, sacrificed—to the idols of self-deification we ourselves have fashioned. Unless, that is, we smash these idols first and cast their broken pieces to " ... the moles and to the bats."

The classical prophets always clung to the hope that the doom they envisaged could be averted by repentance. So can it be with us. But only if we still have ears to hear what they are saying, and only if we—and again I include nonbelievers—can summon up the courage to translate what they meant by repentance into the language of today.

BIBLIOGRAPHICAL NOTE

A MONG THE WORKS I consulted, here are some that were especially useful to me.

On the history of ancient Israel, the most valuable from my point of view was Yehezkel Kaufmann's *History of the Religion of Israel.* I have not read the eight-volume Hebrew original, but I profited enormously from Moshe Greenberg's translation and abridgement of the first three volumes (published in 1960 by the University of Chicago Press under the title *The Religion of Israel: From Its Beginnings to the Babylonian Exile*), and C.W. Efroymson's complete translation of the first two chapters of Volume IV (published in 1970 by the Union of American Hebrew Congregations under the title *The Babylonian Captivity and Deutero-Isaiah*).

Other such works that proved a great help were John Bright's *A History of Israel* (in the revised Third Edition published by the Westminster Press in 1981); Brevard S. Childs's *Introduction to the Old Testament as Scripture* (Fortress Press, 1979); Norman K. Gottwald's *The Hebrew Bible: A Socio-Literary Introduction* (Fortress Press, 1985); Robert M. Seltzer's *Jewish People, Jewish Thought* (Macmillan, 1980); and *A History of the Jewish People,* by several different hands and edited by H. H. Ben-Sasson (Harvard University Press, 1976). My understanding of various special issues was also furthered and enriched by several papers by Jon D. Levenson.

Among the works of general reference I consulted, two were indispensable: *The Encyclopaedia Judaica* in seventeen volumes (Macmillan, 1972), with material added later on a CD-ROM edition; and *The Anchor Bible Dictionary* in five volumes (Doubleday, 1992). Another great resource was the classic twelve-volume *Jewish Encyclopedia* (Funk and Wagnall, 1901), which, though out of date on some points, is still a work of immense erudition and deep learning.

In tracking down rabbinic stories about the prophets drawn both from the Talmud and from the Midrash, I made extensive use of *The Book of Legends,* edited by Hayim Nahman Bialik and Yehoshua Hana Ravnitzky and translated by William G. Braude (Schocken, 1992). The commentaries in the multi-volume Soncino edition of the Hebrew Bible were also a good source of such material.

On the prophets themselves, the books I found most useful for my purposes were Joseph Blenkinsopp's *A History of Prophecy in Israel* (revised and enlarged edition, Westminster/John Knox Press, 1996); Abraham Joshua Heschel's *The Prophets: An Introduction* (Harper & Row, 2 vols., 1962); and *Prophecy in Israel* (an anthology edited by David L. Petersen and published by the Fortress Press in 1987).

On the development and present status of biblical criticism since the nineteenth century, I principally relied on two collections of papers by various authors. One was *To Each Its Own Meaning: An Introduction to Biblical Criticisms and Their Application* (edited by Steven L. McKenzie and Stephen R. Haynes, and published by Westminster/John Knox Press in 1993). The other was *The Literary Guide to the Bible* (edited by Robert Alter and Frank Kermode and published by the Harvard University Press in 1987).

In reading the prophetic books themselves, I consulted a variety of commentaries—Jewish, Catholic, and Protestant—but the ones I leaned on most heavily were those included in the Anchor Bible Series. The general editor of this series, David Noel Freedman, collaborated with Francis I. Andersen in producing editions (complete, like all the others in the series, with new translations and elaborate commentaries) of Amos, Hosea, and Micah. Isaiah 1–39 was done by Joseph Blenkinsopp, and Second Isaiah by John L. McKenzie. For Jeremiah, I used John Bright's edition (which has since been supplanted in the Anchor series). The two volumes of Moshe Greenberg's edition of Ezekiel only cover chapters 1–37, and I therefore also resorted to Walter Eichenrodt's one-volume edition of the entire book in the Westminster Press's Old Testament Library. Returning to the Anchor series: for Zephaniah, I relied on Adele Berlin; for Obadiah, on Paul R. Raabe; for Joel, on James L. Crenshaw; for Haggai and the two Zechariahs, on the two volumes done by Carol L. Meyers and Eric M. Meyers; and for Malachi, on Andrew E. Hill.

A KEY TO CITATIONS

Below is an alphabetical list of the biblical books (including two from the New Testament) cited in the endnotes. The list follows the style adopted by *The New Strong's Exhaustive Concordance of the Bible* (in the King James Version):

Amos:	Amos	Josh:	Joshua
1Chr:	First Chronicles	Judg:	Judges
2Chr:	Second Chronicles	1Kin:	First Kings
Dan:	Daniel	2Kin:	Second Kings
Deut:	Deuteronomy	Lev:	Leviticus
Ex:	Exodus	Mal:	Malachi
Eze:	Ezekiel	Mic:	Micah
Gal:	Galatians	Mt:	Matthew
Gen:	Genesis	Nah:	Nahum
Hab:	Habakkuk	Num:	Numbers
Hag:	Haggai	Obad:	Obadiah
Hos:	Hosea	Ps:	Psalms
Is:	Isaiah	1Sa:	First Samuel
Jer:	Jeremiah	2Sa:	Second Samuel
Job:	Job	Zec:	Zechariah
Joel:	Joel	Zeph:	Zephaniah
Jonah:	Jonah		

Unfortunately, the numbering of verses in KJV is not always precisely the same as in the Masoretic text of the Hebrew Bible. Since the citations in the endnotes all follow KJV, readers looking for them in the Hebrew Bible may have to search in a verse or two above or below.

ENDNOTES

INTRODUCTION

1   of sycomore fruit: Amos 7:14
2   even his Bible: *Culture and Anarchy,* ch. 5
3   most or all: cited in the *Washington Times,* December 11, 2000
3   same as another: Jeff Sheler, *Is the Bible True?,* cited in the *Washington Times,* December 11, 2000
6   kings of Judah: Is 1:1
6   LORD hath spoken: Is 1:2
7   and written transmission: J. Limburg, cited in *The Anchor Bible Dictionary* article on Amos
7   many different prophets: P. Weiner and T. H. Robinson, cited in *The Anchor Bible Obadiah,* p. 16
8   To paraphrase Amos: Amos 7:14
8   of an amateur: "A Critic's Job of Work" (1935)
10   Brevard S. Childs: *Introduction to the Old Testament as Scripture*
10   throughout the centuries: Mary C. Callaway's "Canonical Criticism" in *To Each His Own* provides a good summary
10   jointly edited anthology: *The Literary Guide to the Bible*
10   other than archaeology: *The Literary Guide to the Bible,* pp. 1–2
10   and so forth: *The Literary Guide to the Bible,* p. 2
11   the Authorized Version: *The Literary Guide to the Bible,* pp. 666–667
12   for our God: Is 40:3
13   in academic debris: *Introduction to the Old Testament as Scripture,* p. 431

PART ONE: CLOUDS OF ANCESTRAL GLORY

CHAPTER ONE

19   of ancestral glory: *Encyclopaedia Judaica* article on "Prophets and Prophecy"
20   children of Israel: cited from the tractate *Sukkoth* (7b), in *Encyclopaedia Judaica* article on "Prophets and Prophecy"
20   thou shalt live: Gen 20:7
20   Pharaoh in Egypt: Gen 12:11–20
20   with great plagues: Gen 12:17
20   *his* wife Rebekah: Gen 26:7–11
21   will shew thee: Gen 12:1
21   earth be blessed: Gen 12:2–3
21   in his generations: Gen 6:8–9
22   the Pentateuch, Leviticus: Lev 19:26
22   the job description: *The Anchor Bible Amos,* p. 96
23   in the LORD: Gen 15:6
23   justice and judgment: Gen 18:19
23   of abandoning him: *The Anchor Bible Amos,* p. 93
23   applicable to all: *The Anchor Bible Amos,* p. 91
23   of 'natural law': *The Anchor Bible Amos,* p. 27
23   earth do right?: Gen 18:23,25
23   household after him: Gen 18:19
23   of the earth: Gen 28:14
24   a burnt offering: Gen 22:2
24   by the gods?: Plato's *Euthyphro* 10. See also 1Sa 15:22, to which I refer in both Chapters 2 and 6
26   a jealous God: Ex 20:2–5

26 in the wilderness?: Ex 14:11
26 assembly with hunger: Ex 16:3
27 made with honey: Ex 16:31
27 this stiffnecked people: Ex 32:9; 33:3,5; 34:9
27 the mountain smoking: Ex 20:18
27 we will do: Ex 24:3
27 and be obedient: Ex 24:7
27 finger of God: Ex 31:18
28 before our eyes: Num 11:4–5
28 a slow tongue: Ex 4:10
28 heavy for me: Num 11:14
28 them, they prophesied: Num 11:25
28 people were prophets: Num 11:29
29 spoken by us?: Num 12:2
29 shall he behold: Num 12:5–8
29 unto his friend: Ex 33:11
29 not be seen: Ex 33:20–23
29 life is preserved: Gen 32:30
29 eat and drink: Ex 24:9–11
30 on his left: 1Kin 22:19
30 LORD of Hosts: Is 6:1,5
31 story is deposited: Num 22–24
31 divinely ordained plague: Num 16:31–33, 48–49
31 the Promised Land: Num 20:12
31 search the land: Num 13:2
31 an evil report: Num 13:32
31 return into Egypt?: Num 14:2–3
32 in the wilderness: Num 14:28–32
32 iniquity in Jacob: Num 23:21
32 that curseth thee: Num 24:5–9
33 daughters of Moab: Num 25:1
33 god Baal-peor: Num 25:3
33 act of apostasy: Num 31:16
33 part of Deuteronomy: 2Kin 22–23
34 part very novel: *A History of Israel,* p. 321
34 a slow tongue: Ex 4:10
34 Moses' own "prophet": Ex 7:1
34 in the wilderness: Deut 1:1
34 Leviticus and Numbers: Ex 21–23, 34; Lev 18:24–30; and Num 35 (among others)
34 us this day: Deut 29:14–15
34 the Promised Land: Deut 1:37
35 deliverance from Egypt: Deut 5:15
35 world in six: Ex 20:8–11
35 to their gods: Deut 12:31
35 him to death: Deut 13:8–9
35 midst of thee: Deut 13:1–3,5

36 end of Leviticus: Lev 26:3–46
36 without knowing it: "The Marriage of Heaven and Hell" (c. 1793 C.E.)
36 Near Eastern treaties: *The Schocken Bible Genesis,* p. 974
37 shall ye eat: Lev 26:29
37 all thy gates: Deut 28:53–55
37 in thy gates: Deut 28:56–57
38 in their fathers: Deut 30:4,9
38 seed may live: Deut 30:11–14, 19
38 speeches of Moses: *The Schocken Bible Genesis,* p. 990

CHAPTER TWO

40 of the nation: *Introduction to the Old Testament as Scripture,* p. 236
40 of the prophet: *Soncino Books of the Bible: Joshua,* p. xi
40 shall command him: Deut 18:18
40 hand upon him: Num 27:18
40 hearkened unto him: Deut 34:9
40 nor forsake thee: Josh 1:1–3, 5
41 to give them: Josh 1:6
41 and very courageous: Josh 1:7
41 is written therein: Josh 1:7–8
41 be with thee: Josh 3:7
41 on dry ground: Josh 3:16–17
41 of his life: Josh 4:14
42 congregation of Israel: Josh 8:34–35
42 drawers of water: Josh 9: 27
42 upon their enemies: Josh 10:12–13
43 of a man: Josh 10:14
43 to the left: Josh 23:6 (see also 1:7)
43 yourselves unto them: Josh 23:7
43 traps unto you: Josh 23:13
44 served other gods: Josh 24:2
44 their strange gods: Josh 24:23
44 serve other gods: Josh 24:14–16
45 law of God: Josh 24:26
45 left him alive: Num 21:35
45 named a prophetess: Judg 4:4
46 obeyed my voice: Judg 6:8–10
46 fight against them?: Judg 1:1
47 voice, and wept: Judg 2:1–4
47 that outlived him: Judg 2:7
47 LORD to anger: Judg 2:11–12
47 to teach . . . war: Judg 3:2
47 wars of Canaan: Judg 3:1
47 to deliver them: The Hebrew word is

shofet, which does indeed mean judge, though NJPS translates it as "chieftain."

48   of charismatic leaders: Gershon Bacon in the *Encyclopaedia Judaica* article on Judges
48   of the Midianites: Judg 6:14
48   altar of Baal: Judg 6:26–30
48   down his altar: Judg 6:31
49   the nickname Jerubaal: Judg 6:32
49   of the east: Judg 6:33
49   rule over you: Judg 8:23
49   to his house: Judg 8:27
49   whoring after Baalim: Judg 8:33
49   a burnt offering: Judg 11:30–31
49   cannot go back: Judg 11:34–35
49   and my fellows: Judg 11:37
49   in a year: Judg 11:39–40
50   from the womb: Judg 13:5
51   sight of the LORD: Judg 13:1
51   Spirit of the LORD: Judg 13:25
51   the uncircumcised Philistines?: Judg 14:3
51   against the Philistines: Judg 14:4
51   them a displeasure: Judg 15:3
51   thousand men therewith: Judg 15:15
51   to afflict him: Judg 16:5
51   vexed unto death: Judg 16:16
52   the prison house: Judg 16:20–21
52   my two eyes: Judg 16:28
52   in his life: Judg 16:29–30
52   her for judgment: Judg 4:4–5
53   will not go: Judg 4:8
53   of a woman: Judg 4:9
53   into thine hand: Judg 4:14
53   in his temples: Judg 4:21–22
53   on that day: Judg 5:1
54   neck as spoil: Judg 5:28–30
54   thousand in Israel: Judg 5:7–8
54   over the warriors: Judg 5:13
55   rising in might: Judg 5:31
55   Book of Exodus: Ex 15:1ff.

CHAPTER THREE

56   in the land: 1Sa 3:1
57   a molten image: Judg 17:4
57   do me good: Judg 17:13
57   was in Shiloh: Judg 18:31
57   a graven image: 1Sa 19:13, 16

58   his own eyes: Judg 21:25; see also 17:6, where we find the same words. Various other verses (e.g., Judg 18:1) stress the absence of a king without adding that every man therefore did what was right in his own eyes.
58   of the congregation: 1Sa 2:22
58   their evil dealings: 1Sa 2:23
58   in my mind: 1Sa 2:35
58   make an end: 1Sa 3:11–12
59   LORD before Eli: 1Sa 3:1
59   upon his head: 1Sa 1:11
59   of the LORD: 1Sa 3:19–21
60   thy servant heareth: 1Sa 3:3–6, 8–10
60   and perverted judgment: 1Sa 8:3
60   all the nations: 1Sa 8:5
60   also unto thee: 1Sa 8:7–8
61   in that day: 1Sa 8:11–15, 17–18
61   them a king: 1Sa 8:19–22
62   tribe of Benjamin?: 1Sa 9:21
62   into another man: 1Sa 10:5–6
62   among the prophets?: 1Sa 10:11
63   cunning in playing: 1Sa 16:18
63   of the Philistines: 1Sa 18:25
63   David's enemy continually: 1Sa 18:29
63   came upon Saul: 1Sa 18:10
63   before the LORD: 1Sa 23:16–18
63   his ten thousands: 1Sa 18:7; 21:11; 29:5
63   but the kingdom?: 1Sa 18:8
64   departed from Saul: 1Sa 18:12
64   they prophesied also: 1Sa 19:20–21
64   among the prophets?: 1Sa 19:23–24
64   become "a proverb": 1Sa 10:12
64   shall not continue: 1Sa 13:13–14
65   heavy a punishment: S. Goldman, *Soncino Books of the Bible: Samuel,* pp. 71–72
65   camel and ass: 1Sa 15:3
65   performed my commandments: 1Sa 15:9–11
65   of the LORD: 1Sa 15:13
65   which I hear?: 1Sa 15:14
65   LORD thy God: 1Sa 15:15
66   iniquity and idolatry: 1Sa 15:22–23
66   generation to generation: Ex 17:14–16
66   not forget it: Deut 25:19
67   LORD in Gilgal: 1Sa 15:32–33
68   grey-headed man: 1Sa 12:2

69   He is witness: 1Sa 12:2–5
69   was your king: 1Sa 12:12
69   you a king: 1Sa 12:17
69   us a king: 1Sa 12:18–19
70   you his people: 1Sa 12:20–22
70   the right way: 1Sa 12:23
70   I shall do: 1Sa 28:15

CHAPTER FOUR

72   king over Israel: 2Sa 5:3
72   city of David: 2Sa 5:7
72   Israel and Judah: 2Sa 5:5
72   all his might: 2Sa 6:14
72   dwelleth within curtains: 2Sa 7:1–2
73   is with thee: 2Sa 7:3
73   on every side: 1Kin 5:3
73   in my sight: 1Chr 22:7–8; see also
     1Chr 28:3
73   established for ever: 2Sa 7:16
74   to look upon: 2Sa 11:2
74   flocks and herds: 2Sa 12:2
74   had no pity: 2Sa 12:5–6
74   in his sight?: 2Sa 12:7, 9
74   before the sun: 2Sa 12:9–12
75   man Absalom safe?: 2Sa 18:32
75   son, my son!: 2Sa 18:33
75   of all Israel: 2Sa 16:22
75   of the LORD: 2Sa 12:24–25
76   it unto thee: 2Sa 24:11–12
76   my father's house: 2Sa 24:17
76   now thine hand: 2Sa 24:16
76   of the people?: *Soncino Books of the
     Bible: Samuel,* p. 341
76   men burned them: 2Sa 5:21
78   that hated me: 2Sa 22:18. The entire
     hymn that makes up Chapter 22 is
     included in Psalms 18, with a number
     of variations.
78   his eye sight; 2Sa 22:21–25
78   bring him down: 2Sa 22:28
78   his mighty men 2Sa 23:8
79   of the host: 2Sa 24:3–4
79   rapacious royal power: *The Anchor
     Bible Dictionary,* article on "Samuel:
     Narrative and Theology"
79   which prompted it: *Soncino Books of
     the Bible: Samuel,* p. 342
80   established for ever: 2Sa 7:12–16
80   more, as beforetime: 2Sa 7:10

CHAPTER FIVE

82   "loved" the baby: 2Sa 12:24
83   do this day: 1Kin 1:28–30
83   good and bad: 1Kin 3:5, 7–9
84   lengthen thy days: 1Kin 3:11–14
84   my people Israel: 1Kin 6:11–13
84   I have builded?: 1Kin 8:27
84   that sinneth not: 1Kin 8:46
84   the mother thereof: 1Kin 3:24–27
85   to do judgment: 1Kin 3:28
85   of his wisdom: 1Kin 4:29–31, 34
85   judgment and justice: 1Kin 10:1, 3, 6,
     8–9
85   hear his wisdom: 1Kin 10:24
85   of the country: 1Kin 10:15
85   twelve thousand horsemen: 1Kin
     10:16–18, 21–22, 26
86   these in love: 1Kin 11:1–2
87   unto their gods: 1Kin 11:5, 7–8
87   to thy servant: 1Kin 11:11
87   I have chosen: 1Kin 11:13
87   God of Israel: 1Kin 11:31
88   be "for ever": 1Kin 11:39
88   you with scorpions: 1Kin 12:14
88   unto this day: 1Kin 12:19
88   of the LORD: 1Kin 12:22–24
88   all their days: 1Kin 14:30
88   land of Egypt: 1Kin 12:28
89   man of God: 1Kin 13:1
89   his evil way: 1Kin 13:33
89   with heavy tidings: 1Kin 14:6
89   child shall die: 1Kin 14:7–12
90   Israel to sin: 1Kin 14:15–16
90   the air eat: 1Kin 16:2–4
91   children of Israel: 1Kin 14:22–24
91   David his father: 1Kin 15:11
91   the brook Kidron: 1Kin 15:12–13
91   drinking himself drunk: 1Kin 16:9
91   of his friends: 1Kin 16:11
92   were before him: 1Kin 16:25
92   that were before him: 1Kin 16:31–33
92   bread and water: 1Kin 18:3–4
92   to my word: 1Kin 17:1
92   and hide thyself: 1Kin 17:2–3
92   morsel of bread: 1Kin 17:11
93   spake by Elijah: 1Kin 17:11; 12–16
93   mouth is truth: 1Kin 17:17–24
93   upon the earth: 1Kin 18:1
93   that troubleth Israel?: 1Kin 18:17
94   hast followed Baalim: 1Kin 18:18

PART TWO: ERUPTION

CHAPTER SIX

124   that time on: *The Anchor Bible Amos*,
       p. 90
124   an holy nation: Ex 19:6
125   image of God: Gen 9:6
125   king of Israel: Amos 1:1
125   Carmel shall wither: Amos 1:2
125   instruments of iron: Amos 1:3
125   wrath for ever: Amos 1:11
125   child of Gilead: Amos 1:13
126   word in Amos: Quoted in *Soncino Books
       of the Bible: Amos*, p. 88
126   all your iniquities: Amos 3:1-2
126   Syrians from Kir?: Amos 9:7
126   leopard his spots?: Jer 13:23
126   will not reform: *Soncino Books of the
       Bible: Amos*, p. 121
127   remnant of Joseph: Amos 5:15
127   saith the LORD: Amos 9:8
127   manner of Egypt: Amos 4:10
127   ease in Zion: Amos 6:1
128   saith the LORD: Amos 5:2, 16-17
128   smite the Egyptians: Ex 12:12
128   brightness in it?: Amos 5:18-20
128   kine of Bashan: Amos 4:1
128   in a couch: Amos 3:12
129   shall slay them: Amos 9:2-4
129   not find it: Amos 8:11-12
130   LORD thy God: Amos 9:11, 13-15
130   can but prophesy?: Amos 3:8
130   my people Israel: Amos 7:15
131   and less Greek: "To the Memory of My
       Beloved, the Author, Mr William
       Shakespeare" (1623)
132   house of Israel?: Amos 5:25
132   tradition even here: *The Religion of
       Israel*, p. 365n
132   of that kind: *The Anchor Bible Amos*, p. 59
132   their true God: *The Anchor Bible Amos*,
       p. 71
132   of the people: *The Religion of Israel*, p.
       366
133   God of hosts: Amos 5:26-27
133   my holy name: Amos 2:7
133   of the meek: Amos 2:7
133   of their god: Amos 2:8
133   upon their couches: Amos 6:4
134   flagons of wine: Hos 3:1
134   and new wine: Hos 4:11
134   in sexual orgies: Hos 4:17-18
134   a "dissident intellectual": *Sage, Priest,
       Prophet*, p. 1

134   a "conservative radical": *Jewish People,
       Jewish Thought*, p. 93
134   conditional, not absolute: *The Religion
       of Israel*, pp. 365-67
135   qualities of God: *The Religion of Israel*,
       p. 367

CHAPTER SEVEN

136   of his land: Amos 7:16-17
138   of honest indignation: "The Marriage
       of Heaven and Hell"
138   than burnt offerings: Hos 6:6
138   is cultic only: *The Religion of Israel*, p.
       278
139   Israel to grace: *Encyclopaedia Judaica*
       article on "Hosea"
140   daughter of Diblaim: Hos 1:2-3
140   his name Jezreel: Hos 1:4
140   valley of Jezreel: Hos 1:4-5
140   take them away: Hos 1:6
141   be your God: Hos 1:9
141   from the LORD: Hos 1:2
141   house of Israel: Hos 1:4
141   day of Jezreel: Hos 1:10-11
142   the living God: Hos 1:10
142   and my drink: Hos 2:2-5
143   shall eat them: Hos 2:11-12
143   saith the LORD: Hos 2:13
143   of mine hand: Hos 2:10
143   curses, this therefore: Hos 2:14
143   land of Egypt: Hos 2:15
144   even in faithfulness: Hos 2:19-20
144   available to her: Hos 2:18-22
144   art my God: Hos 2:23
144   be for thee: Hos 3:3
145   the latter days: Hos 3:4-5
146   a single oracle: *The Anchor Bible
       Ezekiel 1-20*, pp. 5-6
147   under their God: Hos 4:12
147   people, like priest: Hos 4:9
147   knowledge of God: Hos 6:6
148   to the LORD: Hos 4:10
148   month devour them: Hos 5:7
148   I bereave them: Hos 9:11-12
148   and dry breasts: Hos 9:14
148   of their womb: Hos 9:16
148   shall eat them: Hos 2:12
148   upon every cornfloor: Hos 9:1
148   things in Assyria: Hos 9:2-3
149   swallow it up: Hos 8:7

149 himself from them: Hos 5:3–6
149 to my place: Hos 5:15
149 return to Egypt: Hos 8:13
149 shall return to Egypt: Hos 9:3
149 them no more: Hos 9:15
150 as a rottenness: Hos 5:12
150 shall rescue him: Hos 5:14
150 shall tear them: Hos 13:7–8
150 god but me: Hos 13:4
150 seek me early: Hos 5:15
151 unto the earth: Hos 6:1–3
151 it goeth away: Hos 6:4
151 bands of love; Hos 11:4
151 to graven images: Hos 11:2
151 midst of thee: Hos 11:8–9
151 make it good?: Num 23:19
151 he should repent: 1Sa 15:29
151 to be king: 1Sa 15:11
152 have made them: Gen 6:5–7
152 clear the guilty: Ex 34:6–7
152 a permanent decision: *The Anchor Bible Hosea,* p. 590
152 for covenant violations: *The Anchor Bible Hosea,* p. 590
153 mercy for it: *The Anchor Bible Hosea,* p. 590
153 be thy destruction: Hos 13:9–10, 14
154 be ripped up: Hos 13:15–16
154 receive us graciously: Hos 14:1–2
154 fatherless findeth mercy: Hos 14:3
154 away from him: Hos 14:4
154 and observed him: Hos 14:8
155 wine of Lebanon: Hos 14:5–7
155 man is mad: Hos 9:7

CHAPTER EIGHT

157 doom was averted: Pesakhim 87a–b, as summarized in *The Encyclopaedia Judaica* article on the Book of Micah
158 meaning eludes us: *The Anchor Bible Micah,* p. 297
158 with thy God: Mic 6:8
160 the Old Testament: Quoted in *The Anchor Bible Micah,* p. 504
160 Prophets of Israel: Quoted in *The Anchor Bible Micah,* p. 504
160 breakthroughs in history: Quoted in *The Anchor Bible Micah,* p. 504
160 church) and ceremonies: *The Anchor Bible Micah,* p. 504
160 in the gate: Amos 5:14–15
160 blood toucheth blood: Hos 4:1–2
161 demand of man: *The Religion of Israel,* pp. 396–97
162 plead with Israel: Mic 6:1–2
162 testify against me: Mic 6:3
162 the high God?: Mic 6:6
163 a year old?: Mic 6:6
163 thousands of rams?: Mic 6:7
163 rivers of oil: Mic 6:7
163 of my soul?: Mic 6:7
163 and his heritage: Mic 2:1–2
163 glory for ever: Mic 2:8–9
164 within the cauldron: Mic 3:1–3
164 in their mouth: Mic 6:10–12
164 Kingdom of Israel: Mic 1:5, 13
164 children of Israel: 2Kin 16:3
165 in their counsels: Mic 6:16
165 oppression and injustice: S. Goldman, *Soncino Books of the Bible: Micah,* p. 183n
165 and social injustice: The Jerusalem Bible: *Micah,* p. 1505n
165 of an harlot: Mic 1:5–7
165 of thy land: Mic 5:11
166 Micah the Morasthite: Mic 1:1
166 destroy thy chariots: Mic 5:10
166 the whole earth: Mic 4:11–13
167 be cut off: Mic 5:4–9
167 sun with fire: 2Kin 23:11; *The Anchor Bible Micah,* p. 491
167 most overt expression: *The Anchor Bible Micah,* p. 491
168 midst of thee: Mic 5:12–14
168 ever and ever: Mic 4:1–5
169 into both books: *The Anchor Bible Micah,* p. 414
169 conquest and control: *The Anchor Bible Micah,* p. 397
170 body in Micah: *The Religion of Israel,* pp. 397–98
170 of the forest: Mic 3:12
171 pronounced against them?: Jer 26:17–19
171 these his doings?: Mic 2:6–7
172 for this people!: Mic 2:11
172 within the cauldron: Mic 3:3
172 war against him: Mic 3:5
172 answer of God: Mic 3:6–7
172 Israel his sin: Mic 3:8
173 come upon us: Mic 3:9–11

174   not drink wine: Mic 6:14–15
174   his own house: Mic 7:5–6
175   behold his righteousness: Mic 7:7–10
175   of the seas: Mic 7:18–19
175   because of thee: Mic 7:10, 15–17
176   upon the heathen: Mic 5:15
176   upon the grass: Mic 5:7
176   mountain to mountain: Mic 7:12

CHAPTER NINE

178   any given verse: *The Hebrew Bible, the
       Old Testament, and Historical Criticism*,
       p. 69
178   have in view: *The Pentateuch and
       Haftorahs*, p. 942
179   of Catholic interpreters: "Introduction
       to the Prophets," in The Jerusalem
       Bible, p. 1125
179   into hopeless chunks: *The Second Isa-
       iah*, p. 13
180   tantalizing in-betweens: *Encyclopaedia
       Judaica*, article on "Isaiah"
181   it has received: *The Anchor Bible Isaiah
       1–39*, p. 73
181   of an ear: Amos 3:12
181   sixth century B.C.E.: *The Anchor Bible
       Isaiah 1–39*, p. 74
181   are getting at: quoted in *The Anchor
       Bible Dictionary*, article on "Isaiah"
181   of Isaiah himself: Quoted in *The
       Anchor Bible Isaiah 1–39*, p. xi
182   reinterpretation and reapplication: *The
       Anchor Bible Isaiah 1–39*, p. 74
182   interpretative religious tradition: *The
       Anchor Bible Isaiah 1–39*, p. 84
183   of its own: *Soncino Books of the Bible:
       Isaiah*, p. v
184   we shall die: Is 22:13
184   LORD, how long?: Is 6:11
184   of the night?: Is 21:11
184   shall lead them: Is 11:6
184   Holy of Holies: *Yadayim* 3:5, quoted
       in *Encyclopaedia Judaica* article on
       "Song of Songs"
185   the social order: W. F. Albright, "The
       Biblical Period," in L. Finkelstein, ed.,
       The Jews, pp. 39ff
186   come unto them: Is 1:16–17, 23
186   become an harlot!: Is 1:21
186   God of hosts: Is 3:13–15

187   instead of beauty: Is 3:16–24
187   touching his vineyard: Is 5:1
187   of the earth!: Is 5:7–8
187   rob the fatherless!: Is 10:1–2
188   abomination unto me: Is 1:10–13
188   will not hear: Is 1:14–15
188   full of blood: Is 1:15
188   be as wool: Is 1:18
189   the faithful city: Is 1:25–26
189   over by "murderers": Is 1:21
190   on the altar?: *The Prophets*, Vol. 1, pp.
       196–97
190   of the cult: *The Prophets*, Vol. 1, p. 196n
190   through the cult: quoted in *The Anchor
       Bible Zephaniah*, p. 83
190   hath no water: Is 1:28–30
192   to the bats: Is 2:6, 8–9, 12, 17–18, 20
192   ships of Tarshish: Is 2:16
192   are lifted up: Is 2:13–14
192   all your iniquities: Amos 3:2
193   of social reform: *The Sociology of Reli-
       gion*, p. 50
194   come to pass: Is 7:7
194   tempt the LORD: Is 7:10–12
194   you a sign: Is 7:13–14
195   his name Immanuel: Is 7:14
195   Prince of Peace: Is 9:6
196   were no wood: Is 10:12–13, 15
196   return to God: Is 10:20–21
196   of his reins: Is 11:1–5
197   cover the sea: Is 11:6–9
197   shall be glorious: Is 11:10
197   kingdom of heaven: Mt 5:17–19
198   seek the LORD!: Is 31:1
198   servant David's sake: Is 37:21–22, 33, 35
199   dwelt at Nineveh: Is 37:36–37
199   calm and confidence: Is 30:15
199   a mighty man: Is 31:6–8
199   be beaten down: Is 30:22, 31
199   to sit still: Is 30:7
200   cease before us: Is 30:8–11
200   Israel mine inheritance: Is 19:21–25
201   reality of judgment: *A History of
       Prophecy in Israel*, pp. 109–10

CHAPTER TEN

203   of the LORD: 2Kin 21:2–4, 6–7,
       16
203   blood flowed forth: Quoted in *The
       Book of Legends*, edited by Hayim Nah-

man Bialik and Yehoshua Hana Ravnitzky, p. 140

203   to preach about: R. Nelson, quoted in *The Anchor Bible Dictionary,* article on "Manasseh, King of Judah"

204   had to do: R. Nelson, quoted in *The Anchor Bible Dictionary,* article on "Manasseh, King of Judah"

204   such a fool: "Notes on Nationalism" (1945)

206   saith the LORD: Zeph 1:2–3

206   the world order: *The Anchor Bible Zephaniah,* p. 83

206   of foreign practices: *The Anchor Bible Zephaniah,* pp. 83–84

206   the LORD's anger: Zeph 2:1–3

207   against their border: Zeph 2:8

207   shall possess them: Zeph 2:9

207   of the heathen: Zeph 2:11

207   lie down in!: Zeph 2:15

207   to the law: Zeph 3:1–4

207   of the LORD: Zeph 3:12

208   make them afraid: Zeph 3:13

208   Berlin, "is reaffirmed": *The Anchor Bible Zephaniah,* p. 148

209   utterly cut off: Nah 1:12–13, 15

209   thou art vile: Nah 1:14

209   wickedness passed continuously?: Nah 3:19

209   trust in Him: *Encyclopaedia Judaica,* article on "Nahum"

209   part of Isaiah: *The Jerusalem Bible,* p. 1137

210   hath spoken it: Obad 1:17–18

211   Jacob and Zion: *The Anchor Bible Obadiah,* pp. 59–60

211   simply political propaganda: *The Anchor Bible Obadiah,* p. 5

211   views and sentiments: *The Anchor Bible Obadiah,* p. 5

211   old-fashioned approach: *The Jerusalem Bible,* p. 1140

211   a great fish: Jon 1:17

212   also much cattle?: Jon 4:11

212   of the gospel: *The Jerusalem Bible,* p. 1141

212   throughout the Book: *Soncino Books of the Bible: Jonah,* p. 137

213   righteous than he?: Hab 1:13

213   wrong judgment proceedeth: Hab 1:2–4

214   terrible and dreadful: Hab 1:6–7

214   unto his god?: Hab 1:11

214   by his faith: Hab 2:4

214   midst of it: Hab 2:18–19

214   glory of God: Hab 2:14

214   versus the idols: *The Religion of Israel,* p. 400

215   of my salvation: Hab 3:18

215   my stringed instruments: Hab 3:19

CHAPTER ELEVEN

217   in this book: 2Kin 23:3

217   his own eyes: Deut 12:2–3, 5–6, 8

220   of his days: *The Religion of Israel,* p. 417

221   ye have peace: Jer 29:7

222   of the earth: Jer 16:1–4

222   same "broken reed": Is 36:6

223   king of Assyria: Jer 50:18

223   it perpetual desolations: Jer 25:12

224   bring upon her: Jer 51:60–64

225   than treacherous Judah: Jer 3:6–11

225   sweet unto me: Jer 6:20

225   offerings or sacrifices: Jer 7:22

225   no absolute value: *The Religion of Israel,* p. 418

225   of the LORD: Jer 17:24–26

226   do sacrifice continually: Jer 33:18

226   do not judge: Jer 5:28

226   in this place: Jer 22:3

226   ever and ever: Jer 7:4–7

226   den of robbers: Jer 7:9, 11

226   to your hurt: Jer 7:6

227   ye know not: Jer 7:9

227   into my heart: Jer 7:30–31

227   fathers taught them: Jer 9:11–14

228   shew you favor: Jer 16:9–13

228   come upon them: Jer 2:2–3

229   *you bend, whore:* Jer 2:20

229   hold no water: Jer 2:11–13

229   shall find her: Jer 2:23–24

230   LORD thy God: Deut 13:6, 8–10

231   thou shalt speak: Jer 1:4–7

231   of his glory: Is 6:3

231   of unclean lips: Is 6:5

231   I; send me: Is 6:8

231   of the land: Is 6:10–12

232   their own hands: Jer 1:15–16

232   of the land: Jer 1:18

232   to do evil: Jer 13:23

254 fire for them?: Eze 16:20–21
254 multiplied thy whoredoms: Eze 16:22–23, 25
254 for thy whoredom: Eze 16:33
255 idols of Egypt: Eze 20:7–8
255 unto this day: Eze 20:30–31
255 in their youth: Eze 23:3
255 of their virginity: Eze 23; 3; see also 23:8
255 she defiled herself: Eze 23:7
256 of mine house: Eze 23:37–39
256 an "everlasting covenant": Eze 37:26; see also 16:60
257 saith the LORD: Eze 37:1–14
258 and Christian communities: *The Anchor Bible Ezekiel 21–37*, p. 749
259 am the LORD: Eze 7:2–4
259 of the mountains: Eze 7:5–7
259 day draweth near: Eze 7:8–12
260 593–586 B.C.E.: *The Anchor Bible Dictionary*, article on "Ezekiel"
261 the "objective correlative": "Hamlet and His Problems" (1919)
261 known unto them: Eze 20:9
262 be your God: Eze 36:17–28
262 known unto you: Eze 36:32
263 idea, his *donnée: The Art of Fiction*

CHAPTER THIRTEEN

268 than 70 units: *Encyclopaedia Judaica*, article on "Deutero-Isaiah"
268 his servant Jacob: Is 48:20
268 as to crawl!: *A History of Israel*, p. 367n
268 the serpent's meat: Is 65:25 (compare 11:6–8)
269 all her sins: Is 40:1–2
269 an unidentified "voice": Is 40:3
270 rough places plain: Is 40:3–4
270 people, my chosen: Is 43:18–20
271 of my righteousness: Is 41:8–10
271 of his understanding: Is 40:17, 22–23, 28
272 know not any: Is 44:6, 8
272 to his time: *The Anchor Bible Second Isaiah*, p. LXIV
272 and false gods: *The Anchor Bible Second Isaiah*, p. LXIV
273 my right hand?: Is 44:9–10, 14–17, 20
273 they could observe: *The Anchor Bible Second Isaiah*, p. LXV

273 was not enough: *The Anchor Bible Second Isaiah*, p. LXV
274 into thine hand: Is 47:6
274 come upon thee: Is 47:8, 10–13
274 the Old Testament: *The Anchor Bible Second Isaiah*, p. LXV
275 from the womb: Is 48:3–5, 8
275 glory unto another: Is 48:9, 11
275 shall be ashamed: Is 45:23–24
276 and shall glory: Is 45:25
276 mediator of blessings: *The Anchor Bible Second Isaiah*, p. LXVI
276 to "many people": Is 2:3
276 for his law: Is 42:1, 4
276 of the earth: Is 49:1, 3, 6
277 of thy feet: Is 49:22–23
277 One of Jacob: Is 49:25–26
277 the desolate heritages: Is 49:7–8
277 hath glorified thee: Is 60:1, 3, 5–7, 9
278 One of Israel: Is 60:10, 12, 14
278 ye boast yourselves: Is 61:5–6
279 with thy iniquities: Is 43:21–24
279 of the LORD: Deut 23:1
279 be cut off: Is 56:3–5
280 upon mine altar: Is 56:7
280 takest no knowledge?: Is 58:3
280 thou cover him?: Is 58:6–7
280 Jacob thy father: Is 58:13–14
281 doing any evil: Is 56:1–2
283 I have chosen: Is 44:1
283 servant, O Israel: Is 49:3
283 in the earth: Is 42:1; 4
283 of the earth: Is 49:6
283 shame and spitting: Is. 50:6
284 acquainted with grief: Is 53:3
284 for the transgressors: Is 53:4–6, 8, 10–12
284 the Old Testament: *The Anchor Bible Second Isaiah*, p. XLIX
284 Servant of Yahweh: *The Anchor Bible Second Isaiah*, p. XLIX
284 to Jesus himself: *The Anchor Bible Second Isaiah*, p. XLIX
284 of the term: *The Anchor Bible Second Isaiah*, p. XLIX
285 of all Israel: *The Anchor Bible Second Isaiah*, p. LIV
285 to Yehezkel Kaufmann: In *The Babylonian Captivity and Deutero-Isaiah*, pp. 128ff
285 covenant with them: Is 57:4–5, 7–8

347   sweet for bitter!: Is 5:20

347   fruitful, and multiply: Gen 2:28

348   come who may: "Howl" (1955–56)

348   the male species: Quoted by Michael
      Schumacher in *Dharma Lion*

349   be fully alive: Review of Cyril Con-
      nolly's *The Rock Pool* (1936)

352   created He them: Gen 1:27

353   ever and ever: Mic 4:5

353   "Home-Alone America": *Policy
      Review,* June and July 2001

355   *of the Theatre: Novum Organum*

356   midst of it: Hab 2:19

356   man humbleth himself: Is 2:8–9

356   ears and hear not: Jer 5:19,21

356   and hear not: Eze 12:2

356   trusteth in them: Ps 115:4–8

356   not forsake them: Is 42:16

356   be "turned back": Is 42:17

357   become "as gods": Gen 3:54

357   *all our woe: Paradise Lost*

357   "one greater Man": *Paradise Regained*

357   any graven image: Ex 20:2–4; Deut
      5:6–8 (where "no" becomes "none"
      and "unto" is omitted)

358   one's self is: "Song of Myself"

358   a bottomless pit: Lawrence, who con-
      sidered Whitman a very great poet (es-
      pecially when writing about death),
      was not specifically referring to him,
      but the remark applies perfectly. Hav-
      ing cited it from memory, I have been
      unsuccessful in trying to track it down.
      There is no doubt in my mind, how-
      ever, that it comes from Lawrence.

359   to the bats: Is 2:20

ACKNOWLEDGMENTS

T HIS BOOK could not have been written without the support of the Hudson Institute, the John M. Olin Foundation, the Lynde and Harry Bradley Foundation, and the Sarah Scaife/Carthage Foundation. I am deeply grateful to all four institutions for their warm encouragement and their great generosity

ACKNOWLEDGMENTS

INDEX

Second Hosea, 7, 10, 137, 146–147, 149

Second Isaiah, 6, 38, 105, 137, 179, 180, 183,
    235, 239, 244, 267–287, 325,
    341–344, 346, 359. *See also* First Isa-
    iah (son of Amoz)
  consolations of, 269–270
  First Isaiah and, 267, 269
  on God's absolute power, 271–272, 274,
    275
  presumed prophecy of birth of Jesus,
    282, 284–285
  return to Jerusalem, 268, 288
  Sabbath and, 280
  sacrifice and, 278–279, 285
  Songs of the Servant of the LORD,
    282–285
  universalism and, 274–278, 281, 282,
    285–287
  war against idolatry and, 272–273,
    285–286

Second Zechariah, 7, 14, 137, 291, 292, 296,
    308, 309
  war against idolatry and, 303–304

Seleucids, 308, 310

Seltzer, Robert M., 134, 345–346

Sennacherib, 170, 198, 199, 266

Septuagint, 4, 195*n*, 214*n*, 219*n*, 316

Seraiah, 224

Shakespeare, William, 68, 131

Shear-jashub, 193

Sheba, Queen of, 85, 86

Shebna, 319

Shechem, 44, 45

Shelley, Percy Bysshe, 36

Shemaiah, 88

Shiloh, 57–59, 170

Shropshire Lad, A (Houseman), 330*n*

Sihon, 45

Simeon, tribe of, 43*n*

Sisera, 52–53

Smith, G.A., 160

Smith, Robertson, 160

Socialism, 131, 336

Society for Ethical Culture, 131, 159

Socrates, 1, 24, 309, 358

Sodom, 23, 77, 78, 121, 134, 151, 187, 247,
    254, 335

Solomon, 61, 65, 73, 75, 82–88, 105,
    217

Soncino edition (Son), 15, 97*n*, 126

Song of Deborah, 53–55, 70

Song of Moses, 55

Song of Songs, 5, 184

Songs of the Servant of the LORD,
    282–285

Sorcery, 192

Southern Kingdom of Judah, 61, 87, 88,
    90–91, 96, 104, 105, 113–115, 118,
    119, 125–127, 136, 155, 165, 166,
    173, 179, 185, 187, 193–197, 199,
    202–205, 210–211, 216–224, 232,
    235, 240, 248–250, 255, 256, 265,
    267–270, 275, 288–291, 303, 307, 324

Spinoza, Baruch, 337

Strauss, Leo, 315

Suicide bombings, 354

Suicide rates, 354

Syncretism, 57, 217, 241

Syria, 127, 193

Talmud, 13, 20, 46*n*, 50*n*, 58*n*, 112, 125, 157,
    160, 239, 243, 258, 309, 317, 319,
    333, 335, 336

Tamar, 75

TaNaKh, 5, 7, 8

Tekoah, 113

Tel-abib, 242, 246, 248

Temple, First or Second, in Jerusalem, 72,
    73, 80, 84, 88, 105, 116, 170, 174,
    189, 191, 202, 203, 215, 216–218,
    222–223, 226, 230, 241–242, 251,
    253, 260, 265–268, 279, 289–292,
    297, 300, 301, 327, 334, 338

Ten Commandments, 25–27, 34, 57, 72,
    121, 123, 227, 245, 247, 357

Ten Lost Tribes, 104, 129, 157, 265

Terrorism, 194*n*, 354–355

Thatcher, Margaret, 194*n*

Third Isaiah, 6, 137, 179, 183, 267, 268, 277,
    279, 288. *See also* First Isaiah (son of
    Amoz)

Third Zechariah, 291

Tobit, Book of, 8

*To Each its Own Meaning: An Introduction to
    Biblical Criticisms and Their Application*
    (McKenzie and Haynes), 9*n*

Torah (*Khumash*), 5, 36, 152, 313

Torrey, C.C., 179, 244